The Family Business in Tourism and Hospitality

The Family Business in Tourism and Hospitality

Donald Getz,
Jack Carlsen

and

Alison Morrison

CABI Publishing

CABI Publishing is a division of CAB International

CABI Publishing
CAB International
Wallingford
Oxfordshire OX10 8DE
UK

Tel: +44 (0)1491 832111
Fax: +44 (0)1491 833508
E-mail: cabi@cabi.org
Web site: www.cabi-publishing.org

CABI Publishing
875 Massachusetts Avenue
7th Floor
Cambridge, MA 02139
USA

Tel: +1 617 395 4056
Fax: +1 617 354 6875
E-mail: cabi-nao@cabi.org

A catalogue record for this book is available from the British Library, London, UK.

Library of Congress Cataloging-in-Publication Data

Getz, Donald, 1949-
   The family business in tourism and hospitality / Donald Getz, Jack
Carlsen, Alison Morrison.
       p. cm.
Includes bibliographical references and index.
   ISBN 0-85199-808-9 (alk. paper)
   1. Tourism. 2. Hospitality industry. 3. Family-owned business
enterprises. I. Carlsen, Jack. II. Morrison, Alison. III. Title.
   G155.A1G439 2003
   910′.68--dc22   2003018338

ISBN 0 85199 808 9

Typeset by AMA DataSet, UK.
Printed and bound in the UK by Cromwell Press, Trowbridge.

Contents

About the Authors

Donald Getz

Donald Getz is a Professor of tourism and hospitality management in the Haskayne School of Business, University of Calgary, Canada. His research interest in family business began with doctoral research in the Highlands of Scotland, as many of the tourism and hospitality businesses studied were operated by individuals and families. He has conducted specific family-business research in Canada, Denmark, Sweden, New Zealand and Australia, involving a number of individual and institutional collaborators. This work has been financially supported in part by the Family Business Research Endowment at the University of Calgary. Professor Getz also does a considerable amount of research and publishes in the area of event management and event tourism, and is the author of the book *Event Management and Event Tourism* (Cognizant, 1997). He has also authored books entitled *Explore Wine Tourism* (Cognizant, 2000), *The Business of Rural Tourism* (with Stephen Page: Thompson International Business Press, 1997) and *Festival Management and Event Tourism* (Van Nostrand Reinhold, 1991).

Jack Carlsen

Dr Carlsen is the Malayan United Industries (MUI) Chair in Tourism and Hospitality Studies within the Curtin Business School, Curtin University of Technology, Western Australia. He received his first grant for Family Business Research in 1998 and has since published papers in the *Journal of Sustainable Tourism*, *Tourism Management*, and *Family Business Review* and presented papers at the International Congress of Small Business, Asia Pacific Tourism Association and the Council of Australian University Tourism and Hospitality Education conferences. Jack has a Bachelor of Economics and a Doctor of Philosophy from the University of Western Australia. His other research interests include tourism economics, tourism management and sustainable tourism. Jack is Founder and Co-Director of the Curtin Sustainable Tourism Centre at Curtin University of Technology.

Alison Morrison

Dr Alison Morrison is Reader in Hospitality Management and Director of Research within Strathclyde Business School, University of Strathclyde. She has attained a BA Hotel and Catering

Management from the University of Strathclyde, an MSc in Entrepreneurship from Stirling University and a PhD from the University of Strathclyde with the thesis titled Small Firm Strategic Alliances: the UK Hotel Industry. Alison has edited and authored five text books in the areas of marketing, hospitality, entrepreneurship and franchising and has published widely in generic business and specialist hospitality and tourism academic journals. She regularly undertakes international assignments teaching and consulting on entrepreneurship within the hospitality and tourism sectors.

Contributors

A number of researchers have contributed cases or research material to this book, and the authors are very grateful for their valuable efforts.

- Chris Ryan, Professor, University of Waikato, New Zealand: author of the case study 'River Valley Ventures'.
- Tage Petersen, Tourism and Regional Research Centre, Bornholm, Denmark: co-researcher with Donald Getz of the family business survey in Bornholm and co-author of a paper on growth-oriented entrepreneurship.
- Per Ake Nilsson, Tourism and Regional Research Centre, Bornholm, Denmark: co-author with Donald Getz of a paper on seasonality, based on the Bornholm data.
- Tommy Andersson, Professor, University of Gothenburg, Sweden: author of the three case studies from Sweden.
- Lynn Batchelor, Griffith University, Australia: co-author of the case study, 'O'Reilly's Rainforest Guesthouse'.
- Shane O'Reilly, of O'Reilly's Rainforest Guesthouse: co-author of the case study, 'O'Reilly's Rainforest Guesthouse'.

How to Use the Book

For Academics and Researchers

Given that this is the first book on family business in the tourism and hospitality industry, it has several academic goals:

- To define and explain the importance of family business studies to the study of tourism and hospitality.
- To present and assess pertinent literature that has previously not been synthesized in the context of family business studies.
- To establish concepts and research directions for advancing this area of scholarship.

The authors also hope to make a contribution to the mainstream study of family business by demonstrating its application to a specific industry, and the many industry-specific modifiers that affect family businesses.

Where can the book be used as a text? Business and management schools with tourism and hospitality programmes are encouraged to incorporate family business studies into their curricula, in recognition of the importance this class of business has in the industry and also because there are increasing numbers of students interested in becoming entrepreneurs. The book could be a stand-alone text or a supplement to more general books on small business management, entrepreneurship, new ventures and even destination competitiveness.

Using Case Studies

The cases developed for this book, most of them original and unpublished elsewhere, are really case histories. They have been a rich source of insights into actual family business operations and related issues. Cases based on in-depth interviews, as they all are in this book, provide a better source of information than surveys because the respondents are directly involved in case preparation and in the end approve of the contents. We also provide original research data from a number of surveys, and the case studies illustrate many of the important findings in those survey results.

The cases do present problems for researchers, as they are essentially reflections of the past, frozen at one point in time. Several of our respondents, for example, have reported major changes in their circumstances subsequent to approving the material contained in this book, while several contributions have been updated right to the last possible minute before finalization of the manuscript. Although several of the cases demonstrate problems and how families must face adversity, the authors believe that collectively they understate the problems faced by families in business. Systematic research comparing success stories with failures would certainly add a lot to our understanding of family businesses in tourism and hospitality.

In teaching applications, individual cases can be used to introduce or illustrate specific issues, such as entrepreneurship, founders' goals, strategies, or barriers to inheritance. The cross-case analysis contained in Chapter 11 ties them all together and yields 30 general issues that apply across some or many of the cases. This analysis can also be used to encourage students to become aware of similarities and differences between cases and the underlying reasons, and in particular reveals remarkable similarities in family business experiences. But it is important to emphasize that the cases were not selected randomly, nor do they reflect best practices or success stories. The cross-case analysis is not generalizable to the whole population of family business in the industry nor in any of the countries.

For Students

This book introduces students to the field of family business studies, with numerous references to the main body of literature. The basic definitions, concepts and themes in family business studies are summarized in Chapter 1, with subsequent chapters focusing on more specific family business issues and how they are applied to tourism and hospitality. The ties to entrepreneurship and small business studies are made explicit in Chapter 2 and these important themes are developed through the book.

Students coming from a family business background will find this book invaluable in helping them make decisions about entering the family business or starting their own. It is a difficult challenge, but countless people around the world seek that challenge and many find it completely fulfilling. At a minimum, the book will help them assess their own ambitions, goals and priorities regarding a professional career versus self-employment and entrepreneurship.

Independent of their own plans, the book will help them understand the numerous family businesses they will encounter, or perhaps work for. Their owners are a special part of the business, and the families face a number of unique challenges. Understanding the family business will also help them appreciate the complexity of the industry when it comes to planning, marketing and fostering growth or innovation.

For Family Business Owners and Managers

Although the book was not designed primarily for the industry, it will prove useful to family business owners and those who manage family businesses. In particular, there are many sections covering the practical management of family businesses, such as ownership and structure, strategic planning, issues surrounding succession and inheritance, and even family branding.

Preface

This is the first book dealing with family business in tourism and hospitality. Given the importance, and in many areas the predominance, of families, couples (called 'copreneurs') and individuals (sole proprietors) running tourism and hospitality businesses, it is long overdue.

The Family Business in Tourism and Hospitality provides a comprehensive overview of this emerging field of study, based on available literature, research by the authors and new case studies. It seeks to make a theoretical and didactic contribution both to the study of tourism and hospitality, and to the generic field of family business studies. Researchers will benefit from new insights on the importance of the family in business management, and the significance of family businesses in destination competitiveness, economic and community development.

Students in tourism and hospitality programmes will benefit from a greater understanding of the opportunities and challenges associated with family business practice in this industry. Many students in these programmes come from a family business background and might even be expected to join an existing family firm. Others will be contemplating entrepreneurial ventures in the industry, and both groups need to be better educated about the management of a family- or owner-operated business. And, of course, just about every graduate will eventually come into professional contact with family businesses and should therefore be cognizant of what businesses in this sector need.

It is not our intention to produce a 'how-to' book for establishing or operating a family business, but there are a number of sections that have very practical applications. We address the business plan, strategic planning, succession planning, marketing, organizational and governance issues, and some financing and investment challenges. The principal purpose in doing so is to show where exactly family considerations intrude on business management, and to discuss (wherever possible) industry-specific issues. These management sections have also been added to increase the appeal of the book to the industry, and to show students and scholars where theory and practice must be brought together.

Objectives and Outline of the Book

The book's specific objectives are:

1. To advance the study of family business within tourism and hospitality, with particular reference to the following perspectives:
   - its scope and significance;
   - management of the family business;

- destination competitiveness;
- economic and community development.

2. To identify the unique opportunities, challenges and issues facing family business in this industry, thereby adding to the generic family business literature.

3. To provide a text or reference work for students in the tourism and hospitality fields.

4. To provide a reference for teachers and academics.

5. To provide a reference work for family business owners and those contemplating a business venture.

The starting point in the Introduction (Chapter 1) is to address the questions of why study the family business, and what exactly it is. We identify generic issues that family businesses face and explain a well-known family business model to shape discussion of the evolution of ownership, the business, and the family. We then examine what is unique about family business in the tourism and hospitality industry and how this relates to the core family business issues. A framework has been developed for this purpose, encompassing 'setting modifiers' (location, level of economic development, and culture) and 'industry-specific modifiers' (the nature of the service, host–guest relations, cyclical demand or seasonality, destination life cycle, and unique business opportunities).

In Chapter 1 we begin to make use of the case studies provided in Chapters 7–10, and the cross-case analysis in Chapter 11. Analysis of the cases led directly to the identification of 30 key family-related issues within tourism and hospitality enterprise, and these are used to inform the more generic and theoretical discussion of family business in Chapter 1.

The aim of Chapter 2 is to recognize family business as a distinct form of entrepreneurship. It makes the connection between entrepreneurship, small and family businesses, focusing on the unique entrepreneurial opportunities and challenges that are inherent in the tourism and hospitality industry. The contribution of key industry-specific and setting modifiers as identified in Chapter 1 is explored within the framework of a model that investigates the extent to which they act as 'filters' to either intensify or dilute the entrepreneurial process resulting in consequential entrepreneurial socio-economic outcomes. Conclusions are drawn that highlight the unique factors associated with entrepreneurship as related to tourism and hospitality family businesses, how they influence the nature and evolution of such enterprises, and competitive and policy implications.

In Chapter 3 the critical issues of motivation and goals are examined first, particularly the contrasts inherent in growth and profit-oriented entrepreneurship versus the more prevalent lifestyle and autonomy motivations. Important antecedents to family business, including the influences of education, experience and training, are considered. Business planning is then examined, as the careful preparation and execution of a business plan is considered to be a major indicator of potential business success, and is certainly associated with achieving growth. Included in this section is an outline of what the plan should include, with emphasis on several family-related issues. Ownership, organization and governance are covered last in this chapter.

The first section of Chapter 4 identifies and examines the meaning of success and failure for a family business, then focuses on specific challenges and causes of failure. Next, arguments for growing a business are addressed, then preconditions and barriers to growth. This is followed by analysis of generic and industry-specific strategies, a section on strategic planning, and separate treatment of strategic marketing and family branding. Research findings are then presented on how seasonality affects family businesses and various strategic responses from a sample of owners in Denmark.

Chapter 5 examines key challenges and issues together with strategies and actions that are actually employed, or are recommended by experts, to achieve a healthy balance. It starts with a discussion of generic challenges and issues for family business, plus some that are specific to tourism and hospitality. Different stages of the life cycle are addressed, including the sole proprietor, coprenurial arrangements, the young business family with children, and the family working together. There are special sections on the family and the environment, and gender issues. Some research findings are presented to demonstrate real concerns from respondents in Australia, Canada and Denmark. Completing this chapter, attention is focused on issues relating to involvement of children in the business, leading to a detailed look at inheritance and succession planning. The concept of a family 'legacy' is discussed in this context.

Chapters 7–10 contain case studies of real family businesses in this industry, organized by sectors of the industry: farm-based; small hotels; resorts; tour companies; attractions. Chapter 11 consists of a cross-case analysis to identify 30 key themes and commonalities.

Two chapters summarize and conclude the book. The first, Chapter 12, draws management implications for the owners/operators of family businesses in tourism/hospitality, as well as implications for tourism destination management, economic and community development. The final chapter draws implications for research and theory, including analysis of gaps in the tourism and hospitality literature pertaining to family business, and a set of detailed propositions that can be used to develop theory. The 30 major themes identified in Chapter 11 are re-visited in the two concluding chapters.

Acknowledgements

The three principal authors are grateful to the earlier named contributors for their valuable contributions to this book. As well, we are sincerely grateful to all the respondents who provided details about their lives, families and businesses in the case studies. None of them requested anonymity, and so their successes and failures can be tracked. This takes some courage, and perhaps faith. The authors are extremely impressed with all the entrepreneurs and families engaged in enterprise, with the risks they take, and the challenges they face daily.

Specific thanks are also owed to the agencies that helped fund or otherwise support the research used in this book. Professor Getz is particularly grateful to the Family Business Endowment at the Haskayne Business School, University of Calgary, and to the Regional and Tourism Research Centre of Bornholm, Denmark. Professor Carlsen acknowledges initial support of the Faculty of Business at Edith Cowan University and more recently the Curtin Business School, Curtin University of Technology. Special thanks also to Ann Hall at Desktop Print for her work on the manuscript.

1

Introduction

Why Study Family Businesses?

Not all businesses are started for growth, profit maximization, or even for permanence – many are established or purchased with the needs and preferences of the owners and their families being paramount. That is the essence of 'family business', and it sets them apart from enterprises in which the owners and their families matter little to the strategy or operations of the enterprise.

Although it is widely accepted that the tourism and hospitality sectors are dominated by small, owner-operated business, little has been written specifically about the family dimension. The thorough review of tourism and hospitality literature contained in this book reveals growing attention to small businesses and entrepreneurship in this industry, but until now the core family-related issues have been neglected. And while many books and manuals have been published to guide families and owner-operators in generic business terms, none have dealt with the unique set of opportunities and issues that stem from owning and operating a business in tourism and hospitality.

Interest in, and research on, family business has been accelerating (Sharma *et al.*, 1996; Smyrnios *et al.*, 1997). This attention is long overdue, given the scale and importance of family businesses in most countries (Lank, 1995; Wortman, 1995). Small businesses predominate in emerging sectors such as nature tourism (McKercher, 1998), and most of these are run by owner-operators and families. Rural studies in general almost inevitably touch on family business matters (see, for example, Page and Getz, 1997).

Why is it important to devote research and a full book to the family business in this industry? There are a number of perspectives to be considered, as explained in the following sections.

Scope and Significance of Family Business

In most countries family business is the dominant form of business ownership and management. Historically, companies and other forms of ownership developed following individual and family-run farms and businesses, particularly to meet the needs of generating larger amounts of capital and dealing with legal issues such as protection against lawsuits and bankruptcy. It was the Industrial Revolution of the 18th century that replaced family-based craft industry with larger manufacturing enterprises. More recently, the rise of a giant service sector generated numerous new opportunities for family ventures.

Although big, public companies tend to attract the most attention, especially in terms of share offerings, stock values and speculation, family businesses will undoubtedly endure as the backbone of enterprise. The desire for autonomy – to be one's own boss – and for family independence, appears to be a basic and unchanging human trait. This motivator accounts for many career-switching entrepreneurs who start up tourism and hospitality businesses to escape what they do not like about their existing work and to steer their own economic future. But in lesser-developed economies there might be little choice – either run a business of your own, or move out. Tourism in developing countries offers numerous opportunities for self-employment and small, family businesses that otherwise would not exist.

Family businesses are especially dominant in rural and peripheral areas because of traditional land-owning patterns and the impracticalities of operating larger corporations in marginal economies. Hence, farm-based tourism and hospitality consists almost entirely of family businesses. Increasingly, individual and family investors are drawn to rural and peripheral areas or small towns for lifestyle reasons, and tourism/hospitality provides the economic means to realize these goals.

The exact scale and significance of family businesses remains subject to definitional and measurement problems, so mostly we have estimates. Westhead and Cowling (1998) reported a number of studies that have found that family firms account for over two-thirds of all businesses in western, developed economies. In Europe, 70% of businesses are family owned or controlled (Thomassen, 1992; Lank et al., 1994). Middleton (2001) noted that in Europe 95% of tourism businesses, generating perhaps one-third of total tourism revenue, are micro-business and most of these are family businesses.

It has been estimated that in the USA family firms generate from 40% to 60% of the gross national product (Ward and Aronoff, 1990) and employ half the workforce (Gersisk et al., 1997). Dyer (1986) and Rosenblatt et al. (1990) suggested that 90–95% of American businesses are family owned or controlled. Shanker and Astrachan (1996) estimated for the USA that as many as 20.3 million family businesses exist, accounting for up to 49% of the gross domestic product and 59% of total employment.

In Australia, Smyrnios and Romano (1999) said that family businesses make up 83% of all private-sector companies and employ more than 50% of the workforce, but the Commonwealth of Australia (1997) noted that about half of all

enterprises qualify as family businesses – that is, businesses where there is more than one proprietor from the same family. Canadian data suggest that family-owned firms constitute about 80% of all businesses (Dunlop, 1993). The consulting firm Deloitte and Touche (1999) said that family firms provided jobs for over 6 million Canadians out of a total population of approximately 30 million.

In many countries statistics on the scope and significance of family businesses are poor or non-existent, partly because of the difficulty in separating self-employment from business ownership, and partly because the term 'family business' is not used or understood. These definitional problems are discussed later.

The business management perspective

The importance of family business as a distinct form of management has only lately been recognized by academics, and has clearly been paid very little attention by tourism and hospitality scholars. Owner-operators and family-owned businesses have been lumped into the categories of small and medium enterprises, which ignores the fact that ownership makes a huge difference and that many are small for very personal, deliberate reasons. Also, the literature is full of references to 'mom and pop operations' which is usually a derisive term stemming from the supposed insignificance of this sector.

Consequently, little is known about the management of the family business in tourism and hospitality. What has been demonstrated repeatedly, in many countries and settings, is that tourism and hospitality attracts many investors for lifestyle and autonomy reasons, including the desire to be self-employed and the opportunity to remain in, or move to, attractive rural and resort areas. And there are many unique opportunities for individual entrepreneurship and family business within the industry.

Accordingly, the motives, goals and business behaviour of owners are different from other business types. Businesses owned and operated by individuals and families are typically not grown for the sake of getting bigger, nor are they managed as if profit-making was the sole objective. Family issues intrude on all aspects of the business, especially with regard to sharing responsibilities, involving the children, and succession (inheritance) within the family. Tourism/ hospitality businesses impose a number of special challenges on the family, particularly seasonality of demand causing cash-flow fluctuations, a high level of host–guest contact, almost unlimited demands on the operators' time, and the intrusion of guests into family space and time.

Do these fundamental differences necessarily make family businesses weak and unimportant? Are there no growth-oriented entrepreneurs among them? This book tries to answer these crucial questions. It is also hoped that family business owners will themselves benefit from increased understanding of their distinctive form of enterprise, and that tourism and hospitality students reading this book will better appreciate the opportunities available to them and the challenges faced by the many family businesses they will inevitably encounter.

Tourism destination perspective

Family business, in many areas, is the foundation of destination competitiveness. Small, owner-operated businesses provide most of the services and attractions in numeric terms, and are the outlets for much of the visitors' spending. The quality of experience realized in these businesses helps to determine perceptions of the destination as a whole. But if family businesses are marginal in terms of profits and sustainability, the destination can suffer.

Economic development perspective

Services, and tourism/hospitality in particular, have become the economic engines in many areas that would otherwise decline or remain impoverished. In a globalizing world that favours huge, transnational corporations, and concentrates wealth in large cities and conurbations, mechanisms are needed to distribute prosperity more widely. People who travel do just that. So do investors who take new money to create wealth-generating opportunities outside the core areas.

There are numerous policy-related issues involving the family business in terms of economic development, not the least of which is the fact that most owners do not want to grow their business and will therefore not create very many jobs. But perhaps some can be tempted and assisted to generate employment for non-family members.

Another concern is the lack of innovation among the majority of tourism and hospitality operators. Many people purchase existing properties and do little with them. Others create services that differ little from countless others. Indeed, tourism and hospitality services by definition are highly substitutable – that is, the consumer can go elsewhere and obtain the same benefits. So where is true innovation and hence long-term viability to come from?

Government and agencies wanting to retain population in peripheral and rural areas need to focus on creating employment. They need answers to the questions posed earlier: is it a sound strategy to assist all small business start-ups? what about people desiring to purchase a business? can the innovator and growth-oriented entrepreneur be singled out for special assistance?

Community perspective

The family is at the heart of many communities. If the family also happens to be in business, its potential contributions to community viability and culture are magnified, and so too are its responsibilities. Family businesses can and do make a visible difference in rural and peripheral areas, in small towns and resorts. Their contributions to cities and the larger community of nations are more difficult to demonstrate, but given the economic significance of the family business sector, are undoubtedly of great importance.

What happens when family businesses disappear and the families move away? At a minimum the community loses continuity and a degree of stability. And if the departers are not replaced by other families, the community loses population – and without children – its future.

Certainly the mechanics of depopulation in rural areas are well understood, as is the potential contribution of tourism in general (see, for example, Getz, 1986). The role of family businesses in particular has not been examined.

Families, their values and actions are also of concern to communities in terms of leadership in economic development and the environment. Because family-business owners tend to be rooted in their communities, or might want to make a positive contribution to their selected homes, they should be expected to provide leadership. The importance of this role is magnified in areas dependent on tourism and hospitality for their economic livelihood, and especially in areas basing their appeal on nature and health.

What is 'Family Business'?

'Family business' has no commonly accepted meaning. Indeed, Sharma *et al.* (1996) and Chua *et al.* (1999) comprehensively reviewed the literature and found 34 definitions. Birley (2001) also argued that in some countries the term 'family business' is not used, nor is it understood. All discussion of family business must therefore start with consideration of definitional issues, and researchers are well advised always to state their operational definitions.

We start with the premise that a 'business' of any kind is a profit-making venture or enterprise (Alcorn, 1982). There are, however, a number of complications, especially within tourism and hospitality, such as part-time businesses (e.g. running tours on weekends while otherwise employed), home-based businesses (which sometimes border on being a hobby), economic activities that are secondary to a main operation (such as farm-based tourism), and a business not easily separated from the family home (such as B&B). Indeed, this industry is somewhat unique in presenting the enterprising person or family with so many business options.

'Self-employment' is a related concept. Owning and operating a business makes one 'self-employed', but a person can be self-employed and not own or operate a 'business'. Provision of services (such as the sex trade or selling things on commission) is not the same as owning and operating a profit-making business. Normally a 'business' is a legal entity owned by

one or more people, although micro hospitality ventures like B&B provision will not usually meet this criterion. It is a fine point, and in this book not too much is made of the real or implicit distinctions.

Definitions of family business

At the most basic level a family business can be defined as '. . . an enterprise which, in practice, is controlled by members of a single family' (Barry, 1975). This definition can encompass businesses that involve only one owner, often called 'sole proprietorship' firms. Definitional complications arise when non-family members are involved in management or ownership (such as a partnership), or when a family firm 'goes public' with a share offering. Other definitions stress the degree of family involvement, whether or not the business has been or will be kept in the family across more than one generation, or a mix of criteria (Westhead and Cowling, 1998). In general, ownership and managerial criteria are both used.

The 1995 Business Longitudinal Survey (BLS) involving about 9000 businesses in Australia (Commonwealth of Australia, 1997) found characteristics of family businesses to be 'somewhat elusive', but the three main elements were said to be: succession (ownership remaining within the family); employment of family members (with or without management involvement); and shared management responsibilities (family members are jointly responsible for running the business).

Chua *et al.* (1999) argued for an inclusive definition of family business which would permit hierarchical comparisons of sub-types, otherwise the lack of comparability between studies will defeat the whole notion of treating family business as a separate field of inquiry. For example, in the research undertaken by Getz and Carlsen (2000) in Western Australia, the sole criterion for including owners in the 'family business' category was that respondents answered in the affirmative to this question: 'Is your business family owned (i.e. owner-operated, or one family owns controlling interest)?' This self-selection method has the advantage of being easily understood by respondents and does not impose a narrow definition. It allows analysis by other factors such as ownership type, participation by other family members, expressed motives and goals, or inherited versus new ventures.

Chua et al. (1999) also argued that the theoretical essence of a family business lies in the *vision* of its dominant family members. The vision must be to use the business for the betterment of the family – potentially across more than one generation. Birley (2001: 75) also concluded that '. . . owner/manager attitude is a more productive approach to describing and understanding the family business sector than the more traditional methods of equity or managerial control.' In this approach the vision (or motives and goals) and behaviour of the firm are differentiated from non-family businesses and from businesses in which family involvement makes no difference to its operations or future development.

In this book we decided to take a very inclusive approach in order to make it relevant to any individual, couple or family involved in owning and operating a business. Our definition is:

> The 'Family Business' consists of any business venture owned and/or operated by an individual, couple(s) or family.

Many family businesses in tourism and hospitality are small, but size is not a factor in our definition. Indeed, 'business venture' applies to micro-businesses such as B&B establishments or other services that might not even possess legal status or hold separate assets. Ownership is also not a hard and fast criterion, as many people in tourism and hospitality manage businesses that they do not fully own, through franchise or lease arrangements.

transference. About 20% of the family business literature is related to this issue of succession (Sharma et al., 1996: 9).

The concept of a business life cycle is well embedded in the family business literature, and it is inherently linked to entrepreneurship. This is because of the profound influence of founders in establishing business goals and organizational culture, and in determining the ultimate disposition of the business through sale or within-family succession. Accordingly, any study of family business must take into account the interactions between family and business over time.

The three-dimensional developmental model of family business by Gersick et al. (1997) is a useful starting point for understanding family business studies. It links three axes concerned with ownership, business, and family (see Fig. 1.1). The business develops through 'start-up' and 'expansion/formalization' to 'maturity'. Ownership potentially evolves from the 'controlling founder' through a 'sibling partnership' to a 'cousin consortium'. Along the family axis are four stages of family development: 'young business family'; 'children in the business'; 'working together'; and ultimately 'succession' (or business termination). As noted by Neubauer and Lank (1998), this $4 \times 3 \times 3$ matrix results in numerous possible combinations, and a given family enterprise could be at more than one stage on any of the three axes.

In the following sections we examine each of the three axes and their interrelationships, including references to pertinent discussions later in the book. We also incorporate issues identified in the cross-case analysis in Chapter 11, because the cases provide real-world insights and elaborate upon the theoretical model.

A Life Cycle Model for the Family Business

Neubauer and Lank (1998: 4) observed that family business studies are academically related to the traditions of research on entrepreneurship, owner-managed businesses, and small and medium-sized businesses. Overlap of these four traditions results in a complex interaction of themes, issues and approaches. The dominant and most unique family-business topic is that of inter-generational ownership

The family axis

In this axis a core concern is with entrepreneurship, foundation motives and goals. Differences can be expected between individual founders and married couples (with or without children) when they establish a business, as families have to be supported through the business and it cannot be treated simply as a financial investment. When the family is placed ahead of the business, sub-optimal business decisions might

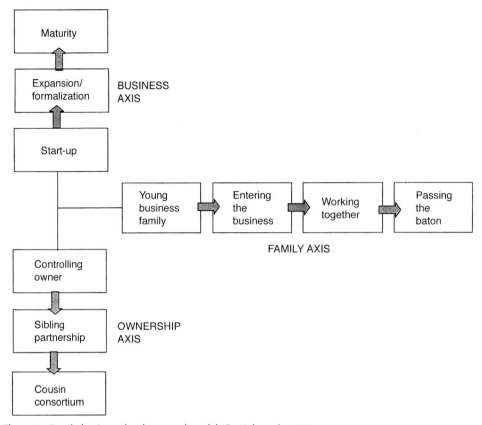

Fig. 1.1. Family business developmental model (Gersick *et al.*, 1997).

result. However, we have discovered that the direct involvement of children in businesses is not at all common, for a variety of reasons, and therefore inheritance of businesses is an option only for a small minority.

Our survey research and case studies reveal that many founders of tourism and hospitality businesses are motivated primarily by lifestyle and locational preferences, sometimes with the needs of children in mind but mostly with their own preferences being paramount. Shared hobbies, leisure pursuits, values and lifestyles lead numerous couples to enter tourism and hospitality businesses and provide them with a measure of cohesion. Strength can be derived for families when work and play coincide in the business.

Ties to the land emerged as an important theme in our research. In rural areas, and especially among farmers, holding on to the farm is a matter of stewardship and its inheritance is viewed as a legacy for the children. When the

farmers add a tourism or hospitality business it can complicate the process of inheritance, as business and land might have to be separated. Nevertheless, it appears that in the industrialized world the greatest number of businesses in this industry are created by urbanites moving to rural areas, and not by the farmers who have always lived there.

Research data also reveal that some founders were highly motivated by profit and growth prospects, and we called these 'growth-oriented entrepreneurs'. They are somewhat different in their values, attitudes, strategies and business practices. For example, they tend to seek out good investments, borrow more money, create companies, and favour larger businesses like hotels and restaurants, but they are also highly motivated by lifestyle and locational preferences. In the conclusions we discuss the importance of these entrepreneurs for community and destination development.

The family life cycle has a potentially profound impact on the business. Bringing children into the business will eventually lead to ownership and control issues. If the children do not want to take over the business, the founders might start planning to sell it, but when and under what circumstances will this fundamental choice become clear?

Family-business interactions are of utmost concern in the service sector, especially where customers are invited into the home or on to the family property. Some owners will be motivated to maximize contacts, while others seek to separate their home and business lives.

The roles of various family members can be an important factor, including age and gender-based differences. Female entrepreneurs are numerous in this industry, partly owing to the secondary nature of some of the businesses (for example, B&B within the family home), and the desire of many women to earn extra money, further their children's prospects, or gain some independence. In some cultures the natural heirs are expected to be males, while daughters face an uncertain future in the family business. As well, a division of labour based on traditional gender roles (e.g. females cook and clean, males do heavy work) might occur naturally without discussion, while in other family businesses a married couple will plan their roles. Several respondents told us that flexibility is a key, with everyone in the family expected to do whatever is necessary and not worry about job descriptions. Yet invariably it was the women who did the financial work and bookkeeping!

Family members have to believe in the business and show a sense of responsibility toward it. The level of family support given to the business, including money and labour, might be critical in assuring its success. The foundation stage requires strong support from all family members, or (as shown in at least one of the cases) all members must at least acquiesce. It can certainly be hypothesized that division over the foundation of a family business will lead to disharmony and problems later.

A related theme is that of internal family conflicts, specifically over goals and agreement on solving problems, plus the issue of finding equal worth within the family business or within the family in general. Dispute identification and resolution mechanisms are needed, and they can be either informal or formal. Open and honest relations were said to be important by some of our married respondents. Responding to adversity was also shown to be crucial, as anything impacting on family or business affects the entire family business system. Sibling relationships were found to be an important issue in our case studies, particularly with regard to their skills, interest in the family business, and level of involvement with it.

Family culture interacts with organizational culture at all levels. Where do the values, traditions and leadership come from, and are they passed on through generations? Are entrepreneurship and innovation hereditary or determined by parental influence? In some families there is a strong desire to create or perpetuate a legacy of land, business or wealth, while in others it is absent. Not only does family culture permeate business decision-making but it sets an emotional climate into which employees and guests enter temporarily. According to Litz and Kleysen (2002: 291) family culture needs more study to develop a theory of the family firm. For example, they asked, '. . . what kinds of family cultures support innovation and what cultures frustrate it?'

Broader cultural factors also affect the family business. In some cultures entrepreneurship is valued and in others it is atypical. Gender roles and inheritance can be greatly impacted by cultural norms.

The business axis

The three stages of business development (start-up, expansion/formalization, maturity) relate to professionalization of the owners and the business, structure, growth, business operations, owner–worker relations, and planning. One of the central questions in family business studies is that of control and stability versus a growth orientation. In other words, do family and lifestyle considerations take precedence over growth?

Most family businesses in tourism and hospitality never evolve beyond the foundation stage. Farm families motivated to secure a little extra income, or B&B operators interested in meeting visitors, are unlikely and often unable to expand. Growth for the sake of growth, or to maximize profit, is often not desired in family firms. Rather, the owners need to carefully weigh the merits of remaining debt-free versus borrowing to expand, and the need to add value to the business in order to generate an adequate income.

Taking on paid staff or retaining professional managers are big issues for small family businesses. Owner-operators in tourism and hospitality often have to hire staff seasonally, but fall back on family members during low-demand periods. Many want to hire managers or lower-level staff to free up the owner's time, but costs and risks intervene.

Lack of professionalism is a frequent complaint levelled at family businesses. In tourism and hospitality, low entry barriers might attract investors with little or no relevant training or education. This can severely limit their potential to grow or prosper. And if family firms grow substantially, should they hire professional managers or establish a board of directors encompassing non-family members? These questions clearly link to ownership and control.

Our research revealed a number of important challenges for operating a family business in this industry. There is a real need for excellent customer service, including family branding and cultivating networks among suppliers and industry partners. Going it alone is difficult, so alliances and cooperative efforts, particularly in marketing, become essential. We observed an over-dependence on word-of-mouth marketing, which works well when demand is steady or expanding, and a weakness in doing segmentation to determine key target markets.

Human resource management is quite different in the family business. Most 'employees' are family members, and they are not always paid a wage or salary. Children might work informally in the business, leading to issues of lifestyle, safety and training. When should they become real, paid employees? Many respondents told us they were hoping to be able to afford to hire paid staff, in order to lift the burden of work, but they either could not generate sufficient and sustained income or they lacked confidence or trust in non-family workers. Managing part-time and casual staff is often required, particularly because seasonality of demand is such an important limiting factor in this industry.

Financial management skills are essential for the family business operator. Mostly it is females who do this work, but where do their skills come from? Formal training in marketing and other management skills helps, but is not always available.

The ownership axis

Some of the key questions along this axis are: what ownership forms are used by family businesses; who in the family is involved in ownership; and how does that evolve and are there gender differences? The model (Fig. 1.1) suggests that siblings take over from founders and ultimately a group of cousins might end up in control of the business.

A central issue for all family businesses is that of control. A family firm can be controlled without total ownership, but many owners might not want to take on partners or issue public shares. Also, if founders are determined to perpetuate family control they need to install legal mechanisms to prevent family shares from being sold externally, such as by establishing a family trust. Many notable family businesses have self-destructed through in-fighting over control and/or asset disposition. Some of our respondents also showed us that partnerships between families can be quite problematic, with one ultimately buying out the other as a solution to disputes.

Financing, ownership and control are interdependent. Equity in real estate, as with farms and houses used in the business, might have to be mortgaged to start and operate a tourism and hospitality business. Property assets might be high in paper value, but the business might generate little in the way of cash flow. This leads to difficulties in both paying family members a proper income and allowing them to 'cash in' on the business or land value. A classic problem is deciding how much income to put back into the business as working capital, as opposed to taking it as income or dividends. It appears that many families plough their earnings back into the business out of necessity or the desire to grow it.

Access to capital is a real challenge for the family business owner, and so most rely on their own or family support plus bank loans and mortgages. Under-capitalization limits profits and growth potential, although this is common to small businesses in general. Too much debt, however, threatens the business and the family's security. Most respondents in our surveys and cases were debt-averse, except for the 'growth-oriented entrepreneurs' who look for and seize financial opportunities. The ability to survive a financial shock, such as a major downturn in demand, is a matter of life and death for small, family businesses. Many fail or consistently under-perform, even in their owners' opinions.

In many cases the land and/or business might have to be sold outside the family because owners need the money for their retirement. But if owners are looking ahead to within-family inheritance of the business, the form of ownership might have to change. For example, potential heirs can be brought legally into the ownership before the founders retire. Problems might arise if more than one potential successor is involved in the business, especially where real property is to be kept separate from business assets.

We found that planning for succession was not at all prevalent, and for many respondents the question of inheritance within the family was not even an issue – it was not desired or not practical. Those who do want their family members to take over a business must plan for it well in advance, especially by getting their children involved at an early stage and giving them increasingly responsible roles to play. Many barriers have been identified, and so it is when a successful succession takes place. Equally, it is unusual to find mutigenerational family businesses in tourism and hospitality.

Using the life cycle model

Table 1.1 summarizes much of the discussion by Gersik et al. (1997) on challenges facing the family business through the life cycle. For each of the three axes of 'business', 'ownership' and 'family', some key challenges within each hypothetical development stage are indicated.

What is particularly useful about this life cycle approach is that it encourages integrative thinking and research about the family enterprise. The business and the family evolve together, with different opportunities and issues to face at each stage. Ownership might have to adapt as children become involved, and ultimately a decision has to be made about keeping the business in the family (i.e. succession), selling out, or dissolving it. Decision-points along one axis affect elements in the others.

This model also clearly points out the need for long-term, strategic thinking in the family business. Do the founders want to create a family legacy, or are children and their future in the business even a consideration? The characteristics of second- or third-generation family businesses are likely to be quite different from those in the early years. Because research in a number of countries has revealed a very high level of start-ups, and a small number of family businesses that have been inherited, less is known about the long-standing family business in tourism/hospitality.

Major themes in family business studies

Table 1.2 provides a broader summary of the main family business themes. A key source for this tabulation is the annotated bibliography produced by Sharma et al. (1996). While all of the main themes are discussed in this book, as well as the key life cycle-related challenges indicated earlier, they are not all treated equally or in depth. This is partly due to insufficient industry-specific material. Also, because the bulk of family businesses in tourism and hospitality never make it to the second or third generation, there is less value in dwelling on succession planning, 'sibling partnerships' or the 'cousin consortium' stage.

A Framework for Understanding Family Business in Tourism and Hospitality

While generic family business issues are applicable, it is also apparent from the research and literature examined in this book that that the tourism and hospitality industry embodies a number of unique or especially important considerations relative to the family business. Figure 1.2 gives a conceptual starting point for understanding the family business in this industry.

Table 1.1.   Challenges through the family business stages of development (from Gersick *et al.*, 1997).

Business	Ownership	Family
Start-up ● Survival (market entry, business planning, financing) ● Rational analysis versus the dream	*Controlling owner* ● Capitalization ● Balancing unitary control with input from key stakeholders ● Choosing and ownership structure for the next generation	*Young business family* ● Creating a workable marriage enterprise ● Making initial decisions about the relationship between work and family ● Working out relationships with the extended family ● Raising children
Expansion/formalization ● Evolving the owner-manager role and professionalizing the business ● Strategic planning ● Organizational systems and policies ● Cash management	*Sibling partnership* ● Developing a process for shared control among owners ● Defining the role of nonemployed owners ● Retaining capital ● Controlling the fractional orientation of family branches	*Entering the business* ● Managing the midlife transition ● Separation and individuation of the younger generation ● Facilitating a good process for initial career decisions
Maturity ● Strategic refocus ● Management and ownership commitment ● Reinvestment	*Cousin consortium* ● Managing the complexity of the family and the stakeholder group ● Creating a family business capital market	*Working together* ● Fostering cross-generational cooperation and communication ● Encouraging productive conflict management ● Managing the three-generation working together family
		Passing the baton ● Senior generation disengagement from the business ● Generational transfer of family leadership

The core of the framework has already been discussed, consisting of the family vision and the three interdependent axes of family, ownership and business evolution. One can look for unique aspects of vision (and related goals), and of the evolution of ownership, family and business that are found in no other industry. Researchers can also try to identify particularly dominant forces within the industry that affect the family business.

The nature of the industry itself acts to modify family business issues. We first address the general business environment for tourism and hospitality, then look at a number of specific modifiers including the nature of the services provided, host–guest relationships, cyclical demand (especially seasonality), the influence of the destination life cycle, and unique business opportunities.

Tourism and hospitality is a truly global industry, and the many settings in which tourism and hospitality businesses exist act as modifiers of the core elements. The setting is important both in terms of location (urban, rural, resort and peripheral are discussed) and with regard to cultural influences and the level of economic development.

The core

Why people get into and stay in tourism and hospitality businesses is a crucial question, particularly when the industry offers so many challenges and often delivers a poor return on investment. For a small minority there is little if any family consideration, but most owners and operators in the industry work with one or more family members and many are preoccupied with family matters. It is vital to understand their motives, goals and family vision, particularly as

Table 1.2.   Major themes in family business studies.

Themes	Specific topics within themes
Definitions	• Criteria for defining a family business • Types of family businesses
Uniqueness of family business	• Their unique strengths (e.g. family branding; loyalty) and weaknesses (e.g. nepotism; lack of growth)
Life-cycle	• Evolution of ownership, the family, and the business
Succession and inheritance	• Succession and estate planning • Barriers to involvement of children
Governance	• Ownership, control and organizational structure • The owner/founder, CEO and Boards of Directors • Family trusts
Strategic management	• Family vision (e.g. taking the long-term perspective) • Strategies and strategic planning
The founders	• Motives and goals • Entrepreneurship • Leadership • Reluctance to 'pass the baton'
Family influence and dynamics	• Family culture (e.g. the legacy; innovation) • Sibling rivalry • Copreneurship (couples working together) • Gender roles • Intergenerational relationships • Nepotism
Culture and ethnicity	• Variations in family business • Influences of culture or ethnicity
Professionalism	• Working with employees • Transition to a professionally managed firm; professional advisers
The family in society	• Social and community responsibility • Environmental attitudes and practices • Social and family networking

Source: Sharma *et al.*, 1996.

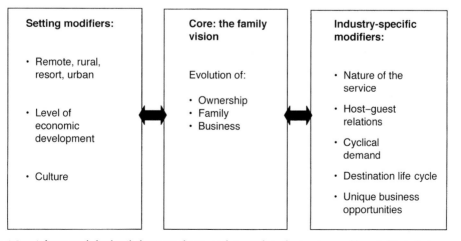

Fig. 1.2.   A framework for family business theory and research in the tourism and hospitality industry.

they might affect business viability and wider economic and community development.

Our examination of core issues begins in Chapter 2 with a detailed discussion of entrepreneurship as it applies to the family business. This theme also figures prominently in Chapter 3 where motives and goals of family business owners in the industry are examined in detail, and again in the case study chapters. Indeed, consideration of family vision and business goals permeates the book. A number of major conclusions about the core vision are discussed in this book's conclusions. By way of preview, the following paragraphs summarize the most important points.

The need for autonomy drives many entrepreneurs, and control-related motives and goals are found to be very important among owners of tourism and hospitality businesses. Autonomy also leads many people specifically to service-sector ventures where they can manage an establishment in a hands-on fashion. Autonomy and lifestyle motives are closely bound.

Lifestyle motives are a dominant reason for setting up or purchasing a tourism or hospitality business, particularly the desire to live in an attractive (often rural) area. Related motives include the desire to stay in or return to family property, and the notion of creating or perpetuating a family legacy. Resorts and other recreational environments attract a lot of people interested in pursuing their favourite sports, while hospitality businesses afford operators the opportunity to pursue life-long interests in a creative environment (e.g. cooking, arts and crafts, flowers, catering, decorating, events production).

Some entrepreneurs and self-employed persons have little choice. They either need extra income (such as to support a farm) or the economy does not provide good employment alternatives. Migrants might find their new environments to be hostile and self-employment is therefore preferred, particularly where family and ethnic networks can be of assistance. Migrants returning home from abroad have been found to be a source of investment in tourism and hospitality, as they can bring back new capital, skills and attitudes.

The profit-maximizing, growth-oriented entrepreneur has been found to be a small minority within family businesses in tourism and hospitality. In most cases, the autonomy and lifestyle goals prevail and the business is deliberately kept small and manageable. Mobilizing the growth-oriented entrepreneur should be a priority of economic and destination development agencies, as should the task of identifying *latent* entrepreneurship among those constrained by a lack of capital or professional advice.

Where is the family vision in all this? First, autonomy and lifestyle motives are a family-first vision, making the business a means towards an end. For a sub-set, the business offers the specific type of family life the owners (typically couples working together) are seeking. Either way, the dominance of these types of family business in tourism and hospitality, at least in highly developed economies, ensures that the sector will remain largely one of small and micro businesses. Second, the family vision as related to children and possible succession is revealed to be of secondary importance and frequently is not an issue at all. As will be demonstrated, most family businesses in this industry do not involve children at all, and very few get inherited.

While motives and goals have been clearly identified, less is known about evolutionary processes within and among the three axes of ownership, family and business. Most do not involve children or make it to the next generation. Researchers will have to focus on selected multi-generational family businesses to determine if they behave differently from other family businesses.

The business environment and industry-specific modifiers

Tourism and hospitality are not always considered together, nor are they universally acknowledged to be an industry, but from the perspective of family business studies they are sufficiently similar to be studied together. For the purposes of this book, the tourism and hospitality 'industry' is defined as consisting of those businesses catering for travellers and persons pursuing leisure activities, including accommodation, catering (food and beverage services), transport and tour services, attractions, activities and entertainment. As well, in many tourist destinations a large number of retailers and arts and crafts manufacturers cater primarily to visitors, so a broad range of enterprises can be included. However, the full extent to which tourism and hospitality services resemble other service-sector family businesses remains to be examined.

The business environment

Westhead and Cowling (1998: 44) discovered through systematic research in the UK that '. . . family companies are over-represented in services activities with low capital requirements.' They are also over-represented in rural areas, and especially in hotels and catering, and are smaller in terms of sales and number of employees.

Part of the explanation for this over-representation of family businesses is the fact that many types of tourism and hospitality business are easy to enter and exit. Either they do not require special skills, lengthy experience, or large amounts of capital, or entrepreneurs think they do. Naivety and over-optimism seem to be commonplace in small family businesses in these sectors. One result is that many such businesses fail to meet owners' performance standards, or fail outright.

Policy regarding economic development generally favours tourism and hospitality investments, at least in designated areas – typically those peripheral to urban and economic centres. Ironically, the industry is also highly regulated and taxed. Consumer rights, health and safety, environmental codes, land use planning and much more impact on small and micro businesses disproportionately.

Tourism and hospitality services are experiential, and therefore highly substitutable. Competition is frequently intense, not only between businesses offering virtually identical products and services, but between all destinations. Large corporations and franchise chains have tremendous advantages, leaving family businesses to find viable niche markets. Small businesses in general can organize to achieve greater efficiencies in operations and a wider market reach, but often there are not enough of them in an area to make a real difference this way.

To some, the tourism/hospitality business environment is typically challenging and often hostile to the family business. It is a tribute to individual and family vision, hard work and persistence that the sector endures and that many families actually prosper.

Nature of the service

Tourism and hospitality are highly experiential in nature. In fact, the family can be an important part of that service, especially when the business brings customers into the family's home or land. Wanhill (1997) noted that families can be part of the tourism experience, and can help to increase customer satisfaction by providing good local information to visitors. When the family becomes part of the attraction it can be said that 'family branding' is occurring, and this could become a powerful competitive advantage. Researchers and teachers in tourism and hospitality have not paid much attention to family branding, but this book contains an excellent case and a pertinent discussion of issues.

Host–guest relations

Many tourism and hospitality businesses require a high degree of host–guest contact, often to the point where family and work become blurred. The owner or owner's family members directly provide guests with accommodation, hospitality, entertainment, information and interpretation, food, or activities. Regardless of their growth orientation, families must usually add value to their business to earn enough money to hire staff so they can gain relief from long hours and constantly being 'on call'. For example, Long and Edgell (1997: 73) observed in their case study of a couple running a campground: 'The owners did note the value of being able to leave the property from time to time and the importance of having dependable employees to look after the operation when they are away.'

Contact between hosts and guests is sometimes a motive for establishing the business, but also a potential source of stress through loss of privacy, handling many demands and complaints, and time pressures. Some of the businesses require a high degree of technical expertise, but many are rooted in 'people skills' like friendliness, helpfulness and integrity.

Cyclical demand and seasonality

One of the hallmarks of tourism is cyclical demand (Murphy, 1985). Many destinations and tourism settings are particularly hard hit by seasonal and weekend peaks, followed by low demand periods. In the Western Australian sample (Getz and Carlsen, 2000), 61% agreed or strongly agreed that their business was highly seasonal. Another 17% were uncertain, which possibly reflects their newness.

The main problems presented by seasonality relate to cash flow and overall profitability, even threatening their viability (Baum, 1998), but it does offer families a lull during which pursuit of family and lifestyle goals can dominate. In fact, Brown (1987) concluded that taking a long, seasonal break from work was a motivator for some family business owners, and this fact impeded growth potential.

Can small businesses survive the potential cash-flow problems? Can families adjust to the peaks and troughs in terms of workload? Is staff available to help out? These represent very serious challenges to the family business owner. A study of seasonality in the Danish island of Bornholm (Lundtorp et al., 1999) revealed some of the pressures that are generated on family businesses. They found that owners relied heavily on summer student workers to meet peak demand, and often worked 100 hours a week themselves over a 16–20 week season. Some took another job in the off-season, while others had to sustain the business (e.g. repairs, marketing).

Seasonality of demand is such a global phenomenon, and usually so predictable, that owners and potential investors in tourism and hospitality have to carefully weigh the implications for business viability and decide whether or not they can handle (or even prefer) the seasonal lifestyle swings. A number of strategies can be employed by family businesses to either counter cyclical demand or adapt to it, as discussed in Chapter 4. All of the options have impacts both on family life and business prospects.

Destination life cycle

The destination life cycle model (Butler, 1980) incorporates an evolution of business investment and ownership with implications for owner-operators and resident versus in-migrant owners. Din (1992) specifically hypothesized that local entrepreneurs dominate in the early stages of development, while Shaw and Williams (1997) suggest that it cannot be assumed that residents have access to capital or are entrepreneurial enough to take advantage of new opportunities. Cooper (1997: 87), commenting on the decline of British coastal resorts, said that many resorts suffer from a lack of investment in the accommodation sector. 'This is due to a combination of seasonality, low occupancy patterns and the characteristics of ownership in the sector, all of which conspire to drive down profitability.'

It remains questionable whether or not any stage in the hypothetical life cycle of destinations presents better opportunities for family business, for residents versus in-migrants, or small versus large companies. A connection between family business and resort decline has been hypothesized and should be tested in a variety of settings.

Unique business opportunities

Tourism and hospitality present a number of unique business opportunities that appear to have specific appeal to individual entrepreneurs and to families. People interested in outdoor recreation can start touring or outfitting companies, or provide facilities. Those with rural property can establish farmstays, campgrounds, and B&B houses, all of which have their own niche markets. Opportunities also exist to meet tourists' needs and desire for fresh produce, antiques, or other merchandise with a unique rural flavour. There is virtually an unlimited scope for creativity, hands-on operations, and provision of new types of services and service environments.

Setting modifiers: location

Although there is a spectrum of settings to consider in geographical terms, most attention within the tourism literature has been given to rural, resort and peripheral settings. Not much has been said about small and family businesses in urban locations.

Urban settings

Urban areas should present numerous opportunities for family businesses, but as discovered by Westhead and Cowling (1998) in the UK, they are actually over-represented in rural areas. Mostly there are no comparative data available on urban versus other business environments for tourism and hospitality enterprises, so it remains a topic in need of study.

The urban environment certainly presents numerous opportunities for family businesses in retailing, catering, accommodation and other services, because of large local and travel markets to draw upon and presumably less seasonality of demand. As most cities have areas or highway strips where motels and restaurants flourish, it can be hypothesized that family businesses will find niche markets and be spatially concentrated in the urban setting. A contrary hypothesis might be that large corporations and chains will dominate urban markets to the point where smaller, family businesses are not competitive.

Rural areas

Many researchers have written about farm and rural tourism, and it has generally been concluded (e.g. Evans and Ilbury, 1992; Page and Getz, 1997) that there has been substantial growth in this industry in recent decades. Part of the explanation for expansion is that of subsidies to farmers for diversification, and partly it is attributable to the lifestyle and locational choices of numerous entrepreneurs.

Komppula (2000) noted that there are about 3600 rural tourism enterprises in Finland, of which three-quarters were originally farms. However, tourism is a major source of income for only about 15% of these mostly family-owned enterprises. They are characteristically part-time owner-operators possessing limited financial resources, low skills and little commitment to development. The businesses themselves consist of cottages and farm buildings for rent, B&B accommodation, farm visits, group catering, holiday villages and recreational activities.

In Denmark about 10% of farms have developed some form of tourism service (Hjalager, 1996). These include farm vacations with access to animals and social contacts with the owners, or merely accommodation. They are usually established to supplement farm income and apparently perform poorly in financial terms.

Numerous issues pertaining to tourism and hospitality businesses in the rural environment have been identified and discussed by Page and Getz (in *The Business of Rural Tourism*, 1997). Some of these are especially pertinent to family businesses, although there has not been any systematic research aimed at making that connection. First, dependency on the natural resource base is high, and often an essential part of the tourism experience. Accordingly there is a need for sustainable development and operations in all businesses, and an appropriate ethic among business operators.

People interested in the environment (and in outdoor recreation) might therefore make better prospects for rural tourism and hospitality investments.

Rural areas are frequently remote from markets and have accessibility problems due to distance or poor infrastructure. In such areas businesses can be highly dispersed, increasing their dependence on intermediaries to connect supply with demand, and on destination organizations or industry partnerships for marketing efforts. Some families living in remote areas might desire the new revenue and social interactions that a tourism business can bring, while others do seek out remoter areas for lifestyle reasons and use tourism as a means to survive there. Remoteness and/or poor accessibility have serious business implications (from extra costs to increased risks of theft and fire) and also impact directly on the family in terms of relationships, shopping, leisure opportunities, schooling, and other essential services. This environment most likely attracts and sustains certain types of personalities, or families with unique backgrounds, and repels others.

Another feature of rural tourism and hospitality businesses identified by Page and Getz (1997) is that of financing difficulties. Many are self-financed, in part to retain control, and partly because of the difficulty in obtaining loans or external investors. This can expose the family business to high financial risks, and can easily limit their ability to grow or adapt.

Peripheral areas

'Peripherality' in the European Union context is based on distance from the economic centre, and implies some or all of the following characteristics (from Nilsson et al., 2004):

- Sparsely populated, and often depopulating.
- Dependent on primary resource extraction or farming; a small manufacturing sector.
- Relatively isolated communities (particularly on islands, along coastlines and in rural areas).
- Costly and/or difficult accessibility.
- Extreme seasonality.
- Potentially high impacts on communities and the ecosystem.

The tourism industry is often of great economic importance in peripheral areas, given the lack of viable alternatives. European Union policies have favoured tourism development (Wanhill, 1997) as an organic solution, with the assumption that farms can add facilities and fishing communities can adapt to recreational activities. However, peripheral tourism typically suffers from high costs, low accessibility, a lack of infrastructure or quality facilities, and a dependence on intermediaries. The local population might not have the skills, capital or inclination to develop tourism, and a dependence on government aid might actually stifle entrepreneurship (Morrison, 1998). Marketing and planning functions for tourism are also likely to be under-developed in these regions.

Morrison (1998: 195) defined 'positives' and 'weaknesses' for the small tourism and hospitality firm in peripheral areas. In addition to the challenges mentioned earlier, these firms (in most cases they are family businesses) face scarce human and constrained financial resources, declining traditional markets (such as the long, seaside holiday in hotels and pensions), and a fragmented industry. On the positive side, small businesses can attempt to capitalize on the appeal of nature and solitude, cultural authenticity, personalized service, and where available, public-sector support. As well, Haber and Lerner (2002) suggested that tourism ventures in peripheral areas might be able to take advantage of under-exploited factors of production, such as existing farm buildings.

The special issues applying to tourism in peripheral areas have been examined in some detail (Brown and Hall, 2000). Island tourism studies, which often embodies peripherality issues, has also produced a number of specific books and special issues of academic journals. Although family-related issues are frequently mentioned in these studies, notably gender roles and the prominence of lifestyle entrepreneurs, nothing systematic has been reported on family business themes in peripheral tourism.

Resorts

Resorts are self-contained settings for vacations or other overnight trip types. By definition they are visitor-oriented and focus on services of all kinds for meeting visitor needs and preferences. They range from small ecolodges in natural areas to fully-planned, integrated resort complexes and major cities. Resort environments should be the richest of all for family businesses in tourism and hospitality, mainly because of the wide range of required services and a huge scope for niche marketing. But are they? Later in this book comparative data are presented from research on family businesses in two resort environments – an island, coastal resort area (Bornholm, Denmark) and a mountain resort (Canmore, Canada). Large, urban resorts have not been studied from the family business perspective, nor have remote eco-resorts.

The nature of the resort attraction base might play a major role in determining family business opportunities (e.g. small tour companies) and of course the markets – such as a preference for B&B or budget accommodation. It might also be that the resort life cycle favours family businesses at the early stage of development, before chains and large corporations make substantial inroads.

The setting: level of economic development

Highly developed, industrialized economies can be expected to generate more and different opportunities and challenges for entrepreneurs and family business. Cultural factors will also vary along the development continuum. One probable difference is the dominance of a life-style orientation among tourism and hospitality owners in developed economies, whereas in poorer economies it can be expected that people have less money and less choice, giving rise to a family business by necessity.

In tourist-receiving societies in less-developed nations, according to Harrison (1992), structures inherited from the colonial period might act against entrepreneurial activity by residents, or restrict them to specific sectors. In-migrants (often retiring in a new location) or returning migrants often dominate the entre-preneurial class. Local elites are often favoured in developing business links with international tourism firms, and these elites might stem from racial or ethnic differences.

Research by Haber and Lerner (2002) revealed that the inherent attractiveness of the location (within Israel's Negev region) was more important than institutional support in explaining business profits, but organizational and managerial variables were the most impor-tant variables. They also examined various types of support that could be utilized in remote areas and lesser-developed economies, including business 'incubators', financial and informational/advisory support.

Resorts often occupy a special place in developing economies. If the resort is a fully self-contained enclave, it might generate few if any local business opportunities. Larger, integrated resort complexes present many opportunities for both 'grey-market' self-employment (e.g. drugs, the sex trade) and local investment in service enterprises.

The setting: culture

Family business in tourism and hospitality will also be linked to culture, although this theme has only been touched upon in the research literature. The core–periphery model was used by Britton (1981) to explain the development of entrepreneurial enclaves in developing nations, and these hypothetically present similar oppor-tunities for family business as those existing in fully industrialized economies. Lundgren's (1973) evolutionary model suggests increasing entrepreneurial opportunities for residents of

the hinterland as a resort or tourist enclave develops.

Culture influences entrepreneurship in general and family business specifically, as some cultures are more open to personal and family business initiatives, and among some cultures continuation of a family business is either shunned or encouraged. For example, Dondo and Ngumo (1998) said that Kenya does not have a culture strongly supportive of entrepre-neurship – it is too conformist, with collective rather than individualistic values predominating. Also, Kenyans tend to live for the moment, lack independence, and are reluctant to accept responsibility. Much of this stems from tribal traditions.

Family business exists within aboriginal or indigenous communities, but it has not been examined in any systematic manner. The tourism and hospitality literature contains many examples of indigenous or aboriginal tourism development, but few deal with individual entrepreneurship or family matters. Getz and Jamieson's (1997) case study of one native entrepreneur in Alberta, Canada, demonstrated special concerns of ownership (i.e. who owns the cultural 'product'?) and the potentially wide extent of family involvement in any business venture. When community ownership of resources prevails, entrepreneurship and family business take on different characteristics.

Notzke (1999) reported on one married aboriginal couple in the Canadian Arctic who were firmly rooted in a way of life tied to the land, but who provided a tourism product for part of the year. This combination maximized the family's ability to maintain their way of life. Many tourists want this type of authentic cultural experience, especially as it provides opportunities for learnig about everyday life in aboriginal communities and families.

In Western Samoa, Fairbairn-Dunlop (1994) concluded that customary land owner-ship results in the necessity that tourism ventures be family or village initiatives. Samoan woman have built successful businesses out of an initial small-scale activity because the endurance of customs has meant that women have received an education, are used to taking initiatives and accepting the consequences, and can use the traditional family system for the benefit of the family and the business.

Frideres (1988) argued that capitalism runs counter to the interests of indigenous people, and that development must be based on community control rather than individual enterprise, but there are many examples of both collective and individual native enterprise in tourism and hospitality, so it remains an issue for research and debate.

Chapter Summary

Issues specific to the family business in tourism and hospitality have long been subsumed under the more general headings of small business and entrepreneurship. What makes the family business unique and worthy of special interest is not merely its almost global significance in terms of numbers of enterprises, nor its typically small size. Rather, it is the vision of owners to start a business to serve personal and family needs, potentially across generations, that sets them apart. Often they are based on lifestyle and locational preferences, plus the desire for autonomy, and do not seek or are incapable of supporting growth and profit maximization.

A greater understanding of the family business and its environment will not only aid in the betterment of this important industry sector, but will provide benefit to economic and community development, and to destination competitiveness. They are so important, particularly in rural, resort and peripheral areas, that ignoring their special goals and needs can potentially be very damaging to industry and community sustainability.

This introductory chapter defines 'family business' and utilizes a well-known life cycle model (Gersik et al., 1997) to establish a framework for examining the inter-dependent evolutionary processes of ownership, family and business. Major themes in the generic family business literature are also summarized, and these are revisited in the concluding chapter in the context of identifying research needs specific to tourism and hospitality.

An industry-specific framework was developed for understanding the family business, starting with the generic core of family vision and the three evolutionary processes of family, business and ownership. It has been argued that the business environment and industry-specific

modifiers make family business somewhat unique in tourism and hospitality. The most important modifiers are likely to be the nature of the service environment, including host–guest interactions that are frequently home-based, the owners and family as part of the experience, cyclical demand (i.e. seasonality), the destination life cycle, and unique business opportunities such as those stemming from farm operations or personal leisure interests and skills. Setting modifiers have also been explored in detail, beginning with the differences imposed by a peripheral, rural, resort or urban location for the family business. The level of economic activity in the environment will have an impact on family business, as will cultural factors.

References

Alcorn, P. (1982) Success and Survival in the Family-owned Business. McGraw Hill, New York.

Barry, B. (1975) The development of organisation structure in the family firm. Journal of General Management Autumn, 42–60.

Baum, T. (1998) Tourism marketing and the small island environment: cases from the periphery. In: Laws, E., Faulkner, B. and Moscardo, G. (eds) Embracing and Managing Change in Tourism: International Case Studies. Routledge, London, pp. 116–137.

Birley, S. (2001) Owner-manager attitudes to family and business Issues: a 16 country study. Entrepreneurship Theory and Practice 26(2), 63–76.

Britton, S. (1981) Tourism, Dependency and Development: a Mode of Analysis. Occasional Paper No. 23. Development Studies, Australian National University, Canberra, Australia.

Brown, B. (1987) Recent tourism research in south east Dorset. In: Shaw, G. and Williams, A. (eds) Tourism and Development: Overviews and Case Studies of the UK and the South West Region. Department of Geography, University of Exeter, Exeter, UK.

Brown, F. and Hall, D. (eds) (2000). Tourism in Peripheral Areas: Case Studies. Channel View Publications, Clevedon, UK.

Butler, R. (1980) The concept of a tourist area cycle of evolution: implications for management of resources. Canadian Geographer 14, 5–12.

Chua, J., Chrisman, J. and Sharma, P. (1999) Defining the family business by behaviour. Entrepreneurship Theory and Practice 24(4), 19–39.

Commonwealth of Australia (1997) *A Portrait of Australian Business*. Department of Industry, Science and Tourism, Canberra, Australia.

Cooper, C. (1997) Parameters and indicators of the decline of the British seaside resort. In: Shaw, G. and Williams, A. (eds) *The Rise and Fall of British Coastal Resorts: Cultural and Economic Perspectives*. Mansell, London, pp. 79–101.

Deloitte and Touche (1999) $1.3 trillion at stake as Canada's family businesses face leadership crisis. www.deloitte.ca

Din, K. (1992) The 'involvement stage' in the evolution of a tourist destination. *Tourism Recreation Research* 17(1), 10–20.

Dondo, A. and Ngumo, M. (1998) Africa: Kenya. In: Morrison, A. (ed.) *Entrepreneurship: an International Perspective*. Butterworth Heinemann, Oxford, UK, pp. 15–26.

Dunlop, M. (1993) Parents' beliefs can cause trouble in family firms. *The Toronto Star* 20 November, pp. K2.

Dyer, W. (1986) *Cultural Change in Family Firms: Anticipating and Managing Business and Family Traditions*. Jossey Bass, San Francisco.

Evans, N. and Ilbery, W. (1992) Advertising and farm-based accommodation: a British case study. *Tourism Management* 13, 415–422.

Fairbairn-Dunlop, P. (1994) Gender, culture and tourism development in Western Samoa. In: Kinnaird, V. and Hall, D. (eds) *Tourism: a Gender Analysis*. John Wiley & Sons, Chichester, UK, pp. 121–141.

Frideres, J. (1988) *Native Peoples in Canada: Contemporary Conflicts*, 3rd edn. Prentice-Hall Canada Inc., Scarborough, Canada.

Gersick, K., Davis, J., Hampton, M. and Lansberg, I. (1997) *Generation to Generation*. Harvard Business School Press, Boston, Massachusetts.

Getz, D. (1986) Tourism and population change: long term impacts of tourism in the Badenoch-Strathspey district of the Scottish Highlands. *The Scottish Geographical Magazine* 102(2), 113–126.

Getz, D. and Carlsen, J. (2000) Characteristics and goals of family- and owner-operated businesses in the rural tourism and hospitality sectors. *Tourism Management* 21, 547–560.

Getz, D. and Jamieson, W. (1997) Rural tourism in Canada: issues, opportunities and entrepreneurship in aboriginal tourism in Alberta. In: Page, S. and Getz, D. (eds) *The Business of Rural Tourism: International Perspectives*. International Thomson Business Press, London, pp. 93–107.

Haber, S. and Lerner, M. (2002) Small tourism ventures in peripheral areas: the impact of environmental factors on performance. In: Krakover, S. and Gradus, Y. (eds) *Tourism in Frontier Areas*. Lexington Books, Lanham, Maryland, pp. 141–163.

Harrison, D. (1992) Social consequences. In: Harrison, D. (ed.) *Tourism and the Less Developed Countries*. Belhaven Press, London, pp. 19–34.

Hjalager, A. (1996) Agricultural diversification development into tourism. Evidence of a European Community development programme. *Tourism Management* 17(2), 103–112.

Komppula, R. (2000) Definitions of growth and success – case studies in Finnish rural tourism industry. Paper presented at the 12th Nordic Conference on Small Business Research, Kuopia, Finland. University of Kuopia Department of Business Management.

Lank, A. (1995) *Key Challenges Facing Family Enterprises*. IMD Publication, Lausanne, Switerland.

Lank, A., Owens, R., Martinez, J., Reidel, H., de Visscher, F. and Bruel, M. (1994) The state of family business in various countries around the world. *The Family Business Newsletter* May, 3–7.

Litz, R. and Kleysen, R. (2002) Old men will dream dreams, your young men will see visions: a conceptualization of innovation in family firms. In: Chrisman, J., Holbrook, J. and Chua, J. (eds) *Innovation and Entrepreneurship in Western Canada: From Family Businesses to Multi-nationals*. University of Calgary Press, Calgary, Canada, pp. 269–298.

Long, P. and Edgell, D. (1997) *Rural tourism in the U.S.: the peak to peak scenic byway and KOA*. In: Page, S. and Getz, D. (eds) *The Business of Rural Tourism: International Perspectives*. International Thomson Business Press, London, pp. 62–76.

Lundgren, J. (1973) Tourist impact/island entrepreneurship in the Caribbean. Cited in: Shaw, G. and Williams, A. (1994) *Critical Issues in Tourism: a Geographical Perspective*. Blackwell, Oxford, UK, p.126.

Lundtorp, S., Rassing, C. and Wanhill, S. (1999) The off-season is 'no season': the case of the Danish Island of Bornholm. *Tourism Economics* 5(1), 49–68.

McKercher, B. (1998) *The Business of Nature-Based Tourism*. Hospitality Press, Melbourne, Australia.

Middleton, V. (2001). The importance of micro-businesses in European tourism. In: Roberts, L. and Hall, D. (eds) *Rural Tourism and Recreation: Principles to Practice*. CAB International, Wallingford, UK, pp. 197–201.

Morrison, A. (1998) Small firm cooperative marketing in a peripheral tourism region. *International Journal of Contemporary Hospitality Management* 10(5), 191–197.

Murphy, P. (1985) *Tourism: a Community Approach.* Methuen, New York.

Neubauer, F. and Lank, A. (1998) *Family Business: its Governance for Sustainability.* Routledge, New York.

Nilsson, P., Petersen, T. and Wanhill, S. (2004) Public support for tourism SMEs in peripheral areas: the Arjeplog project, Northern Sweden. *The Service Industries Journal (in press).*

Notzke, C. (1999) Indigenous tourism development in the Arctic. *Annals of Tourism Research* 26(1), 55–76.

Page, S. and Getz, D. (1997) *The Business of Rural Tourism: International Perspectives.* International Thomson Business Press, London.

Rosenblatt, P., de Mik, C., Anderson, R. and Johnson, P. (1985) *The Family in Business: Understanding and Dealing with the Challenges Entrepreneurial Families Face.* Jossey-Bass, San Francisco, California.

Shanker, M. and Astrachan, J. (1996) Myths and realities: family businesses' contribution to the U.S. economy – a framework for assessing family business statistics. *Family Business Review* 9, 107–119.

Sharma, P., Chrisman, J. and Chua, J. (1996) *A Review and Annotated Bibliography of Family Business Studies.* Kluwer, Boston, Massachusetts.

Shaw, G. and Williams, A. (1987) Firm formation and operating characteristics in the Cornish tourist industry – the case of Looe. *Tourism Management* December, 344–348.

Smyrnios, K. and Romano, C. (1999) *The 1999 Australian Family Business Lifestyle Audit.* AXA Australia Family Business Research Unit, Monash University, Melbourne.

Smyrnios, K., Romano, C. and Tanewski, G. (1997) *The Australian Family and Private Business Survey.* Monash University, Melbourne, Australia.

Thomassen, A. (1992) European family-owned businesses: emerging issues for the 1990s. In: *The Family Firm Institute, Family Business at the Crossroads:* Proceedings of the 1992 Conference, Boston, Massachusetts, pp. 188–191.

Wanhill, S. (1997) Peripheral area tourism: a European perspective. *Progress in Tourism and Hospitality Research* 3(1), 47–70.

Ward, J. and Aronoff, C. (1990) To sell or not to sell. *Nation's Business* 78(1), 63–64.

Westhead, P. and Cowling, M. (1998) Family firm research: the need for a methodological rethink. *Entrepreneurship Theory and Practice* autumn, 31–56.

Wortman, M. (1995) Critical issues in family business: an international perspective of practice and research. In: Proceedings of the 40th International Council for Small Business Conference, Sydney. NCP Printing, University of Newcastle, Newcastle, Australia.

2

Entrepreneurship and Family Business

Introduction

The aim of this chapter is to recognize family business as a distinct form of entrepreneurship and to delve into the more submerged and under-researched variables of importance to enhancing understanding and knowledge. Furthermore, Goffee (1996) cautions against simply attaching 'family' as a prefix without fully pursuing and understanding what distinguishes such enterprises from presumably 'non-family' ones. Thus, the chapter makes the connection between entrepreneurship, small and family business, focusing on the unique entrepreneurial opportunities, challenges and issues that are inherent in the tourism and hospitality industry. The contribution of key industry-specific and setting modifiers as identified in Chapter 1 is explored within the framework of a model that investigates the extent to which they act as 'filters' either to intensify or dilute the entrepreneurial process resulting in consequential entrepreneurial socio-economic outcomes. This three-level filter model is presented in Fig. 2.1 and emphasizes the cyclical nature of the process as negative and/or positive consequences feed through the system, promoting or inhibiting future entrepreneurial activity within a host society. Conclusions are drawn that highlight the unique factors associated with entrepreneurship as related to tourism and hospitality family businesses, how they influence the nature and evolution of such enterprises, and competitive and policy implications. The

Fig. 2.1 model is applied to structure the content of this chapter.

Entrepreneurial Process

The entrepreneurial process represents the level one filter and is an interaction of a complex, multi-dimensional and dynamic set of factors and circumstances. These arise from the characteristics and attitudes of individual entrepreneurs who are motivated to take part in entrepreneurship as a consequence of their genetic make-up and social development within their host community's culture. Discussion surrounding entrepreneurship, culture and entrepreneurs is now explored and understanding developed as to how they combine into an entrepreneurial process.

Entrepreneurship

As with many other academic fields of study, there exists little consensus as to a universally accepted approach to the definition of entrepreneurship. For example, according to Timmons (1994) it is about innovating and building something of value from practically nothing. It is the process of creating or seizing an opportunity, and pursuing it regardless of the resources currently personally controlled. Hisrich and Drnovsek (2002: 175) provide a further useful

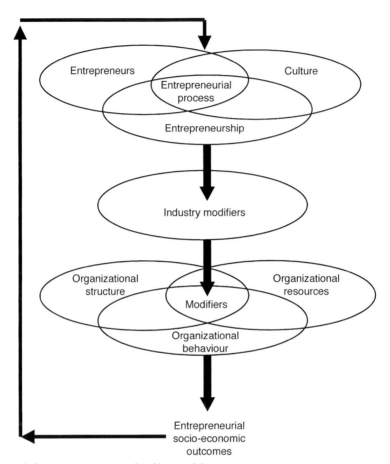

Fig. 2.1. Family business entrepreneurship filter model.

approach in defining entrepreneurship as: the creation and management of new businesses, small businesses and family businesses, and the characteristics and special problems of entrepreneurs. Hence, in these definitions the roots of family business may be taken to originate in the essence of entrepreneurship, with a focus on understanding the interaction of entrepreneur and organizational contexts, structure, behaviour and resources (Craig and Lindsay, 2002).

From a European perspective, entrepreneurship has its roots in classical economic literature as embodied in the seminal research by authors such as R. Cantillon (1680–1734), J.B. Say (1767–1832) and J. Schumpeter (1883–1950). For example, Schumpeter (1934) approaches it from a normative perspective, arguing that entrepreneurs seek business objectives such as profit and growth. However, in the

contemporary world this uni-dimensional, and economically directed, approach is becoming to be regarded as overly simplistic (Greenbank, 2001). It fails to account for non-economic determinants of entrepreneurship including ideology, legitimacy, social mobility and psychological factors (McKay, 2001). This is particularly significant within the context of family entrepreneurship, which Cromie et al. (1999) suggest differs from economic entrepreneurship in that it incorporates a domestic dimension.

Consequently, over recent decades the way of thinking about the process of entrepreneurship has broadened considerably. While it is recognized as being at the heart of an economic development task it is now acknowledged to be driven by the motivations of individuals and families, who are seeking to satisfy their unique social and economic personal goals (Fass and

Scothorne, 1990). Drucker (1986) describes this endeavour as translating into an effort to create purposeful, focused change in a business's economic or social potential, plus the application of distinct entrepreneurial management and strategies. This indicates that entrepreneurship has: 'its foundations in person and intuition, and society and culture. It is much more holistic than simply an economic function, and represents a composite of material and immaterial, pragmatism and idealism' (Morrison, 2000a: 59). Furthermore, interpretations of what represents entrepreneurship are likely to vary cross-nationally according to the distinctive patterning of social values and norms of behaviour (Morrison, 1998a). This highlights the influence of culture in the entrepreneurial process.

Culture

It is tempting to be seduced by the notion that entrepreneurs concerned with family business will behave in a homogenous manner the world over, robotically conforming to theories and insights generated within the worlds of the academic and policy maker. For example, in such a knowledgeable world triggers or cues that result in entrepreneurial behaviour could be isolated and mechanically triggered – by government officials concerned with tourism and hospitality development – to stimulate the process and beneficial economic and social outcomes of entrepreneurship. However, we live in a much more human and unpredictable world awash with rich individual, family and national cultural diversity that cascades a colourful mosaic of cues and behaviours. These often defy academic and policy-maker capture and sense-making. This was alluded to in Chapter 1 relative to the impact of industry and setting-specific modifiers to family business attitudes, values and activities, and a similar stance can be adopted relative to deepening understanding of the role of a host culture in the filtering of what may be considered as a 'pure', undiluted process of entrepreneurship.

Tayeb presents a definition of culture and its scope as:

> a set of historically evolved learned values, attitudes and meanings shared by the members of a given community that influence the material and non-material way of life. Members of the

community learn these shared characteristics through different stages of socialization processes of their lives in institutions, such as family, religion, formal education, and society as a whole.

> (Tayeb, 1988: 42)

Thus, societies can be distinguished from each other by the differences in the shared meanings they expect and attribute to their environment as is evident in the oft cited work of Hofstede (1991). However, Tayeb (1988) and Van der Horst (1996) astutely point out that none of us are slaves to the culture in which we live. There will be those persons who are moved to deviate or escape from accepted cultural norms.

The combination of the terms 'entrepreneurial' and 'culture' has become popular, widely accepted internationally, and is an expression of an attitude towards commerce at a business level. It can be described as one in which a positive social attitude towards personal enterprise is prevalent, enabling and supporting entrepreneurial activity. The existence of an entrepreneurial culture represents societal support for an enterprising spirit that will flourish within certain communities in response to uncertainty and competition (Kirzner, 1979). Gilder (1971: 258) describes this spirit in inspirational terms as it: 'wells up from the wisdom of ages and the history (of the West) and infuses the most modern of technological adventures'. Thus, any explanation of what triggers the release of the spirit of enterprise leading to the initiation of entrepreneurship must work from an understanding of the collectives generally accepted as characteristic of certain societies, and respect and acknowledge the individuality and uniqueness of members of such societies who are personally motivated to act entrepreneurially (Morrison, 1998b).

The following provide some illustrative examples of entrepreneurial cultural norms and diversity.

- **Gender:** strong ideological support for traditional familial labour divisions and societal presumptions of the appropriate roles for both sexes means that deviations from the norms are challenging. For example, an emphasis on the role of women in 'homemaking' in many societies may mean that the provision of hospitality services is deemed to be socially acceptable as a 'female-type' business. Consequently, there is a concentration of women in domestic and personal services-related endeavours, such as, providing B&B for tourists and business travellers (Blackburn, 1999; Cameron and Massey, 1999; Carter et al., 2001).

- **Politics:** in Russia there has not been a history of an entrepreneurial culture. The first law on small business and entrepreneurship was not adopted until 1991. Some individuals managed to overcome the traditional complex of inferiority and lack of creativity and initiative and have created new ventures that are prepared to compete in a market-oriented economy (Hisrich and Grachev, 1995).

- **Economic:** in Tajikistan (former USSR) the economic environment presents little opportunity for legitimate entrepreneurship. Many economic activities are still illegal, and therefore conducted in a covert way in order to avoid punitive measures from law-enforcing authorities. This represents a parallel, underground, officially 'fictitious' economy to that of the formal. It offers a different interpretation of an 'entrepreneurial class' that lives in the shadows in some societies (Dana, 2001).

- **Religion:** many of the Kenyan people are God-fearing and when it is preached from the church pulpits that it is 'easier for a camel to pass through the eye of a needle than for a rich man to get into heaven' it has a profound impact on the societal attitude towards entrepreneurship. Some members of the population might see it as representing selfish capitalism. This attitude is prevalent in a society which prioritises support for the community and extended family, with wealth being shared with 'kith and kin' first, leaving little left over for investment in enterprises (Dondo and Ngumo, 1998).

These examples help understanding of the ways in which culture may filter the entrepreneurial process, either intensifying or diluting it. It has its roots in the dominant politics, history, religion, ideologies and economies. This includes the notion of a potential entrepreneur's evaluation of social legitimacy, desirability and feasibility influenced by cultural values, economic factors, and the relationship between the entrepreneur and their host environment (Jones, 2000). Thus, having a thorough understanding of cultural values, motivations, and aspirations of various cultural sub-groups within populations is critical to increasing the knowledge base about factors that contribute to individuals being influenced to become an entrepreneur (Collins, 2002).

Entrepreneurs

Pearce (1980) succinctly depicts the process of entrepreneurship as a metaphor in comparing entrepreneurs with bees to describe what they do. He believes that, in most respects, entrepreneurs are ordinary human beings, seeking to do good for themselves in terms of material gain and social status. In the process they are unwitting catalysts, as with bees whose strictly private activities are the first cause of almost everything else, as their honey-seeking serves to pollinate. In this respect, entrepreneurs can be regarded as first among equals in the process of wealth creation. In creating their own wealth, entrepreneurs also stimulate wealth creation opportunities for others, and with the potential to bring about positive social consequences in the wider society.

The key to unlocking the process of entrepreneurship would appear to be in the power of these entrepreneurs. Over centuries their endeavours have significantly contributed to change and growth in the business world. They are also credited with most of the material progress in society (Hurley, 1999). Within the tourism and hospitality industry, for example, we can make mention of the likes of Walt Disney, Conrad Hilton and Thomas Cook, all of whom have radically innovated within their respective sectors, significantly redefining the nature of products, services and markets that have contributed to the growth of the tourism and hospitality industry over the decades. In this respect, Day (2000) likens the entrepreneurial process to bush fires. Just as they are natural occurrences that raze forests to the ground, and in the very process engender new life, so do entrepreneurs transform industry and society through their energized and radiating endeavour.

Within academic circles debate abounds as to whether these entrepreneurs are proactive or reactive individuals in the process of entrepreneurship. According to Kuratko and Hodgetts (1998: 97): 'every person has the potential and free choice to pursue a career as an entrepreneur'. However, this underplays the complex and multidimensional interaction of entrepreneurial behaviour 'cues' that are embedded in the contemporary world of the individual, society and economy. These are not necessarily driven by factors such as maximization of a return on investment, or exploitation of a market opportunity. Instead, they may be prompted by the following range of examples of critical incidents that have acted as entrepreneurial behaviour cues:

- 'Buy' themselves and/or family members a job (Harper, 1984).
- Avoid unemployment and respond to economic necessity (Cameron and Massey, 1999).
- Earn enough money to allow them to leave the community to search for a better life (Dahles and Bras, 1999).
- Be a solution to adversity (Dahles, 1998).
- Pursue intrinsic goals such as independence, gaining control over life, and a flexible lifestyle (Middleton and Clarke, 2001).
- Provide an alternative economic means to overcome blocked upward career mobility

experienced within the corporate arena (Smith, 2000).

Table 2.1 summarizes a range of examples of entrepreneurial behaviour cues. Clearly, they represent a complex and somewhat ethereal weave of positive and negative social and economic factors, and those of a psychological nature that may be categorized either as negative or positive dependent on interpretative stance (Morrison, 2001).

As an illustration of entrepreneurial behaviour cues, Collins (2002) provides an historic example of immigrant entrepreneurs to Australia seeking an upward transformation of social class, rather than continuity of what they had experienced in their country of origin. Some came to Australia as refugees from peasant or unskilled backgrounds, others were educated professionals, and there were undocumented immigrants who lived in a shadow world. Discriminatory legislation was introduced in 1896 that confined non-Anglo-Celtic business people to the periphery of the business system. Hence, the likes of the Irish Catholics, Lebanese and Jews were restricted in their access to business opportunities, and faced block employment mobility. This created a movement of the Chinese and many other immigrants such as Italians, Greeks and Lebanese into restaurants, not as a preferred choice but as a consequence of limited options (Glezer, 1988). By the mid-1980s Chinese cafes were an established feature of the Australian suburban and country town landscape. They were the vanguard of encroaching Australian

Table 2.1. Entrepreneurial behaviour cues.

	Positive	Negative
Social	• Role of the family and intergenerational role models • Conducive culture • Supportive networks	• Political/religious displacement • Political unrest • Discrimination • Unhappy with position in society
Economic	• Move towards services • Reversal of highly vertically integrated company structures • Phenomenon of 'dot.com' business	• Corporate downsizing and redundancy • Dissatisfaction with/blocked employment opportunities • Discriminatory legislation • No other way to make money
Psychological	• Entrepreneurial aspirations of independence, wealth, need to achieve, social mobility, etc.	

Sources: Scase and Goffee, 1989; Storey, 1994; Hurley, 1999; Morrison et al., 1999; Morrison, 2000b; Collins, 2002.

cultural diversity as Chinese restaurants provided a culinary diversity in food that did not exist at that time. Thus, it can be seen from this illustration that many of these immigrants used entrepreneurship as a vehicle to break through social and/or economic negative cues of a class or ethnic ceiling, satisfying their psychological needs, and as a consequence transformed industry and society.

Naffziger et al. (1994) contribute to understanding by supplying a useful analytical model that approaches entrepreneurial behaviour cues as an experiential process, and suggest that the initial decision to be an entrepreneur is the result of the interaction of a range of factors as has been presented in Table 2.1. Their model includes the individual's personal characteristics, personal environment, personal goal set, the relevant business environment, and the existence of a viable business idea. This model is attractive in that it combines wider environmental forces with the intrinsic motivations and social context of the entrepreneur, and Fig. 2.2 summarizes the findings from one application to a study of entrepreneurs (Morrison, 2001). Such an approach recognizes that entrepreneurs do not emerge from a vacuum, but that the entrepreneurial process is influenced by the social and business systems within which they are located and conditioned (Carson et al., 1995). It is only when the social and business system-derived cues converge that entrepreneurship will be activated.

It is therefore understandable that existing and emergent entrepreneurs navigate through their respective social and business systems to present themselves in many different guises, as indicated in Table 2.2. Consequently, there is evolving recognition of the need for understanding of different variants, behaviours and dynamics of entrepreneurs (Hurley, 1999; Department

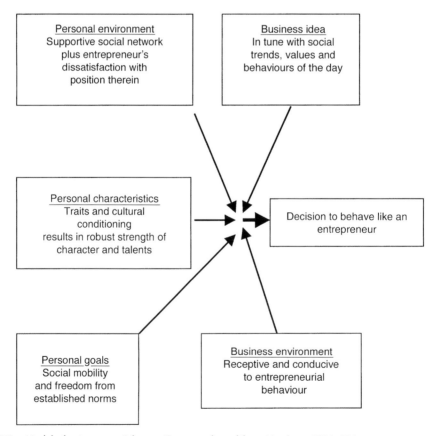

Fig. 2.2. Model of entrepreneurial cues. (Source: adapted from Morrison, 2001: 78.)

of Trade and Industry, 2001). For example, Kets de Vries (1996) proposes that many are, in effect, misfits who need to create their own environment. They do not want to be at the mercy of others, and are motivated to move away from controlling influences. Furthermore, they have difficulties with authority figures and structured situations even after they have moved away from controlling influences. For example, this is often manifested within the tourism and hospitality industry in the form of the rejection of the urban and corporate lifestyle for one that is rural, with relative organizational autonomy achieved through being self-employed.

What is particularly significant within the context of family business is the permeation of 'family' throughout all the entrepreneur guises

with the exception of 'serial'. For example, it would appear that: it is a flexible means to integrate work and family responsibilities; the family acts as a business asset through the 'voluntary' contribution of work; traditional family domestic gender roles transfer to the workplace; and the pursuit and continuity of the family unit and lifestyle is facilitated. Furthermore, it is clear that these typologies of entrepreneur guises should not be regarded as sterile, static and divorced from each other, as many overlap and will change and alternate according to respective family and business lifecycles. These ten guises (Table 2.2) are now discussed in more detail.

- **Copreneur:** many family businesses are established by spouses or life partners,

Table 2.2. Entrepreneur guises.

Guise	Description	Example
Copreneur	Marital and business partners managing work and family responsibilities more effectively	Husband and wife contribute complementary skills and resources to the management of a winery visitor attraction
Ethnic	Entrepreneurs drawn from ethnic minority groups often operating in ethnic niche markets	Chinese, Greek, Italian restaurants in Europe, Australia and North America
Family	Meshing together social and business systems	Multi-generations servicing the tourism market as a means of generating family employment to maintain the family unit
Female	Using business as a vehicle for greater flexibility in managing family responsibilities	Homestay accommodation that enables the combination of commercial, domestic and child-caring responsibilities
Intrapreneur	A family member, other than the founding-entrepreneur, adopts and applies entrepreneurial characteristics within the existing business	Second-generation family member working within a traditional hotel adopts a business re-engineering strategy transforming it into serviced accommodation
Lifestyle	Primary concern is to provide a sufficient and comfortable living to maintain a selected way of life	A ski instructor operates the business for a 4-month season to earn enough to live all year round in a mountain retreat
Micro	Employing less than ten persons deliberately constraining size	Extension of a family home to offer B&B accommodation
Portfolio	Concurrently own more than one business that may bring additional benefits for the entrepreneur and enterprise	Farm diversification into tourism-related businesses such as accommodation and sports activity
Serial	Entrepreneur will own a consecutive series of businesses with entry and exit coinciding with market opportunities	With ICT redefining travel marketing a traditional high street retailer may move into travel consultancy, then a dot.com business
Social	Entrepreneur combines commercial skills with social aims and objectives	Rurally located tour guides that are primarily concerned with environmental preservation and community values

Sources: Scase and Goffee, 1989; Greenbank, 2000; Carter *et al.*, 2001; Carter, 2001.

these copreneurs seeking self-employment in order to achieve greater control over their lives, allowing the flexibility to integrate work and family responsibilities more effectively than would be possible within a corporate environment. They tend to adhere to traditional sex role orientations at home and in the business, with women's traditional family roles as primary caregiver and housekeeper reinforced in the workplace. For example, this is often the case in the provision and servicing of tourism accommodation (Smith, 2000; McKay, 2001).

- **Ethnic:** niche markets are often the seedbed of ethnic entrepreneurship, such as within the independent restaurant sector, which is established as a popular activity for ethnic minority businesses internationally. Accounts of ethnic minorities in business have generated controversy on a number of issues, including: different patterns of self-employment among ethnic groups; relative importance of cultural resources including the support of immediate and extended family; constraining nature of the market environment; and the relationship between ethnic enterprise business and support agencies (Ram et al., 2000; Collins, 2002).

- **Family:** the significant involvement of family in the ownership and management of small businesses has been established, and within the tourism and hospitality industry specifically this is even more pronounced. Examples of this type of entrepreneurship are prevalent within rural, peripheral and resort locations with families often involved in a portfolio of economic activities combining the likes of farming, homestay accommodation and rural tourism experiences (Cromie et al., 1999; Carter et al., 2002).

- **Female:** over the centuries many women have run home-based businesses, frequently attributed to the need to accommodate work and child-rearing roles simultaneously, and this emphasizes the importance of the family and life cycle context. Statistics on female-owned firms are sorely lacking and estimates often exclude the entrepreneurial contributions that women

make to family businesses, which are masked by co-ownership. These businesses tend to cluster in the lower financial turnover categories, use informal sources of finance, and operate in traditionally female sectors of the economy such as hotels and restaurants (Hurley, 1999; Orhan and Scott, 2001; Carter et al., 2002; Collins, 2002).

- **Intrapreneur:** is a person who acts entrepreneurially within the existing family business in terms of re-engineering organizational and economic development. They are concerned with business diversification, innovativeness, self-renewal and pro-activeness, often essential to sustain the family business over generations. Important factors contributing to the emergence of such behaviour are the structural and relational aspects within the environment that may nurture or stifle family members (Carrier, 1996; Antoncic and Hisrich, 2001).

- **Lifestyle:** this represents an extremely elusive and qualitative concept, determined by the values and expectations that the owner-managers largely select for themselves. Their motivations and aspirations relate to the quality of life and place, and economic activity that is bounded by seasonality and profit satisfying rather than conventional measures of financial success, such as growth of sales turnover or number of employees (King et al., 1998; Kuratko and Hodgetts, 1998).

- **Micro:** the majority of family businesses can be classed as 'micro', which is officially defined as employing less than ten persons. In the reality of the tourism and hospitality industry 'micro' dominates and frequently consists of only one self-employed owner-operator or copreneurs. While there may be market opportunities to grow the business, this is frequently not pursued as protection of a specifically selected lifestyle may dominate over rational economic goals (Lynch, 1999).

- **Portfolio:** or multiple business ownership has been associated with a range of benefits for the individual and enterprise. For example, it can be evidenced in agricultural literature relative to farm diversification into tourism, and within urban tourism, entrepreneurs use self-employment in other industry sectors such as financial services to augment the meagre returns from tourist accommodation in low season. These portfolio activities can serve as a means to cross-subsidize economic activities in order to maintain the continuity of the family as a unit (Carter, 2001; Morrison and Teixeira, 2002).

- **Serial:** these entrepreneurs lack an emotional attachment to one business or another. They display strong characteristics associated with market opportunity spotting, speed of action, and versatility to move in and out of business as 'windows' of open-and-shut opportunity. This is not a guise of entrepreneur that is prevalent within family businesses that tend to mesh the family emotional system more closely to that of the business. It tends to lend itself to dynamic market places, such as has been seen in recent years with the development of the Internet which has revolutionized travel distribution processes (Day, 2000; Carter, 2001).

- **Social:** may be considered as active in the 'third sector' or 'social economy', and can be distinguished in that these entrepreneurs combine trading viability with social aims and ownership. The businesses tend to be niche- and locality-focused. Their activities are financed by a combination of earned income from the sale of goods and services (market resources), government subsidies (non-market resources) and voluntary family 'employment' (non-monetary resources). Evidence of this type of entrepreneurship in the tourism and hospitality industry is provided in the form of lifestyle operators, and those concerned with sustainability of the natural environment, who contribute something to communities that have recognized social value (Thompson *et al.*, 2000; Smallbone *et al.*, 2001; Shaw *et al.*, 2002).

Kets de Vries encapsulates the essence of these entrepreneurs as:

Many people have ideas, but very few have the stamina to turn their ideas into action; and as some aspiring entrepreneurs have discovered

the hard way, a vision without action is nothing more than an hallucination. To be successful entrepreneurs must have both vision and drive.
Kets de Vries (1996: 24)

Within the context of family business, vision and drive tends to be directed at the betterment and sustainability of family first, with the business element being a means to that end.

Industry Specific Modifiers

The tourism and hospitality industry specific modifiers act as a second-level filter in the family business entrepreneurial model presented in Fig. 2.1. This industry sector presents itself to entrepreneurs as a potential site for them to apply the entrepreneurial process, rich in many unique opportunities that particularly hold appeal to those attached to the land, rural and natural environments. They will evaluate the feasibility and desirability of entry into this industry sector against opportunities elsewhere, and a persuasive factor is frequently the relatively low capital entry requirements of small service sector operations such as homestays and restaurants. What is unique about the tourism and hospitality industry is that it has held consistently solid appeal to those individuals seeking to combine lifestyle, domestic and commercial activity. Furthermore, as Blackburn (1999) notes, although the family has ceased to be a productive unit in the market economy, it remains one in the domestic economy, such as represented by the tourism and hospitality sectors. For example, within the context of the Scottish tourism industry, it is of significance to note that the majority of tourism accommodation operations are small and often family-run (Lockyer and Morrison, 1999). Many have been lured by the appeal of, often romanticized, notions of the quality of lifestyle that may be experienced. This reflects a naivety as to the 24 hours-a-day, 7 days-a-week service orientation that may place pressure on the founding-entrepreneur and family relationships as family domestic space is shared with commercial customers. Certainly, a significant feature of tourism in Scotland has been inward migration to selected communities with tourism and hospitality market potential by people from outside of the area looking to enter into business. They are often prompted in their choice by initial familiarity with the location through touristic visits. For example, the islands of Mull, Skye and Arran located off the west coast of Scotland are home to communities where a substantial number of in-comer lifestyle families settled during the latter part of the 20th century (Morrison et al., 2001).

This strong lifestyle business entry motivation is reflected in the traditional image presented of small tourism and hospitality businesses. For many, particularly in rural and peripheral locations, maintenance and protection of a certain lifestyle will be prioritized over commercial focus on profit-maximization (Sherwood et al., 2000; Thomas et al., 2000). In this respect, maximization of derived family-value may well be the driving goal rather than that of business-value. For example, Morrison et al. (2001) summarize the following range of lifestyle entrepreneur business entry motivations:

- Meet people and act in a host capacity while still maintaining a relatively unencumbered lifestyle.
- Live in a place that has natural scenic beauty but may be remote and hence few outside visitors.
- Inhabit accommodation and/or location that might be otherwise outside of the comfortable envelope of the proprietors' income.
- Move away from the perceived 'rat race' of modern urban living while having built up

sufficient assets/capital in previous living to move to a peripheral location without significant debt burden; and/or
- Operate a commercial concern, which does not demand 12-month attention but benefits from the effects of seasonality with a 6–8 month annual closed season.

However, the range of possible business entry motivations derived from entrepreneurial behaviour cues (Table 2.1) is endless and any attempt at fashioning a comprehensive list would be a futile exercise. Simplistically they may be categories such as 'opportunity entrepreneurship' – taking advantage of a market opportunity, or 'necessity entrepreneurship' – pursuing the best and often only option available (Ram, 1994; Neck et al., 2001). Furthermore, it could be argued that within the context of the tourism and hospitality industry these categories could be expanded to include 'lifestyle entrepreneurship' and 'social entrepreneurship'.

Table 2.3 summarizes the factors that Morrison (2002) identified to explain the reasons why the small family business endures within the tourism and hospitality industry and those that may endanger certain members of the population in the future. This information should be viewed as a continuum with 'enduring' at one end and 'endangered' at the other, as it is not an either/or situation and there will undoubtedly be differing degrees in between.

Thus, it can be observed that the entrepreneurial process will filter through the industry setting as the entrepreneurs in their various guises assess the feasibility and desirability of it

Table 2.3. Enduring and endangering factors.

Enduring	Endangering
Located in sectors and peripheral geographic and/or economic locations that are unattractive to corporate investment	Located in sites of corporate activity, financial investment and new product development
Providing an 'authentic' tourism and hospitality experience, with clearly differentiated quality products and services to niche markets	Floating product and service within the market place that is undifferentiated and vulnerable to the competitive practices of corporate groups
Lifestyle attraction, low barriers to entry and sustenance of operation despite human and financial resource poverty	Economic climate and general external forces severe, discouraging lifestyle indulgence and unmasking resource deficiencies
Contribution to sustainable regional development and adding value to the economy, society and the environment	Policy makers lack awareness of potential contributions, and neglect to provide appropriate support infrastructure

as a site for the social and economic investment. Evaluatory criteria may include:

- Economic feasibility of combining domestic and commercial domains.
- Aesthetic appeal of a particular geographic location.
- Compatibility with an aspired lifestyle.
- Potential for psychological gratification through the likes of hosting and visitor satisfaction; and/or
- Fulfilment of social and moral obligations such as family cohesion, provision of an inheritance for future generations, sustaining the natural environment or adding value to local communities.

The foregoing provides an explanation of why the tourism and hospitality industry continues to be dominated by the small rural business model in most developed and developing countries (Baum, 1999; Middleton and Clarke, 2001). This is evident in the UK, where the Department of Trade and Industry (2001) indicated that 99.8% of hotel and restaurant businesses employed less than 50 persons in 2000. Thus, what is important is not their contribution to employment, but that their collective critical mass provides the bulk of the essentially local ambience and quality of visitor experiences at rural and peripheral destinations, on which the future growth of overseas and domestic visits depends (Middleton and Clarke, 2001). For guests such businesses can add value socially in that they may reflect the special values of 'place' and 'host encounters' allowing a glimpse into local life and traditions.

Table 2.4 summarizes the negative and positive features associated with small hospitality businesses, which have been identified (Morrison, 2002). The positive features emphasize the value of industry-specific, community and regional contributions that may be achievable, while the negatives illuminate the tensions and contradictions that are involved in the realization of potential. The ease of entry and exit may be regarded as a positive or negative feature according to consequences and perspectives. This summary contributes to the development of a deeper understanding of the contemporary positioning of small businesses within the tourism and hospitality industry.

Setting modifiers

Should the entrepreneurial motivation survive through the second-level filter of the tourism and hospitality industry setting, attention then turns to the organizational setting modifiers of the small family tourism and hospitality business. This represents the third- and final-level filter in the family business entrepreneurial model (Fig. 2.1), and can be analysed relative to the components of organizational structure, behaviour and resources. This approach employs a trinity of definitional approaches to address holistically the multidimensional milieu of entrepreneurship and family business that will ultimately impact on entrepreneurial socio-economic outcomes. This approach corresponds to the Gersick *et al.* (1997) model referred to in Chapter 1 that encourages integrative thinking and research about family business, as decisions within one sphere will impact elements in others.

Table 2.4. Negative and positive features of small hospitality businesses.

Positive	• Valuable element in a tourism destination infrastructure • Respond to market characteristics and demand satisfaction • Sustainable economic, social and environmental contribution • Instrumental to regional development
Negative	• Often ignored in national and regional policy development • Operate out with the hospitality industry • Defy economic logic in their manner of operation • Fragmented sector difficult to co-ordinate and control • Variability and inconsistencies of product quality and visitor experience
Positive/negative	• Low barriers to entry and exit

Organizational Modifiers

Kets de Vries (1996) logically points out that every family business starts somewhere, usually with a founder-entrepreneur who has not only a business concept but also the will and persistence to bring that concept to fruition. He calls these founder-entrepreneurs 'societal misfits'. They are instrumental in structuring the organization, and have a profound influence on it. Carter *et al.* (2002) found that the majority of small tourism and hospitality businesses take the form of partnership shared among spouses, immediate and extended family members. Family members are active in the businesses, taking on roles such as general management, supervision, accounting, cleaning and catering. In many cases it is a husband-and-wife team, or copreneurs, that make all the decisions and deal with most of the work, assisted by very few staff, many of whom are part-time. This reflects one of the paramount organizing principles in many societies, that of gender, and just as it is a dominant factor in families, it is also reflected in the organizational structure of family business (Omar and Davidson, 2001). This leads Goffee and Scase (1995) to refer to it as an 'entrepreneurial family' that functions quite differently from the normal Western pattern of business, for the inextricable linkage of social and business systems means that they cannot be divorced from each other. This will inevitably influence the entrepreneurial process as family values and emotional attachments interact and compete with commercial market-driven values (Cromie *et al.*, 1999).

Other than ownership, organizational structure also manifests itself through the characteristic of 'smallness', which can be regarded as either an asset or a constraint dependent on perspective. Family businesses in the tourism and hospitality industry rarely grow to any significant size and the majority remain as micro. The question why this is so has vexed academics and policy makers over the decades. Explanation can work from a number of different angles as was identified by Morrison and Teixeira (2002) as follows:

- Emotional attachment associated with the physical space, in that it is often also the family home, constrains business growth.

- Concern about market potential and any resultant loss of the distinctive differentiating features associated with 'smallness'.
- Managerial capacity is sufficient to cope with existing size, but growth would bring with it the need to employ from without the family circle, which is not perceived as desirable.
- Financial poverty: while it is relatively easy to raise additional funds for expansion, securing an adequate return on investment to pay back loans was problematic.

Thus, in combination these physical, human and financially derived factors stunt growth and protect the *status quo* of smallness. At best this can be likened to a 'bonsai tree', which presents itself as a specialized, quality niche product whose roots are deliberately and expertly tended to ensure the retention of its defining features. At worst it is a mass market common house plant that has gone to seed and hidden under the soil its roots are stealthily strangling and killing it. Thus, it can be summarized that:

- The heart of the organizational structure contains the founding-entrepreneur, the entrepreneurial family, and their respective family and business value sets, within which social and economic goals are often contested.
- Emotional attachment to predominately family values may dilute the entrepreneurial process, deliberately preserving the 'micro.'
- Alternatively, the family structure could provide the business with a significant entrepreneurial advantage that the corporate organizations may find extremely difficult to mimic.

Organizational behaviour

Brockhaus (1994) defines family business in terms of organizational behavioural characteristics, in that it is represents an enterprise in which family members influence the direction of the business through the exercise of kinship ties, ownership rights or management roles. This definitional approach is supported by

Chua *et al.* (1999). A quote from Kets de Vries succinctly summarizes the spirit and challenge of organizational behaviour in family businesses:

> Founder-entrepreneurs and owners of family firms and their employees are like partners in a dance: the experience can be very exhilarating, but the dancers sometimes fall over each other's feet . . . making the organizational 'dance' gracefully – is the real challenge for all concerned.
>
> (Kets de Vries, 1996: 56)

Goffee (1996) cautions against assuming that all family businesses will exhibit similar behavioural characteristics. Differences will derive from varying structures, cultures and life cycle stages of entrepreneurial families. This was apparent in a study of small family-owned tourism accommodation businesses in Scotland, where Morrison and Teixeira (2002) analysed organizational behaviour through the application of a three-category framework. This focused on the founding-entrepreneur, business and external environment, and resulted in the sets of factors presented in Table 2.5. In concert these interact and impact on the entrepreneurial process within the organizational context as it moves through the various life cycle stages of entrepreneurial families and their respective businesses.

Thus, from Table 2.4 it can be observed how entrepreneurial activities may be further 'filtered' through the interacting range of factors to influence the entrepreneurial process. These can lead to a heavy reliance on family members for managerial talent that may restrict choice and intrapreneurial capabilities. Cromie *et al.* (1997) suggest that this is not a problem. Provided they are trained in technical and managerial areas they can assist in business development. Furthermore, as Kets de Vries (1993) argues, early immersion in the business as a child may provide training opportunities for family members. However, these positive perspectives are challenged by the findings in Table 2.5. They reveal that:

Table 2.5. Factors influencing organizational behaviour.

Founding entrepreneur	• Middle-aged, limited formal education or experience directly related to the hospitality industry • Low professional and financial barriers to sector entry • Perceptions of a 'simple' business to operate • Managerial constraints, limited capabilities and constrained resources to solve gaps in managerial competencies • Business entry decision driven by personal and family-related considerations to the subordination of business • Meshing of personal and business goals may lead to profit satisficing, and/or an unhealthy work/life balance • Limited ambitions and vision, and protection of lifestyle over business expansion
Business	• Family involvement may lead to sub-optimal efficiencies and masked financial viability • Simple organizational structures mean that decision-making is embodied in a few individuals, and management resources are strained • Involvement in multiple income generation activities may detract from commitment to the small business • Failure to attract and manage quality, skilled human resources could impact negatively on the quality of the product and service • Size negates economies of scale, has consequences for financial viability, is physically contained, and deliberately constrained for reasons of product and service differentiation and lifestyle protectionism
External environment	• Industry restructuring to favour the economics of the larger corporation • Weak power position, vulnerable to the micro and macro economic and political environments and natural disasters • Dependent on local human resources that are deficient in satisfying needs • General high dependencies on externalities

Source: Morrison and Teixeira (2002).

- Low entry barriers attract entrepreneurs with limited formal education or experience directly relating to the industry sector.
- There is a significant deficit in management competencies and resources.
- The material and non-material needs of the family tend to dictate the amount of income to which involved family members aspire.
- Businesses operate to sub-optimal levels in terms of profit and growth.

Organizational resources

Habbershon and Williams (1999) adopt a resource-based definitional approach in describing family business resources as the 'familiness' of a given business. More specifically, 'familiness' is defined as the unique bundle of resources a particular business has because of the systems interaction between the family, its individual members and the business. This provides a unified systems perspective on family business performance capabilities and entrepreneurial advantage. Working from a Chinese perspective, for example, Yu (2001) highlights the fact that the cultural and familiness of resources facilitate competitive strategies that are non-contestable by Westerners. Such a definitional approach has advantages in that it may focus attention on the largely hidden contribution of family members, and in particular female entrepreneurs, in enterprise management and development (Carter et al., 2001).

From an organizational resource perspective a family business's founding and ongoing goals can act as both a bonus and a constraint to business. They are instrumental in the making and shaping of the business's resources (Craig and Lindsay, 2002), and a long-term perspective can provide a distinct entrepreneurial resource advantage (Cameron and Massey, 1999). For example, Habbershon and Williams (1999) summarize elements of such a resource base as follows:

- A unique working environment which fosters a family-oriented workplace and inspires greater employee care and loyalty.
- More flexible work practices.

- Family members are more productive than non-family employees.
- A shared 'family language' allows more effective communication.
- Family relationships generate unusual motivation, cement loyalties, and increase trust.
- Transaction costs are lowered.
- Decision-making is informal and efficient.

This emphasizes the significant resource base that an entrepreneurial family has the potential to contribute to a business. Moreover, it has been recognized within the context of the tourism and hospitality industry that it can be a valuable part of the tourism experience as family and customers interact. The significance of this critical asset is intensified within the context of ethnic entrepreneurship. For example, relative to Chinese immigrant entrepreneurs in Australia, Collins (2002) found that both the immediate family, along with the extended 'ethnic family', represent resources critical to entrepreneurial success. Such resources may include moral and financial support, business advice, access to valuable networks and represent an accumulation of social capital that could enhance entrepreneurial knowledge, skills and capabilities (Dana, 2001).

A further significant resource is variously described as the deployment of family members in 'voluntary', 'unpaid', or 'unwaged' employment, and is particularly prevalent in domestic gender division of labour as is often evidenced in the tourism and hospitality industry. This use of family labour is a traditional, important and differentiating feature of the entrepreneurial family (Gorton, 2000). Indeed, according to Scase and Goffee (1989) in the personal service sectors many enterprises, such as small hotels, are only profitable because the overheads are subsidized by unpaid services of family members and by the use of domestic facilities to accommodate business. Thus, in addition, to the appreciation of land and buildings and annual profits, income is derived in kind, because the family lives on the premises, and often 'off the land', as well as any salaries they may pay themselves. As a result it is often difficult to differentiate clearly between profit as return on investment and the emoluments of the owners in the form of cash and non-cash benefits (Medlik, 1994). This suggests that many family businesses operate as social entrepreneurs in a form of 'domestic-economy' as opposed to a 'market-economy' and may represent an economically efficient mode of enterprise with special entrepreneurial advantages (Blackburn, 1999). This represents a vital differentiating feature of family businesses in comparison to corporations. Thus, it can be summarized that organizational resources are composed of economic, market and socially derived capital. This presents a different interpretation from that of strict economic entrepreneurship.

Entrepreneurial Socio-economic Outcomes

Finally, after its journey through the three-level filtering system, the entrepreneurial process reaches the resultant socio-economic outcomes as evidenced within the tourism and hospitality industry. It has been a complex and challenging process and it is perhaps understandable that some of the intensity of the entrepreneurship may have somewhat diminished.

The actual contribution to socio-economic outcomes of small family tourism and hospitality businesses is difficult to gauge accurately (Kovassy and Hutton, 2001), however, Middleton and Clarke (2001) summarize it in economic, social and environmental terms in the following manner. They are embedded in local communities, so the money earned tends to be retained within the community and they provide a vital source of employment. For the guests, they can add value socially in that they may reflect the special values of 'place' and 'host encounters', allowing a glimpse into local life. In expressing the local character of place, entrepreneurs could be more committed than, for example, a corporate group, to sustaining the natural environment for a range of moral, lifestyle and commercial motivations. Furthermore, there is evidence that some family business entrepreneurs act as cultural and/or heritage custodians driven by their commitment to preserving and perpetuating traditions for the next generations of their family. This corresponds with the social entrepreneur guise identified in Table 2.2. Thus, small family businesses have the potential to

contribute social, economic and environmental outcomes to rural and peripheral communities in which they are located by:

- Offering sustainable solutions to economic and social challenges in terms of providing employment and services, purchasing goods and services from local suppliers and traders.
- Preserving the natural environment and heritage in which they locate.
- Attracting inward investment from those persons seeking a lifestyle change.
- Adding value to the social fabric of the community as a whole.

However, Middleton and Clarke counter these positive outcomes in stating that:

> At the leading edge, they embody the entre-preneurial spirit and vitality of places . . . at the trailing edge many exist on the fringes of the industry damaging the environment of the destinations in which they are located, reducing visitor satisfaction and perceived quality of the overall visitor experience.
> (Middleton and Clarke, 2001: 41)

Chapter Summary

Figure 2.3 summarizes key points identified in this chapter relative to the entrepreneurial process. It suggests that understanding of the process, as it interplays with family business, is best served by reference to the cultural, social and business systems within which entrepreneurs are embedded. These combine to filter the perceptions and behaviours of entrepreneurs as to the potential to achieve their aspired material and/or social gain. At full intensity this process will result in outcomes that radically infuse and energize economies, society and industries, creating long-term and sustainable benefits for society as a whole. However, this proposition needs to be treated carefully as it contains an implicit bias towards an idealist vision of entrepreneurship, which may assume that all intentions are morally sound and socially responsible. As has been observed, entrepreneurship by its very nature is concerned with the initiation of change that may challenge, and perhaps destroy, the established order and the complacency of traditional social

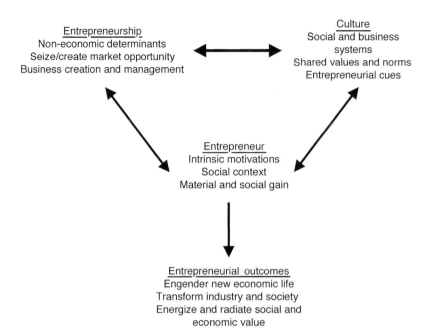

Fig. 2.3. Entrepreneurial process.

and economic systems. Consequently, it would be delusory to accept that all outcomes from the process of entrepreneurship will be positive, even if it is hoped that any, in Schumpeterian (1934) terms, 'destruction' will be creative.

Figure 2.4 consolidates the key findings relative to the tourism and hospitality industry setting, organizational structure, behaviour and resources, and industry-specific entrepreneurial outcomes. Here it is clearly apparent that the intensity of the entrepreneurial process has been significantly diluted by the time it has flowed through all three levels of filters (Fig. 2.1). The nexus between industry setting and family-business organizational modifiers results in an interaction to produce entrepreneurial outcomes of small family entrepreneurial businesses that may lack the energetic intensity depicted in Fig. 2.3.

From the content of this chapter explanations can be drawn that reflect the complex and humanistic dimensions associated with family entrepreneurship in the tourism and hospitality industry, such as:

- Certain impediments to the entrepreneurial process may be self-inflicted, consciously accepted and maintained by the entrepreneurs, while others are out of their control.

- Evaluation of what constitutes entrepreneurship will vary dependent on the socio-economic reference frame used by various stakeholders including entrepreneurs, policy-makers and academics.

- For many entrepreneurs the commercial pursuit of enterprise is a necessary sustenance for, but subordinated to, the pursuit of socially driven lifestyle aspirations.

- The tourism and hospitality industry is characterized by relatively low professional, skill and financial barriers to entry, that readily accommodate a family/lifestyle business model, and as such it is perceived as an attractive mode for those individuals seeking life change.

It is concluded that 'entrepreneurship' represents an extremely broad concept that masks the wide range of variants and degrees of intensity that hide under its umbrella term. Within the tourism and hospitality industry, in their own distinct way, small entrepreneurial families do act as catalysts, stimulating rural and peripheral social communities and local economies. In doing so, they often engender

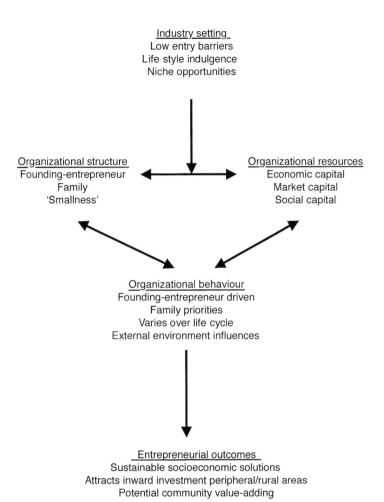

Fig. 2.4. Tourism and hospitality family entrepreneurship.

new life that enables the sustenance and perpetuation of environments, crafts, heritage and traditions that might otherwise disappear. However, the existence and creation of mainly micro businesses is unlikely to transform industry sectors and societies in the same way as the examples given of Walt Disney, Conrad Hilton and Thomas Cook. Nevertheless, small family tourism and hospitality businesses can provide a valuable contribution in embodying an entrepreneurial spirit and vitality that has the potential to contribute significantly to the vitality of place and authenticity of tourism experience.

Thus, it should follow that regional development agencies concerned with the stabilization, regeneration and sustainability of rural and peripheral areas would be well advised to adopt policies deliberately designed to attract and hold families to conducive tourism activity zones. Furthermore, systems are necessary to encourage the active engagement of all stakeholders in the tourism destination infrastructure to connect and work in partnership regardless of size, or public or private sector origins. For as Middleton and Clarke (2001: 463) emphasize: 'Ultimately and ironically, the long-run future of big businesses in mature markets is heavily dependent on the service delivery capabilities of small hospitality businesses over which they have no control'. This signifies the potential for a healthy symbiotic relationship between small and large tourism and hospitality businesses.

References

Antoncic, B. and Hisrich, R. (2001) Intrapreneurship: construct refinement and cross-cultural validation. *Journal of Business Venturing* 16(5), 495–528.

Baum, T. (1999) Human resource management in tourism's small business sector: policy dimensions. In: Lee-Ross, D. (ed.) *HRM in Tourism and Hospitality: International Perspectives on Small to Medium-sized Enterprises.* Cassell, London, pp. 3–16.

Blackburn, R.M. (1999) Is housework unpaid work? *International Journal of Sociology and Social Policy* 19(7/8), 1–20.

Brockhaus, R. (1994) Family business: a blessing or a curse? Keynote Address, Proceedings of the Small Enterprise Association of Australia and New Zealand Conference.

Cameron, A. and Massey, C. (1999) *Small and Medium-sized Enterprises: a New Zealand Perspective.* Addison Wesley Longman, New Zealand Ltd, Auckland, New Zealand.

Carrier, C. (1996) Intrapreneurship in small business: an exploratory study. *Entrepreneurship Theory and Practice* 21(1), 5–51.

Carson, D., Cromie, S., McGowan, P. and Hill, J. (1995) *Marketing and Entrepreneurship in SMEs: an Innovative Approach.* Prentice Hall, London.

Carter, S. (2001) Multiple business ownership in the farm sector: differentiating monoactive, diversified and portfolio enterprises. *International Journal of Entrepreneurial Behaviour and Research* 7(2), 43–59.

Carter, S., Anderson, S. and Shaw, E. (2001) *Women's Business Ownership: a Review of the Academic, Popular and Internet Literature.* Small Business Service, Department of Trade and Industry, London.

Carter, S., Tagg, S., Ennis, S. and Webb, J. (2002) *Lifting the Barriers to Growth in UK Small Businesses.* Federation of Small Business, London.

Chua, J., Chrisman, J. and Sharma, P. (1999) Defining the family business by behaviour. *Entrepreneurship Theory and Practice* 24(4), 19–39.

Collins, J. (2002) Chinese entrepreneurs: the Chinese diaspora in Australia. *International Journal of Entrepreneurial Behaviour and Research* 8(1/2), 113–133.

Craig, J. and Lindsay, N. (2002) Incorporating the family dynamic into the entrepreneurship process. *Journal of Small Business and Enterprise Development* 9(3), 416–430.

Cromie, S., Adams, J., Dunn, B. and Reid, R. (1999) Family firms in Scotland and Northern Ireland: an empirical investigation. *Journal of Small Business and Enterprise Development* 6(3), 253–266.

Dahles, H. (1998) Tourism, government policy and petty entrepreneurs. *South East Asia Research* 6, 73–98.

Dahles, H. and Bras, K. (1999) Entrepreneurs in romance tourism in Indonesia. *Annals of Tourism Research* 26(2), 267–293.

Dana, L. (2001) The education and training of entrepreneurs in Asia. *Education and Training* 43(8/9), 405–416.

Day, J. (2000) Commentary: the value and importance of the small firm to the world economy. *European Journal of Marketing* 34(9/10), 1033–1037.

Department of Trade and Industry (2001) *Small and Medium-sized Enterprise Statistics for the UK, 2000.* DTI, Sheffield, UK.

Dondo, A. and Ngumo, M. (1998) Africa: Kenya. In: Morrison, A. (ed.) *Entrepreneurship: an International Perspective.* Butterworth Hienemann, Oxford, UK, pp. 15–26.

Drucker, P. (1986) *Innovation and Entrepreneurship.* Heinemann, London.

Fass, M. and Scothorne, R. (1990) *The Vital Economy.* Abbeystrand Publishing, Edinburgh, UK.

Gilder, G. (1971) *Spirit of Enterprise.* Simon and Schusler, New York.

Glezer, L. (1988) Business and commerce. In: Jupp, J. (ed.) *The Australian People: an Encyclopedia of the Nation, Its People and Origins.* Angus and Robertson, Sydney, pp. 860–864.

Goffee, R. (1996) Understanding family businesses: issues for further research. *International Journal of Entrepreneurial Behaviour and Research* 2(1), 36–48.

Goffee, R. and Scase, R. (1995) *Corporate realities: the Dynamics of Large and Small Organisations.* Routledge, London.

Gorton, M. (2000) Overcoming the structure-agency divide in small business research. *International Journal of Entrepreneurial Behaviour and Research* 6(5), 276–292.

Greenbank, P. (2000) Micro-business start-ups: challenging normative decision-making? *Market Intelligence and Planning* 18(4), 206–212.

Greenbank, P. (2001) Objective setting in the micro-business. *International Journal of Entrepreneurial Behaviour and Research* 7(3), 108–127.

Habbershon, T. and Williams, M. (1999) *A Resource Based Framework for Assessing the Strategic Advantages of Family Firms, Working Paper Series No. 101.* The Wharton School, University of Pennsylvania.

Harper, M. (1984) *Small Business in the Third World.* John Wiley & Sons, London.

Hisrich, R. and Drnovsek, M. (2002) Entrepreneurship and small business research: a European perspective. *Journal of Small Business and Enterprise Development* 9(2), 172–222.

Hisrich, R. and Grachev, M. (1995) The Russian entrepreneur: characteristics and prescriptions for success. *Journal of Managerial Psychology* 10(2), 3–9.

Hofstede, G. (1991) *Culture and Organisations*. McGraw-Hill, London.

Hurley, A. (1999) Incorporating feminist theories into sociological theories of entrepreneurship. *Women in Management Review* 14(2), 54–62.

Jones, K. (2000) Psychodynamics, gender, and reactionary entrepreneurship in metropolitan Sao Paulo, Brazil. *Women in Management Review* 15(4), 207–217.

Kets de Vries, M. (1993) The dynamics of family controlled firms: the good news and the bad news. *Organisational Dynamics* 22, 59–71.

Kets de Vries, M. (1996) *Family Business: Human Dilemmas in the Family Firm*. Thomson International Business Press, London.

King, B., Bransgrove, C. and Whitelaw, P. (1998) Profiling the strategic marketing activities of small tourism businesses. *Journal of Travel and Tourism Marketing* 7(4), 45–59.

Kirzner, I. (1979) *Perception, Opportunity and Profit Studies in the Theory of Entrepreneurship*. London University Chicago Press, Chicago, Illinois.

Kovassy, M. and Hutton, C. (2001) *Why do restaurants succeed in the Dandenong Ranges tourism region?* Unpublished seminar paper, RMIT University, Melbourne, Australia.

Kuratko, D. and Hodgetts, R. (1998) *Entrepreneurship: a Contemporary Approach*. Dryden Press, New York.

Lockyer, C. and Morrison, A. (1999) *Scottish Tourism Market: Structure, Characteristics and Performance*. Scottish Tourism Research Unit/Fraser of Allander Institute, University of Strathclyde, Glasgow, UK.

Lynch, P. (1999) Host attitudes towards guests in the homestay sector. *Tourism and Hospitality Research* 1(2), 119–144.

McKay, R. (2001) Women entrepreneurs: moving beyond family and flexibility. *International Journal of Entrepreneurial Behaviour and Research* 7(4), 148–165.

Medlik, S. (1994) *The Business of Hotels*. Butterworth-Heinemann, Oxford, UK.

Middleton, V. and Clarke, J. (eds) (2001) *Marketing in Travel and Tourism*. Butterworth-Heinemann, Oxford, UK.

Morrison, A. (1998a) Small firm statistics: a hotel sector focus. *The Service Industries Journal* 18(1), 132–142.

Morrison, A. (ed.) (1998b) *Entrepreneurship: an International Perspective*. Butterworth-Heinemann, Oxford, UK.

Morrison, A. (2000a) Entrepreneurship: what triggers it? *International Journal of Entrepreneurial Behaviour and Research* 6(2), 59–71.

Morrison, A. (2000b) Initiating entrepreneurship. In: Carter, S. and Jones-Evans, D. (eds) *Enterprise and Small Business*. Pearson Education, London, pp. 97–114.

Morrison, A. (2001) Entrepreneurs transcend time: a biographical analysis. *Management Decision* 39(9), 784–790.

Morrison, A. (2002) Small hospitality business: enduring or endangered? *Journal of Hospitality and Tourism Management* 9(1), 1–11.

Morrison, A. and Teixeira, R. (2002) Small hospitality firms: business performance obstacles. Conference paper presented at *International Small Hospitality and Tourism Firm Conference*, Leeds Metropolitan University, Leeds, UK.

Morrison, A., Rimmington, M. and Williams, C. (1999) *Entrepreneurship in the Hospitality, Tourism and Leisure Industries*. Butterworth-Heinemann, Oxford, UK.

Morrison, A., Baum, T. and Andrew, R. (2001) The lifestyle economics of small tourism businesses. *Journal of Travel and Tourism Research* 1, 16–25.

Naffziger, D., Hornsby, J. and Kuratko, D. (1994) A proposed research model of entrepreneurial motivation. *Entrepreneurship Theory and Practice*, Spring, 19, 33.

Neck, H.N., Zacharakis, A.L., Bygrave, W.D. and Reynolds, P.D. (2001) *Global Entrepreneurship Monitor*. Babson College, Massachusetts.

Omar, A. and Davidson, M. (2001) Women in management: a comparative cross-cultural overview. *Cross Cultural Management* 8(3/4), 35–67.

Orhan, M. and Scott, D. (2001) Why women enter into entrepreneurship: an explanatory model. *Women in Management Review* 16(5), 232–247.

Pearce, I. (1980) Reforms for entrepreneurs to serve public policy. In: Seldon, A. (ed.) *The Prime Mover of Progress: the Entrepreneur in Capitalism and Socialism*. The Institute of Economic Affairs, London.

Ram, M. (1994) Unravelling social networks in ethnic minority firms. *International Small Business Journal* 12, 42–53.

Ram, M., Sanghera, B., Abbas, T. and Barlow, G. (2000) Training and ethnic minority firms: the case of the independent restaurant sector. *Education and Training* 42(4/5), 334–341.

Scase, R. and Goffee, R. (1989) *The Real World of the Small Business Owner*. Routledge, London.

Schumpeter, J. (1934) *The Theory of Economic Development*. Harvard University Press, Cambridge, Massachusetts.

Shaw, E., Shaw, J. and Wilson, M. (2002) *Unsung Entrepreneurs: Entrepreneurship for Social Gain*. University of Durham Business School, Durham, UK.

Smallbone, D., Evans, M., Ekanem, I. and Butters, S. (2001) *Researching Social Enterprise*. Small Business Service, Department of Trade and Industry, London.

Smith, C. (2000) Managing work and family in small 'copreneurial' business: an Australian study. *Women in Management Review* 15(5/6), 283–289.

Storey, D. (1994) *Understanding the Small Business Sector*. Routledge, London.

Tayeb, M. (1988) *Organisations and National Culture*. Sage, London.

Thompson, J., Alvy, G. and Lees, A. (2000) Social entrepreneurship: a new look at the people and the potential. *Management Decision* 38(5), 328–338.

Timmons, J. (1994) *New Venture Creation: Entrepreneurship for the 21st Century*. Irwin, Boston, Massachusetts.

Van der Horst, H. (1996) *The Low Sky: Understanding the Dutch*. Scriptum, The Hague.

Yu, T.F.-L. (2001) The Chinese family business as a strategic system: an evolutionary perspective. *International Journal of Entrepreneurial Behaviour and Research* 7(1), 22–40.

3

Starting the Family Business

Introduction

Start-up is the most critical stage in the family business – not growth, and not succession. This is because many founders have little interest in growing, and succession or inheritance is not an issue. The future of the business will always be in doubt, with many strategic options available, but the course of most family businesses is set as soon as the founders make the decision to purchase or create an enterprise. In tourism and hospitality the vast majority, from intent or necessity, will always remain small, hands-on operations.

In this chapter the critical issues of motivation and goals are examined first, particularly the contrasts inherent in growth and profit-oriented entrepreneurship versus the more prevalent lifestyle and autonomy motivations. Research data from Australia, Canada and Denmark are analysed to examine start-up motives and goals in depth. Later in the book (see Chapter 5), data from these same research projects are used to examine family-related and business-development goals, succession plans and related issues.

The third section of this chapter discusses important antecedents to family business, including the influences of education, experience and training. Tourism and hospitality businesses are often easy to enter and many owners lack directly relevant training or experience. On the other hand, previous work in the industry, or exposure through one's upbringing in a family business, might motivate some people to establish their own business. Culture and economic conditions are also antecedents to be considered.

Business planning is then considered. The careful preparation and execution of a business plan is considered to be a major indicator of potential business success, and is certainly associated with achieving growth. Yet a majority of family business founders appear deliberately to neglect the business plan, either out of ignorance or as a reflection of their predominant lifestyle and autonomy motives. Included in this section is an outline of what the plan should include, with emphasis on several family-related issues.

Ownership, organization and governance are covered last in this chapter. Ownership forms and business structure are usually set at the time of business start-up, or absorbed through purchase. Many families prefer uncomplicated forms including single and joint ownership, while various forms of partnership are preferred by others. The profit- and growth-oriented entrepreneur is more likely to purchase or establish a company because of its greater potential to acquire external funds from lenders or investors, and to restrict owners' liability in the case of failure. Of particular interest to the family business is the option of including professionals in managing the business, or at least in a board of directors. Parallel to business governance should be policies and procedures for family management, including a family council and charter.

©D. Getz et al. 2004. *The Family Business in Tourism and Hospitality*
(D. Getz, J. Carlsen and A. Morrison)

Motivations and Goals

Sharma *et al.* (1996: 9) observed that family business goals 'are likely to be quite different from the firm-value maximization goal assumed for the publicly traded and professionally managed firms', but there have been few attempts to identify the imputed differences. At the heart of this issue is whether family business owners will place family concerns over business success or growth, and what impact this has on the business (and by implication, the industry and destination).

Singer and Donahu (1992) touched on this issue by identifying two distinct types: the family-centred business, where the business is a way of life, and the business-centred family, in which business is a means of livelihood. File *et al.* (1994) also categorized family businesses, distinguishing between those which were uninvolved in issues of family dynamics, those balancing family and business needs, some which had family concerns as their primary goal, and others which were most concerned with adapting to changing conditions.

As noted by Westhead (1997), economic theory postulates that the decision to establish a business should be based on an assessment of the best alternative use of the entrepreneur's time, but family business owners are distinguished by providing employment for family members of the management team and by ensuring independent ownership of the business. Dunn (1995) found that it was not uncommon for family businesses to accept lower returns or longer paybacks on their investments, or to sustain a lifestyle, rather than to maximize profits or personal revenue. Gersick *et al.* (1997) concluded that businesses in the start-up stage were characterized by informal organizational structure, owner-manager control and having a single product. When it is also a family business they are more likely to be associated with personal, family or lifestyle dreams than with objective business projections.

Enough evidence has been published regarding motives and goals in the tourism and hospitality industry to conclude that there exist a multiplicity of economic, social and personal reasons. In the following section evidence from a number of diverse sources is presented, then more detailed data and analysis are examined from Australia, Canada and Denmark.

Research Evidence from the Tourism and Hospitality Industry

Quite a lot of evidence comes from research conducted in the UK, where the tradition of family business in tourism and hospitality is very well established. Shaw and Williams (1987), from a study of owners in Cornwall, determined that motivations for leaving their previous job or position were quite diverse. The most frequent (23%) was to be self-employed. Personal or family reasons were given by 19%, while 14% were dissatisfied with previous employment and 10% mentioned the push factor of having been made redundant. An additional 10% wanted to move to Cornwall, while 3.3% were fleeing 'the rat race'. The remainder wanted to make more money (3%) or enhance their career (6%). Asked specifically why they established a business in a particular location (all in Cornwall), the main answers were: the environment, or to move to Cornwall (25%); were in Cornwall anyway (25%); economic reasons (18%); the markets for their business (10%), and luck or chance (14%).

The National Survey of Small Tourism and Hospitality Firms in the UK (Thomas *et al.*, 1997) questioned owners on their motives. Fully 90% of owners gave non-economic reasons for being in business. Few were motivated by the anticipation of greater financial rewards than could be expected from paid employment. The most common reasons given for business ownership were to do what they enjoyed (45%) and the desire for independence (30%). Only 4% considered ownership of their small business to be a form of semi-retirement, while 10% believed they had been driven to self-employment.

Rural and farm-related

Frequently, small farm-based family businesses (e.g. farm-stays, caravan and campsites, B&B operations) are established to support the main farm business (Pearce, 1990; World Tourism Organisation, 1997), but are also set up as a sideline or hobby, often by females (Kousis, 1989; Lynch, 1996; Oppermann, 1997). Other rural tourism researchers have pointed to the goals or rewards of improved social lives (Frater, 1982; Pearce, 1990), and social standing (Pearce, 1990).

A study of farm and ranch tourism in Montana by Nickerson *et al.* (2001) determined that 61% of owners had diversified for economic reasons, while 23% had reasons external to their operations and 16% had social, economic and external reasons combined. Specific economic reasons included: variable and uncertain farm income; providing jobs for family, or helping keep them on the farm; earning extra income; loss of government funding; making better use of assets, and taking advantage of tax incentives. Non-economic reasons included: a desire for companionship; meeting existing demand; educating the consumer, and pursuing an interest or hobby. Apparently imitation of other enterprises was a factor in many of these diversification ventures.

Third World factors

Smith (1998) specifically evaluated small, Third World tourism enterprises, noting that powerful incentives existed for their establishment. These included: taking local control over development; acquiring status; gaining access to clubs and business networks; building equity for a family legacy or retirement assets; hiring family members who might otherwise be unemployable, and being one's own boss. Smith concluded that in the Third World employees of hotels and resorts were often better off than their self-employed neighbours, owing to easier work and higher pay. Accordingly, it can be expected that family business motivations and goals differ greatly between wealthy and poor countries.

Lifestyle motives

In a study of small tourism businesses in Victoria, Australia, Bransgrove and King (1996) found that the top goals of owners/managers were challenge/stimulus, business opportunity,

lifestyle, and long-term financial gain (accounting for 18–24% each), but lifestyle goals were twice as frequent in rural areas. A study of tourism businesses in the Northland region of New Zealand by Page *et al.* (1999) secured data from about 300 operators. Fifty-four per cent of respondents indicated their principal motive for owning a tourism business was enjoyment of their particular line of work, and 20% wanted to be their own boss.

Peters and Weirmair commented on the explosion of tourism in Austria in the mass-tourism-oriented 1970s:

> . . . in Austria those who took over hotels and related businesses from their parents or who entered tourism from agriculture/forestry and who obtained most of their external financing through land collateral frequently fall into the category of 'life style' and/or 'part-time' entrepreneur.
>
> (Peters and Weirmair, 2001)

Many of those who survived are now facing serious financial problems because of high debt loads. In Finland, Komppula (2000) found only lifestyle entrepreneurs in his interviews with rural tourism operators. Growth of the business was not an objective in these enterprises.

Rural Western Australia

In this research, first published by Getz and Carlsen (2000), the sample consisted of a combination of two, mutually exclusive subsets: (i) a general sample of rural tourism/hospitality businesses in Western Australia; and (ii) a more focused sample from one well-known tourist region.

The state-wide sample was partially derived from a list provided by Farm and Country Holidays Association Inc., and augmented by selections from the Royal Automobile Club's Western Australia Touring and Accommodation Guide. Metropolitan Perth and other cities were excluded from the sampling frame. The result was a non-random sampling covering all types of tourism and hospitality businesses. Western Australia is a very large, predominately rural state. Outside the main metropolitan centre of Perth, tourism opportunities abound in small-town, beach, farm, and wilderness settings.

The entire membership of the Augusta-Margaret River Tourist Association was also surveyed, which yielded a few types of business that might not appear to be tourism-oriented, yet membership in the organization suggests that the owners believed they at least benefit from tourism. This tourist region is located south of Perth, approximately a 3-hour drive by car, and includes very popular beaches, wineries, natural areas and small towns. It is more intensively developed for tourism than the majority of the state, and enjoys a reputation for good climate, attractive landscapes and a lifestyle associated with fine dining and wine. Consequently, it has a different character and appeal than most of the rural regions of the state.

The mail-out survey, and a subsequent reminder card, went to 357 businesses in the Margaret River area and to another 455 businesses in the remainder of the state. The response rate was 33% in Margaret River and 20% in the remainder of the state. The total number of useable responses was 210 (for an overall response rate of approximately 26%), but included only 198 family or owner-operated businesses, which have been used in the ensuing analysis.

Respondents and characteristics of their businesses

All 198 respondents used in the analysis indicated that they had a 'family-owned' business, that is, 'owner-operated, or one family owns controlling interest.' They were dominated (66.2%), by businesses owned by a married couple, and 82.2% of respondents were married. Sole proprietors accounted for 14.4%, a partnership of two or more family members 9.7%, limited company 5.6%, a partnership including family members 1.6%, and others 2.5%. Fully 96.4% of respondents reported they were an owner, and it is likely that the others, who said they were 'managers', were family members.

Females were the largest group, accounting for 59% of respondents. This imbalance possibly reflects the dominance of women in B&B and farm-stay operations. In terms of education, the largest group (42.2%) of respondents had high school qualifications, although 19.8% had

received a college diploma, 13.9% a university degree, 11.2% an advanced degree, and another 12.8% a trade qualification.

The dominant age category of respondents was 45–54 (41.4%), followed by 35–44 (24.1%). Only two respondents (1%) were under the age of 25, and only 11 (5.8%) were aged 25–34. The 55–64 category accounted for 19.4% of the sample, and the 65-plus category was 8.4%. Children (ages not defined) of the respondents worked in only 23% of the businesses, although it is likely that parents will not count young children as employees, regardless of any involvement in the business operations. There were 21 respondents with one child in the business, 12 with two, nine with three, and four with four involved children.

Based on the respondents' own descriptions of their business, 75% of the sample were accommodation operators, with the largest block running guest ranches or farm-stays (47 = 25.1%). 'Campground/resort/self-catering' operations was the next largest group (42 = 22.6%), and B&B operations accounted for 40 (21.4%). Only 7, or 3.7% of the businesses were hotels or motels. Other types of operations included: 'food or retail' (13 = 7%); 'tour operation' (12 = 6.4%); 'winery' (12 = 6.4%); 'tourist attraction' (7 = 3.7%); 'other services' (6 = 3.2%) and 'manufacturing' (1 = 0.5%). This breakdown cannot be interpreted as an accurate reflection of the rural tourism and hospitality sectors overall, owing to limitations of the two sampling frames and response rates.

Eighty-three per cent of the respondents had started up the business, with only 4.2% having inherited it. Also, most of the businesses were recently started, with 65.1% commenced in the 1990s, 24.6% in the 1980s, and 5% in the 1970s. Seven respondents (3.5%) indicated the business had started up in the 1800s. Fully 44.4% of businesses had been started within 5 years of the survey. In response to the question: 'how many years have you been involved in the business?', the modal category was 1–5 (54.6%). Only 16.5% had been involved longer than 10 years (with 5.7% under 1 year and 23.2% between 5 and 10).

Most were small and micro businesses. Ninety-five per cent employed 10 or fewer persons, with 4% reporting between 10 and 50 and one (0.5%) reporting over 100 persons. As well,

80% of the tourism and hospitality businesses in this sample reported an annual revenue of under Aus$100,000, while 14% had revenues of between Aus$100,000 and Aus$500,000 and 2.6% over Aus$1 million. Sixty-nine per cent reported fewer than 1000 customers per year.

The Margaret River sample was somewhat different from the overall state sample, although differences on goals were not evaluated because of the quite different sampling frames. Compared to the state-wide sample, Margaret River respondents were less dominated by accommodation and had fewer female respondents.

These data portray a population of mainly middle-aged business operators. They might have had rural roots or connections, but they were mostly not young rural natives taking over family businesses or starting first careers.

Start-up goals

Respondents were first asked an open question: 'Please describe why you got started in this business.' Answers were grouped for coding purposes, with results displayed in Table 3.1. The largest single category (34.1%) concerned lifestyle decisions, and the second main

Table 3.1. Start-up goals of rural family businesses in Western Australia.

Categories	Valid % of total responses
Appealing lifestyle	34.1
Business opportunity/investment	27.6
Worked in related business/ to diversify	9.7
To preserve the home	6.5
Retirement project	6.5
Meeting people	3.8
Recover debt on acquired land	2.7
Assistant to husband	2.7
Build business then sell for retirement	2.2
Thought it would be fun/good idea	1.6
Saw a market need for the business	1.6

Categorized from an open-ended question: 'Please describe why you got started in this business?'; source: Getz and Carlsen, 2000.

category concerned business opportunities and investments (27.6%). Business-related answers were the most frequent.

Table 3.2 presents responses to the question: 'How important were the following goals to you when getting started in this business?' The goal statements were all carefully derived from the family business literature as well as from 12 pre-survey interviews with family business owners covering their motivations and goals. Respondents were asked to tick one box of five beside each of the 12 statements, with the anchors being 'not at all important' and 'very important'.

The researchers first sought to determine the relative importance of the start-up goals. The most striking results were that living in the right environment (mean = 4.51, out of 5) and enjoying a good lifestyle (4.37) were the strongest goals by far, with hardly any respondents not ranking them as 'important' or 'very important'. Other very important goals for these respondents were 'to permit me to become financially independent' (mean = 3.97) and 'to be my own boss' (3.94), both of which express a desire for autonomy. 'To provide me with a challenge' (3.93) and 'to meet interesting people' (3.96) demonstrate that social and personal reasons were important to many respondents. The lowest-ranked goals were 'to gain prestige' (mean = 2.16) and 'to make lots of money' (mean = 2.88).

A second objective of the analysis was to reveal any underlying structure in the 12 goal statements – specifically, which goals go together in defining a lifestyle orientation versus a profit-maximizing orientation? Accordingly, a factor analysis (principal components analysis) was conducted on the 12 goals. The factors were then rotated using Varimax rotation with Kaiser Normalization. This resulted in four factors that explained 60.4% of the variance in respondents' scores; this level of explanation is good, but low enough to suggest that the four factors do not explain all the underlying patterns of responses.

The order of statements in Table 3.2 has been altered from the original questionnaire so that statements comprising the four factors could be grouped together. Each factor was named according to the researcher's interpretation of underlying meaning. The five 'Lifestyle' variables grouped very well together in statistical

Table 3.2. Importance of start-up goals among rural family business owners in Western Australia (*n* = 198).

Goals	1 Not at all important (valid % of responses)	2	3	4	5 Very important	Means	Factors
Lifestyle							
To keep my family together	11.7	6.9	22.3	16.5	42.6	3.71	F1
To keep this property in the family	22.7	4.3	16.2	18.9	37.8	3.45	F1
To live in the right environment	2.1	1.1	8.5	20.7	67.6	4.51	F1
To support my/our leisure interests	11.5	11.0	23.6	17.3	36.6	3.57	F1
To enjoy a good lifestyle	2.1	1.1	12.1	26.8	57.9	4.37	F1
Money							
To make lots of money	17.9	18.4	32.1	20.5	11.1	2.88	F2
To permit me to become financially independent	7.8	5.2	15.1	26.0	45.8	3.97	F2
To provide a retirement income	11.0	9.9	25.7	18.8	34.6	3.56	F2
Stimulation							
To meet interesting people	5.7	5.7	13.5	36.5	38.5	3.96	F3
To provide me with a challenge	5.8	6.8	16.2	31.4	39.8	3.93	F3
Independence							
To be my own boss	7.4	8.4	12.6	26.3	45.3	3.94	F4
To gain prestige by operating a business	45.8	16.1	19.8	13.0	5.2	2.16	F4

Source: Getz and Carlsen, 2000.

terms (they are shown as F1 in Table 3.2), and were by far the most important in light of the mean scores and high factor loadings. Note that F1 explains 21.3% of total variance and includes the two highest means (4.51 and 4.37).

Three goal statements constituted the 'Money' factor (F2; explaining 14.2% of variance), including the second-lowest mean of all – 'to make lots of money' (2.88). The other two goals on this factor were, however, important to the respondents. Factor 3 was called 'Stimulation' (12.7% of variance) and contained two fairly important statements. Factor 4 was called 'Independence' (12.2% of variance), assuming that prestige is one of the appeals of being one's own boss. In hindsight, especially given the results of the analysis from Bornholm and Canmore which follows, Factor 4 should have been called 'Autonomy'. This is because 'being one's own boss' was shown to be an important goal for entrepreneurs and family business owners in its own right.

It was interesting to find that at least one goal in each of the four factors was very important to many respondents, judging by the high mean values. While it can be concluded that lifestyle was, overall, the most important, the findings also reveal that multiple goals were involved in the start-up decisions of these respondents in rural Western Australia.

To determine if there were identifiable differences in the types of respondents according to the way they rated the goal statements, the researchers employed several statistical tests on the individual goal statements. This technique found no statistically significant differences by reference to demographic, business and ownership variables. But what of the four factors – should the groupings of statements reflect some underlying differences in respondents? To answer this important question, demographic, ownership and business-type variables were tested against four new variables consisting of the summed means from statements in each factor. Either analysis of variance (ANOVA) or an independent means *t*-test was employed. The sample size imposed some limitations on this analysis. A much larger sample might have been able to identify more statistically significant differences.

Business type made a difference (after re-grouping to combine the manufacturing, food/retail and 'other services' categories) with regard to the 'Money' factor. Tour operators, compared to the hotel and motel owners, were much less oriented toward making money. Hotel and motel operators probably have invested consid-erable financial resources in their businesses and expect a good return on investment. Although other inter-group differences were not statisti-cally significant, a plausible hypothesis emerges: the more money one invests in the business, the more likely that financial goals dominate. That is not to say, however, that the reason for investing in a rural business was not in part related to envi-ronment and lifestyle considerations. In some of the cases, existing farm operations were probably converted in whole or part to tourism operations (e.g. B&B or caravan park), so the level of investment was less than if a new enterprise was started from scratch.

Another variable found to be significant is that of ownership type. Married couples and sole proprietors displayed statistically significant differences in their responses to the variable that comprises the 'Independence' factor. Sole pro-prietors (i.e. one person owning and operating the business, not a couple or family) were much more likely to agree that being one's own boss and gaining prestige were important start-up goals.

The age of respondents was also important, specifically with regard to the 'lifestyle' factor. Those aged 35–44 had significantly different responses from the 45–54 cohort, with the youn-ger owners displaying much higher agreement with the five statements in this factor. This is pre-sumably linked to the prime family-formation stage, with those aged 35–44 being more likely to have children at home.

As well, both the 25–34 and 35–44 age groups were significantly different from the 65+ group regarding the 'Independence' factor. Younger respondents were much higher in their agreement with the two statements in this component. Apparently the 65+ category, which coincides with normal retirement ages, is less likely to be interested in prestige or self-employment. Younger, sole proprietors favoured these two reasons.

Whether or not this population is similar to that in other rural areas is open to future comparisons. In some traditional communities, for example, it might be expected that most family businesses are inherited rather than new businesses set up by in-migrants. Even within Western Australia differences were noted, as the Margaret River subsample had a different mix of business types. It can be hypothesized that more developed rural tourism destinations attract and sustain different types of businesses and quite likely different types of investors. Developed des-tinations can count on higher levels of publicity and demand, less seasonality, and a broader range of attractions and services.

The Western Australian sample strongly suggests that tourism and hospitality sectors are attracting many middle-aged couples and fami-lies to live and invest, for predominantly lifestyle and family reasons. In addition, there is a group of sole proprietors (who might have informal family involvement in the business) who appear to be motivated more by normal profit-making goals, but who also prefer the rural environment.

Overall, the analysis tends to confirm the presence of both family-oriented businesses and business-oriented families (or sole proprietors) as suggested by Singer and Donahu (1992), but in these rural tourism and hospitality sectors, living in the rural environment, plus family and lifestyle considerations, were significant for almost everyone.

Canada and Denmark

This comparative research (by Getz and Petersen, 2002) of somewhat different resort settings (Canmore, Alberta in Canada and the island of Bornholm, Denmark) in two countries was built on the earlier Australian work, but added several dimensions. The same start-up goals were tested again, and a number of interviews conducted in Denmark to obtain additional insights. Detailed analysis has been performed on these comparative data to search for and characterize profit- and growth-oriented entrepreneurs.

These specific areas were chosen for mostly practical reasons, being immediately accessible to the collaborating researchers. As discussed later, they are similar enough to enable effective comparison of family business owners, yet different enough to yield some significant variations in results.

The resorts

Canmore is a rapidly-growing resort town situated just outside the boundary of Banff National Park, a 1-hour drive west of Calgary, Alberta. Its very recent transition from coal-mining village to tourist destination is attributable to several major factors: staging of part of the 1988 Winter Olympics in Canmore, which generated publicity and a world-class facility for cross-country skiing; a development freeze within the national park, resulting in over-spill development in Canmore; and mounting demand for second homes in the mountains. Consequently, since 1988, tourism has become the town's major industry. Numerous accommodation, retail, tour and other services have opened there.

Canmore's Business Registry, with interpretation by local economic development officials, revealed 1034 businesses of which 61% were considered to be 'family owned', that is owned by identifiable persons, not corporations. A total of 198 tourism-related businesses were identified and it was estimated that 78% of these were 'family owned'. Almost all the 'family-owned' businesses are owner-managed with resident owners, although a very small proportion of owners resided outside the community. A total of 100 respondents completed the survey.

A breakdown of accommodation businesses in Canmore reveals that it is heavily weighted to B&B houses (79 out of 106), and 36 of these B&B owners replied to the questionnaire. All B&B operations were family businesses. In addition there were 27 other accommodation businesses (hotels and motels, plus one campground) of which 16 (59%) were believed to be family owned. The survey yielded nine respondents from these other accommodation types. In analysing the data it was therefore desirable to isolate B&B for a number of comparisons to other business types.

The Island of Bornholm (in the Baltic Sea) is one of the most renowned destinations in Denmark, having been popular since the late 19th century. It has been described as '. . . a mature seaside resort with an established tourism infrastructure dominated by small

enterprises' (Gyimothy 2000: 56). The climate is temperate and often sunny, but winters are harsh and not attractive for visitors. The main attractions are unspoiled rural and coastal scenery, quaint fishing villages, recreational activities (hiking, fishing, yachting, windsurfing, golfing, shopping, bird watching, dining, bicycling, bathing), a number of sandy beaches, historic churches, arts and crafts (especially glass blowing and ceramics), and visiting small museums. The summer season is typically only 2 months in length.

Bornholm is similar to two other Baltic islands, Åland and Gotland. All three islands possess high levels of local ownership and control; Twining-Ward and Baum (1998) concluded that all three had entered a period of decline and were suffering from the ill-effects of seasonally low demand. The problems are augmented by a dominance of small, family enterprises '. . . which in many cases lack the professional training required to secure a high quality of service' (Twining-Ward and Baum, 1998: 135).

Method

Research was undertaken in 2001 by Getz and Petersen, and the Bornholm portion was conducted with co-operation from the Centre for Regional and Tourism Research (CRT) in Bornholm. The main instrument was a self-completion, mail-back questionnaire written in English, then translated into Danish by staff at the CRT, then back-translated into English to ensure consistency. In addition, interviews were conducted in Danish with a sub-sample on Bornholm, but these were not attempted in Canmore.

The sampling frame in both cases was a census of businesses, with owner-managers selected for study. In Canmore the researchers were assisted in this selection by the local economic development agency which possesses intimate knowledge of the community. In Bornholm the researchers relied on detailed personal knowledge and input from local business owners to determine the sample. A few errors might have occurred in this process, but they would be insufficient to bias the results significantly . Sampling also resulted in a few duplications (i.e. owners of multiple businesses), and also a small number of omissions owing to a lack of information. On Bornholm, an unknown number of individual owners of 'summer houses' for rent were not included.

Privately-owned attractions and recreation suppliers were included. Tourist-oriented manufacturing and retailing was included, specifically arts and crafts producers, antique dealers, gift shops and candy manufacturers. Grocery, clothing, furniture and other stores were excluded even though in resorts a portion of their trade would definitely come from non-residents. Private taxi and bus companies were covered. Consequently, the samples can be said to represent all the major elements of the tourism and hospitality sectors within a resort, but not of the industry as a whole, as they exclude major transport companies, chains and corporate investments. The surveys were close to being a census but did not capture 100% of business owners, and under-represent the retailing sector.

An estimate was made by local researchers of the total number of tourism and hospitality businesses in the Bornholm study area, using municipal directories, and the proportion that was family owned (based on detailed local knowledge). As in Canmore, the principal criterion for determining if a business was 'family owned' was the presence of resident, owner-managers. There were 317 identifiable tourism/hospitality businesses in the two Bornholm municipalities covered by the research, of which fully 95.3% were deemed to be family businesses. The main foothold of corporate ownership is that of larger accommodation establishments.

The questionnaire sample of 84 owners on Bornholm is not directly comparable to the business categories used in Canmore, because each respondent was asked to indicate all the different activities of their business and a small number of them ran multiple businesses or multi-activity businesses (such as hotel plus restaurant). Of the 120 activities listed by respondents, accommodation was the largest category (31), followed by restaurants/cafes (22), and then arts and crafts producers (21), (most of which are combined production and retail operations).

Profile of respondents and their businesses

In both resorts (see Table 3.3) the respondents were predominantly married (88–89%), but there were more males in the Bornholm group

(63% compared with 46%), and they were, on average, older. This reflects the older age of the businesses covered by the sample (65% of the Canmore owners had owned their business for 5 years or less, compared with 32% in Bornholm), and in turn the much longer history of tourism development on the island.

Bornholm respondents might appear to be better educated, but a higher proportion of Canmore respondents had university degrees, compared to vocational education in Bornholm. Data on business types are not directly comparable as the industry is somewhat different in these resorts. The largest group in both cases were accommodation operators, but in Canmore there was a high proportion of B&B owners while the Bornholm sample are mostly operators of small hotels and 'pensions' (pensions are typically smaller than hotels, but often indistinguishable). The Bornholm sample also contained a group of 21 arts and craft producers/retailers, but there were none of these in the Canmore sample (one operates in the town).

Ownership was largely in the hands of married couples and sole proprietors. Quite a few families had formed companies, but partnerships were a small minority. There was a higher proportion of sole proprietors in Bornholm and a higher proportion of married couples as owners in Canmore. Exact percentages are not possible because multiple answers were permitted on the ownership question.

In both resorts the businesses were very small, with mostly just the owner(s) being employed. In Bornholm less than half had non-family, full-time, paid employees; only 11 involved children and seven others involved other family members besides spouses. Companies (as opposed to other ownership forms) and non-accommodation businesses had more paid, full-time, non-family employees. In Canmore, less than half had employees and only 17 involved children or other family besides a spouse. Those Canmore businesses owned by companies had more employees, and these were primarily hotels, restaurants, and to a lesser extent tour companies. None of the B&B establishments had non-family, full-time paid employees.

In Canmore, a relatively new resort, 74.5% of the businesses were started by the respondents, compared to 56.3% in Bornholm. There were no inherited businesses in Canmore,

Table 3.3. Profiles of the respondents from a survey of family business owners in Denmark (Bornholm) and Canada (Canmore).

Profile variables	Bornholm $n = 84$ (responses to individual questions vary)		Canmore $n = 100$ (responses to Individual questions vary)	
Gender	Male:	63.3%	Male:	45.8%
	Female:	36.7	Female:	54.2
Marital status	Married:	88.8%	Married:	87.8%
	Other:	11.3	Other:	12.2
Age	Under 25:	1.3%	Under 25:	0
	25–34	5.0	25–34	10%
	35–44	27.5	35–44	40
	45–54	31.3	45–54	28
	55–64	30.0	55–64	15
	65+	5.0	65+	7
Included in the business (respondents were asked to indicate the activities included in their business, yielding multiple answers)	Accommodation:	31	Accommodation:	45
	Restaurant/cafe:	22	Restaurant/cafe:	19
	Attraction:	5	Attraction:	2
	Art/craft:	21	Recreation:	3
	Retail:	8	Retail:	20
	Tour service:	4	Tour service:	12
	Other:	23	Other:	26
Year business started	2000:	2.6%	2000:	10%
	1990s:	33.3	1990s:	67%
	1980s:	14.1	1980s:	14%
	1970s:	12.8	1970s:	3%
	1960s:	15.4	1960s:	1%
	1950s:	7.7	1950s:	2%
	older:	14.1	older:	3%
	(oldest: 1887)			
Number of years in this business (cumulative %)	● 1 or less:	7.3%	● 1 or less:	13%
	● 5 or less:	31.7	● 5 or less:	65
	● 10 or less:	53.7	● 10 or less:	88
	● 20 or less:	79.3	● 20 or less:	96.7
	● 30 or less:	91.5	● 30 or less:	98.9
Purchased or started?	● Purchased:	38.1%	● Purchased:	74.5%
	● Started myself:	56.3	● Started myself:	25.5
	● Inherited:	2.5		
	● Renting:	1.3		
Ownership (multiple responses were permitted)	● Husband/wife:	21	● Husband/wife:	50
	● Ltd. company:	14	● Ltd. company:	29
	● Sole proprietor:	38	● Sole proprietor:	26
	● Partnership no family:	2	● Partnership no family:	5
	● Partnership with family:	4	● Partnership with family:	1
	● Other:	4	● Other:	2
Family involvement (multiple answers were permitted)	Only me:	30	Only me:	25
	With spouse:	41	With spouse:	64
	Child(ren):	11	Child(ren):	12
	Other family:	7	Other family:	5
Paid employees (non-family, full-time)	None:	53%	None:	62.5%
	1:	12.0	1:	6.3
	2–10:	28.9	2–10:	21.9
	over 10:	6.0	over 10:	9.4
	Range: 0–35		Range: 0–35	

Table 3.3.   *Continued.*

Profile variables	Bornholm n = 84 (responses to individual questions vary)		Canmore n = 100 (responses to Individual questions vary)	
Education	Post-secondary:	76.3%	Post-secondary:	66%
Previous business ownership	Yes:	31.2%	Yes:	43.4%
	No:	68.8	No:	56.6

Source: Getz and Petersen, 2002.

but several in Bornholm (2.5%). Previous business ownership was high (31% of respondents in Bornholm and 43% in Canmore), but it is unknown what kinds of businesses they were.

Start-up goals

The 12 goal statements developed for the Getz and Carlsen (2000) research were used again, and three new goals were provided to the Bornholm data in consideration of local conditions. Table 3.4 displays the mean scores (out of 5), and overall, there was a high degree of congruence between the two countries' samples on their start-up goals.

In terms of means, the highest six are the same for each sample, although the ranking is different. Several goals generated differences between the resorts that were statistically significant, as indicated in the table.

The highest mean among the Bornholm respondents was 4.36 for 'to provide me with a challenge', but this was significantly lower in Canmore, at 3.75. The highest mean for Canmore respondents was 4.23 for 'to enjoy a good lifestyle', but it was also important to the Danes at 3.90 (not a statistically significant difference). 'To be my own boss' was second-highest in Canmore (4.20), compared to 3.99 in Denmark (not significantly different). Amazingly, 'to live in the right environment' attracted almost identical and very high means in both samples (4.03 and 4.02). The other very high mean in the Danish group was 'to permit me to become financially independent' at 4.03, compared with 3.95 in Canmore (not significantly different).

Looking at the other statistically different responses, 'to make lots of money' appealed more to the Canadians (mean = 3.18) than the Danes (2.76), as did 'to support my/our leisure interests' (3.73 compared with 3.16), and 'to

provide a retirement income' (3.40 compared to 2.72). None of the three extra items for the Danish sample attracted high means, although 'to move to Bornholm' was apparently a motivator for some of the respondents.

Based on the means, it appears that the family business owners in both resort settings were motivated equally by lifestyle and locational preferences, just as in the rural Western Australian sample. Autonomy goals were also very important to both groups. The Canmore resort setting, however, appears to have attracted more entrepreneurs interested in making lots of money and supporting their retirement, and more owners with specific recreational interests. It might be that the mountains have a stronger recreational appeal than the seaside! Danish owners, on the other hand, appear to be more motivated by the need for challenge.

B&B owners in Canmore

In Canmore, B&B owners (36 in the sample) were the most substantial sub-group and were significantly different from the others. Twenty-seven B&Bs are owned jointly by married couples and nine were owned by sole proprietors, (although 28 of the B&B respondents were female). Significantly (Chi square = 0.005) none of the B&B owners had children working in their businesses, and none had non-family, full-time paid employees. None were under the ownership of a company limited, but 29 of 64 other businesses were. Fully 82% of responding B&B owners reported they started the business themselves.

B&B owners in Canmore were much less concerned with the goal 'To permit me to become financially independent'. Only 39% of them ranked it as important or very important, compared with 82% of the other business

Table 3.4. Level of agreement with 'goals when starting this business'.

Goals when starting this business	Bornholm: means (out of 5) (n = 71–74)	Factor	Canmore: means (out of 5) (n = 92–97)	Factor
(1) To be my own boss	3.99	F2	4.20	F1
(2) To keep my family together	2.99	F4/F5	3.18	F3
(3) To keep this property in the family	2.29	F4	2.12	F2
(4) To live in the right environment	4.03	F1	4.02	F3
(5) To support my/our leisure interests	3.16[a]	F1	3.73[a]	F1
Sig. = 0.016				F2
(6) To enjoy a good lifestyle	3.90	F3	4.23	F1
(7) To make lots of money	2.76[a]	F3	3.18[a]	F2
Sig. = 0.030				
(8) To gain prestige by operating a business	2.06	F3	2.19	F4
(9) To meet interesting people.	3.74	F4	3.84	F4
(10) To provide a retirement income	2.72[a]	F3	3.40[a]	F2
Sig. = 0.002				
(11) To provide me with a challenge	4.36[a]	F2	3.75[a]	F4
Sig. = 0.000				
(12) To permit me to become financially independent	4.03	F6	3.95	F2
(13) To supplement my income (from other sources)	2.10	F5	Not asked	
(14) To avoid unemployment	2.63	F5	N/A	
(15) To move to Bornholm	2.83	F2	N/A	

[a]Indicates significant differences; source: Getz and Petersen, 2002.
N/A, not applicable.

owners. The B&B owners were also significantly less in agreement with the statements 'It is crucial to keep the business profitable' and 'I want to keep the business growing'. For this group, 'To meet interesting people' was a significantly higher motive.

Factor analysis of start-up goals

Similar to the analysis of data from Australia, factor analysis using varimax rotation was performed on both sets of start-up goals. It would be expected that the three samples from different countries would display different results, and they do in some specific ways, but the similarities turned out to be more important. In particular, the lifestyle factor turns out to be paramount in all three samples.

Table 3.5 shows results of the factor analysis for both Canmore and Bornholm. The statements have been kept in their original questionnaire order, and the factor groupings

(described below) for each resort have been indicated with F1–F6. Each factor was given a name based on the researchers' interpretation of underlying meanings. Usually this is indicated, and named after the goal statement with the highest factor loading. When examining these results, particular attention should be given to the congruence of the two goal statements defining lifestyle in both samples, namely 'to enjoy a good lifestyle' and 'to support my/our leisure interests'.

For Bornholm, six factors were derived with a cumulative 72.2% of variance explained. Factor 1 (explaining 24.5% of variance) consists of three goals all clearly linked to 'Lifestyle' considerations, demonstrating the synergistic allure of an island location ('To live in the right environment'), leisure interests and enjoying a good lifestyle. Although two of the three are the same in Canmore's Lifestyle factor, the goal 'to live in the right environment' is more closely associated with family-first concerns among the Canadians.

Factor 2, called 'Challenge' (12.2% of variance), encompasses the top-ranked goal 'To

Table 3.5.   Attitudes and future-oriented goals.

Statements about this business	Bornholm (n = 77–82) Means (out of 5)	Factors	Canmore (n = 96–100) Means (out of 5)	Factors
(1) It is crucial to keep this business profitable Sig. = 0.033	4.73[a]	F3	4.48[a]	F1
(2) I want to keep the business growing Sig. = 0.002	3.54[a]	F3	4.10[a]	F1
(3) Enjoying the job is more important than making lots of money	3.88	F4	3.96	F3
(4) In this business customers cannot be separated from personal life	2.91		2.95	
(5) This business currently meets my performance targets	3.73		3.40	
(6) It should be run on purely business principles	3.11	F3	2.92	F4
(7) I would rather keep the business modest and under control than have it grow too big	3.99	F1	3.78	F3
(8) My personal/family interests take priority over running the business Sig. = 0.018	3.28[a]	F4	3.70[a]	F3
(9) Eventually the business will be sold for the best possible price	3.46	F3	3.57	F1
(10) This business is highly seasonal	4.23		4.23	
(11) I come into daily contact with my customers	4.46		4.24	
(12) It is hard to separate work and family/personal life in a tourism business	3.71		3.69	
(13) I enjoy taking risks	3.81	F2	3.46	F2
(14) After making this business a success I want to start another Sig. = 0.000	1.79[a]	F2	2.84[a]	F2
(15) The business is a legacy for my children	2.01	F2	1.90	F2
(16) I am always trying something new	3.53	F2	3.55	F2
(17) I believe in hands-on management Sig. = 0.049	4.67[a]	F1	4.43[a]	F1
(18) It is best to avoid debt as much as possible Sig. = 0.001	4.65[a]	F1	4.15[a]	F4

[a]Indicates significant differences.

provide me with a challenge' and the highly-rated 'To be my own boss'. There is definitely a high degree of autonomy orientation in this grouping, but it also includes moving to Bornholm, which appealed only to a few.

Factor 3 has been called 'Money Matters' (10.1% of variance) as the highest loading was 'To make lots of money', but it also includes the prestige and retirement-income goals. It is important to note that the means for these three items are all low, indicating that money and prestige were a minor set of goals among the Danish owners. However, it is also possible that in Denmark there is a social/cultural stigma attached to admitting to these goals.

Factor 4, 'Family First' (9.3% of variance), includes 'To keep this property in the family' and 'To keep my family together', both of which were lowly rated. It is unclear why 'To meet interesting people' loads on to this factor, as it was a fairly highly rated goal. Also, keeping the family together was almost equally associated with Factor 5. 'To avoid unemployment' is the important goal in Factor 5 (8.2% of variance), although 'To keep my family together' loads equally here and in Factor 4. Together they have been labelled 'Security'. Factor 6 (7.8% of variance) contains only one item, 'To permit me to become financially independent'. It yielded a high mean in the sample and is therefore important, but conceptually it seems to fit better with 'Security' or 'Money Matters'.

Turning to the Canmore sample, a four-factor solution was derived that cumulatively explains 63% of variance among the responses. As with the Danish sample, Factor 1 is labelled 'Lifestyle' (explaining 26.9% of variance). It contains two of the same goals (lifestyle and leisure), but is associated more with 'To be my own boss', whereas among Danish respondents the third goal in the Lifestyle Factor was 'To live in the right environment'. Nevertheless, all five of these goals were important or very important to both samples.

Factor 2 is called 'Money Matters' (13.8% of variance) as it contains 'To make lots of money' and 'To permit me to become financially independent'. Making lots of money was significantly more important to the Canmore owners (means: 3.18 versus 2.76) whereas financial independence was important in both samples (Bornholm 4.03; Canmore 3.75).

Factor 3 (11.4% of variance) has been called 'Family First'. It includes keeping the family together, keeping the property in the family, and living in the right environment. Of these three goals, keeping the property in the family was unimportant, while living in the right environment was very important.

Factor 4 (10.9% of variance) is termed 'Prestige', but the two goals it contains are a strange mix. 'To gain prestige by operating a business' achieved a very low mean of 2.19 among the Canmore respondents, whereas 'To meet interesting people' was a much higher 3.84.

Characteristics of lifestyle- and money-oriented respondents

Several facts stand out in making a comparison between the Bornholm and Canmore samples. Most important is that 'Lifestyle' is the dominant factor in both, and that the autonomy-related goals (especially the highly-ranked 'To be my own boss' and 'To permit me to become financially independent') were also very important. In Canmore financial independence correlated more closely with making lots of money whereas in Bornholm it stood alone. In some owners' minds, being one's own boss might be a lifestyle consideration (as in Canmore) and to others it is more linked to challenge (as in

Bornholm). Although 'Money matters' emerges as a distinct factor in both samples, it is not very important to a majority of respondents.

Could any differences be detected among respondents favouring lifestyle or money matters? Analysis began with creation of a new variable comprising the summed means of the three goals in the Lifestyle factor. Two of the three Lifestyle goals are identical, but one is different between the two resort samples. Within each sample independent means t-tests were employed to detect significant correlations between the new lifestyle variable and a number of business and ownership-related variables.

In Bornholm, it was determined that sole proprietors ($n = 38$) were significantly more lifestyle-oriented than others. Although gender was not a significantly different variable, it is noteworthy that more females than males were sole proprietors (20 females and 17 males). Owners of arts and crafts establishments were far more lifestyle-oriented than other types (means: 4.36 vs. 3.42). Of the 19 arts and crafts owners, 11 were female. Among Canmore owners, lifestyle start-up goals were so predominant that no significant correlations could be found.

Next, a new variable was created for each sample by summing the means in the 'Money Matters' factors. The goal 'To make lots of money' was included in both Canmore and Bornholm. However, in Bornholm the other goals in this factor concerned prestige and retirement income, while in Canmore it was financial independence and retirement income.

Accommodation owners in Canmore had significantly lower means on the 'Money Matters' goals, no doubt reflecting the dominance of B&B establishments, while restaurant and café owners were significantly more money-oriented than others. Businesses owned by married couples were significantly less money-oriented as were female respondents. Among the Bornholm sample only gender made a difference, with male respondents being significantly less money-oriented. But the very low scores assigned to these goals show that the entire Danish sample was less money-oriented than the Canadian.

Attitudes and future-oriented goals

It is possible that motives and goals change after starting the family business. In particular, owners should be able to articulate goals for the future of the business and the way they want to operate it.

Accordingly, respondents in Bornholm and Canmore were also asked to indicate their level of agreement (on a five-point Likert scale) with 18 'statements about this business' (see Table 3.5). The scales were identical in both samples. The statements were of three types: attitudes that are likely to shape strategy; explicit goals for the future, and some factual statements about the nature of the business. The factual questions (numbers 4, 5, 10, 11, and 12) are not included in the analysis here, but are relevant in subsequent chapters.

As with the start-up goals, the statements pertaining to attitudes and future-oriented goals were based on family business and entrepreneurship literature plus the interviews that preceded research in rural Western Australia. They were intended to reflect a range of possible orientations, and in particular analysis was directed at identifying and profiling those owners who were growth-oriented.

Table 3.5 displays the means achieved for each statement in both samples, indicates statistically significant differences between the two samples, and shows the factors described below. The statement 'It is crucial to keep this business profitable' was highly rated in both samples, but significantly more so in Bornholm. This was a surprise, given that the start-up goals suggested a higher level of profit orientation in Canmore. A likely explanation is that almost all business owners recognize the need for profitable management, and so this statement cannot be used to differentiate respondents. The best single item for differentiating growth-oriented entrepreneurs is the obvious one: 'I want to keep the business growing'. Canmore respondents were much more growth-oriented (with a mean of 4.10, compared to 3.54 for Bornholm), and the difference was statistically significant.

Looking at the other high mean values, both autonomy (i.e. 'I believe in hands-on management') and debt avoidance were highly valued in both samples, but significantly more so in Bornholm. There were two other significant differences of note. The first pertained to family versus business orientation ('My personal/family interests take priority over running the

business'), with both samples agreeing moderately but Canmore respondents significantly more so. Also, both samples were not very receptive to the notion of starting another business ('After making this business a success I want to start another'), but the Canmore respondents were significantly less interested.

Factor analysis of future-oriented business goals

Factor analysis was conducted to reveal underlying dimensions in the future-oriented goals (the five factual statements not being included in this analysis), and to permit identification of respondents associated with each factor, if possible. A four-factor solution was derived for each sample, as shown on Table 3.5. Note that the researchers have to assign items to each factor on the basis of their 'factor loadings' and sometimes there are problems because factor loadings can be negative (as with item 14 for Canmore) or are too low to be statistically significant. Some interpretation is therefore required.

For Bornholm, the total variance explained by the four factors is 55.9%, which is not particularly strong. Factor one, 'Control', explains the most – at 19.5% of total variance. It joins three items related to keeping the business modest, and favouring hands-on management and debt avoidance. All three display high means in the Bornholm sample, demonstrating that a majority were autonomy-oriented.

'Innovation' describes Factor 2 in Bornholm (14.5% of variance explained). This factor includes two significant loadings ('I am always trying something new' and 'I enjoy taking risks'. The means for these statements were 3.53 and 3.81, much less than those for the 'Control' items. Given the overall lifestyle and autonomy-orientation of the Bornholm sample, it is probable that most of the innovation occurs within the business, especially in arts and crafts, rather than in the form of new ventures and growth. Two other items were associated with this factor, but the loadings were too low to be statistically significant: starting a new business and the business as a legacy for children. As well, both those statements yielded very low means.

Factor 3 (12.4% of variance) contains three statements which are interpreted as defining the profit-oriented entrepreneur, and while the goal 'I want to keep the business growing' is loaded in this factor, it was too low to be statistically significant. What this appears to reflect among the Bornholm sample is the majority's desire for a successful business, but one that is under control and does not grow very much – if at all. The fourth factor for Bornholm is 'Enjoyment' (9.4% of variance) and the two statements in it suggest an orientation opposite to that of profit-making.

In Canmore the four-factor solution explains 55% of variance. 'Profit' is Factor 1, explaining 20.8% of variance. Means for the three statements in this factor are high ('It is crucial to keep the business profitable', 4.48; 'I want to keep the business growing', 4.10; 'Eventually the business will be sold for the best possible price', 3.57). This factor appears to define the growth-oriented entrepreneur in terms of attitudes and future goals, so for some owners – in Canmore at least – profit and growth are closely linked. 'I believe in hands-on management' also loads here (although not significantly), thereby suggesting a link between autonomy, profit and growth – unlike Bornholm.

Factor 2 for Canmore has been called 'Innovation' (12.7% of variance). The three statements are identical to those in the same-named Bornholm factor, and again the 'legacy' goal is loaded here but is not statistically significant. Very few respondents in either sample had a legacy in mind.

Factor 3, 'Enjoyment' (10.2% of variance), contains two statements identical to the enjoyment factor in Bornholm. The difference is that in Canmore keeping the business modest and under control is more associated with enjoyment (although the loading here is not statistically significant).

Factor 4 contains one significant loading and has been called 'Debt Avoidance'. The mean for this item in the Canmore sample was a high 4.15, but significantly lower than in the Bornholm sample. The statement 'It should be run on purely business principles' loads here, but not significantly. The statement 'After making this business a success I want to start another' is negatively loaded here, indicating it is viewed as being opposite to debt avoidance.

Who are the profit- and growth-oriented entrepreneurs?

To identify characteristics of the profit- and growth-oriented entrepreneurs the starting point was to create a new variable by summing the means of the items that formed the 'Profit' factors (in Canmore these are statements 1, 2, and 9, whereas in Bornholm they are statements 1, 6 and 9).

Next, a set of independent means t-tests was applied to search for significant correlations. In light of the preceding analysis, it was expected that the Canmore sample would contain more, and clearly identifiable, growth-oriented respondents.

In both Bornholm and Canmore, owners who had purchased their business were significantly correlated with the 'Profit' factor. In Canmore the combined means on the three 'Profit' factor items were 4.47 for purchasers ($n = 25$) and 3.92 for starters ($n = 73$). In Bornholm the means were 4.17 for purchasers ($n = 32$) and 3.55 for starters ($n = 42$). Purchasers are apparently more inclined to seek out the right opportunity, whereas lifestyle- and autonomy-oriented entrepreneurs are more likely to start up a small business.

In Canmore, the one type of business significantly correlated with the profit factor is 'restaurant and cafe', whereas B&B owners are definitely associated with lifestyle and autonomy. In Bornholm, accommodation overall is correlated with the profit factor, while arts and crafts owners are definitely lifestyle- and autonomy-oriented. In Bornholm, copreneurial owners (married couples) were more profit- and growth-oriented than sole proprietors without family involvement in their businesses. In Canmore, owners with children working in their business were significantly correlated with profit and growth. These facts show that family business and profit/growth are in no way incompatible. Indeed, many sole proprietors are more lifestyle- and autonomy-oriented.

Surprisingly, previous ownership of a business is not significantly correlated with profit- and growth-orientation in either sample. Gender of respondents did not matter in Bornholm, but in Canmore males were significantly correlated with profit and growth. Female respondents in Canmore were mostly in the B&B business (28 F and 6 M), retailing (10 F, 8 M) and tour services (6 each), while males were more prominent in hotels (6 M, 3 F) and restaurants (14 M, 5 F). Age was not a significant discriminator on the 'profit and growth factor'.

Examples of growth orientation

Most of the respondents in both samples did not display a growth-orientation. Many small and family businesses add value to their product in order to ensure profitability, but very few in tourism and hospitality actually want to grow their businesses substantially. Those that plan for growth, or are best able to deliver it, are clearly in the minority. These are the owners that can make a big difference in their communities and tourist destinations. Some examples from the interviews in Bornholm (translated from Danish and paraphrased) illustrate a growth orientation:

> Our business has been a success, as we sell all that we can produce. We are now establishing a solid platform . . . to generate a growing sale over the coming years. We sell our products outside Bornholm . . . We have increased the number of employees. We continue to develop our products to improve our competitiveness. We find ourselves in a position to increase business considerably in the future.
>
> (Producer/retailer/exporter of a speciality food product)

> The export (of our craft product) is still growing all over Europe and Scandinavia, and the sale to tourists during the season is of great importance to the firm. To be able to meet the growing demand we have set up a new production facility. We foresee considerable possibilities for more export in the future.
>
> (Producer/retailer/exporter with over 30 employees)

> The owner enjoys seeing a business grow. Therefore he found it very challenging to buy the hotel and make it into a profitable business. He has succeeded, and today the hotel is in a very fine condition and generating a reasonable profit and with a still growing turnover.
>
> (Family member who manages the hotel)

Examples of lifestyle- and autonomy-orientation

It is apparent that most of the owners in these two samples are in these categories. A strong preference for being one's own boss is common to both samples, but this in itself is not correlated with a growth-orientation. Self-employment can be a facilitator of lifestyle choices, particularly leisure pursuits associated with tourism, or can be a reaction against paid employment. Several paraphrased quotes translated from the Bornholm interviews are illustrative of these orientations:

> We are in the business because we like it, and we try to make a living. We are pleased about our work. We stay open from April to October inclusive; the rest of the year we paint and keep the buildings and make bookings for the next season. Maybe we take some vacation too.
>
> (Owner of a small hotel)

> I have only a small business, which I founded as my health did not allow me to continue in my (previous occupation). I therefore do not intend to enlarge my business, as I am pleased the way it is running today.
>
> (Owner of a small hotel)

> My work with horses is my hobby, and it gives us an additional income to the farm. The income does not guarantee a big profit but allows me to combine hobby and work.
>
> (Owner of a recreation business)

'Growth entrepreneurs', as they were labelled by Katz (1995), exist as a minority among owners of small and family businesses in the tourism and hospitality industry. They exhibit certain characteristics such as a preference for purchasing rather than starting up their business, and they can be self-defined by reference to personal goals and attitudes. These profit- and growth-oriented entrepreneurs prefer certain types of businesses that they undoubtedly perceive to present better opportunities for profit and growth. What is of great interest is that the profit- and growth-oriented entrepreneurs are *also* motivated by lifestyle and autonomy preferences. They are most likely *not* to be home-based businesses such as B&B operators (as in Canmore) or small hotels and pensions in which owners live. They are unlikely to be arts and crafts producers/retailers, as witnessed in Bornholm.

'Lifestyle' entrepreneurs are also easily identified in this industry, and they are the majority. Many of them fit the classic 'craftsman' label (Smith, 1967), especially the arts and crafts producers/retailers of Bornholm and the B&B

owners in Canmore. In these businesses there are many more females than males. While B&B businesses in Canmore created no jobs for non-owners, and none for children, a few arts and crafts firms in Bornholm did pursue and achieve growth. Accordingly, it is generally not possible to predict growth by reference only to type of business.

'Autonomy', being the desire for self-employment and control, accompanied both the lifestyle- and profit/growth-oriented entrepreneurs. Almost all respondents wanted business profitability and preferred hands-on management, so these are not good differentiating factors. Innovation was not found to be linked to profit- and growth-orientation in this study. Owners believe they are innovative, but this does not necessarily mean they create new ventures or grow their business. Much of it is likely to be in the form of value-adding for greater efficiency and profit, or artistic innovation.

Regarding Gartner's (1990) definition of entrepreneurship as new venture creation, it is argued that this view is somewhat irrelevant. New businesses in themselves might be of little value to the community, destination or industry, and might even generate over-capacity leading to lowered profitability, less investment, and failure. The profit- and growth-oriented entrepreneurs in Canmore and Bornholm were actually more likely to purchase their businesses, and therefore conform to Smith's (1967) characterization of the entrepreneur as being 'opportunistic'.

Antecedents: Where do Family Business Owners Come From?

Having examined motives and goals in detail, it is useful to focus on the antecedents: where do these family business owners come from, what factors influence them, and are they prepared for business? First we look more closely at educational and experiential background, followed by family, economic, and cultural influences.

Experience and pertinent education or training

In the rural Western Australian sample discussed earlier, as well as the samples from resort settings in Denmark and, Canada, it was found that inheritance of the family business was a very minor precondition. The inherited component was 4.2% of respondents in Australia, 2.5% in Bornholm and none in Canmore. While the samples appeared to be well educated, there were no questions asked on qualifications pertinent to operating a tourism or hospitality business. Previous business experience was queried in Denmark and Canada, and it was determined that 31.2% of the Danish and 43.4% of the Canadian sample had such experience. There were no data collected on the relevance of that experience to their current operations.

Williams et al. (1989) said that most entrepreneurs in tourism and hospitality (based on research in the UK) fell in to one of four categories: (i) ex-entrepreneurs with relevant job or educational experience, plus access to capital; (ii) ex-entrepreneurs with access to capital; (iii) ex-employees with relevant job or educational experience, and access to capital; and (iv) ex-employees with capital. For example, the Shaw and Williams (1987) study of 411 Cornwall businesses found that 70% were owned by sole proprietors. The extent of the owner's previous experience in the tourism/hospitality industry was very low. Only 4.4% were ex-employers, while 8.3% were ex-employees in the industry and fully 54.9% were ex-employees from other sectors. For most owners, it was their first business venture. Shaw and Williams also revealed the importance of migration from cities to the country, at least partially fuelled by the higher costs of urban housing. A similar situation occurs with regard to richer, developed regions/nations and the economic periphery wherein economic and lifestyle migrants can 'cash in' and buy much cheaper property and businesses where they want to live.

McKercher and Robbins (1998: 173), based on data from nature tour operators in Australia, concluded that most '. . . are run by owner/operators who have no formal business or marketing background and no prior experience in the tourism industry.' A study of 232 small tourism businesses (all possessing fewer than ten employees) in New Zealand by Deloitte Touche Tomatsu (1994, reported in Page et al.,1999) revealed that almost half had provided 100% of the start-up capital from personal sources, and only

53% had completed a feasibility study. Some 70% had no previous experience in tourism.

Szivas (2001) studied work patterns prior to entrance into small business ownership in the tourism industry in two parts of England (inland Somerset and the City of Coventry). She found that 106 'entrepreneurs' (as distinct from paid workers), were relatively highly educated, but only 11% had any formal qualification in tourism or hospitality. Although mostly not trained for tourism-related business ventures, this sample had accepted the mis-match in order to gain more control over their work, increased job satisfaction, a better physical environment and a higher standard of living. In the Szivas study, 20% had owned a business outside tourism and another 16% had previous self-employment experience, so about one-third were at least experienced in business. Fully 35% had worked solely in tourism as managers or staff over a 10-year period prior to the research. The respondents did have viable alternatives, so they were not unwilling entrepreneurs. Family tradition was not instrumental in their choices.

The influence of family

The influence of family values and experiences of entrepreneurship is somewhat controversial. What kinds of role models do parents make, especially if they run a family business? Kets de Vries (1996) considered that family influences on entrepreneurs were largely negative, leading to a 'deviant personality'. Such people seek autonomy or prestige as a backlash to their upbringing.

On the other hand, many people believe that family influences encourage entrepreneurship. Quinn et al. (1992) surveyed 124 small tourism/hospitality businesses in Northern Ireland, all owner-managed, and found that 83% were married. There was both a high percentage of female entrepreneurs and copreneurs. When questioned on their motivations for starting a business, the three most common themes were: fulfilling a lifetime ambition; frustration with previous jobs, and inheritance of a business. Other economic choices for women with children were perceived to be low. Of particular interest was the researchers' conclusion (p. 13) that 'The vast majority of

respondents had come from a family where there had been a tradition of self-employment'.

An interesting variation, revealed when conducting interviews for this book, was the family in which two sons both wanted to emulate their father's entrepreneurship, but by starting their own businesses – not seeking work in the father's. This raises the question of legacies and inheritance, which is addressed in detail in Chapter 5.

The influence of economic conditions

The changing nature of work and society in many countries has resulted in large-scale redundancies that have led many professionals from government and business, as well as workers, into business. In many cases these reluctant entrepreneurs have skills, savings and credit to assist them. In other situations, social disadvantage forces people into business. For example Ram and Jones (1998) found that one of the main reasons that South Asians living in the UK go into business is 'blocked upward mobility'. Especially in rural areas, unemployment and under-employment are factors contributing to business ventures.

In tourist-receiving societies in less-developed nations, according to Harrison (1992), structures inherited from the colonial period might act against entrepreneurial activity by residents, or restrict them to specific sectors. In-migrants (often retiring in a new location) or returning migrants often dominate the entrepreneurial class. Local elites are often favoured in developing business links with international tourism firms, and these elites might stem from racial or ethnic differences.

The influence of return migration on entrepreneurship in tourism and hospitality was studied by King (1995). He observed that returning migrants, typically from more- to less-developed economies, could bring back capital, skills and attitudes favouring business investment. These small business owners do not want to return to farming or other poorly perceived jobs. The south of Europe and west of Ireland were given as examples of regions where this phenomenon had been observed. An earlier study in Nazare, Portugal, by Mendonsa (1983) clearly illustrated this pattern.

The influence of culture

Culture influences entrepreneurship in general and family business specifically. Some cultures are more open to personal and family business initiatives, while among others the establishment or inheritance of a family business is either shunned or encouraged. Morrison (1998) explored cultural influences on entrepreneurship and suggested that the 'entrepreneurial culture' featured power distance, individuation and masculinity, uncertainty avoidance, and a long-term versus short-term orientation.

Business Planning for New Family Businesses

A handbook prepared by the Queensland (Australia) Tourist and Travel Corporation (1993: 11) for people setting up tourism business noted that 'one-third of all new businesses fail in the first year, and two-thirds fail by the fifth year.' Tourism Victoria (no date), in its handbook *Starting Up in Tourism*, asks readers why they want to get into tourism and if they are the right type of person for the task. Potential entrepreneurs are advised that it often takes years to generate a profit, it will probably take more hours of work than any office job, guests can be very demanding, and privacy will be scarce. Readers of the Tourism Victoria document are asked (p. 4): 'Have you considered how your tourism business will affect your family?' These, and other advisory documents prepared by tourism agencies around the world, seek to instil a sense of realism, and hopefully prevent future business disasters.

Failure has been linked to the absence of business planning. Given that a majority of family businesses in this industry are lifestyle- and autonomy-oriented, it is no wonder that a minority actually undertake formal business planning.

Elements of the business plan

A 'business plan' should ideally be formulated before deciding on a business purchase or start-up, both to test its feasibility and (if desired) to help raise capital. It can also be completed alongside the strategic plan or in anticipation of an expansion. Once formulated, it becomes a working tool and should be updated periodically.

The main elements of a standard business plan include:

- Business concept, goals and objectives (perhaps emphasizing innovation or any competitive advantages).
- Profiles of the owners/purchasers and their qualifications including past performance in this or other businesses.
- Personal or family equity to be invested.
- Other capital (loans or investments) required for start-up/purchase, and for development.
- Security or collateral offered against loans (the family land or house?).
- Market appraisal (target market segments, market share calculations, marketing strategy, the marketing mix – especially price).
- Development plan (staffing, value-adding, growth, diversification).
- Marketing plan and demand forecasts for target market segments.
- Operations plan (suppliers, equipment, facilities, maintenance).
- Earnings and cash-flow projections and profit/loss calculations by year (5–10 years in advance).
- Pay-back plan for debt; return on investment to investors (if any).
- An operating budget.
- Conclusions as to feasibility and desirability.

A family-business perspective

A business plan must reflect the family vision and the owners' values. For many family business owners, plans will not be shaped around borrowing money and its repayment, as debt is to be avoided, but around realistic financial forecasts and an operating budget. In more complex situations involving investors or substantial debt, the repayment and/or dividends schedule – based again on realistic financial forecasts – can be the crucial element.

A good business plan contains a *feasibility study*, and for many family business owners this entails a cost-benefit evaluation encompassing many intangibles, rather than a straightforward determination of profitability. In other words, the final decision to proceed with the investment or purchase requires a conscious decision about how much lifestyle, autonomy and location are worth.

Cash-flow forecast

This financial tool is pivotal in feasibility studies and should be included in business plans of all kinds. It shows a multi-year period for which revenues, costs and net income are forecast. Assuming that costs can be forecast accurately for each operating unit (e.g. rooms, marketing, administration, food and other supplies), the most likely source of inaccuracy and hence business failure is that of projecting demand and revenue. It cannot be done realistically without careful analysis of the markets, present and future competition, and profit margins. Consultants can be asked to provide their objective assessments, and they typically rely on a combination of published industry performance standards in combination with their experience and original research.

Cash-flow forecasting is also useful on a yearly and monthly basis, especially to indicate exactly when any shortfalls will occur. This form will resemble the business' ledgers and bank accounts in tracing all movements of money. In tourism and hospitality, the seasonality of demand, and other short- and long-term demand cycles, make it difficult to sustain good cash flow over the entire year (see the section on seasonality-related strategies in Chapter 4). Families can be particularly hurt when cash runs out, thereby necessitating good overdraft arrangements with a local banker. They also have to exercise restraint when cash pours in during the busy periods, as much of it has to be put aside for future payments or planned reinvestment.

Capital (financing the family business)

Where do family business owners get the money to start and, if desired, grow their businesses? Capitalization clearly sets family ownership apart from corporations because the risks of failure are often borne directly by the owners and their families. As well, the desire or need to raise money externally always has to be balanced against the risks of losing control of the business or worse – losing the family legacy of land or house.

There are generally a number of options available to any investor or entrepreneur. Personal and family savings or loans from relatives no doubt are at the root of many small business start-ups. Borrowing from institutions is often necessary, and usually some form of collateral (e.g. the family house or farm) is required. Getting business loans without collateral could be difficult, so personal, unsecured loans and overdrafts might be the only option. Venture capital markets are a possible source, but not likely for most of the small family businesses in tourism and hospitality. Venture capitalists look for companies promising rapid growth in profits and invest directly in their ownership.

Once a business is operating there are additional options. Retained earnings are often the preferred source of capital, but many small businesses never generate enough cash-flow or corporate profits for re-investment or new ventures. Finally, some family businesses take the form of partnerships with equity brought in from outsiders, or with growth they might obtain a public listing and sell shares on the stock exchange.

Several researchers have discovered that the bulk of family-business capital in tourism and hospitality comes from personal sources, including savings and the resources of other family members. Hankinson's (1989) report on small hotel owners in England documented an almost equal combination of personal funds and bank loans for financing their investments, but owners reported being reluctant to incur debt. They also had no system for appraising investments, such as a discounted cash flow calculation.

The study of tourism and hospitality businesses in Cornwall by Williams *et al.* (1989) determined that personal and family savings were the main source of capital used, and the only source for 50% of the entrepreneurs sampled. The major study of small tourism and hospitality businesses in the UK (Thomas *et al.*, 1997) clearly revealed that personal funds, bank loans and bank overdrafts were the most common sources, whereas venture capital, partnerships, equity issues and other sources were used by a small minority. It was also found that 56% of the small business owners relied on personal capital for the funding of business development initiatives.

Ozar and Yamak (1997) reported on a study of small hotel owners in Istanbul, Turkey. They were largely (80%) self-owned in terms of both buildings and land, and their initial capitalization was mostly through personal sources and 'informal arrangements'. Institutional debt was rarely used, and ongoing operations were financed mostly by cash-flow from the hotels.

Margerison (1998) concluded that more research was needed to determine if formal business planning really was necessary, or could be linked to improved performance, in small tourism and hospitality businesses. It is possible that many owners do not adopt formal methods because they do not have to report to anyone, not because they are incompetent or disorganized. It is also possible that owners need advice and technical help, but do not get it because they are completely wrapped up in operating their businesses. Growth-oriented entrepreneurs might be more inclined to engage in formal business planning, if only because they need external sources of capital to fuel their ambitions.

Ownership, Organization and Governance

Ownership forms and enterprise organization are closely linked to capitalization. When mostly personal resources are used, which is typical of lifestyle- and autonomy-seekers, it is likely that the start-up business will be small, owner-operated and informally organized. The owner or copreneurs will do most of the work. On the other hand, profit- and growth-oriented entrepreneurs are more likely to purchase a larger business, are not afraid of debt, and will employ professionals as needed. The larger the firm, the more it requires formal management systems including human resources and financial controls. Older, larger family firms might elect to appoint boards of directors incorporating non-family experts (see the O'Reilly's Guesthouse Case Study in Chapter 8).

Carlock and Ward (2001: 119) identified six possible ownership configurations for the family business. These are linked to the life cycle but not necessarily in a linear manner:

- Entrepreneurship
- Owner-managed
- Family partnership
- Sibling partnership
- Cousins' collaboration
- Family syndicate

The cases studied in this book, and the various research findings, show that in tourism and hospitality few family businesses will progress into the more complex configurations involving different branches of the family. The O'Reilly case, however, illustrates one that has advanced to a more complex stage involving multiple generations.

Observed ownership forms in tourism and hospitality

Basic ownership choices for family business start-ups in tourism and hospitality include a number revealed during the Australian, Canadian and Danish research and in case study preparation:

- The business is entirely secondary to the home, farm or other enterprise (i.e. no separate ownership).
- Sole proprietorship (one owner, but family are often involved in operations).
- Copreneurial (joint ownership by couples).
- Partnerships (among family members or involving outsiders).
- Companies with shareholders (to limit the individual liability of owners, and to help generate investment).
- Family trusts (a legal corporation with shares owned by family members).

Ownership and control should not be confused. As the family business grows it often becomes desirable or even necessary to employ professional managers, establish a board of directors, and rely increasingly on non-family expertise. The founders might eventually turn over day-to-day control (as opposed to governance) to the professionals. If family businesses get large enough to form publicly-traded corporations, retaining family control becomes a major issue because of the risk of a take-over.

Over time, ownership shares can get smaller and smaller if each family owner passes on shares equally to all descendants. This could make control difficult, especially if all family shareholders are supposed to vote. An alternative is to make ownership and/or voting rights conditional upon employment within the company, with an ownership agreement stipulating that all shares be redeemed upon death or retirement.

Geeraerts (1984) found that family-owned and -managed businesses in The Netherlands tended to be less horizontally differentiated (i.e. fewer divisions), less formal and with less specialization. Daily and Dollinger (1992) studied manufacturing firms and determined that family-owned businesses were smaller, less growth-oriented, relied less on internal control mechanisms, and achieved lower levels of performance. Organization and management systems in family-owned tourism and hospitality businesses have not been studied in any systematic comparison, but it is suggested from available research that the majority are micro and small in size, owner-operated, informal and do not employ professional staff. A study focusing on larger family-owned firms in this industry is therefore warranted, especially when it has been noted elsewhere that more children are involved in the larger businesses.

Governance

In the early stages, and for most businesses studied in this book, ownership, governance and management are all in the hands of the founders. But while a person or family can own a business and elect not to be involved in its management, they are always involved in its governance.

In the Carlock and Ward (2001) scheme of parallel family and business planning, a board of directors oversees management actions, allocates capital and participates in strategy formulation. On the family side a 'family council' provides the governance structure, leadership, and coordination of family actions.

An 'ownership agreement' can be formulated to shape the ownership and governance of the business in accordance with the family vision and circumstances. Who can hold shares or

stock? Can shares be sold, transferred or inherited? What rights accompany various forms of ownership and employment (e.g. voting, board membership, dividends)?

Liquidity can become a serious issue, as in the case where family shareholders suddenly need cash but their shares cannot be sold outside the family or family trust. Terms and conditions have to be established for internal sales or buy-backs.

Boards of directors

Many authors have recommended the establishment of a board of directors and use of non-family, professional directors to help resolve conflicts and instil greater professionalism. But Sharma et al. (1996) believed there was insufficient research evidence to confirm the imputed benefits.

The supposed advantages, summarized in Sharma et al. (1996: 12), include:

- Fresh perspectives and new directions; catalysts for change.
- Objectivity and fairness.
- Arbitration of disputes.
- Support for new leaders/successors.
- Moral support and sounding-boards for owners.

Others have argued that non-family directors might have little knowledge of the family firm and are only available at meeting times. They might also be beholden to the owners who appointed them, and if they do not have a direct stake in the business their commitment to it might be low.

Boards will consist generally of key family members and senior professional managers, and often external experts. They are to be elected by shareholders and therefore responsible to owners. Carlock and Ward (2001) said that the 'ideal' board of directors for a family business has a majority of independent, non-family members and appoints its own chairperson, but that is likely to be controversial for many families.

Alternatives to the board of directors include the use of professional advisers on a topical, as-needed basis (e.g. accounting, tax planning, succession), and creation of a formal advisory committee.

The family council

In small, informal family businesses, regular meetings or even casual conversations are the basis of coordination and planning. As it grows and develops, formal meetings are likely to be necessary, complete with minute-taking and agendas. To coincide with governance each member of the council would have to be a shareholder, but the participation of children and others without shares might be advantageous in discussing strategic planning and work–family issues.

The family trust

Depending on laws of the land, many families have created family trusts. The case study of O'Reilly's in Chapter 8 illustrates some of the pros and cons of trusts. On the one hand they preserve family ownership and control, preventing family members from cashing-in their shares. As a consequence, despite increasing numbers of generations and descendants, everyone knows that O'Reilly's will endure and individuals can elect to work in the firm or not. On the other hand, there might arise some opposition, or even resentment, where family members cannot benefit from their inheritance except by taking employment in the company.

Chapter Summary

Start-up is the most critical stage in the family business life cycle, because most will not grow substantially and the level of inheritance is minimal. The motivations and goals of founders are critical in setting the future of the family business, with the majority being established for lifestyle rather than traditional entrepreneurial reasons.

Our in-depth research into motivations and goals in several countries revealed the predominance of lifestyle and locational motivations, as well as the strong desire for autonomy (i.e. 'to be my own boss'). Across the industrialized world numerous individuals and couples are moving into rural and resort areas to establish small and micro businesses, with 'living in the right environment' high on their list of locational criteria.

Apparently the incidence of business inheritance in these settings has declined to the level of insignificance, and migration is the dominant force. Most of the family business founders are individuals or mature couples, often getting into a second career, although there are still cases of farmers starting tourism and hospitality businesses as a secondary income source.

We have also been able to identify 'profit- and growth-oriented entrepreneurs' in our research and case studies – owners who are easily differentiated in their response to the simple statement 'I want to keep this business growing'. They are more likely to seek out opportunities and purchase larger businesses (typically hotels and restaurants, not arts or crafts and not B&B establishments), often employing borrowed money and setting up formal companies or corporations. They are also motivated by the same lifestyle and locational preferences, but they are the ones who can be expected to grow the business and generate new jobs. Although many family businesses claim to be innovative, we found that much of this was in terms of value-adding and improving the quality of the business.

Antecedents to establishing a family business in this industry were also examined. There is good evidence in the literature and our research data that a majority do not have previous, directly relevant ownership experience, but that many do have some experience working in the industry or running other types of business. Because capital is required, or credit worthiness, there is a direct connection to land ownership (farmers in particular), and migration – either moving from high-cost to low-cost areas, especially from large cities, or returning international migrants with savings.

Numerous assistance programmes have been directed at the tourism and hospitality sectors, especially in peripheral areas and developing nations, and towards small businesses in general. But is there a case to be made for specific support for the family business in tourism and hospitality? We return to this policy issue in the final chapters. The final section of this chapter provided advice on business planning, and a number of related family business issues are discussed under the headings of ownership, organization and governance.

References

Bransgrove, C. and King, B. (1996) Strategic marketing practice amongst small tourism and hospitality businesses. In: Thomas, R. (ed.) *Spring Symposium Proceedings of International Association of Hotel Management Schools*. Leeds Metropolitan University, Leeds, UK, pp. 29–38.

Carlock, R. and Ward, J. (2001) *Strategic Planning for the Family Business*. Palgrave, Basingstoke, UK.

Dailey, C. and Dollinger, M. (1992) An empirical examination of ownership structure in family and professionally managed firms. *Family Business Review* 5, 117–136.

Dunn, B. (1995) Success themes in Scottish family enterprises: Philosophies and practices through the generations. *Family Business Review* 8(1), 17–28.

File, K., Prince, R. and Rankin, M. (1994) Organisational buying behaviour of the family firm. *Family Business Review* 7(3), 263–272.

Frater, J. (1982) *Farming Tourism in England and Overseas. Research Memorandum 93*. Centre for Urban and Regional Studies, Birmingham, UK.

Gartner, W. (1990) What are we talking about when we talk about entrepreneurship? *Journal of Business Venturing* 5(1), 15–28.

Geeraerts, G. (1984) The effect of ownership on the organization structure in small firms. *Administrative Science Quarterly* 29, 232–237.

Gersick, K., Davis, J., Hampton, M. and Lansberg, I. (1997) *Generation to Generation*. Harvard Business School Press, Boston, Massachusetts.

Getz, D. and Carlsen, J. (2000) Characteristics and goals of family and owner-operated businesses in the rural tourism and hospitality sectors. *Tourism Management* 21, 547–560.

Getz, D. and Petersen, T. (2002) Growth-oriented entrepreneurs and destination competitiveness. Paper presented at the Re-inventing the Destination Conference, Dubrovnik, Croatia.

Gyimothy, S. (2000) *The Quality of Visitor Experience: a Case Study in Peripheral Areas of Europe*. Research Centre of Bornholm, Report 17/2000, Bornholm, Denmark.

Hankinson, A. (1989) Small hotels in Britain: investment and survival. *The Cornell HRA Quarterly* 30(3), 80–82.

Harrison, D. (1992) The social consequences. In: Harrison, D. (ed.) *Tourism and the Less Developed Countries*. Belhaven Press, London, pp. 19–34.

Katz, J. (1995). Which track are you on? *Inc.* 17, 27–28.

Kets de Vries, M. (1996) *Family Business: Human Dilemmas in the Family Firm*. Thomson International Business Press, London.

King, R. (1995) Tourism, labour and international migration. In: Montanari, A. and Williams, A. (eds) *European Tourism: Regions, Spaces and Restructuring*. John Wiley & Sons, Chichester, UK,. pp. 177–190.

Komppula, R. (2000) Definitions of growth and success – case studies in Finnish rural tourism industry. Paper presented at the 12th Nordic Conference on Small Business Research, Kuopia, Finland. University of Kuopia Department of Business Management.

Kousis, M. (1989) Tourism and the family in a rural Cretan community. *Annals of Tourism Research* 16(3), 318–332.

Lynch, P. (1996) Microenterprises and micro-firms in the hospitality industry: the case of bed and breakfast enterprises. In: Thomas, R. (ed.) *Spring Symposium Proceedings of International Association of Hotel Management Schools*. Leeds Metropolitan University, Leeds, UK, pp. 231–236.

Margerison, J. (1998) Business planning. In: Thomas, R. (ed.) *The Management of Small Tourism and Hospitality Firms*. Cassell, London, pp. 101–117.

McKercher, B. and Robbins, B. (1998) Business development issues affecting nature-based tourism operators in Australia. *Journal of Sustainable Tourism* 6 (2), 173–188.

Mendonsa, E. (1983) Tourism and income strategies in Nazare, Portugal. *Annals of Tourism Research* 10(2), 213–238.

Morrison, A. (1998) Small firm cooperative marketing in a peripheral tourism region. *International Journal of Contemporary Hospitality Management* 10(5), 191–197.

Nickerson, N., Black, R. and McCool, S. (2001) Agritourism: motivations behind farm/ranch business diversification. *Journal of Travel Research* 40, 19–26.

Opperman, M. (1997) Rural tourism in Germany – farm and rural tourism operators. In: Page, S. and Getz, D. (eds) *The Business of Rural Tourism: International Perspectives*. International Thomson Business Press, London, pp. 108–119.

Ozar, B. and Yamak, S. (1997) Financing of small hospitality establishments. Paper presented at the Eurochrie Conference on Hospitality Business Development, Sheffield, UK.

Page, S., Forer, P. and Lawton, G. (1999) Small business development and tourism: Terra incognita? *Tourism Management* 20(4), 435–459.

Pearce, P. (1990) Farm tourism in New Zealand: a social situation analysis. *Annals of Tourism Research* 17(3), 117–125.

Peters, M. and Weirmair, K. (2001) Theoretical constructs and empirical evidence of entrepreneurial growth modes in the hospitality industry. Paper presented at the conference Entrepreneurship on Tourism and the Contexts of Experience Economy, University of Lapland, Finland.

Queensland Tourist and Travel Corporation (1993) *Tourism – Taking the First Steps: Getting Started Series*. Brisbane, Australia.

Quinn, U., Larmour, R. and McQuillan, N. (1992) The small firm in the hospitality industry. *International Journal of Hospitality Management* 1, 11–14.

Ram, M. and Jones, T. (1998) *Ethnic Minorities in Business*. Small Business Research Trust, Milton Keynes, UK.

Schein, E. (1994) Commentary: what is an entrepreneur? *Entrepreneurship Theory and Practice* 19, 87–88.

Schumpeter, J. (1934) *The Theory of Economic Development*. Harvard University Press, Cambridge, Massachusetts.

Sharma, P., Chrisman, J. and Chua, J. (1996) *A Review and Annotated Bibliography of Family Business Studies*. Kluwer, Boston, Massachusetts.

Shaw, G. and Williams, A. (1987) Firm formation and operating characteristics in the Cornish tourist industry – the case of Looe. *Tourism Management* 8, 344–348.

Singer, J. and Donahu, C. (1992) Strategic management planning for the successful family business. *Journal of Business and Entrepreneurship* 4(3), 39–51.

Smith, R. (1967) *The Entrepreneur and the Firm*. Bureau of Business and Economic Research, MSU, East Lansing, Michigan.

Smith, V. (1998) Privatization in the third world: small-scale tourism enterprises. In: Theobald, W. (ed.) *Global Tourism*, 2nd edn. Butterworth-Heinemann, Oxford, UK, pp. 205–215.

Szivas, E. (2001) Entrance into tourism entrepreneurship: a UK case study. *Tourism and Hospitality Research* 3(2), 163–172.

Thomas, R., Friel, M., Jameson, S. and Parsons, D. (1997) *The National Survey of Small Tourism and Hospitality Firms, Annual Report 1996–1997*. Centre for the Study of Small Tourism and Hospitality Firms, Leeds Metropolitan University, Leeds, UK.

Twining-Ward, L. and Baum, T. (1998) Dilemmas facing mature island destinations: cases from the Baltic. *Progress in Tourism and Hospitality Research* 4, 131–140.

Westhead, P. (1997) Ambitions, 'external' environment and strategic factor differences between family and non-family companies. *Entrepreneurship and Regional Development* 9(2), 127–157.

Westhead, P. and Cowling, M. (1998) Family firm research: the need for a methodological rethink. *Entrepreneurship Theory and Practice*, Autumn, 31–56.

Williams, A., Shaw, G. and Greenwood, J. (1989) From tourist to tourism entrepreneur, from consumption to production: evidence from Cornwall, England. *Environment and Planning A* 21, pp. 1639–1653.

World Tourism Organisation (1997) *Rural Tourism: a Solution For Employment, Local Development and Environment*. WTO, Madrid.

4

Sustaining and Developing the Family Business

Introduction

Growth is not the preoccupation of most family business owners. Simply sustaining the business is challenging enough and while growth is not necessary, some kind of development is inevitable – all businesses change. The change process can be managed to add value to the business and improve the family's lifestyle, or it can be imposed by external factors.

The first section examines the meaning of success and failure for a family business, then focuses on specific challenges and causes of failure. Next, arguments for growing a business are addressed, then preconditions and barriers to growth. This is followed by analysis of generic and industry-specific strategies, a section on strategic planning, and separate treatment of strategic marketing and family branding. Research findings are then presented on how seasonality affects family businesses and various strategic responses from a sample of owners in Denmark.

Failure and Success

The rate of failure among small and family businesses in general is high. Dunkelberg (1995) said that 67% of new, small businesses in the USA had failed within the first four years. Nilsson *et al.* (2004) noted that a high rate of business failure is typical of small and medium-sized enterprises. They referred to a 'rule of thumb' that indicates only one-third will be

successful, one-third will struggle (and could go either way) and the other third should not be in business in the first place! According to Boer (1998), several studies in the UK confirm that newer firms fail at a higher rate, but there was no compelling evidence regarding tourism and hospitality firms in particular.

In one early study, Shaw and Williams (1987) determined that 60% of hotels and guest houses in Looe, Cornwall, had new owners within the last 2 years, and 28% had been in operation for 2 years or less, so turnover of ownership was very high. Shaw and Williams (1990), in their study of Cornwall, observed many tourism/hospitality businesses with little capital and weak management that were resistant to change or taking advice. These researchers also concluded that many owner-operators lacked experience, and used mostly personal and family savings as their capital. Remaining small and often unprofitable was a chronic condition in the small-hotel sector. Market fluctuations gave rise to many outright failures.

In a Swedish study, Klenell and Steen (1999) correlated lifestyle and the desire not to grow with insolvency. On the other hand, Brown (1987) suggested that owner-operators have an emotional attachment to their businesses that makes them reluctant to abandon the enterprise in difficult times. Because many tourism and hospitality businesses are not the primary or only source of family income, poor performance is perhaps a more typical occurrence than outright failure. Studies of B&B operations in the American Midwest (Dawson and Brown 1988;

Gruidl *et al.*, 1990; Boger and Buchanan 1991) revealed widespread low occupancy rates and poor gross revenue. This can be tolerated by many families, but only if they do not depend on the tourism income.

In purely commercial terms, failure is easy to define: the business does not realize sufficient profit to reward its owner(s) adequately and is therefore closed or sold – or faces outright bankruptcy. Success is generally defined in terms of making a profit, growth (in market share, size of the firm, or share value – if publicly traded), and even its ultimate sale price. But these measures are not always appropriate in family businesses.

What is failure and success?

Success and failure in family businesses can best be evaluated against the owners' needs and goals. In terms of expressed goals of family business owners, obtaining or sustaining profitability is generally ranked highest (Davis, 1996), followed by increasing the value of the business. A study by Tagiuri and Davis (1992) found that the top goals were to make profits now and (equally) to achieve excellence.

For some small hoteliers in England, the owners' measure of success was 'survival' (Hankinson, 1989). If the business at least supports the family, it can be considered a success. If it never grows, but meets all goals of the owners, it can also be considered a success. Failure, on the other hand, is not necessarily implied by low profitability, nor by selling or even terminating the enterprise.

Dunn (1995) examined 'success themes in Scottish family enterprises', finding that definitions of success provided by owners incorporated both objective and subjective criteria. Their definitions centred on achieving quality, the creation of jobs and wealth for family and non-family, sustaining and building the family's reputation within the industry and community, and keeping the business healthy and profitable. What created success? Dunn's respondents identified family values, family dynamics and responsiveness to change as the main success themes. Family values included caring and loyalty to staff and customers, quality enhancements, maintenance of family ownership and

control, stewardship of wealth and employees' well-being, work guaranteed for family members, and preserving the family name and reputation. Family dynamics included good quality work and home relationships (consensus-building), and responsiveness to change covered cautious containment of growth and a long-term perspective on payback.

The matter of a 'legacy' arises here, as in some cultures and families it is considered very important to pass on the family land and/or business to future generations. Other founders might hope that their efforts will be of value and interest to their descendents, so that a family legacy can be created where none previously existed. But most children probably do not share their parents' dreams and have little interest in taking over a family business – especially one that promises hard work and small returns.

A further complication is that family business goals often extend beyond their personal family and business circumstances. Ateljevic and Doorne (2000), from a review of research findings in New Zealand, concluded that a number of pioneering, lifestyle-oriented entrepreneurs possessed social and cultural values that shaped their business. For example, in parts of New Zealand operators of adventure or ecological activities and tours had moved to areas for their own lifestyle reasons but had established businesses that could be described as possessing a strong community and ecological ethic. Furthermore, these pioneers had proved that niche markets were viable, thereby attracting copy-cat businesses.

Again taking a community or destination perspective, it has to be asked if the niche markets occupied by family businesses are in fact restricted to them because of their small size, hands-on family service, lifestyle orientation (profits and growth not being paramount) and concern for social and environmental sustainability. If so, the family business might be the only way to foster tourism and economic development, especially in rural and peripheral regions. In these circumstances, the success of family businesses has to be at least partially evaluated in the context of how they collectively contribute to creating tourist attractiveness, or to its gradual growth and diversification. In other words, each small family business has a part to play in establishing and sustaining the destination. For the community or destination, a high turnover of family businesses (most are purchased by other owner-operators) can result in the absence of stability, innovation and growth, and this might be viewed as a negative phenomenon.

When a family business fails, both the business and the family are in jeopardy. There has been little said about this problem in the literature, and in fact generic business failure in tourism and hospitality has not been well researched (Leiper, 1997). It could be argued that as much can be learned from case studies of failed businesses as from successful ones.

Causes of failure

Small business failure is an under-researched problem, according to Boer (1998). 'Failure' might take the form of bankruptcy, under-performance or voluntary termination. Reasons for failure can be exogenous (e.g. environmental forces) or endogenous (poor management). Boer discussed possible sources of failure for small tourism and hospitality business in general. Poor management might be blamed on the owner/entrepreneur in most cases, owing to the high incidence of owner-operated ventures. This is especially pertinent in tourism and hospitality where so many entrants are not experienced in running a business or in the industry itself. Owners themselves are likely to be biased in their assessment of problems, and might tend to blame external forces beyond their control.

Pizam and Upchurch (2002: 136) commented on failure in the rural tourism sector: 'Clearly, the combination of financial, marketing, human resources, rules and regulatory knowledge, service management, and management is rare combination for the small rural entrepreneur to possess.' They went on to catalogue specific failure causes:

- Lack of proper capitalization.
- Poor identification of a specific target market.
- Insufficient advertising and sales promotions.
- Lack of understanding of service dynamics.
- Inability to compete in a trading area.

The UK National Survey of Small Tourism and Hospitality Firms (Thomas et al., 1997) questioned respondents on 'obstacles to improved business performance'. This gives some insight into problems facing the industry in general, but no specific information about family businesses. The survey found that intense local competition and direct costs (rent, labour and taxes) were the greatest causes of concern. Government regulations were another general area of worry.

Under-capitalization is commonly viewed as a major reason for business failure, and this would appear to be particularly relevant to the family businesses sector where personal funds underpin many business ventures. A related problem is the lack of working capital to keep a business going. Seasonal variations in demand result in periodic cash-flow shortages. Small businesses are highly vulnerable to deferred payments by customers, yet might be required to pay cash, or prefer paying cash, for their own supplies. Inflation, increasing interest rates and economic recession can all have a strong impact on the small firm. Pizam and Upchurch (2002) pointed to low levels of profits in the B&B and farm-based accommodation sectors as being responsible for inadequate working capital.

Boer (1998) distinguished between hotels and catering firms in their vulnerability to potential causes of failure. Hotels, he argued, have a tendency to be more capital intensive, with higher initial investments, longer-term loans, and a longer payback period. They will have higher fixed assets (more are owned, as opposed to leased premises) and higher fixed costs. They might be more susceptible to cash-flow problems because they extend credit to customers. Seasonality might also affect accommodation establishments more than those in the catering business. This means that hotels might have inadequate working capital, even where property assets are substantial. Another factor is that the banking sector holds considerable sway over hotels' financial health, so a credit crunch hurts them more.

Boer also addressed owners' views (from Dorset, UK) on what led to long-term success, separating the hotel and catering sub-samples. Most factors were endogenous, that is, within their own realm of control. Reputation and giving value for money were important to both groups of owners. The hotel sample placed lower emphasis on cash needs and cost control, perhaps because of the catering sector's need for constant inventory replenishment. Other common success factors were location, skills, and luck. The hoteliers also attributed success to good customer communications, low borrowing needs, access to other finance, and limiting the firm's growth. Caterers also attributed success to having good suppliers and staff.

Taylor *et al.* (1998: 59), in discussing the financing of small tourism and hospitality businesses, concluded that 'debt finance should be used cautiously by these firms.' Apparently many owners understand the need for caution because they tend to be very debt-averse, taking it on only when absolutely necessary. Consciously or unconsciously they are sacrificing growth potential and increased quality for a less risky strategy. This might be a reasoned business decision, given the certainty of economic cycles, or merely an innate conservativeness. What researchers have not been able to discern is whether this aversion to debt is in itself a cause of failure in this industry. As discussed elsewhere, many small businesses are inherently too small to be successful.

Research from Ireland (Hegerty and Ruddy, 2002: 19) correlated success and failure in small tourism/hospitality businesses with levels of support provided to them. From a large-scale survey they calculated a failure rate of one in six for sole-proprietor businesses, compared to one in seven for copreneurial businesses and one in ten for businesses involving more family members. Although the study did not explicitly cover previously failed businesses that could not be reached, this intriguing finding raises the hypothesis that having a family in business is a positive factor in ensuring success.

Another complication is the family's willingness and ability to withstand tough economic times in order to sustain their business and lifestyle. When more profit-oriented entrepreneurs would fold their tents and try again another time or place, is the family more likely to stick it out?

Theoretical perspectives on failure

Many authors clearly believe that most failures are due to managerial incompetence or lack of fundamental assets. Indeed, the prevailing wisdom of management experts is that owners and managers make their own success or bring failure upon themselves. Popular competitiveness models such as that of Porter (1980, 1985) encourage this belief. Entrepreneurs are encouraged to develop competitive advantages and take control of their future. This is good advice, but does it ensure success?

'Population ecology' (see, for example Hannan and Freeman 1977, 1984) suggests that individual businesses are at the mercy of broad environmental forces, and that competition for resources guarantees that only some will survive. This is small comfort to the owner or investor, but from a community, industry or destination perspective it makes a lot of sense. The fact that some small businesses are failing is in itself normal and to be expected. The result could be increased quality and competitiveness. Indeed, some authors have gone so far as to suggest that weak businesses be denied support.

When a family's livelihood is at stake, failure should not be taken lightly. More research has to be directed at determining failure and success factors for the family business in tourism and hospitality, because it is not currently possible to make predictions about these matters or even to weigh all the consequences.

Growing the Family Business

A 1997 study of high-growth, family businesses in Australia (Smyrnios *et al.*, 1997) characterized this sub-set as being younger in age, having younger owners, possessing more formalized management structures, involving proportionately fewer family members in management, and showing less family control. One is left with a distinct impression from that research – that growth-oriented owners must make their business less family-oriented and more professional. Indeed, the principal objectives of family business owners in Australia, and especially those of first-generation owners, were to accumulate wealth, increase the value of their business, then sell it at an appropriate time. While their sample was much broader than the tourism and hospitality industry, these conclusions might very well hold true across all family businesses.

Most family businesses in tourism and hospitality remain small, primarily for lifestyle and autonomy reasons, but also in many cases because they lack the capacity to grow. Nor do most of them professionalize by hiring staff – the owners prefer to remain hands-on. Most owner-operators do want to increase their profitability, and this usually leads to a value-adding strategy, carefully balancing the desire to remain small and controllable with the need to increase 'return on effort'. Only a small minority of entrepreneurs in tourism and hospitality do want to grow their businesses, and this requires strategic planning for financing, ownership, organization and management.

Owners with children or other family members who want to be involved in the business have additional challenges: of getting them involved; balancing the needs and goals of potential future owners with the original motives and goals of the founders, and preparing for possible succession. Along the way, numerous family issues will have to be resolved, not the least of which is deciding how much money to take out of the business for family needs, versus reinvestment.

Why grow the family business?

Research on growth-oriented family firms was thought to be almost non-existent by Sharma *et al.* (1996), yet Ward (1987) and Poza (1988) argued that growth is necessary for family firms in order to ensure their survival. The US Small Business Administration (cited in Tagliuri and Davis, 1992) noted that growing companies had a lower percentage of failure than non-growing ones.

There are two basic arguments for growing a family business. The first is economics, namely the need to have sufficient revenue and cash-flow to remain viable and generate profits. Many micro and small businesses in the tourism and hospitality industry are too small ever to be profitable or even to survive. They start out too small and remain that way until the owners realize it is fruitless to continue. Factors that contribute to this common 'size challenge' have already been discussed; primarily a lack of sufficient start-up capital, the pre-eminence

of family and lifestyle goals, and the desire to retain hands-on control.

The B&B business is a clear example. Dawson and Brown (1988) concluded from research that B&B operators in the American Midwest had to spend money on promotion, remain committed to the business, add more rooms and offer private bath facilities in order to increase gross revenue. Pizam and Upchurch (2002) concluded that B&B establishments had to have more than eight rooms to generate a profit. Unfortunately, most operators never have this potential space nor the capital to grow their modest accommodation business.

It should also be noted that legislation in many areas limits the B&B and other rural accommodation establishments to unprofitably small sizes. Examination of regulations applicable to small businesses is therefore essential as an industry priority. The second basic reason for growing the family firm is to create opportunities for children or other family members, particularly if inheritance is a real prospect. Small businesses generally lack either the income potential or challenge necessary to attract and maintain the interest of children and especially heirs. As well, the business assets in tourism and hospitality are often tied up with the family home or farm, making separation difficult or impossible. Children might want to inherit the property, but not continue the business.

Growth and innovation

Upton *et al.* (2001) defined fast-growth family firms as '. . . those that are willing to take risks, to be innovative, and to initiate aggressive competitive actions.' But what exactly does it mean for a family business to be innovative? Litz and Kleyson (2002) argued that intergenerational dynamics must be examined, as innovation can die out with the family firm's founder, or start again with the children. They asked if innovation is a product of family interaction or individual effort. Is it intentional (i.e. do innovators set out purposefully to be creative and change things) or is it serendipitous (i.e. the product of one-time inspiration)?

Little innovation is evident in the purchasing of established businesses in existing destinations, nor is innovation evident in most of the lifestyle-oriented businesses where growth is not pursued. Russell (1996: 116), based on tourism-industry research in Ireland, concluded that 'the pursuit of innovation was not an integral part of most enterprises surveyed and where innovations were claimed these happened to be essential business investment'. In other words, Russell found that the owners were only doing what had to be done, not creating new products or markets. Nor was the business climate at that time supportive of innovation in the tourism industry. A truly innovative culture, according to Russell, would see higher professionalism among business owners/managers (especially in preparing business plans, adopting a marketing orientation and deliberately fostering innovative ideas), better educational opportunities and market information, more sharing of ideas through international contacts and travel, and better support from government agencies.

Innovation and networking

Networking is especially important for small, family businesses, both in terms of extending their marketing capabilities and in fostering innovation – or at least in encouraging the diffusion of innovations (Morrison, 1996, 1998). Networking of a formal, business-to-business type can be facilitated through the efforts of industry associations and destination marketing organizations. Beyond that, owners will be able to develop their own social networks. The family business has a unique potential advantage in this respect, although many family firm owners do not exploit it. They might have deliberately chosen to break off family ties, or their locational preferences might have made it difficult to sustain them. As a family gets established in an area it might become possible to rely more and more on the extended family for support and ideas.

Ethnicity can play an important role in family business networking. Saker (1992) noted that it is family and community that lie at the heart of the ethnic firm's social network. A strong social, particularly ethnic network can provide financial and moral support, but it can

also limit innovation if external influences are neglected.

Preconditions and Barriers to Growth

For most businesses the main precondition for growth is resource availability, either those of internal origin (e.g. savings, other assets such as land) or external (e.g. investors, loans, grants). For the family firm, the foundation is a desire to grow and the commitment to make it happen. In a family business one of the common dilemmas faced is that of reinvestment in the business versus taking resources out for immediate family use and personal wealth creation. Families often do make sacrifices in order to ensure their business becomes and remains successful, but if there is no long-term vision for the business, what is the incentive to reinvest in it?

The 'resource-based theory of the firm' (e.g. Barney, 1991) holds that a business is comprised of its resource bundle, and these are uniquely shaped by ownership and management intentions. The resources held by a family firm can consist of the 'tangible' (i.e. financial capital, information systems, products) and the 'intangible' (i.e. knowledge, skills, brand assets). Attention must be given to the resources owners can control, and to how they are actually deployed. Many family businesses are founded on personal sources of capital that are often inseparable from family assets such as the house or land. Others have little in the way of tangible assets and rely on personal knowledge.

A related theory, the 'knowledge-based' view of the firm (e.g. Nonaka, 1994), holds that businesses are a collection of 'tacit' knowledge (firm-specific) and 'explicit' knowledge (available to all). In family businesses it must be asked what 'tacit' knowledge is held by the owners and their families, and to what extent does it provide a competitive advantage? Does it increase or diminish over time, especially through the succession process? Many tourism and hospitality-related entrepreneurs rely heavily and sometimes exclusively on personal skills to ensure business success. They might be nature-tour guides who possess intimate knowledge of a natural area and its wildlife, or arts and crafts producers with creative talents. But all these personal sources of knowledge are potentially shared by many, or can become general knowledge over time, thereby eroding competitive advantages.

From either theoretical perspective – resource- or knowledge-based views of the firm – many family businesses in tourism and hospitality are essentially weak. They have neither the resources, the desire nor the knowledge to innovate or grow.

Storey (1994) identified a clear association between 'limited company' status and fast growth, but it was not clear which came first. Do growth-oriented entrepreneurs seek company status in order to raise capital and protect their own assets? He also identified common barriers to growth, specifically lack of motivation, limited financial resources, lack of skilled labour, and government controls. These, and other barriers noted by Poza (1988) are now discussed.

Lack of motivation or vision

The family vision, placing personal or family needs ahead of growth, or placing autonomy and hands-on management above growth potential, results in a very widespread lack of ambition to grow family businesses. But there is another kind of vision problem, rooted in the inability to see real opportunities that might be realized even within the scope of the family vision. Owners can be educated or at least encouraged to 'think beyond the box', particularly by examining other family-business success stories. This is where many entrepreneurship and small business programmes fail, because they need first to recognize the dominance of the family vision and how it constrains innovation and growth. The best people to undertake the training might be successful family business owners, backed by 'best practice' case studies.

Failure to communicate

Poza (1988) argued that maintaining distance from customers, employees, the competition, or family could impede growth. This is not just a matter of information flow or market intelligence, but also a behavioural and cultural issue.

Finances

Having large overheads and poor cash-flow prevents many owners from saving money for re-investment or growth. Are there ways to grow a family business without incurring a risky debt-load or giving up family control? Again, these options have to be placed before the owners and their families for consideration and weighing of the costs and benefits. At a minimum, practical 'value-adding' investments must be demonstrated, especially where new technology is involved. Indeed, financial assistance offered to establish or grow family businesses in tourism and hospitality is often going to miss the mark, whereas concrete help with technology and other value-adding systems (such as yield management, relationship marketing or inter-business networking) could have tremendous results.

Family impasse

Families might not be able to resolve their internal needs and goals, thereby falling into a non-growth option by default. This is the exact place and time for outside advisers to make an impact. It might be a simple matter of getting family members to share their ambitions and fears, or it might involve strategic and financial planning in depth.

Market area

Most small and family businesses rely on local or regional customers, as they lack the means to reach farther afield with effective marketing. The only solution to this universal problem is to form marketing alliances. Destination marketing organizations should examine how they can specifically cater to the needs of small and family businesses, whether it be for a collective website, special promotions, or 'piggybacking' on major advertising campaigns. On the other hand, owners have to realize that the destination has to be competitive first, then individual businesses can draw on increased tourist demand.

Laws or regulations

Often for good reasons, laws and regulations artificially limit the size or scope of small and family businesses, thereby preventing many from prospering. Why allow B&B establishments, for example, but limit them to so few rooms that they can never be more than a sideline or hobby? Every jurisdiction desiring growth in the small and family business sector should conduct an audit on its own laws and regulations to reveal problems, even if they are only paperwork issues. Beyond that, economic development agencies need to examine the best ways to help this sector given the known limitations.

Strategic Planning

Research by Rue and Ibrahim (1996) found that families that set goals for growth planned to grow first through equipment purchases, then marketing efforts, followed by hiring key staff, and finally by developing new products or physical expansion. But if the business is never going to grow or change in any fundamental way, there is little need for a strategic plan.

Indeed, Ward (1987) described strategic planning as '. . . the process of developing a business strategy for profitable growth'. The original business plan should suffice to see the owners through enterprise start-up or purchase and related financial and management issues. But owners with a longer-term perspective on growth and development need to think and plan strategically.

Key planning issues

Carlock and Ward (2001) argued that five pivotal variables demanded policies and plans in the family business:

- Control (management, ownership and decision-making).
- Careers (the family pursuing careers or other roles in the business, with advancement and rewards based on performance).
- Capital (systems and agreements so that family members can reinvest, harvest or

sell their investment without damaging other family members' interests).
- Conflict (addressing conflicts arising from work and personal lives intersecting).
- Culture (using family values to guide plans and actions).

These are all important elements in balancing business and family life and are discussed again in the next chapter. In tourism and hospitality, a number of unique considerations enter the strategic planning process:

- The business might be a secondary or seasonal source of income, with little growth potential.
- It might be more of a hobby than a serious way of earning a living.
- Its profit-making potential might be too limited to support paid staff or the formal involvement and inheritance by children.
- The nature of the work might very well be unattractive to children, and parents might prefer their children to live or work elsewhere.
- Only larger businesses, such as hotels or restaurants, have the potential to generate substantial cash flow and ultimately profits upon its sale.

To Ward (1987), the really big strategic issues were threefold: to keep or sell the business; to grow it or not; and to determine the extent of family involvement, including the potential for inheritance. Ward also argued that family issues *must* be incorporated into the strategic plan, and he recommended a formal, open process for developing the plan.

Getting professional advice

Most experts agree that getting professional advice is essential for family businesses. The case studies presented in this book also highlight the importance of advice as divergent as banking, accounting, marketing, business and strategic planning, estate and tax planning. Other areas of available family business advice concern group dynamics, health care and related costs, and raising capital.

Many firms specialize in family business advice, and they can be found through a simple internet search of the term 'family business consultants'. Astrachan (1993) suggested that family business consultants act as facilitators to help the family develop appropriate skills, and such advisers should be generalists with expertise in many areas. Once a trusting relationship has been established, it might pay the family to keep their advisers for as long as possible. Another source is the family business institutes that exist in universities, typically attached to business schools. And there are a number of family business associations that owners can join for mutual support and learning.

Why would owners not use external advisers? It could be a simple matter of the cost, but in many instances it is likely to stem from the founders' values and attitudes. A reasonable hypothesis is that the more autonomy-oriented the owners, the less likely they are to ask for or accept external advice.

Process and elements of strategic planning for the family business

Carlock and Ward (2001) advocated a 'parallel planning process' for integrating and balancing family and business concerns. The family side of the model contains 'core values', 'family commitment', 'family vision' and the production of a 'family enterprise continuity plan'. These interact with strategic business planning, so that values affect the 'management philosophy', family commitment corresponds with 'strategic commitment', a shared future vision leads to identification of a 'business vision', and the result is a 'business strategy plan'.

The 'family enterprise continuity plan' (Carlock and Ward, 2001: 16) addresses a series of goals, the first group of which pertain to securing family commitment. Does the family vision include a desire to perpetuate the business? How committed are all family members to this vision, and is it based on strong core values or philosophy? The second set of goals relates to family participation, in which fairness and conflict resolution is considered. This might entail family meetings and formal agreements. The third group of goals deals with the special case of preparing the next generation of leaders and owners, and the fourth cluster of goals covers the

development of effective owners, encompassing consideration of the family and business life cycle and related organizational and governance options.

The 'business strategy plan', according to Carlock and Ward (2001), has three groups of goals. The first set covers 'assessing strategic potential', based on environmental scanning, auditing, and market appraisal. Next is a set of goals relating to 'exploring possible business strategies'. Basic strategic options include renewal, reformulation or regeneration of the family business, but using unique strengths of family businesses should permeate the evaluations. Finally, the third set of goals pertains to finalization of 'strategic and reinvestment decisions'. An assessment of the business's health through a SWOT analysis (i.e. its Strengths, Weaknesses, Opportunities and Threats) is often a useful tool in strategic planning.

Alternatives must be considered, including those relating to capital, markets, staff, organization and ownership. For the family firm, usually a long-term perspective can be taken on these strategic issues. Then goals, both personal and family, must be factored into the strategy, and finally specific business strategies selected.

Mission statements

These are statements of why the business exists. Is its purpose to perpetuate a family legacy, or to make the family rich? Herremans and Welsh (1999) developed a case study of an ecotourism business 'mission statement' that is highly instructional. 'Treadsoftly', an 'Environmental Education Company' (see: www. treadsoftlycanada.com) is a family business located in the Crowsnest Pass area of Alberta, Canada. It began in 1997, and built into its initial business plan the increasing involvement of family members. What is unique is that the founders wanted to establish the business with an ideology reflecting sustainable development and community responsibility. It is committed to respect for the environment, co-operative efforts within the community, use of an environmental management system to link strategic planning to environmental issues, and to proactive environmental conservation efforts

including cumulative effects monitoring. The
mission statement reads as follows:

> To delight our guests. We promote environ-
> mentally and socially responsible travel that
> respects our natural and cultural resources,
> and educates our participants during a first
> hand nature experience.

By stating core values in this unambiguous way,
the family business provides direction and
stability through its evolution.

Vision statements

The importance of the 'family vision' (Chua
et al., 1999) has already been emphasized. This
is the vision to employ the business for the
benefit of the family, and potentially across the
generations through inheritance. Visioning can
be conducted informally by the owners and
family, or formally with the help of advisers.
According to Carlock and Ward (2001: 38), the
vision should cover five dimensions:

- Desired business accomplishments (innovation, growth, service).
- Possible family legacies (ownership, social
  responsibility).
- Benefits for the family (wealth, recognition,
  meaningful careers).
- Responsibilities to the business (investment,
  governance, philanthropy).
- Responsibilities to other stakeholders (employees, customers, suppliers, communities).

A good 'business vision' statement provides
a clear picture of the business at some point in
the future, say 5 or 10 years forward. It is important to base the vision on core values, or a formal
mission statement. For example, because most
family businesses in tourism and hospitality are
not profit- and growth-oriented, it is the rare
vision that will be expressed in terms of profit
maximization or continuous growth. Rather, the
vision might relate to future profitability, family
and business being in balance, and desired
value-adding. For the profit- and growth-
oriented entrepreneur, the vision might
relate more to a desired company size, target
market share, growth in sales and profitability,
professionalization through staff hiring, or
development of family skills.

Goals

General goal statements are derived from
the mission and vision. They are normally
expressed in terms of things to attain, such as
increased profitability, finding more leisure time
for the family to be together, or developing the
skills of children to eventually take over the firm.
Goals can also be expressed in terms of things
to avoid, such a high debt load, overwork, or
loss of control.

Many owners are reluctant to develop or
express their goals, according to Tagiuri and
Davis (1992), for several reasons. Some fear that
stating goals might lead to missed opportunities
or inflexibility. Goal-setting could cause conflict
over strategy, and if goals are not met, blame
might be assigned. In other cases, a multiplicity
of family- and business-related goals might make
it difficult to balance or prioritize them.

'Goal incongruence' (or disharmony) can
occur within families, such as when children
and parents cannot agree on the future of the
business (Peiser and Wooten, 1983). This is a
'life cycle' problem that is likely to occur at
a particular point in the evolution of the
family business. Possible consequences include
the professionalization of the business, in order
to avoid family indecisiveness, or a loss of
strategic orientation because of stalemate.
In contrast, Poza (1988) described 'intrapre-
neuring' as a revitalization process that occurs
just prior to or during the tenure of the 'next
generation' (i.e. the inheritors). In these cases
the children or other inheritors, with or without
the support of the founders, adopt innovations
or make radical changes to company finances,
organizational structure or family-related
systems.

Implementation, monitoring,
evaluation and revision

What management systems must be established
or refined to achieve the goals? Owners
must anticipate the practicality and costs of
implementing their strategies, together with
the necessity of monitoring progress, conducting specific research or analyses to evaluate
outcomes, and refining the plans as necessary.

Strategic Options

Strategies are the courses of action necessary to achieve major goals. There are no optimal or correct strategies to follow, only choices. We start this section with some generic business strategies that could apply, in theory, to any venture. We then examine family-specific strategies and related issues.

Generic business strategies

Miles and Snow (1978) developed a typology of business strategies that has also been used in the study of family businesses (e.g. Daily and Dollinger, 1992; McCann et al., 2001). The 'Defender' strategy is sticking to what the firm knows best. An 'Innovator/prospector' strategy embodies taking risks in order to provide new products or services, and applies to the growth-oriented entrepreneur. Following closely on the heels of innovators, the 'Analyser' strategy seeks competitive advantage by adopting proven strategies. The 'Reactor' strategy is one of adapting only when change makes it necessary.

However, these classic strategies look more like attitudes than concrete courses of action a business might take. Lifestyle and autonomy-oriented owners are generally conservative and therefore can be expected to be 'Defenders' rather than 'Innovators'. The tourism and hospitality industry in general displays a great deal of the 'Analyser' strategy in that successful products and services get widely copied, often to the point of standardization. What is poignant about the 'Reactor' strategy is the likelihood that many tourism and hospitality business cannot adapt in a timely or adequate manner and therefore are constantly at risk.

Building strategy upon the unique advantages of family business

Donnelley (1964) suggested that family businesses contain several inherent strengths and weaknesses:

Strengths:
- available family resources;
- family sacrifice;
- networks within family and the community;
- loyalty and dedication to family, staff and business;
- unified management under the owners;
- social responsibility;
- continuity and tradition, including family myths and legends;
- integrity;
- special knowledge;
- ability to capture niche markets; and
- long-term orientation.

Weaknesses:
- conflicts between family interests and business interests (e.g. taking money from the business versus reinvesting in its development or growth);
- lack of discipline over profits and performance (e.g. lack of firm cost controls);
- failure to adapt or react quickly to challenges or opportunities (similar to inherent conservatism: Ward, 1998); and
- nepotism versus performance (employing or advancing family members without regard to ability).

To Donnelley, most successful family businesses place institutional restraints on family prerogatives and these are backed by rigid tradition.

Carlock and Ward (2001: 192) suggested that additional competitive advantages can be gained in family businesses. Long-term payoffs can be pursued, even to the point of experimenting with options. But while this is possible for successful family businesses seeking permanence, it is not for those struggling to survive. Furthermore, some family members might be inclined to oppose anything that limits their immediate gratification. In tourism and hospitality, families can sometimes afford to sit on their real-property assets waiting for eventual payback even while cash-flow and profits are weak.

Flexible organization is another potential advantage. Assuming a shared vision and unified control, the family business can avoid bureaucratic infighting, react quickly to seize opportunities, change direction fast, and be innovative. One of the secrets of successful entrepreneurs is to move before their competitors, even when the decision involves a degree of risk. This principle seems to apply when individuals with insider knowledge and specialist skill are the first to offer touring or guiding services, are quick to exploit a new target market segment, or terminate a product when it fails to meet expectations.

A strong commitment to quality, based on family pride and social responsibility, can result in loyal customers and strong family-branding, as in the O'Reilly case. Who is better to deal with unhappy or demanding customers than an owner-operator? Who, other than family business owners, is a tangible part of the product? As a strategy, creating a family brand will require patience, commitment to quality and clever marketing. It does not hurt to have strong personalities and colourful characters in the business.

Niche market positioning is a mainstay of small, family businesses. In tourism and hospitality the limitations of being restricted to local and regional markets make it essential to develop strong relationships with one or more niches. These might be affinity groups and local companies, other family businesses, or well-known repeat visitors. To find real advantage in these small markets, the family business has to have cost, product quality or service advantages over larger competitors.

Investment in people is also a hallmark of the family business, both for family members and staff. Having trustworthy employees is a plus, especially when they can be relied upon to adhere to the family values and vision. When employees become 'part of the family' additional benefits accrue. In a tactical sense, this might permit the family business to save on recruitment and training, and in terms of strategy it might permit investment in developments that require a very high service component, such as catering or five-star accommodation.

Strategic options: renew, reformulate or regenerate

Given an existing course of direction or strategy, any strategic thinking will first face the question of whether to continue or depart from the current direction.

Renewal

Capitalizing on existing strategy is the renewal option (Carlock and Ward, 2001: 180). It does not imply a total absence of change, but focuses the owner's attention on getting more out of current capabilities and markets. It can be thought of as value-adding if the current strategy is to avoid debt and growth.

Reformulation

Improving the strategy is the essence of reformulation. Owners can examine how to strengthen their capabilities and develop new markets. Are there assets to be harnessed?

Regeneration

The position of many family companies in tourism and hospitality, upon reflection, is likely to be weak. A new owner, having purchased a business, or an inheritor, might be confronted with these weaknesses all of a sudden and have little choice but to come up with a new strategy or a radical reformulation of the old one. New investment might be required.

Given the research evidence and the case studies in this book, many owners in the tourism and hospitality industry will be looking to sustain their business, that is to keep it profitable but not to grow it. Others will want to add value in order to increase profitability, and only a few will desire substantial growth or diversification. Other fundamental choices are to sell the business, take in external investment, or to hand over control to professionals.

These options are now looked at in greater detail.

Sustainability option

Owners of family businesses can, and usually do, elect to remain small and controllable. Because that option is predominant, and probably always will be, it cannot be dismissed as being unimportant to the industry or to destinations. Effort must be directed at understanding this choice and helping the owner-operator ensure that the business remains viable enough to support the family. This will be termed the 'sustainability' option. Beyond this basic model, options include value-adding, growth measured in terms of diversification or physical expansion, and the plan-to-sell option. Planning for inheritance (the 'succession option') is considered in detail in Chapter 5.

An old adage applies to owners who elect to keep their family business unchanging: 'if you do not grow, you will inevitably fall behind'. The essential problem with staying the same is that nothing else remains constant! How can a small business compete in such an evolving environment – one in which innovation brings on new choices for consumers all the time and the number of competitors increases? And if the business fails to improve at all, will it not simply decline? This can easily result in a downward spiral which, as stressed by Shaw and Williams (1997) can seriously harm the entire tourist destination and render it uncompetitive.

To remain viable (i.e. competitive and profitable for the owners) in the absence of growth requires several strategic responses. The first is reinvestment to ensure that the physical plant remains modern and attractive. An inherent difficulty is with owners who purchase old properties because they are affordable or in the right location, without considering the investment that will be required to maintain and upgrade the property. Another problem is with cash-flow, in that owners of small family businesses might have to take out too much of the profit for their own subsistence.

Attention to changing market characteristics and consumer preferences is important. It is always a mistake to assume that what is now desired or even popular will remain so. Several authors have documented how fundamental changes in tourism have resulted in a revolution from mass markets to custom markets (Poon, 1993), and how this change has led to many business failures (Peters and Weirmair, 2001).

A small, static business in the tourism and hospitality industry can potentially retain its competitive advantage indefinitely if it meets one or more of the following conditions:

- Uniqueness (there are few options to this product or service; it is one-of-a-kind).
- Ideal location (the business has the best location).

- Superb service quality (customers rave about the service, the food, the hosts).
- Cost advantage (competitors cannot keep their costs as low).
- Price advantage (better expressed as perceived value for price – i.e. customers think they are getting more than they pay for, relative to competitors).

What should be clear, however, is that few family businesses actually possess or can retain these enduring competitive advantages without changing. Often the owners merely think they have advantages, but they are not informed about what is happening around them. If they do learn about competitive threats, they are often unwilling or unable to adapt.

Value-adding option

Improvements in management systems and marketing can achieve higher profitability without necessarily requiring physical growth. In several of our case studies the owners explicitly realized the need for value adding, and devised ways to achieve it within their goals framework and operational constraints; sometimes this led to modest growth. The following are generic value-adding options.

Using technology

Much attention has been given to the use of computers in enabling sophisticated management systems for small businesses, and of the internet in improving small-business marketing. Employing readily-available accounting software should result in better cost control, quicker billing of customers, and improved cash flow. Internet marketing, particularly when implemented in partnership with destinations or business allies, should result in an extended customer base.

Efficiency gains

The 'learning curve', or how owners apply what they learn over time, should result in reduced costs and higher outputs. Applying 'yield management' formally (with the help of sophisticated software) or informally, based on specific knowledge of the business and markets, should generate higher profits.

Adding new services and products

This is likely to be the most viable value-adding strategy for family businesses in tourism and hospitality. Owners can follow the leaders by watching what products and services appeal to their target markets, or they can try out their own new ideas.

Moving up-market

Improvements to the physical plant, adding new products and services, and constantly improving service quality can enable the owner to charge higher prices and attract higher-yield customers. For example, taking a modest B&B establishment, the reduction of rooms in favour of room upgrading (e.g. adding en-suite bathrooms and antique décor) could enable the owner to charge more.

Diversification option

One of the characteristics of small, family businesses is that most of their trade is local or regional in nature. This applies in tourism, as it is difficult to compete with chains and major players in attracting tourists from afar, and in hospitality firms that must rely on residents for steady business. This makes diversification difficult.

The Bornholm (Denmark) research, reported later in this chapter, revealed that a small proportion of owners were engaging in diversification strategies. Some fall into this naturally, while for others it might only come about through careful research or trial and error. There are several patterns to diversification, and what differentiates these from 'value adding' is the related growth of the business.

New markets

On Bornholm, several owners were able to commence export of their products off the island to other parts of Denmark or globally. Others decided to pursue both the resident and the tourist markets, mainly because of the extreme seasonality of demand concentrated in two summer months.

New products and services

A common response to seasonality of demand is to use business infrastructure for different purposes, such as hosting private functions and producing special events. This can be simple value adding, but might very well require growth in staff, investment in specialized equipment, and modification of infrastructure.

New ventures

Tourism provides the opportunity for entrepreneurs to own or even manage more than one business simultaneously, such as a hotelier who adds a restaurant or tour service. This 'vertical integration' generates value by bringing more sources of revenue from tourists into the same company. Knowledge of the 'tourism value chain' is essential for this strategy to work, so owners familiar with different aspects of tourism will have the advantage. Rarely, an owner buys or develops counter-cyclical businesses – that is, operating in different parts of the world with opposite or complementary seasons. An example would be for a family in Bornholm to run their business for several months, then move to a warmer climate to operate a different business the rest of the year.

Webster (in Thomas, 1998a) cautioned that diversification can present problems for the small business operator. It might be better to stick to the core business if diversification stretches one's financial resources, time and skills. Poza (1988) went further, arguing that 'Most diversification outside the products, manufacturing processes, and markets that firms know well fails.'

Physical expansion option

Adding to the size of the establishment might have the effect of increasing the need for paid staff or professional managers. The owner-operator and family must carefully consider how much they can manage in terms of physical space (e.g. number of rooms to clean in a motel), time commitment (hours per day and week), resources available (equipment, computers, vehicles) and variable costs. This issue of fixed versus variable costs is crucial in terms of yield management.

Taking external investment in the business

How much investment can be handled without losing family control is an important issue. The additional capital might make the difference between remaining too small and growing to the optimum level, or in having an adequate reserve to weather low cash-flow periods.

Plan-to-sell option

Many, perhaps even most, owners in tourism and hospitality, plan to sell their business and hope to get the 'sweat equity' out of their efforts. In other words, the business might not be profitable in strict accounting terms, but it supports the owner or family until such time as a major capital gain can be generated through sell-off. This might even be the only retirement plan available to owners, but it is assuming a lot about the future value of land or other assets and is therefore risky.

Professionalization option

If the family business gets too big, complex or demanding, or if the owners want to try something else, they might opt to hand over operations and even control to professional managers. Owners might also consider the absence of potential heirs to be an adequate reason for bringing in paid professionals.

According to Goffee and Scase (1985), a 'quasi-organic' management structure often occurs where owners retain the right to intervene at any time, but management is nominally in the hands of professionals. As a transition stage, this structure entails some risk of inefficient interference by owners and owner-manager conflict, so a board of directors might be necessary to make it function smoothly. The family business literature is not firm on just how much conflict arises in such transition periods (Sharma et al., 1996).

As family firms grow and become more professional in their management, does innovation and entrepreneurship decrease? Mintzberg and Waters (1990) suggested that planning and procedures might replace vision and entrepreneurial activity, but there is an absence of evidence on this matter that applies to tourism and hospitality, probably because so few family businesses in this industry get big or make the transition.

Strategic Marketing and Family Branding

Marketing is inherently challenging for small businesses (Friel, 1999), and typically the owner takes a short-term (less than 1 year) perspective. Other weaknesses include:

- narrow scope and range of marketing activities;
- simplistic and haphazard efforts;
- reactionary, not innovative;
- informal; and
- opportunistic rather than systematic.

All marketing efforts should be based on market intelligence, yet the UK national survey of small tourism and hospitality businesses (Thomas et al., 1997) found that only 50% did market research. Of those that completed some research, the focus was on customer needs and service, while the business environment was least researched.

These weaknesses stem from a combination of limited resources, lack of training and skills, and the inherent difficulty of small businesses in having any kind of impact on the marketplace. Consequently, a number of strategies suited to small businesses should be contemplated, namely niche marketing, relationship and cooperative marketing, plus the family branding option. Marketing strategies also must be considered in light of the broader options discussed under strategic planning.

Niche marketing

Many owners rely on the popularity of the destination to bring in customers year after year, and fail to consider what their own specific appeal might be. They offer completely undifferen-tiated products (typically accommodation and dining), but without differentiation, every business is completely substitutable. Morrison (1998: 194), commenting specifically on hotels in peripheral areas, argued that '. . . product differentiation and extension, market diversifi-cation and flexible specialization' are necessary strategies.

The aim of niche marketing is to focus on one or several market segments that desire, and will pay, a premium for the kind of customized product, personal service and unique experi-ences that a family business can provide. Differentiation for niche markets can be based on several advantages. The first is geography, including the always-wise strategy of building strong community ties. Or the owner might have personal knowledge about, or contacts in, a more distant marketplace that can be exploited.

Providing a unique service or experience is advantageous. Historic accommodation estab-lishments with antique décor stand out from the ordinary. Tour operators with detailed knowl-edge and access to special places are likely to be more appealing than large tour companies. Families that are part of the product offer some-thing extra. The secret is to think about the total visitor experience and the specific benefits customers derive.

Relationship marketing

Being customer-focused should result in the establishment of excellent relationships with loyal customers. While it is desirable always to have new customers (who then spread positive word-of-mouth recommendations to others), repeat business is of tremendous value. The underpinning philosophy of relationship marketing for the family business is that the owner and guest connect on a personal level, and the business and guest engage in a permanent dialogue.

When an inquiry is made, a potential customer approached, or a real person buys the service on offer, the opportunity exists for relationship building. In wineries, for example, every person who shows up to taste the product is a potential long-term customer. All too often,

however, wineries let people come and go without even attempting to engage them in conversation, learn their preferences, get their name, or add them to a mailing list.

Relationships require effort, and the customer will only make that effort if rewarded by quality service, great experiences and specific bonuses. A computer database and mailing list are the basic elements, but the customer does not want to be bothered with a lot of useless contacts. Specific requests for feedback from customers are important.

Pricing and packaging

Competing on price is a potential trap. As a strategy, it is usually better to find ways to cut costs (leaving a higher profit margin) and improve perceived value than to cut prices. Dependence on a single tour operator can bring in volume, for example, but they might require an accommodation operator to cut prices to the bone in order to maximize tour-company revenues.

Hankinson (1989: 82) observed from research that 'Most of the hotels followed a policy of rigid target-return pricing which exem-plifies a behaviour pattern closely approximating survival'. Similarly, simplistic cost-plus and follow-the-leader pricing are tempting for unsophisticated owners and managers, but pricing should follow from a broader strategy and incorporate both packaging and yield management.

Packaging is a way of expanding the market appeal of many small businesses. Customers can be sold a standard package at a given price, or they can be given the option of assembling their own from a menu. The allure of packaging to the customer is a combination of perceived value (they think it costs less than all the elements would cost individually, but this is not always the case), convenience (someone else has done the hard work for them) and uniqueness (getting a complete experience that is otherwise difficult or impossible to arrange on their own).

The basic approach to packaging is for an operator to pull together elements of the travel or leisure experience, focused on the specific business. For example, an accommodation operator makes a stay at their establishment the centrepiece for a package, encompassing room, recreation and meals. The recreation component can be sub-contracted or a simple matter of booking a tee time for the customer and including the price of golf in the package.

More complex packages require business-to-business relationships or the intermediary power of a marketing alliance. The idea is to offer potential visitors a destination package allowing a choice from many accommodations, attractions and services offered by small and family businesses in the area. This approach might have to be developed in conjunction with a business accreditation system to ensure quality, and a booking system that allows customization.

Yield management

Even the smallest of businesses can benefit from the practice of yield management. A number of special considerations apply to small and family businesses. Yield management begins with realization that unused capacity represents a major loss of potential revenue for the business. For example, accommodation units that are unused and empty seats on a bus can never be replaced – they are 'perishable' commodities. Other businesses with high fixed costs, including restaurants that are fully staffed but sometimes devoid of customers, can also benefit from yield management. With this in mind, owners and managers often seek ways to reduce operational costs, such as by cutting back on the hours of operation or keeping staff levels to a minimum. Cyclical closure of the business is often practiced, but in most cases these strategies are a form of capitulation and it would be preferable, financially, to attract more paying customers.

The simplest form of yield management occurs through price reductions in off-peak demand periods, such as winter-season specials at resorts and mid-week lunch discounts in restaurants. Combined with attractive packaging, new business can be generated within market segments that are sensitive to price and responsive to 'specials'.

Raising prices when it is anticipated that demand will be high is less appealing to many owners, but generates substantial profit enhancements to the businesses that employ it. Based on historical demand patterns, which are often highly predictable, the business takes advantage of the fact that many customers (particularly travellers) cannot or will not change their plans. It works best for hotels and transport companies that can continuously revise their schedule of fares for specific dates. Others will have to make do with seasonal or weekday–weekend price changes.

Yield management has to be integrated with policies on reservations, advance payments and refunds, over-booking and length of stay. For example, many accommodation providers want two-night minimum stays for weekends. Companies practising yield management also have to be concerned about customer reactions, as variable pricing inevitably produces situations where customers have paid different prices for the same experience. The principle benefit they received for higher prices is a guaranteed reservation exactly when they wanted it.

The very basic decisions that have to be made about growth or value adding are linked to yield management. What is the sense of building new accommodation units, for example, if it is easier and cheaper to fill up available capacity through more aggressive marketing including discounts, packaged prices and other incentives? Owners have to examine their operations to see if the forecast benefits of expansion are worthwhile and necessary in order to add value and profit to the enterprise.

Accounting for family labour enters the yield management picture as well. All too often family labour is devalued (relative to wage and benefit levels for employees), or not accounted for at all. This makes it difficult to determine the true costs of various operations, and therefore makes it hard to implement yield management. For example, additional accommodation units would potentially generate more revenue, but are all labour costs being calculated? Is it assumed that family members will simply work harder? The same applies to determining the potential benefits of price reductions to fill surplus capacity – each additional room filled will also have a marginal labour cost.

Co-operative marketing

Clarke (1995) observed that farm accommodation operators tend to be isolated, engage in rivalry and exchange little information, but this might be typical of small and family businesses in tourism and hospitality. To overcome many inherent limitations of being small and isolated, the business owner has to engage in co-operative marketing and consider other forms of strategic alliance.

Co-operative marketing can take several forms, from simple to complex. Informally, many business operators agree to a mutual referral system in which potential customers are given specific referrals to other businesses. This works well during peak-demand periods, or when customers want advice on what else to see or do in an area.

More formal arrangements are usually organized by tourist boards, chambers of commerce and the like. Normally it is the destination that is promoted through these mechanisms, with individual members being a secondary consideration. Such member-based alliances allow the pooling of resources for additional marketing reach, plus the sharing of market intelligence or formal training.

Evans and Ilbery (1992) described producer cooperatives among farm-based accommodations that have arisen on order to produce or purchase more cost-effective advertising. These are also called 'product clubs' or 'marketing consortia', where the same types of business jointly promote their services (e.g. a marketing consortium of ecotour operators).

Advantages of a co-operative marketing effort were listed by Morrison (1998: 194):

- networking;
- achieving greater economic scale;
- obtaining professional advice;
- access to better technology;
- support for training and education; and
- pooling of resources.

For the larger business, buying into a franchise gets both a name brand and its marketing strength, while joining an exclusive association (e.g. luxury inns or historic country restaurants) provides marketing power and a form of branding.

Family branding

The most prominent family-dependent issue in marketing is that of exploiting the family-firm status, or the family name, for competitive advantage. The term 'family branding' can be used to describe a family of brands, such that the same brand name is used on every product the company makes or on every service it offers. If the overall brand name has value in terms of acceptance by customers, then all the products and services using that name should be well received. On the other hand, if a brand associated with quality is later applied to a low-price product, the consumer might begin to think that the entire family of brands has lowered its standards.

Dunn (1995: 21), based on analysis of successful Scottish family businesses, concluded that some of them used their family status for marketing purposes to imply quality, care, and special attention to customers. Because the 'brand' is often the family name, it should ideally communicate all the following brand attributes:

- Quality and value (service; good value for money; reliability) based on past performance and the assumption that a family takes pride in all it does.
- Tradition (we have a long history; we are rooted in the community and we care about you).
- Personality (we are a family, different from corporations, with our own way of doing things; we offer all our clients customized experiences and a personal touch; we are always ethical in our business dealings).
- In some cases the attributes can also signify culture or tradition, as in an ethnic business. Whatever the name, customers should be made to feel they personally know and understand the family behind it.

There are potential negatives associated with exploiting one's name and family-business, status, including the fact that some people associate family business with a lack of professionalism and nepotism. As well, there might be a fear of attracting unwanted attention to the family and thereby of including some risks.

Networking

Families should have advantages in dealing with other families, especially when based on blood and marriage relationships, but also when there are solid roots in a community. Networking works at two levels, both social and business-to-business. It can be formal, as through membership in marketing organizations, or informal. Network theory has been applied to the study of both social and business connections. Dodd (1997) examined formal social networks in the UK and concluded that business success might be linked to membership in social organizations. Business owners tended to be more active this way than employees or the self-employed. Littlejohn et al. (1996) found that small business owners placed more value on social or informal networks than on structured consortia.

Birley and Cromie (1988) suggested that the early stage of enterprise development is characterized by heavy reliance on an informal network of friends, family and local social contacts, with increasing reliance over time on professional links. Ram (1994) determined that ethnic or minority networking provides both strengths and weaknesses to the business, with a real risk being the exclusion of external assistance and contacts.

The Seasonality Challenge and Strategic Responses in Bornholm

Because cyclical demand fluctuations are such a global concern for the tourism and hospitality industry, how businesses and families react is of utmost importance. In this section the seasonality problem is explored in detail, and results presented from research in Denmark to illustrate strategies being employed by family businesses.

Seasonality and its causes

Seasonality in tourism demand is a universally recognized phenomenon (BarOn, 1975; Baum and Hagan, 1997; Baum and Lundtorp, 2001).

It results in fluctuations in tourism volumes over the calendar year, and must be differentiated from longer-term business cycles and short-term changes related to weekly and daily travel patterns. Seasonality of demand is typically caused by institutional and/or natural factors, with the pattern usually remaining stable over many years. This predictability of seasonality makes it possible for businesses, lenders and investors to anticipate many of its impacts.

Baum and Hagan (1997: 2) listed the main causal factors:

- climate or weather;
- social customs, especially holidays;
- business customs, such as meetings and events;
- calendar effects, including important dates;
- supply side constraints such as labour availability; and
- alternative uses of facilities.

Butler (1994) added 'inertia' to the list of causes, and later (2001) separated 'demand factors' from 'supply attributes'. A set of 'modifying factors' such as pricing can be employed by destinations and businesses. All these interactions necessitate differentiating between demand (customer) and supply (business) fluctuations when discussing seasonality in a given area.

BarOn (1975) examined arrivals data from 16 countries over a 17-year time frame and concluded that some areas have a '. . . very strong high season with negligible tourist activity during the rest of the year' (p. 2). 'Extreme months' (p. 16) were said to be those deviating from random irregularities by more than 1.5 standard deviations. Jeffrey and Barden (2001: 123) in their analysis of seasonality in hotel occupancy rates in England observed that 'Seaside and remote or peripheral hotels generally have . . . pronounced or extreme seasonality.'

'Extreme seasonality' remains a somewhat subjective and elusive concept. While it can be approached as a statistical problem, using various measures such as those of demand amplitude or inequality (see, for example: BarOn, 1975; Wanhill, 1980; Yacoumis, 1980; Lundtorp, 2001), the numbers do not necessarily shed light on the implications for various businesses or the destination.

The challenges of seasonality

Seasonality of demand is often referred to as a problem (Allcock, 1989), and destinations generally work hard to reduce it. For individual businesses the negative impacts or costs can include:

- peak-period crowding and high work loads;
- cash-flow problems;
- unused capacity and lower profitability during low demand periods;
- difficulty in attracting and keeping skilled employees;
- need for seasonal workers and part-time staff;
- difficulty in attracting investors and lenders.

An overview of seasonality in Europe (McEeniff, 1992) discussed patterns (e.g. domestic tourism is much more peaked than international arrivals), trends (greater spread of demand was occurring over time) and potential solutions (such as all-weather resort facilities). Coopers and Lybrand Consulting (1996: 1), in a report for the Canadian Tourism Commission, described seasonal variations in tourism demand as '. . . one of the biggest challenges currently faced by the Canadian travel industry.'

A major analysis of seasonality in occupancy rates among English hotels was reported by Jeffrey and Barden (2001). Some hotels did better than others, depending principally on their target markets. Those oriented toward business travellers and conventions, or group tours, displayed significantly less seasonality. Practising yield management definitely helped, but deep price discounts did not. They concluded (p. 123) that '. . . most hoteliers could extend their seasons' through better marketing, but some would find seasonal closures to be the most cost-effective solution to pronounced seasonality.

Unfortunately, many attempts to reduce seasonality fail. Butler (1994) observed that growth in demand often occurs in the peak season, dwarfing attempts to improve seasonal balance. In the northwest of Scotland he found that the pattern of seasonality had not changed appreciably since 1970, although shoulder-season volume had increased. In Ireland, Kennedy and Deegan (2001: 51) observed that 'Many businesses in Irish tourism experience long periods of low usage and short periods of high usage', although there were some signs of improvement.

The common lack of success in defeating seasonality suggests that destinations should look more carefully at other strategies. The most profound change in common practice would come from a focus on yield, rather than volume. For example, Kennedy and Deegan (2001: 68) suggested that Ireland should preferentially attract markets with a 'high propensity to travel out of the peak season, spend the most money per capita, stay the longest and travel throughout the country.'

Another possibility is to carefully examine supply with a view to eliminating old, surplus capacity (Lundtorp et al., 1999), thereby improving occupancy rates for all remaining businesses. Flognfeldt (2001: 110) suggested that some destinations must learn 'how to live with strong seasonality', and his basic idea is to 'fit different types of tourism production into the seasonal patterns of other production activities, including an adjustment of some public services.' He also noted a number of business strategies in place in rural Norway, including mixed employment (e.g. tourism and agriculture or tourism and teaching), use of student and migrant workers, developing new products to expand the season, taking long holidays, getting into export markets, and moving away to work or study in the off-season.

Seasonality and the family business

For family businesses seasonality can mean severe personal and financial stress, an impediment to having children take over the business, and a disrupted leisure and social life. Families face a heightened risk from extreme seasonality, in light of the following considerations:

- The family house and property are often an integral part of the business (e.g. small hotels, farmstays, B&B or guest houses, campgrounds on family land).

- Families often depend completely on a single business venture for their income.
- Family businesses tend to minimize labour costs by maximizing their own inputs, resulting in long hours of hard work.
- Many parents want to leave a tangible legacy for their children in the form of a viable business or other real property.

Cooper *et al.* (1993) said that in order to justify remaining open, a business must at least cover the variable costs associated with staying open. These could be heating, labour and insurance. In the case of family businesses, this rule does not fully apply. Families that provide all the necessary labour can avoid payroll costs altogether. When they live in the accommodation, as many do, at least some of the costs of staying open can be considered as family subsistence costs. Families can employ strategies used by other companies, but there are also some unique options available to them. These will be explored through assessment of the Bornholm example.

Seasonality in Bornholm

Bornholm (population 45,000), like many resorts, and particularly islands, experiences greater seasonality than other types of destination (Butler 1994). Peripheral regions at higher latitudes also find it more difficult to influence seasonality in demand (Lundtorp *et al.*, 1999). Furthermore, islands frequently rely on natural attractions, particularly the beach and water sports, which in temperate and high-latitude climates experience huge temperature swings.

Bornholm is one of the most renowned destinations in Denmark, popular since the late 19th century. It has been described as '. . . a mature seaside resort with an established tourism infrastructure dominated by small enterprises' (Gyimothy, 2000: 56). Sixty-four per cent of all visitors come for holiday reasons, and this figure rises to 90% in the summer. The key markets are regional, namely Danes, Swedes and Germans.

A hotel survey on Bornholm by Sundgaard *et al.* (1998) found that 43% of hotels were small, family owned, and opened in the peak-season only (the actual percentage is higher, owing to

non-response). Twenty-three per cent of larger hotels were seasonal and owned by limited liability companies. Almost all the campsites and youth hostels were closed off-season, plus 88% of holiday centres, 65% of large hotels, 84% of medium hotels, and 65% of small hotels. Some restaurants and other catering businesses were also seasonal. Most owners were residents, and most businesses were small in size.

Bornholm is similar to two other Baltic islands, Åland and Gotland, in both its history and current seasonality. All three islands possess high levels of local ownership and control. Twining-Ward and Baum (1998) concluded that all three had entered a period of decline and were suffering from the ill-effects of seasonally low demand. The problems are augmented by a dominance of small, family enterprises '. . . which in many cases lack the professional training required to secure a high quality of service' (p. 135).

Lundtorp (2001) summarized the extreme seasonality problem on Bornholm by noting that for 9, slow months of the year the island attracts only 33% of total demand, and over 10 months the figure is only 50%. Bornholm and other parts of Denmark, he suggested, display 'high seasonal amplitude' (p. 31). Lundtorp (2001) also concluded from his analysis of tourist trends that there had been no substantial pattern change in seasonality for Denmark or Bornholm in the 1989–1998 period. Lundtorp *et al.* (1999) concluded from their analysis that seasonality could not realistically be eliminated, and not even substantially reduced. A major reason was the uniformity of visitors and their behaviour – Bornholm's shoulder seasons attracted the same types of loyal visitor as the peak season, for the same reasons and length of stay. Most recently, increases in volume have occurred, but this has not altered the extremeness of seasonality. It remains to be seen if a volume increase in itself can alter the seasonal responses of local businesses.

The seasonality 'problem'

Over half (46 or 57.5%) of respondents in Bornholm indicated their business closed for part of the year. For seasonal operations, the

most typical 'width' of the open season was
7 months (14 indicated April–October), with
6 months (May–October: seven respondents) or
5 months (May–September: ten respondents)
also being common. The typical seasonal
business on Bornholm therefore experienced
a 2-month peak tourist season, from 3 to 6
shoulder months and 4 to 7 closed months.

Respondents were asked if their business
was 'highly seasonal' (as one item in a set of
statements about the business), and 68.3%
selected 'fully agree' on a scale of five
(mean = 4.23) while only 10% checked 'fully
disagree'. In a separate question, respondents
were asked if highly seasonal demand was a
problem for the business, and only 18.3%
checked 'a serious problem' while 53%
indicated it was 'somewhat of a problem' and
34% said it was 'not a problem'. From these two
responses it can be concluded that for many
owners extreme seasonality was not a serious
problem because they closed and did not worry
about it. In other words, they were coping.

A selection of quotations from the interviews helps to understand the nature of the
seasonality problem for family business owners,
and especially its impact on profitability. Of
course, some of these problems also relate
to small size and competition:

> We have to be very careful about our business,
> as the profit of our activities is low. It puts a
> limit for what we would like to do. We have
> to take small steps forward.
> (Campground; sole proprietor; closed part year;
> married but children work elsewhere)

> We keep an eye with our expenses, as it is not
> possible to increase our prices because of the
> competition . . .
> (Campground; sole proprietor; no children;
> open April to November)

> It is not possible to extend the opening season
> because of the climate but we could use more
> of our capacity in shoulder seasons.
> (Married couple; hostel and tour operators)

> The problems on Bornholm are the same as
> in the rest of the country. Eighty per cent of
> the business should be closed. The earnings
> are too low, and the amount of risk-willing
> capital also too low. The companies are so
> weak that it is impossible to develop new
> products.
> (Hotel/restaurant owner and former banker)

Responses to seasonality

Respondents staying open all year were asked
how they dealt with the low season economically. Four choices were provided, and respondents could select more than one, plus a space
was provided to write in 'other' actions. The
main response was dismissal of staff (25
responses), followed by 22 who supplemented
their income from other sources. Fourteen drew
on savings and six took out loans to survive the
low season. 'Other' actions mentioned: arrange
parties (three respondents); and (one response
each) take a vacation; have personal guests;
rely on social security, use private financing,
and work alone. It is clear that being open all
year is not the same as being active or profitable
all year.

The remainder answered the question of
what they did when their business closed part
of the year, with five categories provided and
space allowed to write in 'other' actions. There
were 76 responses from the 57.5% of the sample
who closed part of the year. The main activity
was maintaining or improving the property
(21 mentions). Eighteen respondents owned
another business and nine took another paying
job. Only 16 said they enjoyed the leisure time.
No-one selected 'unemployed'. 'Other' activities
were: produce stock (five mentions); take
courses (one mention).

Coping strategies

Selected quotations from the interviews
illustrate a variety of 'coping strategies', being
defined herein as closure of the business *plus*
the absence of attempts to expand. These
owners accept extreme seasonality and try to
cope with its impacts:

> We close when season is over and use the rest
> of the year to keep up the facilities of the site.
> (Campground)

> Our open season is from 1 May to 1 October.
> The rest of the year I plan for the next season,
> renovate, do some marketing and make
> bookings and reservations. I also have another
> occupation out of season.
> (Sole proprietor; hotel and restaurant;
> no children)

Opening season is 1 April to 1 November. The rest of the year we keep up the facilities – take some vacation as we have long working hours during the summer.

(Married couple; hostel and tour operators).

We rent our flats in high season for about 13 weeks. Outside tourist season we paint and repair the flats and make them ready for the next season. Then we also use our time for our primary income: the farm.

(Married couple; three flats on farm)

'Coping' is not just for micro businesses, as witnessed by the example of two brothers who own and operate an inherited hotel with restaurant. The wife of one of the brothers also works full-time in the business. The hotel and restaurant are 'closed for the winter' but they do open for conferences or functions, on demand. In the slow season the family runs the business without regular paid staff and occupy themselves with maintenance, planning the next season and taking bookings. High-season requires employment of three more staff plus six or seven students during their holidays. Their strategy seems to be mostly 'coping', with a little 'combating'.

Combating

Many business owners try to defeat seasonality, or at least expand the shoulder seasons for enhanced profitability, although they might still be forced to close for part of the year. The main criteria for inclusion in the 'combating' category are attitude and action, as the following quotations reveal:

We continue to develop our concept . . . We would like to have more guests in the shoulder seasons. In the high season we have a full house.
(Sole proprietor; campground; closed part year)

I would like to be able to make more investments and enlarge my business. It is my intention to establish ten more beds in the next year and also a hall for conferences.
(Married couple; farm-based accommodation; closed part year)

Our concept is very popular among locals as well as tourists. In winter we have many arrangements for the locals, and in high season many of the locals recommend us to tourists

asking for a place to eat . . . Our business is running well, and we have a lot to do in high season, where the capacity is fully used. We could use more guests in the shoulder season, which we would like to be extended by 1–2 months.
(Restaurant owner; open all year; one daughter works in the business)

Our firm is very solid with a fine yearly net profit . . . This (fish smokehouse) is very popular with tourists and our sale for tourists is substantial but not as big as our export. We also export a lot to private people in Denmark. Who order by phone or e-mail . . . We find ourselves in a good position on the market and expect a good profit in the future. Our business gives us a satisfactory income, and we do not intend to enlarge our volume.
(Married couple; children live off-island; open all year)

The export (i.e. products) of the firm is still growing all over Europe and Scandinavia, and the sale to tourists during the season is of great importance to the firm. The demand for our production is still increasing year by year. To be able to meet the demand we have set up a new production (factory) . . . We foresee considerable possibilities for more export in the future.
(Owner of a craft production and retail company; open all year for production, sales and marketing)

Our business has been a success, as we can sell all that we are able to produce. We sell our products outside Bornholm, but of course we also have a considerable sale to tourists visiting the area. We therefore see us as both a sales business but also as an attraction in the area . . . We continue to develop our products to improve our competitiveness.
(Family-run producer/retailer of a luxury food product; open 11 months a year)

Capitulating

Shrinking, terminating or selling a family business in response to extreme seasonality can be called 'capitulating', but it might also stem from personal preferences or the absence of heirs. For example, the C. family business is very unusual in Bornholm, having been developed and expanded successfully from a farm base, and passed on to the third generation. However, the older married couple who own and operate this attraction are selling out and their children – who have already moved off-island – do not want to take over. It is seasonal, opening May–September. Resident demand is insufficient to warrant a longer season as staff and operating costs are quite high. They employ six permanent, all-year staff and 50 seasonal workers. Repairs, maintenance and improvements are made over the whole year, and the owners have always tried to add something new before each season. The business is neither big nor small enough to allow the owners the luxury of relinquishing all-year management. Would a longer season and higher profits make a difference? It is impossible to say.

In the following example, the owners are undecided about their business viability and its future. The H. family opened their own craft manufacturing and retail business on the island, following a period of paid employment by the husband at a (now) competing business. The premises are rented, and both capital and operating costs in this line of work are high. Unfortunately, the tourism season is very short, as their market is primarily that of longer-staying German visitors who come mostly in the warm, short summer. Competition is high and increasing, as Bornholm seems to attract many arts and crafts entrepreneurs. Almost all the businesses in their little seaside community are locally owned and have to close for a lengthy part of the year, and while some owners can afford to go away on vacations over the closed season the H. family do not generate sufficient revenue. The husband spends part of the winter off-island to earn additional income, and they both manufacture crafts for later sale. In the summer, students are employed in the shop. Their child is still at school and not employed. Although they love living in this area, increasingly they see that they might have to move away to earn a decent living.

Quite a few respondents were micro businesses with no option of staying open all year, and many were always intended to be secondary sources of income. Although some family business owners undoubtedly prefer to close for the season, because they are lifestyle oriented or place the family first, the evidence from Bornholm strongly suggests that most prefer otherwise. The majority of business owners surveyed and interviewed wanted a longer, more profitable tourism season, and many stayed open all year despite the severe downturn in tourism demand.

In terms of impacts on the family, this research revealed that strategies for 'coping with', or 'combating' extreme seasonality have profound implications for the owners and their families. Many family business owners were apparently successfully 'coping' by way of seasonal closure and alternative revenue generation, but in some cases business viability was at risk. Most respondents would prefer to expand the peak tourist season, as this would undoubtedly improve their financial positions a great deal.

One other possible consequence of extreme seasonality on the family business was revealed by the very low number of children involved in these businesses and by the high level of expectation that the businesses would not be passed on within the family. This deserves further study, as continuity in family businesses should have positive consequences for the community and the industry.

What remains are the following options, directly aimed at the small and family business sector:

- Focus on building demand in the shoulder seasons with the hope of generating sufficient revenues to sustain the business and the family.
- Develop niche markets that can keep some businesses open all year (i.e. residents, sport tourists, business travellers).
- Create export products.
- Generate counter-seasonal income from non-tourism ventures.

Chapter Summary

Owing to the widespread preference to keep the family business small and under control, yet profitable, owners face many challenges. This chapter started by discussing the notions of failure and success in the family-business context, noting that both should be viewed in the light of owners' goals and needs. It is readily observable that small businesses in tourism and hospitality frequently turn over their ownership or fail outright, but it is less certain if the family vision is responsible – failure can often be attributed to generic factors affecting all small businesses, and to the often-harsh business environment.

There are good reasons for growing a family business, including the additional revenues that come from increased business volumes and the enabling of increased family involvement in the business – including potential inheritors. Various barriers and preconditions for growth were discussed, starting with resource availability and encompassing the lack of related vision or goals.

Family-business owners are in need of strategic planning, even if they want to avoid growth. After presenting a basic strategic planning process for family firms, including the need for parallel family and business visions, this chapter outlined a number of generic strategies as well as options specific to the family enterprise. A number of unique advantages are held by the family business that can be exploited, such as the ability to take a longer-term perspective on return on investment, and the special resources families and their networks can bring to the business. Strategic marketing was then discussed, highlighting the need for most family businesses to develop profitable niche markets and to forge marketing partnerships. The pros and cons of family branding were noted.

The final portion of this chapter was devoted to an examination of strategic responses by family businesses in Denmark to extreme seasonality of demand. It was revealed that some owners merely coped with seasonality, including shutting down for part of the year, while others endeavoured to combat it through diversification of products and markets. This research identified a number of specific strategies that were working for family businesses in Bornholm.

References

Allcock, J. (1989) Seasonality. In: Witt, S. and Moutinho, L. (eds) *Tourism Marketing and Management Handbook*. Prentice Hall, London, pp. 387–392.

Astrachan, J. (1993) Preparing the next generation for wealth: a conversation with Howard H. Stevenson. *Family Business Review* 6(1), 75–83.

Ateljevic, I. and Doorne, S. (2000) Staying within the fence: lifestyle entrepreneurship in tourism. *Journal of Sustainable Tourism* 8(5), 378–392.

Barney, J. (1991) Firm resources and sustained competitive advantage. *Journal of Management* 17(1), 99–120.

BarOn, R. (1975) Seasonality in tourism: a guide to the analysis of seasonality and trends for policy making. Economist Intelligence Unit, Technical Series No. 2, London.

Baum, T. and Hagan, L. (1997) Responses to seasonality in tourism: the experience of peripheral destinations. Conference paper, International Tourism Research Conference on Peripheral Area Tourism. Research Centre of Bornholm, Denmark, pp. 8–12.

Baum, T. and Lundtorp, S. (eds) (2001) *Seasonality in Tourism*. Pergamon, Amsterdam.

Birley, S. and Cromie, S. (1988) Social networks and entreprenurship in Northern Ireland. Paper presented at the Enterprise in Action Conference, Belfast, UK.

Boer, A. (1998) An assessment of small business failure. In: Thomas, R. (ed.) *The Management of Small Tourism and Hospitality Firms*. Cassell, London, pp. 39–57.

Boger, C. and Buchanan, R. (1991) *A Study of Bed and Breakfast Facilities in Indiana*. Indiana University, The Indiana Extension Service, Indianapolis, Indiana.

Brown, B. (1987) Recent tourism research in South East Dorset. In: Shaw, G. and Williams, A. (eds) *Tourism and Development: Overviews and Case Studies of the UK and the South West Region*. Working Paper 4, Department of Geography, University of Exeter, UK.

Butler, R. (1994) Seasonality in tourism: issues and problems. In: Seaton, A., Jenkins, C., Wood, R., Dieke, P., Bennett, M. and MacLelian, L. (eds) *Tourism: the state and the art*. John Wiley & Sons, Chichester, UK. pp. 332–339.

Butler, R.W. (2001) Seasonality in tourism: issues and implications. In: Baum, T. and Lundtorp, S. (eds) *Seasonality in tourism*. Pergamon, Amsterdam, pp. 5–22.

Carlock, R. and Ward, J. (2001) *Strategic Planning for the Family Business*. Palgrave, Basingstoke, UK.

Chua, J., Chrisman, J. and Sharma, P. (1999) Defining the family business by behavior. *Entrepreneurship Theory and Practice* 23(4), 19–37.

Clarke, J. (1995) Sustainable tourism: marketing of farm tourist accommodation. PhD thesis, School of Hotel and Catering Management, Oxford Brookes University, UK.

Cooper, C., Fletcher, J., Gilbert, D. and Wanhill, S. (1993) *Tourism: Principles and Practice*. Pitman, London.

Coopers and Lybrand Consulting (1996) *Special report on off and shoulder season marketing.*

Canadian Tourism Commission, Ottawa, Canada.

Dailey, C. and Dollinger, M. (1992) An empirical examination of ownership structure in family and professionally managed firms. *Family Business Review* 5(2), 117–136.

Davis, J. (1996) Values and mission statements. In: *The Family Business Management Handbook*. From the editors of Family Business Magazine. Family Business Publishing Co, Philadelphia, Pennsylvania, pp. 20–23.

Dawson, C. and Brown, T. (1988) B&Bs: a matter of choice. *Cornell Hotel and Restaurant Administration Quarterly* 29(1), 17–21.

Dodd, S. (1997) Social network memberships and activity rates: some comparative data. *International Small Business Journal* 15(4), 80–87.

Donnelley, R. (1964) The family business. *Harvard Business Review* 42(2), 93–105.

Dunkelberg, W. (1995) Presidential address: Small business and the US. *Business Economics* 30, 13–18.

Dunn, B. (1995) Success themes in Scottish family enterprises: philosophies and practices through the generations. *Family Business Review* 8(1), 17–28.

Evans, N. and Ilbery, W. (1992) Advertising and farm-based accommodation: a British case study. *Tourism Management* 13 (4), 415–422.

Flognfeldt, T. (2001) Long-term positive adjustments to seasonality: consequences of summer tourism in the Jotunheimen area, Norway. In: Baum, T. and Lundtorp, S. (eds) *Seasonality in Tourism*. Pergamon, Amsterdam, pp. 109–117.

Friel, M. (1999) Marketing practice in small tourism and hospitality firms. *International Journal of Tourism Research* 1, 97–109.

Goffee, R. and Scase, R. (1985) *Women in Charge: the Experiences of Female Entrepreneurs*. George Allen and Unwin, London.

Gruidl, N., Cooper, R. and Silva, D. (1990) *Structure, Conduct, and Performance of the Bed and Breakfast Industry in Wisconsin*. Recreation Resource Center, University of Wisconsin- Extension.

Gyimothy, S. (2000) *The Quality of Visitor Experience: a Case Study in Peripheral Areas of Europe*. Research Centre of Bornholm, Report 17/2000, Bornholm, Denmark.

Hankinson, A. (1989) Small hotels in Britain: investment and survival. *The Cornell HRA Quarterly* 30(3), 80–82.

Hannan, M. and Freeman, J. (1977) The population ecology of organizations. *American Journal of Sociology* 82, 929–964.

Hannan, M. and Freeman, J. (1984) Structural inertia and organizational change. *American Sociological Review* 49(2), 149–164.

Hegarty, C. and Ruddy, J. (2002) The role of family in entrepreneurial development in Irish rural tourism. Paper presented at the conference: Re-Inventing the Destination, Dubrovnik, Croatia.

Herremans I. and Welsh, C. (1999) Developing and implementing a company's ecotourism mission statement. *Journal of Sustainable Tourism* 7(1), 48–76.

Jeffrey, D. and Barden, R. (2001) An analysis of the nature, causes and marketing implications of seasonality in the occupancy performance of English hotels. In: Baum, T. and Lundtorp, S. (eds) *Seasonality in Tourism*. Pergamon, Amsterdam, pp. 119–140.

Kennedy, E. and Deegan, J. (2001) Seasonality in Irish tourism, 1973–1995. In: Baum, T. and Lundtorp, S. (eds) *Seasonality in tourism*. Pergamon, Amsterdam, pp. 51–74.

Klenell, P. and Steen, M. (1999) I am in charge – small business problems and insolvency in Jamtland. Cited in: Public Support for Tourism SMEs in Peripheral Areas: the Arjeplog Project, Northern Sweden.

Leiper, N. (1997) *Tourism Management*. TAFE Publishing, Melbourne, Australia.

Littlejohn, D., Foley, M. and Lemmon, J. (1996) The potential of accommodation consortia in the Highlands and Islands of Scotland. Proceedings of the IAHMS Spring Symposium, Leeds Metropolitan University, Leeds, UK, pp. 55–66.

Litz, R. and Kleysen, R. (2002) Old men will dream dreams, your young men will see visions: a conceptualization of innovation in family firms. In: Chrisman, J., Holbrook, J. and Chua, J. (eds) *Innovation and Entrepreneurship in Western Canada: from Family Businesses to Multinationals*. University of Calgary Press: Calgary, Canada, pp. 269–298.

Lundtorp, S. (2001) Measuring tourism seasonality. In: Baum, T. and Lundtorp, S. (eds) *Seasonality in Tourism*. Pergamon, Amsterdam, pp. 23–48.

Lundtorp, S., Rassing, C. and Wanhill, S. (1999)The off-season is 'no season': the case of the Danish island of Bornholm. *Tourism Economics* 5(1), 49–68.

McCann, J., Leon-Guerrero, A. and Haley, J. (2001) Strategic goals and practices of innovative family businesses. *Journal of Small Business Management* 39(1), 50–59.

McEeniff, J. (1992) Seasonality of tourism demand in the European Community. *Economist Intelligence Unit, Travel and Tourism Analyst* No. 3, 67–88.

Miles, R. and Snow, C. (1978) *Organizational Strategy, Structure, and Process*. McGraw-Hill, New York.

Mintzberg, H. and Waters, J. (1990) Tracking strategy in an entrepreneurial firm. *Family Business Review* 3(3), 285–315.

Morrison, A. (1996) Small firm cooperative marketing in a peripheral tourism region. *International Journal of Contemporary Hospitality Management* 10(5), 191–197.

Morrison, A. (1998a) Small firm statistics: a hotel sector focus. *The Service Industries Journal* 18(1), 132–142.

Morrison, A. (ed.) (1998b) *Entrepreneurship: an International Perspective*. Butterworth-Heinemann, Oxford, UK.

Morrison, A. (2000a) Entrepreneurship: what triggers it? *International Journal of Entrepreneurial Behaviour and Research* 6(2), 59–71.

Morrison, A. (2000b) *Initiating Entrepreneurship in Enterprise and Small Business*. In: Carter, S. and Jones-Evans, D. (eds) Pearson Education, London, pp. 97–114.

Nilsson, P., Petersen, T. and Wanhill, S. (2004) Public support for tourism SMEs in peripheral areas: the Arjeplog project, Northern Sweden. *The Service Industries Journal* (in press).

Nonaka, I. (1994) A dynamic theory of organizational knowledge creation. *Organization Science* 5(1), 14–37.

Peiser, R. and Wooten, L. (1983) Life cycle changes in small family businesses. *Business Horizons* 26(3), 58–65.

Peters, M. and Weirmair, K. (2001) Theoretical constructs and empirical evidence of entrepreneurial growth modes in the hospitality industry. Paper presented at the conference Entrepreneurship on Tourism and the Contexts of Experience Economy, University of Lapland, Finland.

Pizam, A. and Upchurch, R. (2002) The training needs of small rural tourism operators in frontier regions. In: Krakover, S. and Gradus, Y. (eds) *Tourism in Frontier Areas*. Lexington Books, Lanham, Maryland, pp. 117–140.

Poon, A. (1993) *Tourism, Technology and Competitive Strategies*. CAB International, Wallingford, UK.

Porter, M. (1980) *Competitive Strategy*. The Free Press, New York.

Porter, M. (1985) *Competitive Advantage*. The Free Press, New York.

Poza, E. (1988) Managerial practices that support interpreneurship and continued growth. *Family Business Review* 1(4), 339–359.

Ram, M. (1994) Unravelling social networks in ethnic minority firms. *International Small Business Journal* 12(3), 42–53.

Rue, L. and Ibrahim, N. (1996) The status of planning in smaller family owned businesses. *Family Business Review* 9(1), 29–43.

Russell, B. (1996) Innovation in small Irish tourism businesses. In: Thomas, R. and Shacklock, R. (eds) *Spring Symposium Proceedings of International Association of Hotel Management Schools*. Leeds Metropolitan University, Leeds, UK, pp. 116–120.

Saker, J. (1992) cited in Ram, N. Network in small firms. *International Small Business Journal* 12(3), 42–53.

Santarelli, E. and Pesciarelli, E. (1990) The emergence of a vision: the development of Schumpeter's theory of entrepreneurship. *History of Political Economy* 22(4), 677–696.

Sharma, P., Chrisman, J. and Chua, J. (1996) *A Review and Annotated Bibliography of Family Business Studies*. Kluwer, Boston, Massachusetts.

Shaw, G. and Williams, A. (1987) Firm formation and operating characteristics in the Cornish tourist industry – the case of Looe. *Tourism Management* 8, 344–348.

Shaw, G. and Williams, A. (1990) Tourism, economic development, and the role of entrepreneurial activity. In: Cooper, C. (ed.) *Progress in Tourism, Recreation and Hospitality Management*, Vol. 2. Belhaven Press, London, pp. 67–81.

Shaw, G. and Williams, A. (eds) (1997) *The Rise and Fall of British Coastal Resorts: Cultural and Economic Perspectives*. Pinter, London.

Shaw, G. and Williams, A. (1998) Entrepreneurship, small business, culture and tourism development. In: Ioannides, D. and Debbage, K. (eds) *The Economic Geography of the Tourist Industry: a supply-side analysis*. Routledge, London, pp. 235–255.

Sherwood, A.-M., Parrott, N., Jenkins, T., Gillmor, D., Gaffey, S. and Cawley, M. (2000) Craft Producers on the Celtic Fringe: Marginal Lifestyles in Marginal Regions? paper presented at 15th International Society for the Study of Marginal Regions Seminar, Newfoundland, Canada.

Smyrnios, K., Romano, C. and Tanewski, G. (1997a) *The Australian Family and Private Business Survey*. Monash University, Melbourne, Australia.

Smyrnios, K., Romano, C. and Tanewski, G. (1997b) Distinguishing Factors of High- and Low-Growth family Firms. Working Paper Series, AXA Australia Family Business Research Unit, Monash University, Melbourne, Australia.

Storey, D. (1994) *Understanding the Small Business Sector*. Routledge, London.

Sundgaard, E., Rosenburg, L. and Johns, N. (1998) A typology of hotels as individual players: The case of Bornholm, Denmark. *International Journal of Contemporary Hospitality Management* 10(5), 180–183.

Tagiuri, R. and Davis, J. (1992) On the goals of successful family companies. *Family Business Review* 5(1), 263–281.

Taylor, S., Simpson, J. and Howie, H. (1998) Financing small businesses. In: Thomas, R. (ed.) *The Management of Small Tourism and Hospitality Firms*. Cassell, London, pp. 58–77.

Thomas, R. (ed.) (1998a) *The Management of Small Tourism and Hospitality Firms*, Cassell, London.

Thomas, R. (1998b) An introduction to the study of small tourism and hospitality firms. In: Thomas, R. (ed.) *The Management of Small Tourism and Hospitality Firms*. Cassell, London, pp. 1–17.

Thomas, R. (1998c) Small firms and the state. In: Thomas, R. (ed.) *The Management of Small Tourism and Hospitality Firms*. Cassell, London, pp. 78–98.

Thomas, R., Friel, M., Jameson, S. and Parsons, D. (1997) *The National Survey of Small Tourism and Hospitality Firms*, Annual Report 1996–97. Leeds: Centre for the Study of Small Tourism and Hospitality Firms, Leeds Metropolitan University, Leeds, UK.

Twining-Ward, L. and Baum, T. (1998) Dilemmas facing mature island destinations: Cases from the Baltic. *Progress in Tourism and Hospitality Research* 4, 131–140.

Upton, N., Teal, E. and Felan, J. (2001) Strategic and business planning practices of fast growth family firms. *Journal of Small Business Management* 39(1), 60–72.

Wanhill, S. (1980) Tackling seasonality: a technical note. *Tourism Management* 1(4), 243–245.

Ward, J. (1987) *Keeping the Family Business Healthy: How to Plan for Continuing Growth, Profitability, and Family Leadership*. Josey-Bass, San Francisco, California.

Yacoumis, J. (1980) Tackling seasonality: the case of Sri Lanka. *Tourism Management* 1(2), 84–98.

5

Balancing Family and Business through the Life Cycle

Introduction

Numerous challenges and issues face the family business, and finding the right balance between family and business throughout the life cycle is critical for success. This chapter examines key challenges and issues together with strategies and actions that are actually employed, or are recommended by experts, to achieve a healthy balance. It starts with a discussion of generic challenges and issues for family business, plus some that are specific to tourism and hospitality. Different stages of the life cycle are addressed, including the sole proprietor, copreneurial arrangements, the young business family with children, and family working together. There are special sections on the family and the environment, and gender issues. Some research findings are presented to demonstrate real concerns from respondents in Australia, Canada and Denmark.

Later in this chapter attention is focused on issues relating to involvement of children in the business, leading to a detailed look at inheritance and succession planning. The concept of a family 'legacy' is discussed in this context.

Generic Challenges and Issues

A study of family businesses in the UK by Birley et al. (1999) found three distinct attitudinal clusters related to the balancing of family and business:

- The 'Family Rules Group' wanted children to be involved in the business at an early age, and believed successors should be chosen from the family.
- The 'Family Out Group' held opposite attitudes towards family involvement.
- The 'Family-Business Jugglers' did not have strong views but were seeking a balance between family and business issues.

In part, this threefold typology reflects different values and visions for the business. Some owners simply do not want, or feel it important, to involve children. For many others it is irrelevant because there are no available children. However it must also be asked if those owners who do not formally involve any other family members in ownership or management can still remain free of family influences on the business.

Carlock and Ward (2001) specifically discussed the generic problems of balancing family needs and wants with business requirements and opportunities. They identified five pivotal variables requiring plans and policies: control, careers, capital, conflict and culture.

Control

In many family businesses a single founder/owner makes all the decisions, which is neat and simple. Add one person to the equation, either a spouse or child, and complications set in. How will families working and living together make decisions to control the business? One idea is the family council, discussed later.

Careers

Are both partners in the copreneurial firm equal in their responsibilities and rewards? Do children or other family members get involved on a casual basis, or develop careers within the business? Appointment, advancement and rewards should ideally be based on accomplishments, but in some families they tend to be viewed as rights.

Capital

Although many families struggle to eke out a living from their businesses, others prosper. Every family business has to face the trade-offs between reinvesting income in the business or 'harvesting' it for family use, and ultimately that of inheritance or selling the business. Will all family members benefit equally? Money issues can easily lead to conflict.

Conflict

Procedures are needed to identify potential sources of conflict and to deal with them. Because friction is a fact of family business life, there is no advantage in hiding conflicts nor in putting off their resolution.

Culture

A number of authors have observed the importance of family culture. For example, Carlock and Ward (2001) described 'collaborative' families that work together, while 'conflicted' families find it difficult to get along. Dyer (1988) identified four types of family business culture. 'Paternalistic' families were hierarchical with power in the hands of leaders who are usually the founders. The *laissez-faire* culture is also hierarchical, but while family members are given preferential treatment, employees are given scope to implement the family vision. In 'participative' families, which are relatively rare according to Dyer, the family's status is de-emphasized in favour of group decision-making inclusive of employees. The fourth culture was termed 'professional' and denotes the turning over of management to non-family professionals. Dyer said that paternalistic owners often fail to prepare their successors for leadership.

The style of founders who keep all information and make all important decisions can be thought of as 'paternalism', while Dean (1992) and Tsang (2002) talked about 'autocracy' as a common leadership style associated with the founder. The founding values tend to endure, but might eventually be challenged and replaced by successors. Peiser and Wooten (1983) referred to this as the 'life cycle crisis' which is precipitated when goals of the founding generation and those of the second generation conflict.

Family values can be the foundation of plans and actions, even if they are not articulated. In strategic planning, however, there is the opportunity to state the values, principles and vision that drive the family and its business.

Seasonality and other cycles

This is an issue of particular importance to business families in the tourism and hospitality industry. As detailed in the preceding chapter, extreme cyclical demand poses a potentially fatal threat to the business and has profound implications for the owners and their families. Many families simply cope with the problem by shutting down for part of the year or treating the business as part-time and/or secondary to other economic activities. Those that elect to combat seasonality employ a variety of strategies that are more entrepreneurial and often innovative, including diversification of products and markets – even getting into the export market.

To many families the off-peak periods of the business year are welcomed, and even necessary, for maintaining their mental and physical well-being. McGibbon (2000), writing about a resort community in Austria, observed that work routines are less intense in the summer than in the peak skiing season, for both genders. Mothers enjoyed more time with their children, and whole families could spend more time together. As noted by Twining-Ward and Twining-Ward (1996), destinations and residents might benefit from low-demand seasons in several ways:

- residents might need and welcome a period of rest;
- environmental pressures are reduced, and recuperation is possible in damaged environments;
- infrastructure can be repaired or improved; and

- traditional social and cultural activities can be resumed.

Whole communities have to make the seasonal adjustments. Those that become all-year destinations gain in economic terms, but suffer from the expansion of other problems.

It might be a useful line of research to compare all-season resort communities and rural/peripheral areas with extreme seasonality on various economic and socio-cultural impact measures, with family issues clearly in focus. Presumably many families in business are equally pressured by weekday–weekend fluctuations in demand.

Family business and home life

Numerous families operating tourism and hospitality businesses share their home space with customers, and this impacts substantially on their work and family life. As well, high-contact services are provided by many family businesses, regardless of location. Consequently, host–guest relations have been identified as an important issue in the tourism and hospitality literature.

Lynch and MacWhannell (2000) have examined the relationships between 'home and commercialized hospitality'. They identified three types of home accommodation, namely: (i) within the family home and sharing public spaces (such as B&B establishments); (ii) the owner lives on the premises but in separate quarters (as in many hotels); and (iii) the owner provides self-catering rentals in accommodation sometimes used as a second home. One could easily extend that typology to cover the many owners who provide completely separate accommodation units but are directly involved in their operation and maintenance and therefore contact guests regularly.

Several themes in the literature were identified by Lynch and MacWhannell (2000), including a feminist perspective on 'women's work', female entrepreneurship, social relationships, and the home as 'refuge'. Those authors (p. 111) suggested that researchers '. . . might wish to rethink traditional business strategy concepts when analysing and devising policies for small accommodation enterprises in order to reflect the importance of home and its influence on business strategies.'

Family business owners, especially women (see the gender section, following), have frequently complained to researchers of long hours, minimal financial rewards, and disruptions to family and community life. Stringer (1981), based on a study of B&B establishments, observed that the relationship between hosts and guests extended beyond remuneration and included social elements. The ability to preserve privacy is a major issue when the home environment is offered to visitors (Stringer, 1981).

McGibbon (2000) found that women running guest houses in St Anton, Austria, had little free time and worked long hours in the peak winter tourism season, leading to sleep deprivation. They also suffered from a lack of private space, as guests failed to respect 'private' designations.

Kousis (1989) studied tourism development in rural Crete, revealing growth in family tourism businesses by spouses, with children and parents helping out. Social activities of families were affected, and parents helped newly-weds to set up businesses. Females ran most of these family tourism businesses, with men working elsewhere.

The Western Australian research by Getz and Carlsen (2000) documented areas of satisfaction and difficulty among rural family business owners. The positive features stemmed from working together as a couple or family, pride in the business, pleasing customers, and independence. Major perceived difficulties included time pressures (e.g. lack of free time or time with partners), balancing family and work life, and the need to find space away from customers.

A study by Mendonsa (1983) of family tourism businesses in Portugal concluded that running tourism businesses put considerable strain on families, and especially on the women who did most of the work. Mendonsa (1983: 235) found that 'families have consciously altered their patterns of behaviour in order to cope with and benefit from tourism.'

The family life cycle

Many of the balancing challenges and issues are specific to stages in the family life cycle, including the unique situation facing sole proprietors who might or might not involve family members or consider family implications. Although mentioned here, the crucial issue of involving potential heirs and the succession process is dealt with later in this chapter.

The sole proprietor

The sole proprietor might be a founder without family, or an entrepreneur who keeps family and business as separate as possible. Nevertheless, many do involve family members informally and others will eventually have to face the fact that their business and family affairs are overlapping. Hegarty and Ruddy (2002: 16) observed in Ireland that 'Entrepreneurs operating their enterprise single-handedly tend to rely on family support at a secondary support level through employment'. Sometimes, working for the owner was considered to be a favour or an obligation.

Copreneurs

Numerous married couples operate businesses together without the involvement of children. Hegarty and Ruddy (2000: 16) found that 36% of their Irish sample were spouses or couples working as partners, with one not being subservient to the other. Baines and Wheelock (1998) reported that in half of their sample of microbusinesses, both husbands and wives, were highly involved and that distinct gender roles were observable. Women tended to provide formal administration, marketing and secretarial services and men offered technical support. As evidenced from the literature cited, and the case studies contained in this book, gender roles can evolve naturally from roles performed before the business, or can be a function of who starts the business and its nature.

Couples might be in the pre-family stage, 'empty-nesters' engaging in a career switch to fulfil a life-long ambition, or older adults in the retirement or pre-retirement stage of life. A special case encountered by the authors is the homosexual couple running a business. These arrangements are more widespread and numerous than might be thought, mainly because the literature has ignored this phenomenon. Indeed, many researchers would not even consider single-sex couples to be a family, yet increasingly they are gaining family-equivalent legal status and many do have children.

For couples, the principle challenges are to find ways to work together as partners, and this might be the very attraction of establishing the business. It can be difficult to escape stereotypical gender roles in copreneurial businesses, particularly because the tourism and hospitality industry is full of so-called 'women's work'. In the Western Australian sample (Getz and Carlsen, 2000), a goal was for couples to be working harmoniously together. Finding equal-value tasks for husbands and wives was also a major consideration.

The young business family

When children are young the founder or couple running a business have special challenges. McGibbon (2000: 171) noted that 'Running a business at home is particularly stressful when children are young, which often coincides with when couples are building up their business.' Unique problems facing the accommodation provider might include children being displaced from bedrooms in order to accommodate paying guests, an inability to keep guests and children physically apart, and exposure of children to unruly guest behaviour. In many hospitality situations children will be exposed to guests' drinking and partying.

Marriages will be strained when women have a disproportionate share of the burdens of managing both family and business. Making joint decisions about the balancing of work and family life is therefore a necessity. Sometimes working out relationships with the extended family will become an issue, especially where more than one generation lives together. The presence of grandparents can, for example, provide essential baby-sitting or cause additional stress.

Family working together

Massachusetts Mutual Life Assurance (1993) found that in 81% of family businesses in the USA some family member(s) worked on a day-to-day basis, with spouses and sons most often involved. Working with family members poses a number of challenges, typically related to couples sharing the responsibilities and parents working with children. As noted by Cromie *et al.* (2001), family members are simultaneously members of a family system with relationships based on affection and other family bonds, and a work system organized on the basis of 'threat and exchange'. This can cause role conflicts, and they cannot be 'left behind at the office'.

Children growing up within a family business environment might be exposed to guests and the services provided by their parents at a very early age. Our case studies show that in some families it is considered normal and appropriate that very young children have the run of the establishment, meet and even entertain guests, and do odd jobs suitable to their ages. If the children are interested they might eventually receive remuneration for their contributions, but the parents we interviewed were very concerned about the differences between casual (helping out) and formal (paid) involvement.

Strategies for balancing family and business

A number of strategies or actions are suggested in the literature and in our case studies for balancing family and business life.

Boundaries

For many families in tourism and hospitality businesses it is difficult (some feel it is impossible) to separate work and family life. Yet boundaries might have to be established to sustain a healthy family–businesses balance. The literature and case studies suggest some options:

- **Fences**. The old adage that good fences make good neighbours probably also applies to hosts and guests. Physically separating home from the visitors' environment will at least discourage over-familiarity and possibly result in a psychological differentiation as well. If home is not a refuge from one's guests, it will cease to be comfortable.
- **Locks on the door**. B&B operators, and others who share their living space with paying guests, have to lock out their guests from private quarters. Signs have to be posted saying 'private', or intrusions will

occur. This imposes a serious obligation, however, because someone always has to be on call for emergencies. Will guests know where to turn for help?

- **Employees**. Hands-on owners enjoy their craft, but frequently need relief that only paid staff can provide. It is both a matter of money (can we afford employees?) and trust. Family business owners trust other family members the most. Small hotel owners in England were found to employ a minimum of paid staff from outside their immediate family, and as a result family members at most operations reported very long working hours – at least 50 hours a week (Hankinson, 1989).

A common worry about family firms is that family members not only receive preferential treatment, but that each family member can act like a boss over staff. However, Cromie *et al.* (2001) surveyed family firms in the Scottish Highlands and Islands and found that, contrary to the literature, roles were generally allocated clearly to family members and to staff, thereby minimizing disagreements.

Dunn (1995) reported that many family business owners not only felt a strong sense of responsibility for their families but also for their employees and their families. This community-minded spirit might be expected to be particularly important in rural or small-town areas where families are deeply rooted and everyone knows everyone.

Time management

Certain times of the day, week and year have to be reserved for privacy and family affairs. There will always be the temptation to keep working, always to be on call, or never to delegate responsibilities, yet private time has to be found. Employees hired to free up time might in fact become a burden if they require training and supervision. Technology should be used to save time, but learning how to use it is often very time consuming.

Attitude

A business owner can be both professional and friendly and at the same time communicate to customers the need to preserve private time and personal space. This is a skill that presumably can be learned, but is also a reflection of personality.

Formal mechanisms

Carlock and Ward (2001) describe the Family Enterprise Continuity Plan, and it has been described in the strategic planning section. Family meetings are suitable for small families, while formal Family Councils might be required for larger enterprises or where more than one family branch is involved. Conflict–resolution measures might be needed, including the role of an external arbitrator. Family businesses with boards of directors might have this function built into the board's responsibilities. In other words, directors will be trusted to help resolve family disputes.

Formal Family Agreements are another tool. They establish principles, rules and procedures based on family consensus, and can thereby carry the weight of a constitution. Ideally they are understood and adhered to by all family members. Changes are made only after due deliberation and input from all the stakeholders. A specific example is the rules governing family employment, remuneration, advancement and ownership. This is only likely to become controversial when more than one child is involved, and could be an issue when many family members are potentially employable in the business.

A code of conduct might be desirable, either within or separate from the family agreement. What are the expectations for behaviour, both among family members and between the family and customers or other stakeholders? The code is a good tool for fostering a positive working environment, a strong customer orientation, and avoiding many potential conflicts.

Family business and the environment

Another balancing act occurs between the family business and the environment. This issue of environmental responsibility could also be considered under the heading of family culture, or strategic planning: do family businesses make better stewards of natural resources and the environment because they are owned and operated by families?

Carlsen et al. (2001) examined data from a survey of Western Australian family businesses from the perspective of sustainable tourism. The basic premise to be tested was that families and owner-operators would be inclined to protect the resource base upon which their (rural) businesses were founded; some support was found for that hypothesis. Researchers in Spain (Garcia-Ramon et al., 1995) concluded that women in farm tourism businesses developed new attitudes in support of preserving the physical and cultural landscape. On the other hand, McKercher's (1998) evaluation of nature tour operators in Australia, all of whom were owner-operators or family businesses, revealed a disturbing practice. Some of these small businesses willingly accepted fines for disobeying park regulations on visitor numbers in order to profit from higher volumes of customers.

Lynch (1996: 233) argued that 'B&B establishments fit squarely into the concept of sustainable tourism.' They preserve old buildings, may help improve the housing stock and have low environmental impact. Genuine host–guest interaction is facilitated, and they are very flexible forms of accommodation. This logic should extend to almost all small, family-owned accommodations.

Twining-Ward and Baum (1998) observed high degrees of local ownership of tourism and hospitality businesses on three Baltic Sea islands and concluded that this was advantageous in reducing leakages. They argued that local ownership also gives the islands more control over cultural and environmental protection. While not specifically addressed by those authors, it is clear that local ownership and control stems from owner-operator and family businesses.

Herreman and Welsh (1999) prepared a case study of a family-operated ecotourism business in which the founders' values and goals led to a high degree of environmental sustainability. The family in question has ties to the area in Alberta, Canada extending back five generations. Other evidence concerning the importance of personal or family values has been provided by Ateljevic and Doorne (2000) based on research in New Zealand. They concluded that some entrepreneurs, whom they call 'lifestyle entrepreneurs', consciously limit the scale and scope of their businesses in order to balance economic performance and sustainability in sociocultural and environmental terms. In particular, they want to be close to nature (e.g. cave rafting) and involved in community life. To survive requires capturing a viable niche market, and re-conceptualization of 'success' to encompass non-economic measures. The researchers also observed that while innovators were lifestyle-oriented, later imitators were more focused on profit maximization.

Gender Challenges and Issues

Several books and a special issue of the journal *Annals of Tourism Research* have been devoted to 'gender issues' in tourism. Major themes include the predominance of females in certain occupations and enterprises, motives of women establishing a business, costs and benefits, impacts on the family, barriers to female entrepreneurship and a feminist perspective on power, exploitation and development.

Many researchers have noted the preponderance of women operating small tourism and hospitality businesses, typically accommodation, and the evidence comes from many countries and regions (e.g. Walton, 1978; Stringer, 1981; Whatmore, 1991; Cukier *et al.*, 1996; Lynch, 1996). For example, Armstrong (1978) determined that the B&B accommodation sector in the Scottish Highlands was primarily associated with women because of the supposed domestic nature of the service. Armstrong also noted that these women had difficulty being heard in the public domain and so had to establish their own voluntary organization in order to lobby.

Danes (1998) concluded that farm tourism, as well as off-farm work, can be motivated by women's desire for increased status. Quinn *et al.* (1992), studying female entrepreneurs in hospitality in Northern Ireland, determined that self-employment offered a better choice for wives and mothers, perhaps related to frustration with a previous job, but for many the business was a realization of a lifelong ambition.

A detailed study of family-operated hotels and pensions in St Anton, Austria by McGibbon (2000) found most to be run by women, while the men of the household sought employment outside the home in tourism (e.g. ski instructors or mountain guides), other sectors, or even other

family-owned business (such as retail or taxi services). For these business-women, the distinctions between public and private space, employment and housework, work and leisure were unclear. The Baurenhof figures prominently in this environment, being the large combined home and commercial accommodation that supports the extended family and is intended to be passed down through the generations.

Values underlying this system are deeply rooted in the Tyrolean culture. In addition to the long hours of hard work and interference with motherhood and family duties, the female accommodation-operators of St Anton sometimes faced a more serious problem. According to McGibbon (2000), husbands tend to ignore the daily operation of the hotels and pensions, but do insist on controlling the finances and holding ownership. Many women who operate these businesses are legally considered to be employees. Over time, however, young people in St Anton are deciding not to take over such businesses but to pursue education or employment elsewhere.

Jennings and Stehlik (1999) interviewed women involved in farm tourism in Queensland, Australia, and determined they all wanted to earn extra income for families under financial stress. As well, some enjoyed the work and especially the resultant socializing, while others reported feeling more worthwhile. A number of problems or challenges were also generated. These often stemmed from the increased workload, including interference with farm work and family time. They also reported a loss of privacy and the intrusion of other priorities into their lifestyle. Female entrepreneurs were not always supported by their partners, giving rise to potential stress or conflict. As well, some of them needed information or training with regard to their new business ventures.

Researchers have written about female entrepreneurs in farm-based tourism in Spain (Garcia-Ramon *et al.*, 1995; Caballe, 1999; Velasco, 1999). The studies revealed that all such businesses were initiated and operated by women who tended to be married, with children at home. Some were residents trying to supplement farm incomes and some were in-migrants from cities who prefer to live in the country and have taken up farm-tourism as their primary source of income. Many Spanish women in these entrepreneurial positions had limited job opportunities and often poor accessibility, so they preferred working at home where flexibility was permitted.

Several family-related issues were observed, including potential opposition to the business, the need to consult with husbands on all economic decisions, and the delegation of certain tasks to other family members. Husbands, mothers and children contributed in various ways, although it was the women who started and took responsibility for the tourism enterprise. Perception of increased economic independence and self esteem were recorded. Caballe (1999) concluded that gender roles were modified and that women can take on new economic and social roles through involvement in farm-tourism.

Velasco's research on ten women entrepreneurs in Andalusia, Spain (1999), found that farm-tourism businesses were initiated to earn extra money and to refurbish the home. The sample were all married or in relationships, with children. Most (six out of ten) did not participate in farm activities, and their characteristics and behaviour were thought to be unorthodox in cultural terms. Rural tourism took place mostly on the weekends, and seasonality also greatly affected their lives. Despite hard work, and resentment at being tied to the farmhouse while other family members enjoyed leisure time, respondents were usually quite positive about their work and displayed a high level of satisfaction.

Long and Kindon (1997) assessed Balinese village tourism and found that all but one of the 25 homestay establishments they surveyed were owned by resident couples. Half were staffed by family members alone, seven by hired labour, and three by a combination, but women in the household did the hospitality work even though males and females co-managed the businesses. Males were mostly employed elsewhere. Generally, tourism did not alter existing gender-related social and family patterns.

Scott (1996) studied a number of family accommodation businesses in northern Cyprus, a culture in which there was no tradition of female entrepreneurship. She found that the accommodation places families operated were separate from their personal homes, and that pluriactivity (multiple employment) was common. Only a few women actively managed

the establishments, and males and females tended to hold other jobs.

Breathnach et al. (1994) sampled female B&B operators in Ireland whose greatest dislikes were long hours and being tied down by the job. Meeting people was a benefit, and the work suited their lifestyle. Leontidou (1994) examined the impacts of seasonality on Greek women in business, many of whom had to dismantle their homes seasonally in order to let them out to tourists. Dernoi's (1991) study of farm tourism in Austria revealed that 81% of the women involved in tourism also had to participate in farm work, and almost all of them had housework.

Walker et al. (2001) determined that trekking in Nepal resulted in numerous lodges and teashops being created, with women managing a majority and owning some of them, but females do not have control over family income, so they are limited in starting a business independently. Out-migration of males had created a niche for women to fill, plus capital could sometimes be obtained from men who had migrated for their families to start the business. One consequence is that women's status has improved in both the family and the community. Another benefit is that women were freed from farm work and felt an increase in free time, especially in low demand periods.

Much of the gender-specific research has focused on small-scale accommodation establishments where women are the predominant entrepreneurs. In these businesses sometimes only the females of families participate, because in many cultures hospitality is perceived to be an extension of housework (i.e. so-called 'women's work'). There is ample evidence to conclude that these female entrepreneurs have different issues to face, but on the matter of motives and goals it is not clear that they differ from males. On this point, the Western Australia (Getz and Carlsen, 2000) survey found no significant differences between males and females in their motives for start-up, growth and ultimate disposition of the business. However, that research included mostly copreneurial couples, so it is possible that women working alone to establish or operate a business will have different goals.

While it is helpful to look at female-specific issues, especially in the context of fostering entrepreneurship and potential benefits for development in general, family business studies are more about family relationships. Consequently, more research has to be devoted to couples as business partners, and to issues facing sons and daughters within family businesses.

Research Evidence from Western Australia

Results of this research by Getz and Carlsen (2000) shed light on a number of family-related issues. The methodology and other results have been presented elsewhere in this book.

Family-related goals

Respondents were asked, 'How important were the following family-related goals for you?', using a five-point scale from not at all important to very important. The most important family goal was the sharing of key decisions, which 82% of respondents (the majority of whom are co-owning spouses) indicated was somewhat important or very important (mean = 4.34). This relates closely to the goal of preventing disharmony among family members (73% rated it as somewhat or highly important; mean = 3.86). Earning enough money to support the family was rated fairly highly, as 68% rated it as somewhat or very important (3.86).

Least important was 'elevating our family position in society' (mean = 1.18), although a small percentage did find it important. Creating employment for family members and training children for future ownership of the business were also of minor importance overall. The largest neutral or uncertain response was for the goal 'ensure the family has lots of free time together'. It was somewhat or very important to only half the respondents, so either a lot of respondents were uncertain whether they were going to be able to have a lot of free time together, or it was not a major concern. To some extent time spent working together might obviate the need or desire for families to spend leisure time together, and a complete break from the family unit might be more appropriate for some of the respondents.

Respondents were also asked to include other important family-related goals for the business. A total of 62 were listed, from which several groupings seem to be important. The largest (14 mentions) was related to the enjoyment of working together or allowing time to enjoy the family. Eleven pertained to having children growing up working in the business. Sharing the financial reward with family was mentioned by eight respondents, as was having work that suited one's lifestyle. Another seven specified the ability to shape children's education.

Satisfaction and problems

A great deal of insight into the nature of the business can be gained by examining what aspects of the business generated the greatest satisfaction or difficulties. Responses on satisfaction can be grouped into three main themes: working as a family (time spent working together and team work); pride in the business (of ownership, developing the business and satisfying customers); and independence, or making one's own decisions.

Expressed difficulties of family businesses can also be grouped into several themes. The most important are time-related: the number of hours worked; lack of free time, and time lost with partners. Related to this problem is the difficulty in balancing work and family life, and the need to find space away from customers. Another theme is that of internal family conflicts, specifically over goals and agreement on solving problems, plus the issue of finding equal worth within the family business or within the family in general. Specific business problems were also a theme, including doing the administrative and financial tasks, marketing and promotion, and providing good service at all times.

Nature of the business

Two important elements relating to the nature of tourism businesses were examined. Seasonality of demand is a typical rural tourism problem, and in this sample 61% agreed or strongly agreed that their business was highly seasonal. Another 17% were uncertain, which possibly reflects the newness of many of these businesses. The main problems presented by seasonality relate to cash flow and overall profitability, but it does offer families a lull during which pursuit of family and lifestyle goals can dominate.

Close contact with customers is central to small hospitality and tour companies, and is almost inescapable in B&B operations. Sometimes this causes trouble for owners, resulting in stress and a desire to separate themselves from their guests, whilst others crave meeting new people and engaging them in conversation. Of this sample, 37.5% disagreed or strongly disagreed that 'In this business customers cannot be separated from personal life' (mean = 2.97), while 36% agreed or strongly agreed. This mixed result could indicate real differences in business or merely of perception. It can be interpreted better by looking at responses to the statement 'I come into daily contact with customers', to which fully 80% agreed or strongly agreed (mean = 3.92).

Involving the Next Generation and Succession

It seems ironic that the core of family business literature concerns the succession issue (Sharma et al., 1996) when, in fact, so few businesses are inherited (Ward, 1987; Westhead and Cowling, 1998). Beckhard and Dyer (1983) said that 90% of all businesses in the USA are family businesses, and research shows only 30% survive past the first generation. In Sweden, only 15% of businesses are expected to be inherited, while in Germany the figure is 37% (Bjuggren and Sund, 2001). For the UK, Handler (1994) and Stoy Hayward Consulting (1999) claimed that only 24% of family businesses transfer to the second generation and 14% reach the third.

What are the reasons for this low level of inheritance? There is a large body of literature on the succession process, and generic barriers to inheritance have been identified. However, it is probable that barriers vary in nature or importance by industry, type of business and the business environment. In tourism and hospitality a number of unique business opportunities exist and peculiar environmental forces make it both attractive to family businesses yet difficult for success and inheritance.

Inheritance is not necessarily a good or bad thing. It might be expected in some cultures that land and business assets are to be passed on to the next generation, while in others the emphasis will be placed on enabling children to pursue their own interests. Inheritance can enable families to build a strong company over time, but also might result in stagnation if no changes are made, or in intra-family conflict regarding ownership and wealth. The low level of succession within family businesses is important for a number of reasons. First, it is uncertain if this fact reflects a failure on the part of owners, or is not important to parents or children, or even that parents do not want children involved. If it is a failure, reasons must be identified and strategies put in place by the owners to combat barriers.

The legacy

'Legacy' means that which is bequeathed in a will, typically real property or money, but it can also refer to something more intangible, such as a 'family legacy' of values, or of knowledge and contacts that can assist subsequent generations in running the business. Many people focus on the legacy of land, and those with close ties to the land – such as farmers – often have a strong desire to ensure it is inherited.

The number of family businesses that get inherited is most likely on the decline in developed nations. For example, evidence from Ireland (Hegarty and Ruddy, 2002) suggests that family take-overs are rare, with rural tourism and hospitality businesses started by women who marry and then migrate, or owners following lifestyle and locational preferences. Another likely reason is that young people in many countries are better educated than ever before, and have more choices available to them. Also, most family businesses are not started out of necessity, but out of choice. People are less tied to the land or their home community than ever before, and mobility for education, work and pleasure continues to increase.

Yet in certain families, the idea of building a 'legacy' or of continuing the family business tradition remains strong. Why is that? Carlock and Ward (2001: 19) reported on a survey of 75 family-business owners and spouses who were specifically working to ensure family perpetuation of their businesses. These people believed that ownership benefits the family, and might keep it together. Their children could enjoy the same opportunity for wealth, freedom and growth that they experienced. Inheritance would also perpetuate the family's tradition and business heritage.

The business owners' pride appears to be important, although pride is not something everyone will admit to. Assuming the business is a success and wealth has been created, the owners can certainly be forgiven for feeling that this accomplishment should not be lost or squandered away. This might explain some aspect of the desire for children to take over the business, and might lead to problems when the parents expect more than the children wish to give. Obligation might motivate some children to assume the family business. It can be a negative thing, as where parents drill their children to feel obligated, or a positive thing arising from a belief that other family members are dependent on them.

A related concept, or ideal, is that of 'stewardship'. Carlock and Ward (2001: 145) described this philosophy as the values and vision that each generation should pass on the business in a healthier and more valuable condition. Thus, owners become stewards who think about all subsequent generations. For example, the family council would explicitly consider the impact of decisions not only on short-term business performance but on the assets (tangible and intangible) available for all future generations. This is akin to the goal of ensuring 'inter-generational equity' that underlies 'sustainable development', and it encourages very long-term thinking.

In Christian doctrine, individuals are encouraged to be 'good stewards' of the earth. In the case of farmland and other rural holdings, children might very well grow up with a strong attachment to the land, or to nature in general. This can motivate them in later life to protect and sustain the resources. The notion that family businesses might be more environmentally conscious is explored elsewhere.

Is the desire for creating or perpetuating a family legacy based on race, ethnicity or culture? Will it become increasingly rare in a globalized economy? Can it be fostered through education or indoctrination by parents? These questions have not been adequately addressed by researchers.

Barriers to Inheritance

A number of generic barriers to inheritance are discussed in this section, with industry-specific research evidence following.

Absence of heirs

Inheritance presupposes potential heirs within the family, but sometimes they do not exist or cannot be considered. In cases where there are no children owners can look for heirs in their wider family, but many will simply not even consider the possibility of succession.

What has not been addressed in the literature is the question of whether or not certain types of business or business environments facilitate a greater or lesser degree of family involvement and potential inheritance.

Life-stage factors

The absence of viable heirs might relate to life-stage factors. Demographics play a part in determining the probability and nature of inheritance or joining a family firm. Davis (1968) considered life-stage and succession, noting that sons aged between 17 and 25 preferred to break away from family businesses in order to create their own identity. Davis and Tagiuri (1989) suggested that children in their 20s strive for independence and success in the professional world, while fathers in their 40s may be confronting mid-life anxieties and doubts about their achievements, leading to intergenerational conflicts.

Through examination of student intentions, Birley (1986) found that older students had a higher interest in joining their family firm. Firm size did not affect intentions, nor did gender or birth order. Cory (1990) believed that offspring made up their minds about joining the family business by the time they reached teenage years.

Ward (1987) identified the ideal transition period for a family firm, namely the time when parents are in their 50s and children are 27–33 years of age. However, it is quite possible that the children have already made major commitments by the time they turn 27, thereby precluding (re)involvement in the parents' business.

Many businesses are created by older entre-preneurs, perhaps as a second career or even with retirement in mind. In these cases there might never be an opportunity for children to get involved, or the potential heirs might already be committed to other careers and locations.

The dream dies

Lansberg (1999) highlighted the importance of a 'shared dream' in shaping succession within family businesses. This dream is a '. . . collective vision of the future that inspires family members to engage in the hard work of planning and to do whatever is necessary to maintain their collaboration and achieve their goals' (p. 75). While the 'dream' is clearly a powerful force in leading to inheritance, it is not a given constant in all family businesses.

Attention has also been paid to the 'next generation's perspective', such as A. Patrick's (unpublished, The Fielding Institute, 1985) study of children's satisfaction and working relation-ships with their owner-fathers. Blotnick (1984) concluded that there is high resistance on the part of children to being in the parent's business. Handler (1994: 141) argued that 'positive suc-cession experiences' for children flow from ful-filment of three needs (career interests, psycho-logical needs and life-stage needs) and from relational influences (between generations and siblings, commitment to family business perpetu-ation, and separation strains owing to family involvement).

An international survey of university students by Stavrou and Winslow (1996) dis-covered that they had a low degree of willingness to participate in their family firms, and most wanted to start their own. Males were more will-ing to consider the option of joining the family business than were females. Stavrou (1999) later surveyed 153 college students in the USA con-cerning voluntary intentions of joining the family firm. The majority had no intention to join (except among Asian respondents), and the main reasons were as follows: preference for other opportunities; desire to create their own business; need to discover their interests or prove their capabilities; pursue education; and develop their own identity. It is noteworthy that these reasons are based on preferences.

Founders' reluctance to let go or to plan for succession

Davis and Harveston (1998) conducted a large-scale study of succession planning processes among family businesses, especially the influence of the family on the process across generations. Some potential barriers to succession were identified, including:

• Conflicts arise when family and business roles have not been clearly defined.
• Generational envy.
• Family politics spill over into business, resulting in conflicts that impede sound business decisions.

They suggested that owners wanting a smooth succession should employ more close family members in positions of responsibility, as they become the main voice of the family. The corollary might be that owners operating the business without family involvement at a high level will find it more difficult to pass on the enterprise.

In a major review of the literature on succession, Handler (1994) examined different research approaches and theoretical perspec-tives on the succession process and concluded: 'The ongoing health of the firm, quality of life, and family dynamics are critical to the success of the succession process.' (p. 134). The role of the founder, and underlying psychological factors, is also critical to the process. Founders might be reluctant to let go of power or to prepare potential successors and heirs adequately (Lansberg, 1999).

Handler and Kram (1988) presented a model of resistance to succession in family businesses, juxtaposing 'factors promoting resistance' with 'factors reducing resistance'. At its core is 'succession planning', and pertinent resistance factors were categorized as following:

• individual level (owners and children);
• interpersonal group level (trust, communi-cation, power);
• organizational level (culture, stability, structures); and
• environmental level (influences on the business).

Heirs 'actively and capably involved in the business', and 'one child as potential heir' were identified as factors reducing resistance.

Negative perceptions of the business or the work environment

Alcorn (1982) said that negative impressions of the business while growing up discouraged many children from joining a family business. Negativity might stem from observations of parents' working hours and conditions, or the absence of money. There is also debate in the literature about the influence of entrepreneurs on their childrens' values and goals: do such parents provide good role models or does the experience of working in a family business turn children off the prospect of taking over?

Birley (2002) concluded from research on potential heirs that the top reason for not joining the family firm was a lack of interest in that particular business, followed by perceptions that the business would not allow the children to use their talents or training.

Gender and culture

Gender is sometimes an impediment, with daughters being treated prejudicially (Dumas, 1992; C. Iannarelli, unpublished, University of Pittsburg, 1992). Some researchers have concluded that first-born children, particularly males, are more likely to join and inherit a family business (Goldberg and Wooldridge, 1993). Daughters in many cultures apparently are less likely to get involved or be assigned important duties in family businesses.

The business is not viable

Involvement and inheritance by other family members might be precluded by the business itself. Many small and micro businesses are likely to suffer from low turnover and profits, or periodic cash-flow problems. This barrier could be absolute, as in the case where a great debt load or tax burden makes inheritance of a going concern impossible, or a matter of degree –

potential heirs perceive the business as lacking potential to support successors. Bjuggren and Sund (2001) argued that both taxes and legal matters were barriers to inheritance in Swedish firms.

Research Findings from Australia, Canada and Denmark

The research methods and profiles of these three samples of family businesses have already been described. In this section the data pertaining to involvement of children and succession plans are examined.

Western Australia

Almost half (46.5%) of the respondents were uncertain about the ultimate disposition of their family business. One-fifth had no plans to keep it within the family, while one-quarter planned to will it to children or family members upon their death. A small portion (1%) had already involved children in ownership of the business, while another 7% planned to do so by means other than a will. In total, only 33% were planning to involve, or had already involved, children or other family members in ownership. Children worked in only 23% of these businesses.

Canmore and Bornholm

Family-related goals are shown in Table 5.1. Training children for future ownership of the business was considered to be important (combining the number who indicated four and five on the five-point importance scale) to only about 21% of the Danish respondents and 15% of the Canadians. Providing jobs for family members was also more important in Denmark, with about 37% rating it highly compared to 15% in Canmore. On the inheritance question, just over 21% of those in Bornholm and 17% of the Canmore respondents thought it important to 'pass on the family business to children/family'.

Extent of family involvement (Table 5.2)

In both resort areas the businesses were very small, with mostly just the owner(s) being employed. In Bornholm less than half had non-family, full-time, paid employees; only 11 involved children, and seven others involved other family members beside spouses. Companies (as opposed to other ownership forms) and non-accommodation businesses had more paid, full-time, non-family employees. In Canmore, less than half had employees, only 12 involved children and five involved other family members beyond a spouse. Those Canmore businesses owned by companies have more employees, and these are primarily hotels, restaurants, and to a lesser extent tour companies. None of the B&B establishments had non-family, full-time paid employees.

Only a very small number of respondents indicated that keeping the family together or preserving family property was an important start-up goal. Those that planned for growth, or were best able to deliver it, were clearly in the minority. However, because of their desire to grow the business they might very well be the most likely to create a viable inheritance scenario.

Problems regarding inheritance, and succession plans (Table 5.3)

Among the Danish respondents taxes were thought to be a serious problem by 50% of those answering a question about barriers to inheritance (there were 18–20 respondents). About one-quarter of the respondents thought it serious that the children either did not want to live there or did not want to own the business. There was also a suggestion that the business could not support children financially, as 42% determined it was 'somewhat of a problem'. In Canmore the highest-ranked item was taxes, which attracted 48% of the respondents in the 'somewhat of a problem' category.

Disposition plans (Table 5.4)

Disposition plans were explicitly examined for all respondents. Most were uncertain about the

Table 5.1.   Family-related goals, Bornholm and Canmore.

Goals	Bornholm (% rating the goal important) (*n* = 28–31)	Canmore (% rating the goal important) (*n* = 46–49)
Prevent disharmony among family members	73.3	81.3
Share all key decisions with the spouse or family	74.2	71.4
Train the children for future ownership of the business	20.7	15.2
Provide family members with jobs	36.7[a]	14.9[a]
Share the work equally with my spouse	46.7	37.2
Pass on the family business to children/family	21.4	17.0
Earn enough to support the family	67.7	75.0
Elevate our family position in society	16.7	12.5
Ensure the family has lots of free time together	27.6[a]	75.5[a]

[a]Significant differences between the samples.

Table 5.2.   Family involvement, Bornholm and Canmore.

Extent of family involvement	Bornholm (*n* = 84)	Canmore (*n* = 99)
No other family members work in the business besides me	30 (35.7%)	25 (25.3%)
A husband and wife work together in the business	41 (48.8)	64 (64.6)
One or more of the owners' children work in the business	7 (8.3)	5 (5.1)
Other family members beside spouse or children work in the business	7 (8.3)	5 (5.1)

Table 5.3. Problems regarding inheritance. Q: If you wanted your children to inherit your business, would any of these factors be a problem? (multiple answers permitted).

Problems	Bornholm (n = 18–20; valid percentages)			Canmore (n = 26–27; valid percentages)		
	1	2	3	1	2	3
Taxes	4.00	10.0	50.0	37.0	48.1	14.8
Children do not want to live here	63.2	10.5	26.3	61.5	26.9	11.5
Children do not want to own the business	66.7	11.1	22.2	56.0	32.0	12.0
Children do not have the necessary skills	78.9	15.8	5.3	58.3	33.3	8.3
It is not able to support them financially	57.9	42.1	–	69.2	19.2	11.5
There is too much debt	78.9	21.1	–	66.7	25.9	7.4

1 = Not serious
2 = Somewhat serious
3 = Serious

Table 5.4. Disposition plans (multiple responses).

Disposition plans	Bornholm (n = 84)	Canmore (n = 99)
Part ownership of the business has already been transferred/sold to one or more children or family members	2	0
Ownership will be transferred/sold in the future to one or more children	8[a]	0[a]
The business will be sold, but not to children/family	22	31
Ownership is to be willed to children/family	5	4
Uncertain	50	62

[a]Significant difference.

future of their business, but it can be concluded that this uncertain group (50 of 84 in Bornholm and 62 of 99 in Canmore) do not include many viable inheritance scenarios. In fact, the biggest response category was that the business will be sold, but not to children or family. The one significant difference in this comparison was that eight respondents in Bornholm definitely planned a sale or transference of ownership to family or children, compared to none in Canmore. In addition, there were five in Bornholm and four in Canmore who were planning to will the business to children or family.

By totalling the three responses related to inheritance it can be seen that it was occurring or planned in 15 of 84 in Bornholm (18%) and only four of 99 in Canmore (4%). Both proportions are minor, but the higher rate of inheritance in Bornholm can probably be attributed to culture and the longer history of tourism.

By way of summarizing the data, it is clear that inheritance was a minor concern among the two samples, although more of a prospect in Bornholm than in Canmore. Most of the owners did not have children in the business or living with them. The fact that many respondents were older and in second careers suggests that life-stage is a real barrier in this industry. Specifically, many get into the tourism and hospitality business too late to involve their children. The small size of many of the businesses is also a real impediment.

Evidence from interviews

A separate but overlapping sample of 33 owners was interviewed in Bornholm. Some respondents completed both an interview and a questionnaire. Selected quotations from the interviews illustrate a number of key points on the involvement of children and barriers to inheritance, in response to a question on succession plans.

Three main scenarios emerged: inheritance is not possible; it is possible but not planned or desired; or it is desired and/or planned. In addition, a summary follows of the specific barriers mentioned by respondents. The following quotations are translated and paraphrased from the Danish.

Scenario A: Inheritance is not possible

My wife and I run the business seasonally. I have to work at another job in the quiet season to make enough money. We like living and working here and it is a good environment for our young daughter, but we think about moving because it is so difficult to make a decent living. Our daughter has no interest in the business. I have other children from a previous marriage but they live in Copenhagen and abroad.

(Producer and retailer of a craft product)

The farm is too small to generate a living for the next generation.

(Owner, farm-based accommodation)

None of my children are working in my business. They do not want to. They have high educations and jobs outside Bornholm. They do not want to go back to Bornholm either.

(Hotel owner)

Our children do not live in Bornholm and have their income elsewhere.

(Campground owner)

My father turned his father's hobby (on the farm) into a business. I took over the tourism business and my brother the farm. Our own children have moved away and are not interested in the business. My wife and I are definitely selling it and will retire.

(Farm-based, seasonal tourist attraction)

Scenario B: Inheritance is possible but not desired or planned

My wife and I are from Bornholm. We built this business from the profits of our first restaurant. My wife runs it seasonally, and we both run this one the rest of the year. In my family it is a tradition to be business men, and my father and brother are also entrepreneurs in different firms. I wanted to create my own, not follow in my father's. We have no plan for our own children to take over.

(Owners of two restaurants, one seasonal)

We are unlikely to still own the business when our children grow up.

(Owners of an accommodation business)

Our children are not interested in this business because of the long working hours in high season.

(Hostel owners)

During the summer only we have children working in the business. But they have their own careers and will not take over from us.

(Hotel owners)

Scenario C: Inheritance is possible, and desired or planned

Perhaps we will pass on the business to the daughter, who has some interest and is in the area.

(Owners, farm-based accommodation)

I have no children in the business, but my son-in-law is my right hand and is running the daily business. The plan is that he is going to take over the business.

(Hotel and restaurant owner)

The children are grown up now and work (elsewhere in Denmark). They do not want to take over the operations of the business – but maybe the ownership on basis of stocks in the company.

(Owner of a recreation attraction)

My son and daughter are working in the business today. They are interested in a takeover, when I want to retire in some years. They know all about it, so they are fit for takeover.

(Attraction owner)

Scenario A consists of businesses that cannot viably be inherited (no heirs, too small, no real or separable assets, too much debt) and those that must be sold (parents need the proceeds). In Bornholm, many of the owners had children who were gone and could not realistically be considered for taking over the business. Bornholm, like many remote and rural areas, sees most of its children leave the island for education and jobs, and most do not want to come back or cannot financially make it work. A related barrier is linked to life-stages in that parents start or purchase the business later in life, perhaps with retirement in mind, and the children are already long gone. In the case of farms, tourism businesses are usually created for supplementary income and so are not inheritable as separate entities.

Scenario B consists of many businesses in which inheritance is at least possible, specifically because of the involvement or presence of children, but it is unlikely to occur. The nature of the business is a barrier, because of hard work, seasonality and low levels of income. This results in a negative perception of the business by children. Many micro businesses never have the potential to support a growing family or subsequent generations as they are created in the first place to supplement farm or other income sources. Yet some do foresee inheritance by children, and determining what ultimately makes this happen should be a research priority.

In scenario C, inheritance is desired and/or planned. Even so, there is uncertainty about its feasibility. One interesting case reflected the separation of ownership and owner-operation (children might want to assume ownership of a profitable business, but do not want to operate it). In such cases many of the potential benefits of family businesses for the community are lost.

Planning for Involvement and Succession

The topic of preparing for succession is one of the hallmarks of family-business literature, and so there is no shortage of advice on how owners should handle it. What is evident in much of this advice is that attention must first be paid to the involvement of children or other family members in the business so that they can be prepared for succession.

Ward (1990) and Handler (1994) described succession as a process, rather than as an event, and Handler conceived this process in terms of transition theory. At each stage in the process, the actors (typically parents and their children; often fathers and sons) play roles that must evolve if the succession is to take place. The founders and potential successors must engage in mutual role adjustment whereby founders decrease their level of control while successors increase their involvement to the eventual point of taking over. In particular, there must be a transfer of leadership experience, authority, decision-making power and equity.

The most basic and common reasons for a failure in the succession process relate to the inability of founders to give up control, and the lack of willingness or ability of children to take over. A variety of strategies can be employed by founders to decrease deliberately their involvement, notably taking on new ventures. In many instances, external advisers or intervention might be necessary to ensure that all parties in the process engage in rational planning, rather than putting off the necessary decisions. But who is to initiate such an intervention?

According to C. Iannarelli (unpublished, University of Pittsburgh, 1992), there are a number of factors critical to developing the interest of children in running the family firm:

- spending time with the parents in the business;
- exposure to various aspects of the business;
- parental encouragement and positive attitudes;
- making an individual contribution to the team; and
- the time at which the opportunity to join the firm is presented.

Iannarelli also found that young girls are often treated differently from their brothers during this business socialization process, resulting in less time being spent in the business and lesser skill development. Parents wanting their daughters to get involved will therefore have to offer more encouragement to daughters, while daughters wanting to get involved might have to make a special effort to be taken seriously.

Ambrose (1983) and Astrachan (1993) are among those authors who have advocated early involvement in the firm by heirs in order to develop their interest and their likelihood of joining the firm.

Lansberg (1988) identified the basic tasks in succession planning as follows:

1. Formulating and sharing a viable vision for succession.
In many tourism/hospitality businesses the vision must take into account a separation of home/farm from the business. What exactly is to be inherited, especially when one child is interested and another is not? In many cases the small size or low profitability of the business will make inheritance a non-starter.

2. Selecting and training the successor(s) and the top management team.
How do children get involved and trained if they go away for education? At what age is it wise to start children working in a service-oriented environment? Can work and home be separated?

3. Designing a process to transfer power.
This could be done informally, between the generations, but often will require impartial and expert advice.
4. Developing an estate plan for asset and ownership inheritance.
External advice will undoubtedly be needed regarding the legal and tax implications of transfer. A special consideration is that of family 'brands' whereby the family name has value in itself.
5. Designing structures to manage the changes, such as a family council, task force or board of directors.
The majority of tourism and hospitality firms will be too small to permit or require elaborate mechanisms or boards of directors, but it is possible that those most suitable for inheritance will be large enough to warrant these methods.
6. Educating the family regarding the rights and responsibilities that come with new roles in the business.
Founders have the obligation to inform and consult with children about all family and business matters, and especially about succession options. As discussed elsewhere, one major issue facing families is the trade-off between reinvestment in the business and taking out funds for immediate use. Regarding inheritance, there is sometimes a fear in the minds of parents that their inheritors will pillage or sell the business to realize a quick income boost.

Additional relevant advice comes from Ward (1990) who recommended 15 key guidelines to help with the transition process:

- Present a balanced perspective on business to children.
- Present the business as an option, not an obligation.
- Successors should get outside experience.
- Successors should be hired into an existing job in the family business.
- Encourage the development of complementary skills in the successor.
- Teach successors the foundations of the business.
- Start the successor with mentors.
- Designate an area of responsibility for the successor.
- Develop a rationale why all the effort is worth it.

- Recognize that you (the owners and heirs) are not alone.
- Have family meetings.
- Have a business plan, estate plan and succession plan all together.
- Establish an advisory board.
- Set a retirement date.
- Let go!

Handler (1994) identified a number of research needs concerning the succession process, including study of cultural or ethnic differences, the role of family dynamics and gender, and resistance factors to succession effectiveness. To this list must be added the industry and setting-specific factors discussed previously, as it is clear that tourism and hospitality enterprises present some special challenges.

Estate planning

All family businesses must consider the ultimate disposition of their assets, and when inheritance is contemplated, estate planning is required. A workable form of ownership has to be created for the heir(s), with options ranging from one heir as total owner to distribution of shares among many family members. It might even be desirable to transfer voting and non-voting stock or to create a family trust. Gifting of assets over a period of time, well in advance of the legal change on ownership, might save taxes.

One of the most serious issues facing founders and all subsequent owners is creation of their personal retirement fund, separate from transferred assets. For example, how much are the parents going to need to live independently through retirement, and will there be enough earnings potential left in the business to support the next generation? Many businesses in tourism and hospitality do not have the potential to support two generations at once, leaving the owners with no option but to sell the firm as their retirement fund.

A framework for investigating industry-specific barriers to inheritance

A number of generic and industry-specific barriers to inheritance have been identified, but research on other industries, settings and business types is bound to reveal more. How are they to be explored and evaluated? A framework is provided in Table 5.5.

The model developed by Shapero and Sokol (1982) for examining entrepreneurial events (i.e. firm creation) is useful here. Those authors hypothesized that both negative displacements (such as forced migration or job loss) and pull factors led to new firm creation, but perceptions of desirability and feasibility intervened. This type of thought process is also likely to be crucial for the inheritance/succession process: the situation of the potential heir must be considered (such as age, gender, work experience), then perceptions of desirability (is it an attractive career option?) and – perhaps simultaneously – viability and perceptions of feasibility (can the family business support me?).

A number of research needs are suggested by the research findings and the framework. One line of research would be to examine the experiences, attitudes and plans of tourism and hospitality students towards that industry and family businesses in particular. Studying how children are brought up in service-oriented businesses, especially where home and work are combined, would be very revealing. Selecting a sample of multi-generational businesses will enable analysis of barriers and success factors. Why do some hotel businesses in Europe, for example, survive many generations in the same family? Is it due to culture, succession planning, or a favourable business environment? Different settings should be compared.

Tourism and hospitality businesses in remote islands and small towns might differ considerably from those in large cities or resorts. It is possible that children are more likely to enter a family business if it is located in a resort or city. In more general terms, different industries and business types should be compared. Use of the suggested framework will permit systematic data collection on key points affecting succession and inheritance.

Chapter Summary

The life cycle model provided the framework for assessing challenges associated with balancing family and business. A number of these challenges are generic, and several industry-specific ones were presented – especially seasonality of demand and combining home-life with guests. Specific issues facing the sole proprietor, copreneurs, young business families and older business families that involve children were then examined.

Strategies for managing or balancing family and business were detailed, including very specific advice on how to separate guests from private spaces and private times, and formal mechanisms such as establishing family agreements, family councils and codes of conduct. The special case of gender issues has been discussed in detail, along with the family and the environment. Research evidence from Australia, Denmark and Canada was presented to illustrate many of the challenges and strategies for coping.

We then turned to the challenges of involving the next generation, and ultimately succession of the business. In this context the idea of a family 'legacy' was addressed. A number of generic and industry-specific barriers to inheritance were presented, ranging from the obvious (no heirs; the business cannot support inheritance) to life-stage factors, such as couples

Table 5.5. A framework for examining industry-specific barriers to inheritance.

Situation of potential heir(s)	Perceptions of desirability	Perceptions of feasibility
• Being brought up in the family business	• Desirability of the potential lifestyle	• Current and potential earnings from the business
• Work experience (within and outside the family firm)	• Desirability of the location/setting	• The legacy (real property; family brand)
• Education specific to the industry	• Desirability of the nature of the work	• Potential to grow or diversify the business
• Ability to work in and/or control the business	• Desirability of the business as a career	• The business environment (competition, long-term viability)
• Education and career goals		• Practicality of inheritance (taxes, legal problems)

establishing businesses when children have already moved away for their own careers and families. Founders might be reluctant to let go of their business, but equally the children might simply not share the dream of autonomy and lifestyle through operating a family business.

Research findings confirmed a low rate of succession planning and potential inheritance of the businesses examined in Australia, Canada and Denmark. Specifically drawing on the Bornholm, Denmark, sample, several scenarios were developed: inheritance is not possible; it is possible but not desired or planned; it is possible and desired or planned. The latter scenario is observed infrequently.

After discussing how owners can plan for involvement of their children and eventual succession, this chapter concludes by presenting a conceptual framework for investigating industry-specific barriers to inheritance. The three main factors to consider are: situation of the potential heir(s); perceptions of desirability of inheriting or taking over the business, and perceptions of the feasibility of inheriting or taking over the business.

References

Alcorn, P. (1982) *Success and Survival in the Family-Owned Business*. McGraw Hill, New York.

Ambrose, D. (1983) Transfer of the family-owned business. *Journal of Small Business Management* 21(1), 49–56.

Armstrong, K. (1978) Rural Scottish women: Politics without power. *Ethnos* 43(1/2), 51–72.

Astrachan, J. (1989) Family firm and community culture. *Family Business Review* 1(2) 165–189.

Astachan, J. (1993) Preparing the next generation for wealth: a conversation with Howard H. Stevenson. *Family Business Review* 6, 75–83.

Ateljevic, I. and Doorne, S. (2000) Staying within the fence: lifestyle entrepreneurship in tourism. *Journal of Sustainable Tourism* 8(5), 378–392.

Baines, S. and Wheelock, J. (1998) Working for each other: gender, the household and micro-business survival and growth. *International Small Business Journal* 17, 11–16.

Beckhard, R. and Dyer, W. (1983) Managing change in the family firm – issues and strategies. *Sloan Management Review* 24(3), 59–65.

Birley, S. (1986) Succession in the family firm: the inheritor's view. *Journal of Small Business Management* 24, 36–43.

Birley, S. (2002) Attitudes of owner-managers' children towards family and business issues. *Entrepreneurship Theory and Practice* 26(3), 5–19.

Birley, S., Ng, D. and Godfrey, A. (1999) The family and the business. *Long Range Planning* 32(6), 598–608.

Bjuggren, P. and Sund, L. (2001) Strategic decision-making in intergenerational successions of small- and medium-sized family-owned businesses. *Family Business Review* 14(1), 11–23.

Blotnick, S. (1984) The case of reluctant heirs. *Forbes* July, 134, 180.

Breathnach, P., Henry, M., Drea, S. and O'Flaherty, M. (1994) Gender in Irish tourism employment. In: Kinnaird, V. and Hall, D. (eds) *Tourism: a Gender Analysis*. John Wiley & Sons, Chichester, UK, pp. 52–73.

Caballe, A. (1999) Farm tourism in Spain: a gender perspective. *Geojournal* 48(3), 245–252.

Carlock, R. and Ward, J. (2001) *Strategic Planning for the Family Business*. Palgrave, Basingstoke, UK.

Carlsen, J., Getz, D. and Ali-Knight, J. (2001) Environmental attitudes and practices of family businesses in the rural tourism and hospitality sectors. *Journal of Sustainable Tourism* 9(4), 281–297.

Cory, J. (1990) Preparing your success: family ownership. *Hardware Age* July, 74.

Cromie, S., Dunn, B., Sproull, A. and Chalmers, D. (2001) Small firms with a family focus in the Scottish Highlands and Islands. *Irish Journal of Management* 22(2), 45–66.

Cukier, J., Norris, J. and Wall, G. (1996) The involvement of women in the tourism industry of Bali, Indonesia. *The Journal of Development Studies*, 33(2): 248–270.

Danes, S. (1998) *Farm Family Business*. University of Minnesota Extension Service, Minnesota.

Davis, J. and Tagiuri, R. (1989) The influence of life-stage on father–son work relationships in family companies. *Family Business Review* 2(1), 47–74.

Davis, P. and Harveston, P. (1998) The influence of family on the family business succession process: a multi-generational perspective. *Entrepreneurship Theory and Practice* 22(3), 31–53.

Davis, S. (1968) Entrepreneurial succession. *Administrative Science Quarterly* 13, 402–416.

Dean, S. (1992) Characteristics of African American family-owned businesses in Los Angeles. *Family Business Review* 5(4), 373–395.

Dernoi, L. (1991a) About rural and farm tourism. *Tourism Recreation Research* 16(1), 3–6.

Dumas, C. (1992) Integrating the daughter into family business management. *Entrepreneurship: Theory and Practice* June, 41–55.

Dunn, B. (1995) Success themes in Scottish family enterprises: philosophies and practices through the generations. *Family Business Review* 8(1), 17–28.

Dyer, W. (1988) Culture and continuity in family firms. *Family Business Review* 1(1), 37–50.

Garcia-Ramon, D., Canoves, G. and Valdovinos, N. (1995) Farm tourism, gender and the environment in Spain. *Annals of Tourism Research* 22(2), 267–282.

Getz, D. and Carlsen, J. (2000) Characteristics and goals of family and owner-operated businesses in the rural tourism and hospitality sectors. *Tourism Management* 21, 547–560.

Goldberg, S. and Wooldridge, B. (1993) Self-confidence and managerial autonomy: successor characteristics critical to succession in family firms. *Family Business Journal* July, 60–65.

Handler, W. (1994) Succession in family businesses: a review of the research. *Family Business Review* 7(2), 133–157.

Handler, W. and Kram, K. (1988) Succession in family firms: the problem of resistance. *Family Business Review* 1(4), 361–381.

Hankinson, A. (1989) Small hotels in Britain: investment and survival. *The Cornell HRA Quarterly* 30(3), 80–82.

Hegarty, C. and Ruddy, J. (2002) The role of family in entrepreneurial development in Irish rural tourism. Paper presented at the conference: Re-Inventing the Destination. Dubrovnik, Croatia.

Herremans, I. and Welsh, C. (1999) Developing and implementing a company's ecotourism mission statement. *Journal of Sustainable Tourism* 7(1), 48–76.

Jennings, G. and Stehlik, D. (1999) The innovators are women: the development of farm tourism in central Queensland, Australia. Proceedings of the International Society of Travel and Tourism Educators Annual Conference, Vancouver, Canada.

Kousis, M. (1989) Tourism and the family in a rural Cretan community. *Annals of Tourism Research* 16 (3), 318–332.

Lansberg, I. (1999) *Succeeding Generations: Realizing the Dream of Families in Business*. Harvard Business School Press, Boston, Massachusetts.

Leontidou, L. (1994) Gender dimensions of tourism in Greece: employment, subcultures and restructuring. In: Kinnaird, V. and Hall, D. (eds) *Tourism: a Gender Analysis*. John Wiley & Sons, Chichester, UK, pp. 74–105.

Long, V. and Kindon, S. (1997) Gender and tourism development in Balinese villages. In: Sinclair, T. (ed.) *Gender, Work and Tourism*. Routledge, London, pp. 91–119.

Lynch, P. (1996) Microenterprises and micro-firms in the hospitality industry: the case of bed and breakfast enterprises. In: Thomas, R. (ed.) *Spring Symposium Proceedings of International Association of Hotel Management Schools*. Leeds Metropolitan University, Leeds, UK, pp. 231–236.

Lynch, P. and MacWhannell, D. (2000) Home and commercialized hospitality. In: Lashley, C. and Morrison, A. (eds) *In Search of Hospitality: Theoretical Perspectives and Debates*. Butterworth-Heinemann, Oxford, UK, pp. 100–117.

Massachusetts Mutual Life Assurance (1993) *Major Findings of the Family Business Survey*. Springfield, Massachusetts.

McGibbon, J. (2000) Family business: commercial hospitality in the domestic realm. In: Robinson, M. *et al.* (eds) *Reflections on International Tourism: Expressions of Culture Identity and Meaning in Tourism*. Business Education Publications, Sunderland, UK.

McKercher, B. (1998) *The Business of Nature-based Tourism*. Hospitality Press, Melbourne, Australia.

Mendonsa, E. (1983) Tourism and income strategies in Nazare, Portugal. *Annals of Tourism Research* 10(2), 213–238.

Peiser, R. and Wooten, L. (1983) Life cycle changes in small family businesses. *Business Horizons* 26(3), 58–65.

Quinn, U., Larmour, R. and McQuillan, N. (1992) The small firm in the hospitality industry. *International Journal of Hospitality Management* 1, 11–14.

Scott, J. (1996) Chances and choices: women and tourism in Northern Cyprus. In: Sinclair, T. (ed.) *Gender, Work and Tourism*. Routledge, London, pp. 60–90.

Shapero, A. and Sokol, L. (1982) The social dimensions of entrepreneurship. In: Kent, C., Sexton, D. and Vesper, K. (eds) *Encyclopedia of Entrepreneurship*. Prentice-Hall, Englewood Cliffs, New Jersey, pp. 72–88.

Sharma, P., Chrisman, J. and Chua, J. (1996) *A Review and Annotated Bibliography of Family Business Studies*. Kluwer, Boston, Massachusetts.

Stavrou, E. (1999) Succession in family businesses: exploring the effects of demographic factors on offspring intentions to join and take over the business. *Journal of Small Business Management* 37(3), 43–61.

Stavrou, E. and Winslow, E. (1996) Succession in entrepreneurial family business in the US, Europe and Asia: a cross-cultural comparison on offspring intentions to join and take over the business. *Proceedings of the International Council for Small Businesses World Conference 1996*, Vol. 1. ICSB, Stockholm, pp. 253–273.

Stoy Hayward Consulting (1999) *Staying the Course: Survival Characteristics of the Family Owned Business*. Vantage point, London.

Stringer, P. (1981) Hosts and guests: the bed and breakfast phenomenon. *Annals of Tourism Research* 8(3), 357–376.

Tsang, E. (2002) Learning from overseas venturing experience: the case of Chinese family businesses. *Journal of Business Venturing* 17(1), 21–40.

Twining-Ward, L. and Baum, T. (1998) Dilemmas facing mature island destinations: cases from the Baltic. *Progress in Tourism and Hospitality Research* 4, 131–140.

Twining-Ward, L. and Twining-Ward, T. (1996) *Tourist destination development: the case of Bornholm and Gotland*. Research Centre of Bornholm, Report 7/1996, Bornholm, Denmark.

Velasco, M. (1999) Andalusian women and their participation in rural tourist trade. *Geojournal* 48(3), 253–258.

Walker, S., Valaoras, G., Gurung, D. and Godde, P. (2001) Women and mountain tourism: redefining the boundaries of policy and practice. In: Apostolopoulos, Y., Sonmez, S. and Timothy, D. (eds) *Women as Producers and Consumers of Tourism in Developing Regions*. Praeger, Westport, Connecticut, pp. 211–234.

Walton, J. (1978) *The Blackpool Landlady – a Social History*. Manchester University Press, Manchester, UK.

Ward, J. (1987) *Keeping the Family Business Healthy: How To Plan For Continuing Growth, Profitability, and Family Leadership*. Josey-Bass, San Francisco, California.

Ward, J. (1990) The succession process: 15 guidelines. *Small Business Forum* 8, 57–62.

Westhead, P. and Cowling, M. (1998) Family firm research: the need for a methodological rethink. *Entrepreneurship Theory and Practice* Autumn, 31–56.

Whatmore, S. (1991) *Farming Women: Gender, Work and Family Enterprise*. MacMillan, Basingstoke, UK.

6

Farm-based Family Businesses

Introduction

This chapter introduces three case studies of farm-based family businesses in Canada and Australia. Alborak Stables Inc. is a family-first business with lifestyle motivations, located in the foothills of the Rocky Mountains of Alberta, Canada. Taunton Farm in the south-west of Western Australia is also a business that builds on family farmlands, with the aim of keeping ownership of the land as paramount. The final case of Old MacDonald's is a campground on a family farm in Alberta, which was also started as a complement to rural living. In all three cases, family farming is the common ground and the decision to start a family business in tourism was a pragmatic response to the needs of the farm and the family.

Case 6.1 Alborak Stables

Background

Alborak Stables Inc. is a family-owned and -operated business located 35 km west of the Calgary, Canada city limits, in the foothills of the Rocky Mountains. The Donnelly family established this business to be devoted to the 'Olympic' disciplines, or English horse riding (i.e. dressage, show jumping and eventing), and they offer training, lessons, clinics, horse stabling and management, and commission sale horses. The main facility, completed in 1998, is

a 2222 square-yard (1856 m^2) indoor heated arena with 38 boarding stalls; two tack rooms, washrooms and shower, offices, rider's lounge, and bedrooms and kitchen for staff (on a second level). The Stables also offers an outdoor sand ring, round pen, paddocks, pastures and trails over the 800-acre farm. As discussed later, farm and Stables are legally separate entities.

Alborak is situated in a fairly isolated location along an unpaved private road leading to the main Trans-Canada Highway. Its regular clients are attracted from the city, surrounding rural areas, and Banff and Canmore to the west. The operation can be described as a rural and agricultural land use, but from the customer's perspective it is primarily recreational, entailing a high degree of direct customer service. There is potential for tourism development, but it remains uncertain if the Donnelly family will move in that direction.

The farm consists largely of forest with some improved pasture. The traditional agricultural business of cattle grazing and horse breeding remains part of the family's economic activity. Currently they run 50 cow–calf pairs, but the land does not have additional agricultural potential.

Sandra and Mary work full-time at the stables, with Sandra being in charge of the horse-related operations and Mary handling most of the office responsibilities. She recently received permission to run a B&B establishment, which would be restricted to two bedrooms in the family house. The demand comes from clients who would like occasionally to stay overnight.

©D. Getz et al. 2004. The Family Business in Tourism and Hospitality
(D. Getz, J. Carlsen and A. Morrison)

John works from the family home as a private consultant, and provides financial advice to the Stables. Karen's involvement has also been part-time and related to marketing the business.

In addition to family, the stables have two full-time employees, one full-time working student, and two to four part-time working students, depending on the season.

Family dimensions

The Donnelly family consists of John and Mary, who own the land and facilities, daughter Sandra who is President of Alborak Stables Inc. (and leases the facility from her parents), and younger daughter Karen who lives and works in Calgary. The family has agricultural roots in Alberta dating back to 1886, and the farmland has been in the extended family since the 1940s. Mary Donnelly inherited it. The private access road, owned by a natural gas company, was built only in the 1970s, and the current family house was built in 1981.

Horses have always been an interest to family members and a focus of family activities. Their love of horses logically led to the establishment of the Stables, but more specifically it occurred because of Sandra's ambition to run her own operation and her parents' desire to see that happen.

The decision to proceed was made internally and by consensus. They are obviously a 'hands-on' family that has both set and implemented an ambitious vision. Having made the decision to develop the stables, the Donnellys obtained legal advice, especially regarding equine law, and prepared a business plan. Detailed cost estimates were received and projected along with pro-forma financial statements. A full feasibility study including marketing evaluation was not completed, and the family realized there were risks associated with the venture.

They did understand the competition, however, which consists of 12–15 other English-style stables in the region. This led them to decide to build a top-quality facility in order to stand out immediately. Three target markets were clearly identified, related to services offered: horse breeding, training and sales; horse

and rider coaching for both recreation and sport, and horse management. It was not conceived as a tourism-related business, but the possibility of adding tourism attractions and services has been recognized all along.

Start-up financing involved bank loans with the farmland as collateral, and the selling of some acres of logs for cash. For a variety of reasons, including financial risk, Alborak Stables was created as a separate, incorporated business that leases the land and facility from John and Mary Donnelly. If the worst-case scenario occurred in terms of the stables, land could be sold to pay off debt.

However, for the parents the land, and now the stables, is a family legacy that will some day be inherited by their daughters. With this goal in mind, why not develop the business there? Mary initiated the idea, knowing that Sandra was looking to lease a stable to begin a business on her own.

Sandra had been doing teaching and horse training in different locations, and she had definite ideas about design and operations. Living on the farm and near to her parents is a nice bonus, but her main motivation was to start up a successful business and live on a farm.

John did not see a big role for himself in running the business, although he anticipated it would involve some of his time as business adviser and general handyman.

Karen was more oriented toward completing her graduate degree in planning and commencing a professional career in the city, where she lives. She enjoys working with family and helping in the business on a part-time basis, but was not motivated to develop or run the business.

The decision to develop the stables was made by the parents, who had to provide the land and secure financing, in consultation with the two daughters. Sandra, naturally, was party to the detailed planning process. Karen was interested and supportive, but was not intending to be part of the business full-time. Everyone agreed it would be fun, and they all looked forward to some degree of participation.

Having made a family decision, the Donnellys had to develop their individual roles in the business and work out a number of family-business inter-relationships. At one level, 'everyone helps with everything', in order to get things done. However, there are some clear separations of duties and responsibilities, and a belief that everyone needs something significant to do.

Sandra, as President, has overall responsibility for stable operations. She has a full-time employee who acts more like a partner in day-to-day operations. Sandra also shares accommodation with staff on the upper level of the stable, so staff must fit into the family atmosphere. She often works long hours, including evenings and weekends, so that work and personal life tend to merge. She takes Mondays off and gets 2 or 3 weeks of holiday each year.

John and Mary currently handle most of the business operations. Mary feels she will stay involved for some time in the same capacity, doing general office work like invoicing, and even tractor operations. John provides financial advice, and Karen has contributed to promotions and plans to construct a website. Karen might consider more involvement in the management of the business in the future, but views the horse-related activities more as leisure than ideal work.

Business dimensions

The Stables are running at near physical capacity already, although there is considerable scope for revenue enhancement. First-year targets were exceeded, but generating a surplus is a multi-year effort.

There seems to be a family consensus regarding the short-term in not making the business much bigger than at present, but to make it profitable. A number of years have gone by in which costs have exceeded revenues. Sandra has not been able to take a pay cheque out of the business, but does earn some personal commissions stemming from horse breeding and consulting to horse owners. Profitability is linked to developing a good reputation and developing a loyal client base. Raising young horses for sale should become profitable.

A paid stable manager might be feasible in the future, thereby leaving family members freer to enjoy the horse- and customer-related activities. Sandra might also consider taking on a formal business partner.

John would like a slower lifestyle and less need for financing the company. Ultimately it should repay the initial investment and operate self-sufficiently. More horse sales and training fees, and not physical expansion, would generate the desired profits.

Possible developments have been articulated, and relate to both the Stables and the property in general. The stables could benefit from a cross-country course, more sheds, pastures and shelters, and perhaps a retail shop. Other possibilities include a country inn or retreat, restaurant, and more diverse recreation activities. More development would require municipal planning permission and would probably not be feasible as long as the access road is private. Developing the road to municipal standards seems prohibitively expensive, and might encounter opposition from area residents. Already the Alborak sign at the entrance to the private road has gone missing.

Decision-making involves the whole family, which can be a unifying force, although within a family opinions are likely to be expressed frankly and with emotion. Formal Alborak Stables meetings are scheduled, at which goals are set and measured.

Keeping family relationships good is an important concern for all family members. 'Family life has merged with business life', according to one member of the Donnelly family, but in many ways the effort has drawn the family much closer together. There is a clear sharing of goals and considerable pride in the family's accomplishments with the business. Most family interaction now takes place 'either at the workplace or in discussions about the workplace'. Other get-togethers became rare.

Recruiting and keeping a good workforce is an issue, especially 'to internalize the goals and aspirations of the family.' As well, there is constant pressure from clients, many of whom like to socialize with the family. For the most part this is an enjoyable aspect of the hospitality business, but finding privacy can be a challenge. Also, 'social demands of patrons at times make it difficult for family and staff to complete their chores.'

An attachment to the land is a driving force in this family business. The stables provide added value that could not otherwise be attained, given the low agricultural potential of the farm. Keeping the land and business within the family, and through the next generation, is an important value base.

This type of business is not particularly seasonal in that the horses have to be boarded all year round, as do training and lessons. Remoteness has its advantages and disadvantages. A horse-based business could not work well with lots of neighbours, and a large acreage is necessary for grazing. Customers are prepared to drive a reasonably long distance for the special services offered, and there is little direct competition in this area west of Calgary. Being in the forested foothills allows unique trail-riding opportunities. It is a customer-service business, so that good relations with clients are essential.

It is a 7-days-a-week business, so someone with responsibility always has to be on site. It is a long way to get supplies and services, so some costs are higher. The initial investment was probably higher to compensate for extra driving time on the part of clients – it had to be of high value right from the beginning.

Neighbours, although few and far between, can be problematic when setting up a business that attracts new traffic into a quiet, rural area. Signage for the stables, posted at the main road, has disappeared, although clients are provided with maps to help find the stables.

- Commitment by the entire family.
- A strong knowledge base in the (horse) industry.
- Relatively strong business knowledge.
- Strong financial resources (within the family).
- Top quality facilities.
- Access and closeness to population centres.

Case 6.2 Taunton Farm Holiday Park

Background

Taunton Farm is a caravan and cabin park on the Bussell highway, near the town of Cowaramup in the south-west corner of Western Australia. It offers powered and unpowered sites, caravan and limited cabin accommodation and is located on a working farm in the heart of the Margaret River district. It has excellent facilities for guests, including a rustic shed and barbecue facility complete with ovens, refrigerators and modern conveniences. The park is run with great enthusiasm by the farmer Rob Saunders and his wife Julie, although they do employ a couple to manage the park reception area.

Ownership dimensions

As evidenced by this case, compared to public companies private businesses can more easily do long-term planning without the pressure of generating short-term profits for the sake of shareholders. Furthermore, planned inheritance of the business by children ensures continuity.

Ultimate disposition of the farm and the stables has not been formally planned. It is assumed that the two daughters will share the farm and land inheritance, and the family all agree that this is important. Given that the land is separate from the stables in terms of ownership, a number of options exist. Coming to an agreement on this sensitive issue is difficult in most families, and the Donnellys do not view it as a current priority.

The Donnelly family identified several critical success factors for this business:

Family dimensions

Rob Saunders' personal reasons for establishing Taunton Farm Holiday Park were based on survival of the family farm, which he inherited from his parents. As farming sheep and cattle had become less and less viable due to increasing competition and lower prices for primary produce, alternative sources of income were needed to service loans and cover the running costs of the farm. Rob has a strong desire to continue to work in agriculture and clearly has a strong affinity with the land. Rob's wife Julie shares the same goals as Rob, with a strong desire to raise their family (ages 20, 18 and 13) on the farm.

Interestingly, growth of the business was not an initial goal as Rob decided to take a cautious approach to business development and 'play it by ear'. Rob's family would continue to 'live off the farm' in terms of their food, accommodation and transport requirements. Any profit from the Holiday Park would be re-invested into improving the park and 'adding value' through provision of additional facilities (to be discussed later). Thus expansion was never a goal for the business, but improvement of existing facilities was always pursued.

In 1991, when Rob was considering whether to build a holiday park on the road frontage of his 330 hectares (825 acres) estate he consulted widely with tourism and farming people in the south-west region of Western Australia. Local and regional government departments were contacted to provide information on the feasibility of caravan parks. However, only one proved to be beneficial, the South West Regional Office of the Western Australian Tourism Commission. They provided a computer model which could be used to predict the optimal number of caravan berths to build (which was 60) and the cost and revenue flows associated with that scenario.

Rob found that business advisers and 'how to' feasibility seminars were mostly a waste of time and involved individuals who were seeking to 'sell' their services and products rather than deal with specific business issues.

A critical decision faced by Rob was whether to build chalet-style accommodation and target wealthy tourists or to provide a value-for-money holiday park for travellers on a budget. He discussed this problem in detail with his neighbours, who were keen caravanners, and they agreed that a caravan park would be attractive to the many holidaymakers travelling through the region.

Based on his discussions with as many people as possible, combined with his own 'gut feeling', Rob decided to build the caravan park. In hindsight this was the correct decision, as there has been an explosion in chalet-style accommodation in the south-west region and approximately 300 new establishments opened in the 1990s. However, Taunton Farm Holiday Park remains one of the few caravan parks in the region which targets the lower-income end of the market. Rob believes 'it is better to be different than it is to be better'. In other words, he has resisted participating in the rush to build 'up-market' accommodation and has chosen to be unique.

The decision as to whether the children will take over the business will be made in consultation with the whole family. The children will only take over the business if they so desire. So far, the eldest child (a 20-year-old boy studying architecture at university) has not shown any interest in taking over either the business or the farm. It is possible that the next eldest child (an 18-year-old girl) may be interested, in the future. The youngest child (a 13-year-old girl) shows some interest in farming. Thus there is no clear disposition plan, but the business disposition will be determined according to the needs and aspirations of each family member. Rob is adamant that he will not sell the farm or the business, but would consider a lease arrangement, as long as the lessees were suitable. Rob considers that any lease arrangement would have to be regulated to avoid any problems developing between the owners and the lessees. A third option is the appointment of full-time managers and the reversion of Rob and Julie's role to owners, with no involvement in the day-to-day running of the business. Whatever the disposition plans are, Rob is keen to leave an inheritance for his children in the form of the farmland and the business.

Business dimensions

Rob chose to participate in a franchise arrangement with Big 4 Holiday Parks, the largest chain of caravan parks in Australia. Big 4 is an affiliation of some 160 parks in Australia, offering units, cabins, villas, caravan and camping sites to suit a range of tastes and budgets (http://www.big4.com. au/). Big 4 charges a franchise fee based on a percentage of turnover, which for Taunton amounts to Aus$2000 to Aus$3000 per annum. Holidaymakers are invited to join the Big 4 Club for Aus$30 for 24 months' membership and qualify for a 10% discount on tariffs in Australian Big 4 parks as well as in affiliated parks in the UK (The Best of British), New Zealand (Top 10 Holiday Parks) and Italy (Network Camping). Based on the discount rate revenue that Taunton receives, Rob estimates that this franchise generates approximately Aus$20,000 worth of business per annum so revenue from the franchise arrangements is far in excess of the costs.

There are also consumer loyalty benefits associated with the Big 4 franchise, as franchise parks refer their visitors to other Big 4 parks around Australia, thereby keeping people 'within the chain'. Big 4 offers a free reservation and book-ahead service which guarantees accommodation at the next Big 4 park, as long as the booking is made as you leave a Big 4 park and pay a deposit. Big 4 also provides a money-back guarantee if guests are not satisfied with the facilities or service. All franchisee parks have to apply to Big 4 and are inspected a number of times before they can affiliate with Big 4.

Being part of a larger chain initially helped Taunton to counter competition from other parks. A Western Australian company, Fleetwood Corporation, has been expanding into ownership of caravan parks in order to obtain sites for the setting up of their park homes (mobile homes placed on longer-stay and permanent sites). Fleetwood Corporation is a major promoter of caravanning and camping in WA and operated over 1600 caravan sites in eight holiday parks in 1999. They are one of the largest wholesalers and retailers of caravans and caravan accessories in WA, and the largest manufacturer and supplier of park homes to the WA market. However, Fleetwood recently affiliated with Big 4 and no longer poses a direct threat to his clientèle.

Rob continues to nurture customer loyalty through personal contacts (by telephone) and an annual Christmas card mail-out. As many as 50% of his 'local' clientèle (from within WA) are repeat visitors, and word-of-mouth, although slow to take effect, remains his most effective communication channel. Rob estimates that it took about four years for the reputation of Taunton Farm to spread, but this latter channel is now very effective not only within WA but also across Australia. This may reflect the nature of the camping and caravanning holiday market, where the park's visitors spread its reputation as they travel to other parks of Australia and talk with other caravanners and campers.

Rob considers that there are some unique aspects of their Park and farming activities. Principally, the unique mix of having a working farm and a holiday park on one site creates opportunities for specialized tours such as horse riding, dairy and shearing operations and farm-yard animal viewing. However, Rob is reluctant to expand into these areas without the specialist knowledge and infrastructure needed. In any case, other farm operators in the region are providing these services.

Another unique aspect and an underlying business philosophy is the emphasis on personal contact with customers and staff. Rob and Julie are always prepared to talk and socialize with their visitors, and encourage their staff to be friendly towards visitors at all times. Personal contact takes precedence over any operational matters. For example, Rob does not mind if 'it takes one and a half hours to empty the rubbish bins' if he is engaged in conversation with visitors. This creates an issue of how to complete the daily tasks of running the park without being caught up in conversations all day. Rob jokingly suggested he needs lessons in how to get away from people.

Coupled with the emphasis on personal contact is the high level of pride in Rob and Julie's achievements at Taunton Farm. Their success as an affordable, friendly and comfortable holiday park was recognized in the 1997, 1999 and 2000 Western Australian Tourism Awards when they won in the category of Camping and Caravan Parks. In 2001, Taunton Farm was the first caravan park in Western Australia to be inducted into the Tourism Hall of Fame after winning their category three times.

Rob has many development plans, but the cautious approach to expansion is still prevalent. Any future development will be based on the financial aspects of the business – turnover and occupancy rates. As a general rule, Rob believes that once an average 60% occupancy rate has been reached it is time to expand, or run the risk of turning away business. This principle applies specifically to the cottages within the park, which generate the most revenue for the business. Rob commenced with two cottages (cabins) in 1992, but has since increased to ten. Next year more cottages will be built on land overlooking the park and the pond/recreation area. Interestingly, the cottages cover their costs at just 20% occupancy rate and make a profit at 40% occupancy rate.

Other plans for the park include a swimming pool and more caravan berths with their own en suite bathrooms attached. Rob is also considering extending the park office to include a tearoom or licensed restaurant, which will overlook the pond and pool area. Another plan involves production of bottled rainwater, which will be produced and sold in the park. While these plans involve expansion and diversification of the business, Rob views these developments as adding value to the park, rather than deliberate growth.

Ownership dimensions

For Rob's family the decision to borrow money to invest in the park was relatively low risk. Rob was well aware that the improved value of the land after building the park would be far in excess of his borrowings, which were approximately Aus$300,000 in 1992. In other words, if the park was not viable, Rob could recoup all of his investment (and probably make a profit) by selling the park as an established business. The value of the land was higher than the capital cost of the holiday park and land values in the region have continued to escalate during the 1990s. However, there is always some risk, and for Rob it was the threat of losing the land, which he viewed as a part of his heritage, which should be passed on to his children in the same way that his parents bequeathed him the farm. Rob would always be reluctant to sell any of his land, as he believes that 'once it is gone – it is gone'. Again, his links with the land provide the main underlying philosophy of the family and the business. The park land remains a part of the farm holding and the mortgage is secured over the farm.

Rob will continue as owner/manager with his wife Julie well into the future. They are both young (around 40 years of age) and will continue to be involved as owners. However, they have reached a point where they must now appoint a paid manager of the park as Rob is keen to devote more time to farming. He has decided that the business justifies a full-time paid manager, a considerable departure from the casual arrangements he has had in place. He currently employs a young couple as paid managers for five days per week and only works at the park during their days off or when it gets busy. All decisions regarding the management of the park are still made by Rob and Julie.

Case 6.3 Ol' MacDonald's

Background

Ol' MacDonald's Resort is located on Buffalo Lake, Alberta, about a 2-hour drive from either Edmonton or Calgary. It is very rural, not on a main highway, and therefore can be considered to be a destination resort based on the attraction of the large lake and peaceful environment. The owners can boast of a full house in summer, and that 80% of their customers are repeat visitors or referrals from customers.

The resort started as a 25-site campground on forested family land and has been ambitiously developed by the MacDonalds to become a family holiday destination. The resort offers many attractions and services:

- 270 serviced and unserviced pitches for recreational vehicles and tents;
- group camping areas;
- cabins;
- motel;
- rental recreation vehicles;
- washroom and laundry buildings;
- cafe ('home cooking') and store, combined with the office;
- gift shop combined with indoor mini-golf and museum, pool tables and arcade;
- large tents for group use;
- catering on- and off-site;
- sandy beach, boat rentals and boat launch; beach concession;
- playgrounds and ball diamond, horseshoe pits, volleyball net, obstacle course, crafts for kids;
- farm animals;
- fire pits and firewood;
- hay-wagon rides and horse riding;
- special events; and
- church services.

The general area offers a golf course, hunting and fishing, bird watching, and abundant wildlife.

The most recent development was the purchase of a large nearby house that is rented to groups for functions or as deluxe, all-year accommodation. The family also possesses janitorial and maintenance contracts for three nearby provincial parks. They have also sold residential lots nearby, where a small subdivision has been developed. The actual resort site is 50 acres in size.

The resort business is highly seasonal in Alberta, with winters being unsuitable for camping and lakeside recreation. The MacDonalds have no ambition to run any of the resort during the off-season (from October to April) but hope to develop off-site catering and the new house as all-year revenue sources.

Family dimensions

Jean MacDonald came up with the idea of developing a campsite, partly as a reflection of her own mother's unfulfilled dream to start a business. She admits this was largely an emotional motive, and also believed that farm income was not enough, and wanted to make her children's lives better. She could develop a legacy that could be handed down to them in the future, all within the context of remaining a farm family with strong ties to the land.

With her earlier experience working as secretary–treasurer of a county recreation board, and financial experience in running a park, Jean felt she could run a campsite business. There was also the need for a challenge, and she was motivated even more by being told her idea would not work. Banks would not lend money for a rural tourism business, especially when provincial parks on the same lake provided free camping. Why would anyone pay?

Daughter, Joanne MacDonald shared their mother's original goals, but some of the others did not. There was no real opposition, however, and Sam was simply too busy to contribute. The decisive factor in getting started was the availability of a federal grant programme. Jean applied and received money in 1984, which made it possible to hire workers and clear bush land for roads and 270 camping pitches. If the grant had not been available Jean feels she would have eventually got it done, but the site would have been much smaller, and it would have been completed at a much slower pace.

Jean describes the family as 'conservative', thrifty, and always saving. Hence they retained her grandparents' possessions, which now constitute the on-site museum. The ideal of leaving a physical legacy of value for future generations runs deep in the MacDonald family.

Sam was originally reluctant to set up a resort business, as he was farming 2000 acres (800 hectares) and had little time to spare. For the first 2 years he had no direct involvement in the resort operations, but supported the idea of its development because it looked like it would work. He subsidized the resort's development from the farm income, and although the farm operations have been greatly diminished he still does some outside consulting work for additional income. Now they own 1400 acres and continue to raise 120 cattle. The resort now commands all his efforts during the peak season. Sam admits he is a farmer at heart and could never live in the city.

The resources, consisting of ample forested land, and attractive waterfront with beach, were part of the original farm and presented a natural opportunity for some kind of recreational and/or residential development. There was no specific plan for ultimate development of the land, and the concept evolved over time. Sam never believed it would get to its current size and complexity, and it grew very fast.

Joanne was excited about her parents' decision to develop the resort, and had confidence in its success. She was involved from the beginning on a part-time basis, and set up the registration process. Recently she quit her full-time job at a high school in a nearby town to commence full-time at the resort. The other daughter, Roxanne was living and working in Red Deer when the start-up decision was made. She was not involved in the initiation of the resort, but saw the potential for extra income. She visited frequently and helped out a little, then moved back to Buffalo Lake in 1994 with her two children. It was her goal to raise children in the country, and she built a house on the nearby subdivision being sold off the family farmland. In 1995 she started to work three-quarters of her time at the resort. She did not know how much the business really entailed and never seems to get finished with work and responsibility.

The land and resort business is owned by Sam and Jean MacDonald as a limited company. Two daughters are employed, and three of their children have worked in the business seasonally, so it is supporting three generations. Previously, their son Murray, along with Joanne, was being groomed to take over management of the resort, but in 1998 he and two staff members were killed in a car accident. This tragic incident delayed the retirement plans of Sam and Jean, and required a major re-assessment of where the business was heading and who would run it. A 2-year period ensued that has been described as a 'plateau', and a time of healing and introspection.

Business dimensions

Sam has to be jack-of-all-trades around the farm and the resort, all year round. He is the only one familiar enough with the resort infrastructure (e.g. where do the water lines run?) to handle much of the maintenance. The workload is high and can be very demanding, especially because the family's strategy has been to improve the resort continuously, with frequent expansions made to the physical plant.

Jean functions as office manager. She handles the financial and marketing side of the business, but also works in the cafe and catering areas.

Joanne is the reservations manager and deals with 90% of their customers through the front office. She has done some staff management and payroll work, but registration is really a full-time job. Dealing with people can be difficult, but it is the part she enjoys most. Eventually she would like to take over more of the general management and relieve her mother of her workload. Her eldest daughter is 16 and has been working on site; she would like to study tourism and enter the family business full-time.

Roxanne runs the gift shop, museum, arcade, mini-golf and petting animals. The indoor facilities are all in one building and constitute a vital profit centre for the resort.

Three grandchildren (two daughters and one son of Joanne and Roxanne) work seasonally at the resort; one has been employed full-time and the other part-time over the summer. They work in the store and reception areas. Kevin, another son of Sam and Jean, has not been involved in the resort.

This case illustrates how the family business keeps a family together, especially through adversity. Family members agree that ability to work through problems together is a must, and the crisis following Murray's death reinforced this

conviction. Not all differences of opinion have been easy to resolve, but in a family context there is the knowledge that they must and will be resolved eventually. Emotion is a key element in this family business, and it has its positive side in generating commitment. Working with loved and respected family members makes for a good environment and the family's accomplishments foster pride.

Even disagreements can be lived with, but at least one family member would like to see more formal and effective organization, with regular meetings and better communications. For example, sometimes staff receive different instructions from various family members, so the question of who is in charge needs sorting out.

Ownership dimensions

To the parents, this family business provided the opportunity to work with family and to see children grow in age and ability. It provides personal happiness to have children at home or nearby. Long hours and hard work are inherent in the family business. The owner–parents are never free of responsibility and getting a day off is always difficult. Children have to decide if that is the lifestyle they want.

Chapter Summary

One common characteristic for all farm-based family businesses is strong ties to the land. These are not only based on farming traditions or love of the land, but also financial ties that compel farming families continually to work the land to make it viable and support the family. This situation had driven the families into diversification into tourism perhaps as 'reluctant entrepreneurs'. This is a very difficult transition to make from an industrial perspective – from being a primary producer to being a service sector operator. From a business perspective farming and tourism are complete opposites – farming is supply-driven, tourism is market-led; farmers are cost-cutters, tourism businesses are revenue-maximizers; farmers produce single standardized products at a given price, tourism businesses diversify into many products and offer a range of prices. Perhaps the only thing that farming and tourism have in common is seasonality, although tourism operators can adopt strategies to cope with seasonality. These three cases illustrate how farm-based family businesses have negotiated the difficult transition from farming to tourism based on careful decision-making, family commitment and most importantly, appropriate use of the farm land.

7

Family-owned and -operated Small Hotels

_____

Introduction

Running a small hotel places families at the centre of the tourism experience and as such, places extra demands on both family members and the business. Working hours are long and guests demanding, and the rewards can be insufficient for family members working in the business. The three cases in this chapter demonstrate that family-owned hotels represent the quintessential family businesses in tourism and hospitality, in that the true character and strength of the family is reflected in the fortunes of the business. Case 7.1 demonstrates that hard work and commitment are needed to maintain a family business that provides accommodation, and owners must in some cases be willing to work in all aspects of the business, including construction, maintenance and cleaning, for a limited financial return. The lifestyle rewards identified earlier in the book are clearly sufficient to offset any lack of remuneration for the founders of the business, but the next generation are not always willing to make such a trade-off. Case 7.2 also demonstrates that hard work and imagination can transform a heritage building into a hotel and restaurant and prove to be a financial success. However, even when opportunities are realized by family businesses, rewards are not always distributed equitably, generating some level of resentment amongst family members. Case 7.3 illustrates a young

family business, yet to face some of the challenges of balancing family and business dimensions, and one in which ownership and succession is not yet an issue.

Case 7.1 Gunnar and Maude Bergstedt, Åre, Sweden

Background

Located in the mountains of central Sweden, the resort town of Åre is primarily devoted to the winter sports of downhill and cross-country skiing. In the surrounding rural area are several smaller ski facilities and a range of accommodation, including the self-catering cabins owned by the Bergstedt family.

Gunnar and Maude Bergstedt operate five cabins containing ten units, and three of the cabins are considered to be at the executive level of quality for the purpose of advertising to the German market. They are all situated in a wooded subdivision of 20–25 lots that lies adjacent to a small resort operated by friends of the Bergstedts (it is also a family business) that contains a restaurant. Nearby is a ski hill and hotel complex, and the area contains many groomed cross-country ski trails. Gunnar helps his neighbours maintain and groom the ski trails through the winter season, as they are the main attraction.

©D. Getz et al. 2004. _The Family Business in Tourism and Hospitality_
(D. Getz, J. Carlsen and A. Morrison)

Family dimensions

Gunnar's grandfather's grandfather established the family farm, and when the railway came to Åre in 1882 he recognized the potential for tourism development. He built a shop and a hotel, which have not continued in the family, but this initiative certainly imbued a family interest in tourism. What has been passed on through the generations is the farm, and the separate landholding on the mountain.

In 1963 Gunnar's own father started the subdivision that today contains the cabins, some 20–25 in total. Gunnar is not alone in this line of business, as both his brothers have also developed cabins and homes on the family land.

When Gunnar was about 20 years old he had a vision of this development. He expected that building and renting ten cabins would make him financially comfortable, and that he could be his own boss with flexible time. Of course it proved rather more difficult! He entered a career as a schoolteacher and is now retired after almost 30 years in that profession. Maude also worked locally, and both incomes were needed to support the family and development of the cabins.

Over the decades he and his brothers built their separately owned cabins one at a time, using wood from their own forest, cut at their own small sawmill. The two brothers and their families live on the mountain in houses they built, while Gunnar and Maude live on the farm during summer, and spend winters on the mountain – to be close to their rental cabins and ski trails.

Business dimensions

It is a highly seasonal business, with the peak months being January–April. Summer demand is slight, and in the autumn there is hunting for moose and birds in the surrounding forest. The Bergstedts' neighbour operates over 20 snowmobiles for tourists, but they are considered to be incompatible with the ski trails and require a separate system.

Maude and Gunnar operate the cabins themselves, and he admits it is a lot of work for little financial return. They have no employees and say that labour costs in Sweden are far too high and therefore paid staff are unaffordable. This means all the physical work (cleaning and maintenance of cabins) must be done by Maude and Gunnar.

Lack of marketing is an admitted weakness. The Bergstedts rely on repeat business, which is a strength, and on word-of-mouth recommendations. Some clients return year after year to the same cabin. As well, the nearby ski resort sometimes books cabins for them, for a commission.

Their only advertising is through a German travel agency network, and this consists of a small profile with one photograph placed in a catalogue that contains many competing accommodations throughout Scandinavia. They do not have a brochure for distribution.

When their son, Jon, was studying at university his personal website was utilized to generate some business for the cabins, and now the family wants to develop a separate website for the cabins. Gunnar believes this will be successful and acknowledges the need to generate more business.

Ownership dimensions

Jon has been educated in computer programming and does not want to enter the business, and a daughter who lives in Stockholm is not involved. Another son, Jacob, was killed in a car accident several years ago and that tragedy permanently changed the family. Jacob was a champion snowboarder who wanted to live in the area and take over the family business. Now there is no apparent successor within the immediate family.

Most of the cabins have been financed personally, with some bank loans. Ten years ago, after their tenth and last cabin was constructed, the property market was in crisis owing to over-supply and bankruptcy sales. Gunnar believes he only avoided bankruptcy because his debts were small. His father had instilled in the sons a philosophy of self-reliance, and this value seems to explain why the Bergstedts have not applied for available European Community grants to subsidize their development – that, and the fact that Gunnar has not got around to the necessary paperwork!

The entire Bergstedt family, including the three brothers, have a long and deep attachment to the land. In part this is attributable to being successors to many generations of inheritance, and in part to the rural culture and lifestyle in central Sweden. This involves annual hunting parties for birds and moose, resulting in supplies of meat for the entire year. Skiing is an essential ingredient, and more recently snowmobiling, and for the younger generation, snowboarding. Living and working in the forest, including tree cutting and sawing, fits the preferred lifestyle.

Very recently the three brothers, Gunnar's son Jon, and two nephews, together purchased 1000 acres adjacent to their mountain landholding. They will cut lumber for a pulp and paper mill in Norway, thereby generating revenue. This might also facilitate future property developments, and will definitely ensure continued hunting privileges for the family.

Farming is no longer a subsistence activity in this region, but rural traditions associated with farming and forestry endure. Gunnar recognizes that his family cabin business is related to a lifestyle preference, and wants this to continue through his retirement. However, the future of the business is not certain.

Would Gunnar recommend this type of business to another family? He is doubtful, citing hard work, minimal financial returns and the normal challenges of working with close family members. He thinks his arrangement, with the brothers and other family members, is somewhat unique and definitely not typical of family businesses in this region.

With the loss of their son and intended business heir, the Bergstedts are uncertain about continuing this tourist-cabin business. For 2 years the family business was essentially frozen, because of the tragedy. Now it is time to get it back on track and plan for the future.

However, Gunnar does not want to build more cabins, given the costs and work involved. The Bergstedts' goals remain lifestyle-related and Gunnar would ideally like to maintain his traditional farming life in the mountains of mid-Sweden. There is the possibility of selling cabins, but once they are gone the potential earnings from the remainder might be inadequate for their needs. Another option is to sell the whole operation as their retirement fund.

Case 7.2 Cricklewood Hotel

Background

Cricklewood Hotel, originally built in 1885 as a coachhouse, is a popular restaurant and accommodation establishment in the village of Bothwell, Scotland. It offers a relaxed family-oriented restaurant, a conservatory and a beer garden. An extensive menu is available and food is served from 11 a.m. to 11 p.m. each day.

Cricklewood is an attractive Victorian property, set off the main Hamilton to Glasgow road, with parking and a garden area that was originally built for the manager of a local colliery in 1890. In 2002 one of the leading hospitality and leisure companies in the UK bought the six-bedroom Cricklewood Hotel. It is located in the conservation village of Bothwell, Scotland, which is 15 miles from Glasgow and 40 miles from Edinburgh, and has a population of 6000, mainly composed of professionals. Plans are afoot to transform it into a leading-edge entertainment venue, the likes of which the region has never previously experienced. This is a far cry from 1979 when its lease was put on the market at the price of £15,000. At that time it was being run as a B&B with a turnover of £11,000 per year, which was mainly derived from a contract with British Gas to accommodate long-term unemployed men who were being retrained.

Family dimensions

Still with little in the way of adequate finance as a young couple, Alison and Colin, then in their early 20s, were supported by Colin's grandfather who stood as guarantor to secure funds from the Bank of Scotland. Business advisers were drawn from the circle surrounding their parents and were of the same older generation of family lawyers and accountants not up to date with modern-day commerce.

Although business entry had been made financially easier through the lease arrangement, it had been drawn up and approved by the family lawyer who would have been duped into agreeing to certain clauses by the landlord – including responsibility for all internal and external repairs to Cricklewood. The building was old, sick and had not been designed to withstand commercial usage; understandably repair and maintenance costs were extensive. As Colin and Alison worked harder and the turnover increased, so did the rental. By 1981 they had two sons under the age of 2 who they rarely spent time with due to the hours, demands and complexity of the ever-growing business. The work/life balance was becoming increasingly problematic and stressful. Alison tried a partial withdrawal from the business to care for the children in the recently purchased family home, but felt excluded from the 'partnership'. The couple were faced with a real dilemma: they have created a thriving and ever-flourishing business that is stretching their capabilities to effectively manage it, and at the same time to maintain harmonious marital and family relationships.

Business dimensions

Local competition was negligible. Into this virgin market Colin and Alison imported a Canadian coffee shop concept and incorporated it into the bar and restaurant area of the hotel, quickly creating a popular meeting and socializing place for local residents. By 1984 turnover had reached £250,000 – the concept was a significant success . . . but life was not without its challenges.

Ownership dimensions

In 1984 they reached the difficult decision to sell to Colin's younger brother Nigel, who had worked with the couple for 5 years since he was 17 years old. The selling price for the lease was set through the emotional criteria of: wanting to give the brother a good start in business at a young age; his view of the hotel as his 'home'; and a desire to get out of the business deal without the hassle of putting the lease on the open market. The lease was handed over to Nigel for a 'family gift' price of £25,000.

Turnover at Cricklewood Hotel continued on an upward trajectory with little or no alteration to Colin and Alison's original concept. Nigel managed to negotiate with the landlord to buy the property outright for £300,000 and sold it on to a Plc. in 1992 for £1 million. On reflection, Alison in particular feels bitter about how things worked out, and often agonizes on what might have been in wealth terms if she and Colin had persevered, and resents Nigel's success based on what in effect was intellectually their property.

Case 7.3 Millestgården

Background

Johan and Malin Antman own and operate a small hotel called Millestgården outside the village of Duved near the Swedish resort town of Åre. Their 1 ha property lies close to the main highway to Norway and overlooks a beautiful river valley, with ski hills only a short drive away, and ski trails within 200 m. It is also adjacent to a historic site with a monument that is well marked on the highway and which attracts visitors to drive right by the hotel.

Millestgården has 23 rooms with 60 beds, a restaurant and small conference room. At peak times there are around 50 guests on average. It is a pensionnat, normally providing room plus two meals per day. Showers and toilets are shared (not en suite), so the hotel caters to more budget-conscious families and groups, including business meetings. There is also a sauna, billiards and table tennis for guests.

An inn was located on this site in 1880, serving passing highway trade, while the current hotel was built in 1945 and expanded in 1965. The previous owner went bankrupt after having invested heavily in the property, particularly by completely renovating the restaurant. Johan, who was then living on an adjacent farm, saw the opportunity and purchased the business for much less than it would otherwise have cost. He and his wife have owned it for 3 years.

Family dimensions

Johan came to the Åre resort area in 1991 as a ski instructor and decided to stay. It was his idea to own a business and take root. He previously managed the Backpacker's Inn, located in the centre of Åre, and continued to run it for the first year after purchasing the hotel. Neither he nor Malin had formal training in hotel management, but Malin is now completing chef courses since she does the restaurant cooking. Johan is learning the business as he goes, drawing on friends and even the previous owner for advice. He still does some work in winter for the ski school, and in summer they take bookings by telephone for a local adventure company. When possible, he uses this service to attract additional hotel business.

The primary motivation for purchasing the business was to provide the family with the opportunity to stay permanently in the area. The Antmans have three young children, aged 2, 3 and 6, and this presents them with a challenge. Usually the children go to a day-care facility, plus babysitters are brought to their private quarters at busy times when both Johan and Malin are working. Occasionally there are difficulties in balancing work and family life, but Johan feels he is able to spend more time with the youngest than he did with the two older children, because they are nearby. On the other hand, the work means they do not always get the free time with the children that they want.

Johan and Malin were at first apprehensive about working together on a daily basis, after holding separate jobs, but they say it has worked out perfectly. Johan tends to get up early and make breakfast for the family, while Malin works more in the evenings. This 'shift work' was not planned but developed naturally.

During winter the days are very long and sometimes stressful as they are constantly on call. Contacts with friendly customers can sometimes interfere with work, while at other times the children might get in the way of guests. This year they took a holiday for two weeks in mid January when demand was low, and this is only possible by completely shutting the hotel. The children went to stay with grandparents while Johan and Malin went skiing on the continent.

The best aspect of running a family business, at least for Johan, is the ability to manage his own time. Some jobs are dirty and undesirable, but there is a lot of variety. Guests are friendly, and so work can be very enjoyable. 'If it wasn't fun, I would not do it' comments Johan.

The children like to help with little things in the hotel, but of course are too young to stick to any task for very long. When they get older,

perhaps 15, the parents might employ them in paid work in a part-time capacity, thereby reducing the need for other staff. Johan says these would be 'real jobs'.

Johan could not think of any other families in the area, with children, who were running tourism businesses. He is currently the chairman of the Duved industry group and so he personally knows most of the operators nearby. He feels parents might be afraid of taking the big step, whereas brothers and sisters might find it easier to get into business together.

Business dimensions

The winter season is dominant, owing to the popularity of skiing and other winter sports. The Antmans more or less close the hotel in the quiet months of May, June, September and December, but as they live on the premises they open it for functions or groups if there is demand. They employ no full-time staff and do most of the work themselves. When demand is high they use local, part-time workers to help out – usually in the evenings including dinner time.

The winter season is busy and financial performance so far has been good, but as with many businesses in this area cash flow becomes a problem late in the year (autumn). That is when banks extend credit to small operators to see them into the winter peak season. If summer demand could be improved, this family could hire one or two permanent staff to lift the heavy workload burden.

Marketing is mostly done through Åre's main promotion and booking company (www.areresort.se), and because this service is owned by the dominant ski-lift and hotel company, small operators worry that they are not necessarily getting equal attention. On the other hand, this company has considerable resources for promotion and development of the resort.

In the main Åre promotional booklet Millestgarden has a small photo and profile within the Duved section (the company promotes 'One ski resort, five villages') It is described as an 'authentic regional pension in a natural and quiet environment at the Carolean soldier's monument 2.5 km west of Duved.' Packages including skiing and accommodation are offered.

They also have their own Internet site (www.millestgarden.se), but it is not set up to take direct bookings. Their own 1-page flyer describes the hotel as a 'genuine Jämtlandish guesthouse in scenic and quiet surroundings located 2 km west of central Duved in western Jämtland. Our speciality is traditional cooking from Jämtland. This includes fresh fish from the lakes and rivers of Jämtland, reindeer, moose and many more locally grown products.' It promotes local recreational activities, including fishing in the river, mountain biking, sightseeing, golf, Sami cultural attractions (the region's native people), rafting, caving, climbing and boogie surfing on the river.

Duved needs to be marketed better as a destination distinct from Åre, according to Johan. Their tourism industry group, of which he is chairman, finance a tourist information bureau, but more cooperation is needed to build demand during the 2.5 months of summer that is currently a low period.

Expansion of activities and decreased seasonality are desired, rather than any expansion in bed capacity. In fact, the Antmans are contemplating the elimination of ten beds in order to allow the addition of small meeting rooms to help develop the business meetings segment.

The property includes an old, unoccupied house, and a barn, which both figure in the Antmans' expansion plans. In the house could be developed a small cafe, souvenir shop and information centre to take advantage of the adjacent historical site. There is a Carolean trail concept along the highway linking Sweden and Norway, recounting a failed invasion hundreds of years ago. Some European Community funds might be available to help develop the house as part of this tourism concept, specifically for the audio-visual component, and the Åre Kommun government might also contribute to refurbishment of the house to help develop tourism infrastructure.

The barn can be incorporated, but turned into a venue for historically themed (1700s) functions. This would also be aimed squarely at the conference market, including those staying on site or elsewhere. The family plans to do all the work, and is looking 5 or 6 years into the future for completion.

Ownership dimensions

Succession or disposal of the property is not currently an issue, as the Antmans are still in the developmental stage. The children are too young to participate in the business, but the parents would like them to be able to continue to live in this attractive rural area.

Chapter Summary

There is much to be learned from these three cases in terms of family, business and ownership dimensions of small hotels. Commitment of family members is paramount in the hotel business, as the demands are high and the work hours long. Some businesses can call on the extended family to assist with the business (as does case 7.1), or use the business to give extended family members a start in business life (case 7.2). This is especially useful when it is recognized that not all family businesses have the cash-flow to employ non-family members (case 7.1). In fact if revenue did improve, these businesses would employ more casual or permanent staff to ease the work load of family members (case 7.3). In case 7.3, work arrangements evolved naturally among the family, with a shift-work approach to running the business being the most agreeable arrangement between the husband-and-wife team. Their children are too young to work in the business and if they ever do so it will be as paid employees. Business lessons are evident in these three cases, in terms of having a vision or recognizing a business opportunity, establishing the business and developing it successfully. Perhaps the most tangible lessons in this chapter are in terms of ownership, which must be handled carefully to avoid financial or family problems. In case 7.1, borrowings were kept to a minimum and that prudent approach enabled the family to retain the business, in spite of a family tragedy and business problems of seasonality, property price deflation and bankruptcy. Retention of ownership would, in retrospect, have been a better option in case 7.2 for the family concerned, and any family business disposition will always involve some agonizing on the part of the founders.

8

Family-owned Nature-based Resorts

_____

Introduction

These case studies cover a number of topics relevant to all family businesses as well as some specific issues related to family businesses in or adjacent to natural areas such as national parks and waterways. The motivations for establishing resorts adjacent to natural areas are usually lifestyle-related, but in two cases the families have held a long-standing attachment to the area over several generations. These two cases are O'Reilly's Guesthouse in Queensland and River Valley Ventures on the Rangitiki River on the North Island of New Zealand. The rise in popularity of nature-based tourism experiences in countries like Australia and New Zealand also provides a compelling reason for family business start-up in areas that offer ecotourists, backpackers and the pleasure/holiday visitors a unique holiday resort experience in a natural area. Crystal Creek Rainforest Retreat is a unique rainforest lodge that accommodates a range of visitors from Australia and overseas.

property adjoining the World Heritage listed Numinbah nature reserve in northern New South Wales (NSW). The facilities include luxury accommodation, walking trails, fine cuisine and a functions centre. In keeping with the theme of peace and tranquillity, accommodation is limited to seven couples at any one time, and each bungalow provides total privacy amidst the rainforest. Bungalows all have modern facilities and guests can order fine cuisine prepared on the property by Judy and served by Ralph. The CCRR has won several regional and state tourism awards since 1994, and in 1999 won a national tourism award in the category of Unique Accommodation.

The CCRR attracts mainly couples from the nearest capital city, Brisbane, seeking to enjoy the rest and relaxation in the rainforest. The retreat also holds workshops for birdwatchers, botanists, natural healers and artists during the year. It also offers a small function centre that can cater for small weddings and corporate groups.

Case 8.1 Crystal Creek Rainforest Retreat (CCRR)

Background

Owners Ralph and Judy Kramer established CCRR in 1992 after retiring from their respective careers. CCRR is described as a 140-hectare (360-acre) sub-tropical rainforest

Family dimensions

Ralph and Judy were both seeking a career change and change of environment, from the industrial city of Newcastle in NSW. Ralph had a long-held interest in nature and wildlife and was active in the conservation movement. Judy had involvement in the arts and ran her own art gallery in Victoria. Together they shared a desire to live and work in the rainforest of Northern NSW where they could combine their interests. Having the concept of a rainforest retreat in mind, they then sought the right location and engaged a number of professionals (architects, engineers and business planners) to guide the project.

After 6 years of running the business, Ralph and Judy are seeking less 'hands-on' running of the business and would like to employ more staff. Currently they employ four part-time cleaners and one full-time maintenance person, although two part-timers also assist with maintenance of the extensive gardens that surround the retreat. There are also two daughters currently working in the business (Fiona and Jude) on a part-time basis; they are acquiring the skills and experience to work in tourism and hospitality. Jude is completing a business degree in tourism management and should graduate in the next 2 years. Rather than moving straight from there in to a management position at CCRR, Ralph would prefer that she worked for a larger tourism enterprise for a while in order to broaden her work experience. Ralph and Judy agree that training the children to take over running of the business is a difficult task, because, in Ralph's opinion . . . 'you can't treat your children like employees'. He has observed that the children do not appear to be as committed to the business as both he and Judy are, which makes the issue of disposition and succession a difficult one.

Fiona also works part-time in the business and has gained some previous experience in tourism management as an employee of the local tourism industry association. Her main interest is in the horseracing industry, and she maintains that interest through her partner's horseracing enterprise in the neighbouring town, where she works 3 days per week. Fiona has a very business-like approach to CCRR and considers that running at a profit is the most important business issue. She has ideas for developing greater efficiencies in the business, such as installation of a computerized reservation system to replace the manual system currently in use. She finds guests of the retreat demanding, as they require the full service of bungalows (daily cleaning and meals). Fiona's preferred option would be to run the administration and office of the business. She is currently completing a small business management course at the local college, acquiring such skills as basic book-keeping, business planning and business negotiation skills.

Other family members have worked at CCRR in the past but are currently pursuing their own careers. Christine (aged 26) is living in Brisbane and studying for a degree in Psychology. Mandy (aged 32) lives with her husband and child in London and works with her husband managing a small hotel. Another daughter, Sharon (aged 25) works as a Human Resource manager in Sydney, for the Furama Hotel. She is also completing a degree in Industrial Relations.

Business dimensions

In order to support more full-time staff (such as a full-time chef to replace Judy), their revised business plan indicates that 15 bungalows would be required to accommodate additional guests who would make use of the fine dining service. This would need a significant capital investment and borrowing would have to increase substantially, an option that Ralph and Judy do not wish to pursue at this time. Currently, seven bungalows achieve 80% average occupancy, with long weekends booked well in advance. There is a concern that additional bungalows and guests on site would compromise the peace and tranquillity of the retreat. Consequently, there is a level of capacity that has to be achieved in order to be financially viable, whilst avoiding the destruction of the theme and ambience of the retreat.

Ralph and Judy received requests for bungalows with spas (an almost universal requirement in the luxury accommodation category), despite the fact that a natural spring-fed creek meanders through the property. All bungalows have been fitted with spas, requiring an additional investment of Aus$35,000 per bungalow. Even at the current tariffs of Aus$245 per night, the payback period for this investment is considerable. Ralph also has plans for a day-spa for guests, requiring an additional Aus$50,000 investment, but this could be financed out of the business funds.

Finance and investment are major issues for CCRR in an environment of uncertainty with regard to the internal and external factors that can impact on business profitability. While the owners are confident in the current internal business operations, they also recognize that there are a number of external factors (such as interest rates and economic conditions) which can affect their business plans and operations. While the constraint may be financial, the opportunities are unlimited for value-adding through new products and services to cater for new markets, such as corporate retreats and natural health. There is also extensive land available to accommodate new value-adding ventures with only about 5 ha currently used for accommodation. Ralph and Judy have imprinted their personalties and vision on the business and the uniqueness of the experiences and personal interactions that they offer. They have strived for recognition in the region as an authentic ecotourism business and are sensitive to any suggestions and feedback from their guests and the wider rural community. As previously discussed, recognition has been achieved in the form of awards at the regional and national level, which has provided for a positive marketing and promotional image for CCRR. They have also sought constant improvement in the standard of accommodation, the level of services and the presentation and interpretation of the rainforest experience.

Guest feedback (from in-house surveys) indicates a very high level of satisfaction with the CCRR accommodation and services, although requests for more extensive walking tracks are not uncommon. The construction and maintenance of extensive walk-track systems is an expensive exercise that can be undertaken in national parks, but it is unreasonable, in Ralph's view, to expect this of private operators.

Ownership dimensions

The future of CCRR as a unique business offering a luxury rainforest experience is bright. Bookings are made 12 months in advance for peak periods and there is a growing interest in new markets for corporate retreats and natural healing workshops and programmes. The important decisions that the owners are confronted with are:

- Expansion of accommodation – currently seven bungalows, but prospectively 15

needed to support future plans for business expansion.
- Succession – what succession or disposition arrangements should be put in place over the next few years as Ralph and Judy approach retirement age?

Within the two issues are a number of related factors in terms of finance, investment, training, protection of the rainforest and maintaining the uniqueness of CCRR. These issues remain 'on the table' and are openly discussed with staff and other family members. Ralph and Judy are unsure about their plans for disposition of the business. They have enjoyed living and working in the rainforest environment and would find it difficult to move away. The nature of the CCRR business is such that it would require a unique set of skills to take over running of the business successfully, and both Ralph and Judy feel that they have not yet found anyone who possesses those skills. There is also a deep commitment to maintaining the environmental integrity of the rainforest, which would have to be considered in any disposition decision. Ironically, the very peace and tranquillity that motivated Ralph and Judy to live in the rainforest (and has been the basis for their business success) have been compromised in the face of the growing demands of running CCRR.

Ralph and Judy feel that Mandy and her husband (who is an Italian chef) could take over running of the business as they have the necessary skills to meet the customers' requirements. However it is unlikely that they will move from London at this time, so succession plans remain uncertain. In the meantime CCRR continues to enjoy success in business and a growing reputation for excellence at the national and international level.

Case 8.2 O'Reilly's Rainforest Guesthouse

Background

O'Reilly's Rainforest Guesthouse is an internationally acclaimed ecolodge situated in Lamington National Park (a World Heritage reserve), Queensland, Australia. It is also a unique family business now into its fourth generation of ownership.

The Guesthouse is located a 2-hour drive south of Brisbane, capital city of Queensland, Australia, and about 1.5 hours west of the famous Gold Coast resorts. It is surrounded by the Lamington National Park, a World Heritage reserve. The Guesthouse lies at 930 m altitude and is reached by a twisty, narrow, but sealed mountain road. The national park service has a campsite and information centre very close to the guesthouse. Day visitors use a large car park next to the Guesthouse. In 2000, 22% of their visitors were from overseas.

The Guesthouse business started in 1926 but stems from a pioneering settlement on the land in 1911. It has been kept in the family through four generations. Many family members currently work in the business, and it is expanding in new directions. The O'Reilly family name is so legendary in Australia that it has become a valuable brand.

The year 2001 marked 75 years of continuous operation of O'Reilly's Rainforest Guesthouse. It remains a successful, growing, family business with a number of unique ownership and management features. The modern, tourism-award-winning enterprise bears little resemblance to the original bark-clad guesthouse that provided the original shelter for visitors to Lamington National Park.

Accommodation:
- three canopy suites (luxury level);
- 61 view rooms; and
- communal guesthouse: six rooms.

Facilities:
- spa, sauna and massage;
- plunge pool;
- games room;
- dining room;
- bar;
- bistro;
- lounge;
- guest laundry;
- theatre for 120 persons;
- conference, wedding and function facilities;
- retail shop (Gran' O'Reilly's Store); and
- library and historical Stinson display.

Bus Service: Five buses are owned and operated by the Guesthouse to transport guests to walks and beauty spots. There are daily buses from Brisbane and the Gold Coast, operated by other companies. A 'meet-and-greet' service is available for Gold Coast Airport.

Guided activities are included in room tariffs, including bird walks, bush dances, 4-wheel drive bus trips, guided night walks, a 'flying fox' ride across a canyon, history and nature presentations. Special interest weeks and weekends are promoted, including Bird Week in November when all other guest activities are suspended in order to host 'birders'. Outdoor team-building activities are offered to groups. The Scrub Club provides activities for children.

Family dimensions

Pioneering origins and development of the Guesthouse have been documented by the O'Reilly family in a publication entitled *The O'Reilly Story* (to order it, see their website: www.oreillys.com.au). It is a story of four generations, beginning in 1911, with no less than eight O'Reilly boys from two related families securing 100 acres each of mountainous land for dairy farming and sheep grazing in the far hinterland of the state capital, Brisbane.

The McPherson Range was at that time wilderness, with loggers not far away, and the state government had the foresight to establish a national park. This new park was designed to surround the O'Reilly lands. In 1914 the Stockyard Creek Track was carved up the mountains to provide access to the new park (proclaimed in 1915), leading to 20 years of daily horse-trains carrying cream and wool 15 km to the valley below, and increasing tourist traffic up the mountain to experience the remaining rugged wilderness.

Early park visitors had little choice but to stay in O'Reilly huts ('humpies' made from tree bark), and the boys acted as guides into the rainforest. Trails were cut to scenic spots for horseback guests. Herb, Luke and Bernard were appointed as honorary park rangers, while Mick became overseer and accordingly the state's first 'national park ranger'. Mick and his new wife, Annie, left in 1930 to establish their own farm.

The government had required each settler to construct a hut on their specific acreage, but the boys preferred to share one house and that made two others available for visitors. A hospitality business started to develop, and it looked rather attractive compared to the alternatives. So in 1926 the first purpose-built 'guesthouse' was established, and three O'Reilly sisters moved in to help run the business, although it was seen as a temporary measure to boost cashflow until improved road access would make the farm more profitable.

A major part of the O'Reilly legend stems from a famous air crash in 1937. A Stinson airliner, just taken off from Brisbane and heading south to Sydney, disappeared in the McPherson Range. Almost a week went by before the O'Reillys heard of the tragedy, so it was an unexpected triumph when Bernard O'Reilly trekked into the forest and saved two survivors after a full 10 days of isolation. This story of courage and skill was very big news, making Bernard into a celebrity. He later published a book entitled *Green Mountains* to meet the public interest. A statue of Bernard and the rescued survivors has been erected at the Guesthouse site.

In 1944 Mick and Annie returned to the mountain with two sons, Vince and Peter, and these boys later became the second generation to run the guesthouse. Mick was Manager of the operation, beginning in 1946, while Annie ran the little store that was established in 1951. Both of them passed away in 1979.

The two sons of Mick and Annie were both married in 1961 and together they established the third generation. Vince married Lona Murphy and they had ten children, while Peter married Karma England and they had five children.

In 1947 the first road was built to the Guesthouse, finally allowing motor vehicles to bring in tourists and supplies. By 1960 bus tours were snaking their way up the oft-muddy road, but the greater connection with the outside world came in 1967 when the electricity line was extended to the guesthouse, replacing the old generator and wood-fired hot water system. A year later Land Rovers were purchased to cater to the needs of older guests who could not do vigorous backcountry hiking, and in 1975 these were replaced when O'Reilly's acquired its own four-wheel-drive bus.

As the business expanded and increased in complexity, family members have had to adapt. If they cannot cope with their responsibilities, family membership is no guarantee of a job. On the other hand, the board of directors will pay for a complete university education for family members wanting to enter the business in a professional capacity.

Full-time family members of staff share the marketing responsibilities when it comes to geographic areas. Shane handles Europe, Peter has North America, Greg is responsible for Singapore and Catherine looks after Australia. Under Peter, there are regular marketing meetings, and a lot of travel is undertaken.

Business dimensions

A major building project occurred in 1977 to expand the Guesthouse, and its first bar was constructed in 1984. The popular Tree Top Walk was constructed in the rainforest near the Guesthouse in 1987. Major physical improvements occurred in 1991, the same year in which the approach road was finally sealed over its entire length. In 1997 the kiosk (called 'Gran's') was expanded to handle the growing volume of day-trip visitors, providing both a retail shop and restaurant.

A major expansion was brought to fruition in 1999 with the opening of Canungra Valley Vineyards. This tourist-oriented facility lies along the approach road to the national park in an attractive valley-floor setting. It is 90% owned by the O'Reillys, although the venture originally had another partner who has been bought out.

The biggest expansion ever to the Guesthouse was realized in 2000, adding 21 guest rooms, a relaxation centre and new staff accommodation.

O'Reillys sought and was awarded advanced ecotourism accreditation from the Ecotourism Association of Australia. Although they do not use the term 'ecolodge', it does fit their operation in a number of ways. Perhaps the biggest difference is that the Guesthouse has continued to move up-market into the luxury accommodation category.

Capitalizing on the family brand is ongoing. Gran O'Reilly's Store, at the Guesthouse, includes a bistro, gift shop and other provisions. It is very popular with day-visitors to the park.

There is now an O'Reilly's line of clothing, gifts, nature videos, and wine from the Canungra Valley Vineyards.

Ownership dimensions

In the early days all eight O'Reilly boys owned separate properties, but built and operated the Guesthouse collectively. A public company was formed in 1931, but this action threatened family ownership. In 1948 Mick, then manager of the Guesthouse, organized a share buy-back and de-listed the company, returning it to family ownership. This covered the guesthouse and combined properties. Mick's sons, Vince and Peter, became directors of the company in 1957.

In 1994, two family trusts were established, reflecting the fact that brothers Peter and Vince owned 90% of the shares, with Lona and Karma holding the remaining 10%. Joe, the longest surviving of the original O'Reilly generation on the mountain, died in 1989. In the next decade the third generation started to take charge. Shane, the current Managing Director, was appointed director of the company in 1995; a year later his uncle Vince retired, then in 1998 his father Peter retired.

Today, with ownership under two family trusts, O'Reilly's remains a flourishing family business. Fifteen third- and fourth-generation family members work in it. However, there might be a problem looming in maintaining harmony and sustaining family control.

The family trusts work this way: all descendants of the two brothers, Vince and Peter Sr, automatically become beneficiaries. However, it is totally up to the two trustees of each trust as to who gets annual dividends and how much. The first dividends were paid only four years ago, with Aus$20,000 paid from each trust in equal allocations. Shane believed this to be a perfect model when it was introduced, but now he has some doubts.

The family trusts serve to keep ownership and operational control within the family, but they also ensure that no one can realize a direct benefit other than wages or dividends as determined by the trustees. This arrangement is being questioned by some of the third-generation O'Reillys who find they have almost no rights to manage the company or inherit shares. In effect, the tangible assets of the company are locked away forever.

One potential problem raised by the family trusts is that of pressuring family members to work in the company when they would rather not. If they could be issued shares or provided with a cash settlement, they might be happy to leave ownership and control to others. The risk, as recognized long ago by Mick, is that family control might gradually, or even rapidly, slip away.

The company is managed by a Board of Directors including family members (two from each of the two trusts) and two non-family directors. This board makes operational decisions under guidance of the chairperson and executive director (who are non-family). Structured, monthly board meetings are held.

The non-family trustees are vital, both in helping to avoid in-family management problems and in counselling individual family members. They were sought by the family after a process of setting out desirable attributes. Personal relations already existed with the two external directors before they were asked to sit on the board.

The board, however, has made important strategic decisions that did not conform to the non-family directors' advice, as in the case of taking dominant ownership in Canungra Valley Vineyards. Family businesses tend to take a long-term perspective on everything, whereas traditional company directors often focus on short-term returns. Regular family meetings are held (every six months) to keep everyone informed and to get their input.

The O'Reillys believe in professionalism, to the point of bringing in non-family trustees, a general manager, and other professionals. Jobs are advertised by the human resources manager and both family and outsiders can apply. A written 'family employment policy' covers this issue.

The dilemma of the family trusts will have to be resolved. At issue is the means to extract value for family members while maintaining family control. Dissolving the trusts and issuing shares, which could include retention of majority control, might still have a serious cultural impact on the company through dilution of family influence on the board of directors.

Going completely public could eventually result in the O'Reilly name remaining only as a brand, a commodity to be bought and sold. A number of expansions are contemplated, primarily to increase accommodation for both guests (two-bedroom, spa villas) and staff (self-contained units), and to continue moving up-market. Approval has been obtained to construct up to 50 cabins 1 km from the Guesthouse, but the recent improvements took priority. Now an equity partner is being sought for the cabins, but approval will lapse in 2002. The company also plans to sell 50% of Canungra Valley Vineyards.

Case 8.3 River Valley Ventures, New Zealand

Background

River Valley Ventures Ltd is situated along the Rangitikei River on the North Island of New Zealand. It is a remote setting some 32 kilometres from the nearest town, Taihape, which is located on State Highway 1. To the north is Auckland, the main tourist gateway to the country, and to the north-west lies Lake Taupo and Rotorua, both major tourist destinations. Most highway traffic passes through the Rangitikei.

Family dimensions

River Valley Ventures was founded in 1982 as a registered company by Brian and Robin Sage to provide white-water rafting. It was a sideline to their farming operation, made possible by ownership of 1.5 km of river frontage and control over the best landing zone. Other rafting operators had used the road to the river (which had been constructed by the Sages) on an *ad hoc* basis. Initially the Sages provided meals and refreshments to these operators and collected a toll. Their rafting company began with the purchase of two rafts. However, by 1990 Brian and Robin Sage sold their farm to cover the most pressing debts and sold the

rafting business and Lodge to their daughter Nicola and her husband Brian Megaw.

Brian and Nicola are shareholders in River Valley Ventures Ltd and Brian is Managing Director. A number of shares have been placed in a family trust, and the Megaws want to move all their tangible assets into this device to afford protection to the family against business failure and to facilitate inheritance. When the transfer has been completed, River Valley will lease back the physical assets from the trust.

The Megaws have three daughters, one of whom, Jane, aged 22, is currently working in the business. Kate (aged 19) works part-time in the Lodge, but concentrates on her school studies. Melissa, 20, is a cook in the Lodge. River Valley is a second-generation family business in which extended family ties are an important element. Nicola's father, Brian Sage, continues to be involved in the business through contractual provision of vans to carry rafters to the drop-off zone up-river. Mr and Mrs Sage live in a new house on the cliff overlooking the Lodge and river.

Nicola's role has not changed as much, but computerization of their business systems has eliminated the need for manual bookkeeping. Nicola's brother, Richard, is an expert kayaker and uses this vehicle to take action photographs of rafters and other kayakers. This is a profitable, sub-contracted element of the business. Richard also develops and sells kayaks.

The horse trekking operation is contracted to Brian's sister, Shona. River Valley makes the bookings and takes a commission. The treks are a very popular feature and can be purchased with other activities in a package.

The Megaws have never lived at the Lodge, but own a house 2 km away. This provides a necessary escape from the constant demands of staff and guests and keeps family life somewhat separate from business life. In the early years they both worked at all jobs, all the time, and dreamed of employing a manager to relieve their personal burden. They first took a family vacation from the business in 1995, for a couple of days and a trip to America to visit their daughter.

Brian originally micro-managed the business and took parties rafting five days a week. He has reduced rafting to 1 day a week and now finds himself doing mostly macro-management.

Staff are able to do more, and do not require the level of supervision they once did, although he finds delegating authority difficult.

Brian elaborated on the vision: 'First and foremost, River Valley needs to keep being fun! Not only for people who visit, but also for staff.' A 'hands-on involvement by management leads to an in-depth understanding of the business, its opportunities and threats. With this understanding we can provide the leadership required to strive for ongoing improvement, and excellence.'

The Megaws' extended family is an important feature of this case study. Who better to get involved, and to trust, than family members? This network might be a somewhat unique feature related to their isolated location, but it suggests that family connections could be important both in start-up and development of the family business.

Brian Megaw was wishing he was back on the river, guiding a white-water rafting tour down the raging Rangitiki, but he was managing director of a successful family business owned with his wife Nicola, and his rafting days had long since been reduced to once a week, if he was lucky. A major decision weighed on his mind, as it involved a NZ$250,000 loan to construct new chalets at River Valley Lodge. The chalets had the potential to generate substantial profit and to reduce his dependency on a single market segment. However, the history of this family business included one major financial disaster, and although it had been followed by a complete recovery, taking on such a large debt involved another great family risk. Was the timing right? Is there ever a good time to borrow so heavily for a family tourism business? These are some of the questions that emerge from this case study when establishing and expanding a family business in tourism.

Business dimensions

At first the rafting business went well, but in 1987 the Sages decided to expand, and constructed a loan-financed lodge by the river. River Valley Lodge has a beautiful site in a deep valley, with views of a waterfall and native forests rising above. It still offers dormitory-style accommodations plus four double/twin rooms and a large open area for meals and relaxation. Showers, toilets and changing facilities for rafters were provided outside. A diesel generator was first used to provide electricity.

Unfortunately the budgets that formed the basis of the expansion bore little relationship to the reality of the situation. By 1990, despite turnover of NZ$350,000, the annual operating loss had also grown to NZ$40,000 and the company was unable to service its debt. The family went through difficult times as creditors sought repayment of loans. Finally, Brian and Robin Sage sold their farm to cover the most pressing debts and sold the rafting business and Lodge to their daughter Nicola and her husband Brian.

After taking over from Nicola's parents the immediate objective was a financial turnaround. Now, sustainable growth and profitability are pursued. The owners want to position River Valley 'firmly at the top of our industry segment, both in profitability and in quality of product.' This means River Valley has had to create and continuously promote itself as a destination in its own right.

Once the company became financially sound, improvements and expansions were undertaken. Electricity was brought to the Lodge, thereby relegating the diesel generator to stand-by status. Tree planting was accelerated for aesthetic reasons, to screen working areas and improve the views. The original Lodge, originally used mostly by schools and groups for outdoor management courses, was upgraded. The plan had been to convert dormitories into meeting rooms to accommodate management team-building groups, but that plan is now obsolete.

Outdoor management training for groups has been discontinued, although it once accounted for about 20% of the business. Multi-day rafting trips have also been discontinued, leaving the focus on shorter, white-water adventures. These changes have been made in response to the partnership with Kiwi Experience (discussed later).

Other recent additions have been the golf course, an expanded tenting area and a riverside stage for events. Major growth is not being contemplated, nor is it desired. A plan to build three chalet units is the only physical development on the horizon, and the emphasis is now on improved yield. To meet the needs of older, more quality-conscious tourists, River Valley is planning to borrow NZ$250,000 to construct three chalet-style units on a view-site separated from the Lodge. Brian calculates that they will become profitable above 20% annual occupancy and will therefore add substantially to revenue whilst broadening their market appeal.

The Megaws have been approached with the idea of franchising their successful formula elsewhere in New Zealand, but they declined. Opportunities for new challenges might exist for Brian elsewhere in the tourism sector. A single, contractual partnership with Kiwi Experience in 1995 dramatically changed the fortunes and plans of River Valley. Brian had known the potential of this market segment, but it took a visit from Kiwi Experience, and a subsequent offer, to cement a deal.

Kiwi Experience is one of several coach/bus companies that cater to the rapidly growing backpacker market in New Zealand. Visitors, mostly young and foreign, can use the bus service (7 days-a-week in summer, 5 in winter) to access a range of destinations and accommodations all over New Zealand.

River Valley is featured as an overnight and adventure destination exclusive to Kiwi Experience (see their website: www.kiwiexperience. com). The southbound bus (from Auckland to Wellington) stops automatically at River Valley, and Kiwi Experience promotes the adventure activities in its own marketing, so there is a strong likelihood that travellers will spend a night there. In fact, the average length of stay at River Valley is now one night. Occupancy rates are growing at 4% a year, on a 10,000 person-night base.

Surveys of Kiwi Experience users consistently show River Valley to be 'recommended' accommodation. White-water rafting and horse trekking are two of the most popular and highly recommended activities by this same travel segment.

River Valley's market segments changed dramatically with initiation of this partnership. Previously, independent overseas tourists accounted for about 10% of the customer mix, tour groups were 20%, schools 30%, and the remainder came from social groups, clubs, family outings and the like. Kiwi Experience, however, brings mostly young, foreign

backpackers to River Valley so that the overseas segment (mostly from Europe) has grown quickly to account for 80% of customers.

This new, guaranteed backpacker market has substantially increased River Valley income, but has also required substantial adjustments. A new accommodation block featuring simple bunk-house arrangements had to be built to accommodate the increased numbers, and the product was changed.

The partnership contracted with Kiwi Experience in 1995 changed the marketing picture completely by focusing attention on the growing backpacker market and their needs, and by causing the Megaws to get concerned about potential over-dependency on this one source of customers. Marketing expenditure as a percentage of sales has been falling, from approximately 10% in 1997, to 6% in 2000. This reflects greater success in attracting customers and more effective communication techniques, especially through their website.

Brian has determined that only 55% of guests are purchasing an activity, so clearly many backpackers view their visit as purely for accommodation or sightseeing. He realizes that daily expenditure has to be increased, given the one-night average length of stay. This led to development of the pitch and putt golf to provide guests with a relatively inexpensive (NZ$10) activity. Food packages, Internet access and merchandise for sale are other examples of value adding.

There is also a joint marketing arrangement that provides visitors with an additional adventure activity, similar to the popular two- and three-activity packages found in Queenstown in the South Island (New Zealand's self-proclaimed adventure capital).

Rangitikei River Ventures, by agreement with River Valley, runs scenic and camp-out rafting trips but not white-water experiences. The two companies refer customers to each other for commissions. Farmstay accommodation had been obtained through partnering with the Powell family. The house is situated close to River Valley Lodge on the Powells' working sheep farm and guests had the option of either participating in farm activities or simply enjoying the rural tranquillity. However, the farmstay is now used for seasonal staff accommodation only.

In the early years, marketing occurred by word of mouth, limited advertising, partnering with tour companies, and 'serendipity'. For example, River Valley worked with one Australian tour operator who brought skiers to the volcanic slopes of Mount Ruapehu 2 hours to the north. A director of the company arrived at River Valley as a client and was so thrilled with the product that he incorporated the rafting experience into his own package. However, rafting was secondary to the skiing, and therefore business from this source was dependent on ski conditions. When the skiing was bad, rafting demand increased. An added complication was that bad weather required extra transport costs to get customers to suitable river areas.

Monitoring of advertising in magazines revealed that only 8% of demand was generated this way, yet it accounted for 80% of River Valley's promotional expenditure. That had to change, so in 1996 they cut back on magazine ads, increased their production of brochures from 20,000 to 30,000, and employed targeted brochure mail-outs using their customer and contact database. More careful targeting of intermediaries who could bring their customers to the Lodge was also attempted. Joint marketing through the Rangitikei Tourism Association at trade shows was initiated, including participation in New Zealand's annual Tourism Rendezvous (TRENZ) where inbound tour operators and suppliers meet.

Another marketing initiative was the familiarization tour, wherein River Valley brought in car rental staff, tourist information centre personnel and others to visit the site. 'Farm' tours are now offered to accommodation providers who see the Kiwi Experience backpackers earlier in their New Zealand tour, so that recommendations can be made concerning accommodation and activity options.

Branding has become important to River Valley, now that they are a success. Their branding effort is built on the constructs of quality, the river, excitement, and an outdoor adventuring New Zealand experience that is at once safe and fun. In 2000 a new logo captured the essence of this brand; it has an authentic New Zealand feel to it, reminiscent of Maori designs. Their new posters, website, and merchandise push a consistent message. A new poster features their

website address and the slogan 'what are you waiting for?' River Valley phone cards and the occasional production of CDs complement the marketing effort.

River Valley's website (www.rivervalley.co. nz) is viewed as their primary offer of information, replacing brochures. The number of unique users of their website has grown to over 300 per week (March 2000). The website is used mostly for information-gathering, and like many other tourism operators River Valley has found resistance to on-line bookings.

Did the Megaws seek to create opportunities for personal fulfilment through economic activity? (see for example: Morrison et al., 1999). What role does the founder play in operating the business, and does that change over time? Is entrepreneurship an inherited personality trait? Above all else, consider the nature of risk-taking in establishment and growth of a business, and the possible pitfall of over-confidence in one's own capability.

This case is rather unique in that it provides a longitudinal examination of the company's development and of a family business successfully inherited and developed by the children. Furthermore, this case presents a clear success story from a purely business perspective, while at the same time generating questions regarding small business strategy and the future of the company and its family owners. It provides many insights into the nature and challenges of developing a rural tourism/hospitality business.

The case illustrates how an easy-to-enter, sideline rafting business quickly took over the Sages' lives and resulted in a financial disaster. The absence of a business plan, lack of cost controls, excessive personal debt and inexperience in operating and marketing a growing tourism business were all contributing factors. High revenues at first hid the problem, leading to development without sufficient cash reserves to ride out a lengthy period of asset building. The farm and house were sacrificed, although sufficient land and the Lodge were retained to permit a fresh start.

What is amazing is that the business was salvaged by the children who grew it into a financial success. Inheritance of family businesses in the rural tourism and hospitality sectors is believed to be rare (see Getz and Carlsen, 2000), for several possible reasons. Many such businesses are based on high levels of debt and/or 'sweat equity', and while they can sustain a family they do not often present an attractive or viable option for the next generation. Furthermore, many rural tourism and hospitality businesses are rooted in lifestyle choices that might not be shared by younger adults, or in the need to generate some additional income for farmers – inheritance of a farm does not necessarily entail continuation of the sideline business.

Ownership dimensions

The decision of the children to take over the business was not made lightly. Brian had met Nicola while both were students at university in Auckland, but when married they returned to their rural roots. By 1982 Brian was managing a sheep-shearing gang, and had little relationship with the rafting business. Brian and Nicola had contemplated starting their own sea-kayaking business in the Bay of Islands and had already followed their leisure interest by exploring that area and its potential. They had even drawn up budgets. With the financial crisis at hand, however, Nicola's parents were threatened with losing both the farm and their home. Given that the rafting operation had made money, it was decided to try to save the business.

In the Megaws' case family loyalty, ties to the land, and personal leisure interests combined to make the salvage attempt attractive. Much hard work and worry followed, but the family was able to capitalize successfully on their effort, talent, and vision of what the business could become.

Brian persuaded the creditors to keep the business going, arguing that its assets were insufficient to pay the debt. The only way out was to turn it into a profitable business, and it had certainly shown its potential to generate revenue. Most of the problems, according to Brian Megaw, were created by poor cost controls, accounting and management practices. It was a case of good ideas on the part of the Sages, but inexperience in the practicalities of operating a tourism business.

Brian and Nicola sold their own house and its 5-acre plot to raise capital, and for a year they juggled debts, paid cash for everything, introduced proper accounting procedures, saved and scrimped, argued and survived. By 1994 a small net profit (after tax) of NZ$30,000 was realized on turnover of NZ$230,000. This represented a decrease in total revenue, but owing to retrenchment, a firm profit on which to build.

Since then it has grown into a profitable business and has become a destination for adventure activities and backpacking, attracting over 10,000 visitors annually. River Valley operations in the year 2000 generated for the first time NZ$1 million in annual sales.

Brian is not yet ready to contemplate retirement, and in fact has ambitions to improve the business in other ways. He has thought about succession and thinks that at least one of their daughters might have the vision and drive to take over some day. A real question is whether the children will have the necessary management skills to run such a business, with more and more technological skills being required. Creation of the family trust will ultimately facilitate inheritance of all the tangible assets, while in the meantime it pays allowances to the children. Whether or not any of the daughters take over the business, Brian feels that the experience of growing up with it has broadened their horizons considerably.

Chapter Summary

These three cases illustrate that establishing and running a family business specializing in tourism in the natural environmental is a very attractive option. All of these businesses offer unique opportunities for guests to immerse themselves in nature at the same time enjoying a high standard of accommodation and service. It is apparent that the natural environment is the basis of these business activities and the traditional family connections with the environment (in cases 8.2 and 8.3) and personal values (in case 8.1) are the prime motivators for the family businesses. Ironically, the success of these businesses acts to limit the amount of time the families can actually spend enjoying the natural area, which attracted them in the first place.

References

Getz, D. and Carlsen, J. (2000) Characteristics and goals of family and owner-operated businesses in the rural tourism and hospitality sectors. *Tourism Management* 21, 547–560.

Morrison, A., Rimmington, M. and Williams, C. (1999) *Entrepreneurship in the Hospitality, Tourism and Leisure Industries.* Butterworth-Heinemann, Oxford, UK.

9

Family-owned and -operated Tour Companies

Introduction

These three case studies cover a number of topics relevant to all family businesses as well as some specific issues related to family-owned/-operated tour companies. The reasons for establishing a tour business in these three cases seem to be in response to an opportunity that is recognized and pursued by the founders and their families. It may be that design and delivery of land, marine and adventure tours attracts more creative and entrepreneurial family businesses. The capital-intensive nature of these businesses introduces particular issues for funding the establishment of the business. In most cases, founders have had a working life before going in to business that provides them with the capital, skills and motivation (in the form of a desired career change) to commence in business. Once in business the challenges of further expansion, marketing, staffing, seasonality and customer interaction are confronted with the same degree of enthusiasm and commitment that was evident at business start-up.

Case 9.1 Wild Over Walpole (WOW)

Background

WOW Wilderness operates cruises with two tour vessels on waterways of the Walpole-Nornalup National Park on the south coast of Western Australia. The 2.5 hour Wilderness Cruise departs at 10 a.m. every day from the town jetty in Walpole and returns at about 1.00 p.m. The current costs are Aus$20 for adults, Aus$10 for children under 14 and free for children under 5 years old. The 3.5 hour Sunday River Cruise operates in the summer and costs Aus$25 for adults, Aus$15 for under-14s and free for under-fives. Both tours include a detailed interpretation of the natural, social and historical aspects of the area and guided walks at selected sites. Active participation is encouraged in all aspects of the tour and interaction and discussion over tea and homemade cake is a feature of the tour. Current capacity is 18 passengers on the smaller vessel *The Naughty Lass* and 48 passengers on the larger vessel *Rainbow Lady*.

Family dimensions

WOW is a family-operated boat tour company owned by Ross and Marion Muir, who started the firm, together with their son Gary as a partner. There have been seven generations of Muirs in the area as farmers and WOW is the first tourism-oriented venture. Marion is financial manager while Ross and Gary handle the cruises, but roles are not fixed and do overlap. Gary has considerable professional experience working with the Department of Conservation and Land Management (CALM), the state land management authority. He also does outside consulting, computer-assisted design, environmental science and guiding, all under the Wild

©D. Getz *et al.* 2004. *The Family Business in Tourism and Hospitality*
(D. Getz, J. Carlsen and A. Morrison)

Over Walpole Wilderness Services business name. He is poised to take over the tour business when his parents retire and hopes to expand it by diversifying the products offered under the WOW umbrella. His vision is to expand the business his parents created, possibly in partnership with his cousin, Rob, whose family currently operates a houseboat and B&B business in Walpole.

Ross has a farming and fishing background and brings a wealth of historical knowledge to the WOW cruises, which he takes when Gary is not available. Since starting WOW, Ross has been active in the local business community and was president of the Walpole Tourist Association for 2 years. Ross has also managed a number of land management projects in the area, including a tourist boardwalk project in the Tingle forest.

Marion manages the finances of WOW and has developed considerable skills in managing farm finances, which are now applied to the business. She is also becoming proficient in the use of computers and account-keeping software, which she enjoys. Gary conducts most of the daily tours and works with local land management agencies on projects that support the mission of WOW. He has initiated a range of projects that will enhance the WOW experience and will develop new products and services including accommodation, foods (based on local bush tucker), outdoor adventure and scientific research expeditions into the wilderness.

Business dimensions

Ross and Marion Muir set up the business as an opportunity to generate income in their retirement and as a self-employment opportunity for themselves and their son Gary. The Muir Family has had a long association with the region around Walpole, commencing with farming and later in retail. The goal of living and working in the region that their family pioneered and helped to establish was important and the historical and personal links with the region are themes that run through the Muirs' family and business life. Traditional cattle farming in the region was becoming less viable in the 1990s and although the family retained ownership of extensive farm lands, only the eldest son and his

family continue to operate the family farm on a full-time basis. Ross had tried other forms of employment after leaving the farm, including a stint as a commercial fisherman, during which time he renewed his interest in the ocean and inlets surrounding Walpole. When the opportunity to purchase their first tour boat, *The Naughty Lass*, presented itself in 1994, Ross and Marion embraced the idea. Within one week of that purchase, a second considerably larger tour vessel became available and Gary, who was working as a land manager with the Department of Conservation and Land Management, was included in the decision to acquire it. Gary had considerable experience and training in environmental management and interpretation; combined with Ross's extensive knowledge of the social history of the region and Marion's skills in financial management the WOW business was formed.

The first few years of operation were on a limited basis and tours were conducted mainly in the smaller of the two boats. Gary had committed to a major project in the region and had limited time to devote to the business. Consequently Ross conducted the tours and kept the business operational. Upon completion of the project in 1996 and the gaining of a coxswain's certificate, Gary was ready to make a full-time commitment to the business. The project that he managed, the construction of a major nature-based tourism attraction in the Valley of the Giants near Walpole, provided a significant boost for tourism in the region. This is indicated by the increase in visitation to the Walpole Tourist Bureau after September when the Tree Top Walk opened in 1996 (see Table 9.1) and provided direct benefits for the WOW business. After 1997 interest and awareness of WOW grew through favourable word of mouth, television programmes featuring the Tree Tops Walk and WOW, and some advertising through tourism promotional magazines and brochures.

The initial capital investment in the business was drawn from Ross and Marion's retirement funds so it is essential that the business generates sufficient retirement income for Ross and Marion as well as an income for Gary. This financing arrangement, whilst avoiding the need for investment loans from financial institutions, does not mean that the investment decision is less risky. On the contrary, as Ross and Marion reach

Table 9.1. Visitation numbers for the Walpole Tourist Bureau, January 1994–April 2000.

	1994	1995	1996	1997	1998	1999	2000	2001	2002
January	2,427	2,149	2,560	**6,503**	**7,679**	**8,438**	**9,594**	**11,656**	**11,887**
February	1,872	1,720	1,892	**3,111**	**3,327**	**4,264**	**4,616**	**5,526**	**6,294**
March	1,611	1,602	1,511	**4,758**	**4,008**	**4,453**	**5,503**	**6,796**	**7,812**
April	1,761	2,176	2,819	**4,718**	**6,620**	**7,249**	**7,459**	**7,822**	**7,302**
May	1,002	972	2,500	**2,486**	**3,387**	**3,549**	**3,890**	**4,396**	**4,475**
June	912	847	1,087	**1,667**	**2,027**	**3,007**	**2,952**	**3,350**	**3,358**
July	600	622	981	**2,465**	**3,100**	**3,958**	**3,006**	**4,304**	**3,792**
August	467	1,109	1,317	**2,013**	**2,750**	**3,279**	**2,957**	**3,968**	**3,539**
September	1,127	1,271	**3,109**	**4,621**	**5,811**	**6,923**	**6,407**	**6,773**	**7,125**
October	2,721	2,911	**4,017**	**5,516**	**5,978**	**7,313**	**7,062**	**8,830**	**8,643**
November	970	1,159	**4,610**	**3,,461**	**4,132**	**4,848**	**5,257**	**6,236**	**6,897**
December	1,921	2,071	**5,418**	**4,629**	**5,320**	**5,952**	**6,926**	**7,977**	**7,705**
Total	**17,391**	**18,609**	**31,821**	**45,948**	**54,139**	**63,233**	**65,629**	**77,634**	**78,829**

Note: Bold type denotes Tree Top Walk opening.
Source: Derrin Foster, Manager, Walpole Tourist Bureau.

retirement age there is added impetus to ensure that the business is profitable into the future.

Periodic injections of funds are required for running the boats and new motors have had to be purchased for both vessels in the last 2 years. In the near future the larger of the two vessels is marked for a re-fit, with major modifications to the hulls and to the waste water storage tank held within the hull. The vessel should have a larger capacity after re-fit and should also generate higher revenue. At present WOW turnover is about Aus$125,000 per annum based on about 8000 passengers. Fortunately, the major re-fit can be funded through 'plough-back profit' or reinvestment, rather than through any new financial injection.

The long-term goal for the business is continued growth. This will be based on the larger capacity of the *Rainbow Lady* that will allow it comfortably to handle coach-loads of patrons on a daily basis in addition to the current fully independent traveller/tourist market. Presently, the majority of visitors are from within Western Australia (WA) and are mostly self-drive tourists from Perth (Perth is the capital city of Western Australia), a five-hour drive from Walpole. WOW has had some success in attracting coach tours from provincial centres within WA and plans to continue to grow this market. Older persons predominate WOW's visitors. The tours are promoted through the local Walpole Tourist Bureau and also through accommodation providers in Walpole and other towns within the region.

Supporting the attainment of this long-term goal is a detailed set of goals and objectives for the product and the business. WOW's mission statement is . . . 'To be leaders in sustainable nature-based environmental tourism offering our clients a blend of ecological, cultural and adventure opportunities.' WOW's objectives are to provide visitors with high quality experiences based on the natural environment, to implement best practice in environmental management and to expand, protect and restore the land and wildlife. A number of projects are already in place that will result in the restoration of biodiversity of the wilderness areas visited on the cruise as well as research aimed at increasing scientific knowledge of wilderness. Gary has a vision for WOW that encompasses a team of specialists that will each contribute to a greater understanding of the biological, cultural and traditional significance of the wilderness. This knowledge will then be imparted to visitors thereby encouraging deeper appreciation of the historical impacts of European settlement on the environment and aboriginal inhabitants of the area. Gary's interpretation of the natural and cultural history of the area carries a very powerful message that promotes friendship, tolerance and understanding between cultures and people.

Ownership dimensions

All family business members agree that Gary will eventually take full control of the running of the business. Gary has a high level of commitment to the mission and objectives of WOW and will pursue his plans for expansion and growth under the WOW 'umbrella' name. He has spent 5 years developing and recruiting a group of friends who have specialist skills in interpretation, scientific research, traditional use of natural flora and fauna for foods and medicines (called 'bush tucker') and outdoor adventure. He is also keen to include his cousin Rob in the future business structure, but he alone will retain ownership of the WOW business name, and hence it will remain a family business. He has made a substantial emotional investment in the business, as well as a financial investment in the expansion of WOW. On the other hand, Ross and Marion have a purely business approach and would mainly like to see a financial return at the end of the day. That is not to say that they are completely detached from the business. Indeed, all three family members hold a great deal of pride in WOW as well as a deep love of the Walpole region and all that it holds. This theme runs right through the business. Ross and Marion will continue to operate a small B&B as part of their private residence in Walpole, which they can comfortably maintain in retirement. The succession and structure of WOW has yet to be finalized and it may be the case that Ross and Marion draw an annuity from the business.

Should Ross and Marion bequeath to Gary a business that is unencumbered with debt, it would provide an ideal platform upon which Gary can realize his vision for WOW and the Walpole wilderness area. Ross and Marion realize that Gary has a great deal to offer, as well as to learn, and are keen to see him succeed. However, their enthusiasm is balanced with the pragmatism that they have inherited from generations of Muirs who farmed and ran businesses in the region. In many ways it was farming and business that was the genesis of WOW, and the Muir family farm remains an important link with the past as well as a key to the future of WOW.

WOW is much more than a family-owned and -operated tour boat operation, as it represents a substantial component of the social, economic and environmental fabric of the Walpole region. An Australian songwriter, Paul Kelly, once penned a song titled 'From Little Things, Big Things Grow' and this truism could equally be applied to the WOW business. Many lives and many more miles of wilderness have been touched by WOW's activities in a positive way, and maintaining that positive interaction and contribution to the wilderness remains a unique vision shared by Gary Muir and his family and friends.

Case 9.2 Minnewanka Tours

Background

Minnewanka Tours is a family-owned, seasonal business within Banff National Park, Alberta, Canada. The Mackie family, consisting of husband and wife Ian and Brenda, and niece Diane, have an exclusive lease from the park authority to operate a marina and boat tours on the park's largest lake (and the only lake in the park where motor-boating is permitted). They handle 40,000–50,000 customers a year.

The business consists of the following:

- three tour boats;
- 21 rental motorboats;
- marine gas sales; and
- snack/retail shop (tackle and souvenirs).

In addition, the family owns a chartered fishing company with six boats, operating out of the same lakeside facility and utilizing the same staff. The Mackies lease office space in the nearby town of Banff, and also have office space in their home in Banff. In addition they have a leased house at the lake where up to eight seasonal staff stay. Operations are permitted for only 5 months of the year, but actual business at the lake occurs for only about 4 months (May–September) owing to prohibitively freezing conditions.

Lake Minnewanka is the subject of a book by R. Sandford, who describes the history of recreational use of this beautiful body of water. It was prepared with the co-operation of the Mackies and includes a number of photos of theirs and previous tour boats. The book's introduction by Ian and Brenda states:

For more than a hundred years, visitors to Banff have been enjoying boat tours on Lake Minnewanka. The same stunning scenery that enticed passengers off the train to visit the lake in 1889 still attracts people to the Lake of the Water Spirits. We are proud and fortunate to be the stewards of the lake and its boating tradition today.

Family dimensions

The Minnewanka Tours Co Ltd was formed in 1977 when Ian and Brenda purchased the operation from an acquaintance. Originally there was another married couple involved, but that partnership did not work well and the Mackies bought them out after the first year.

Following a career with a major company involving a variety of engineering and managerial experiences (in tourism and recreation), Ian was looking for self-employment. He wanted a 'hands-on', challenging venture, which he describes as being 'vital' to his life. He explained: 'If I put the same energy and time into my own business as I gave to the company, I knew it would be successful.' Also, he wanted it to be a family business in which both he and Brenda would work together.

Ian was not particular about the type of business or location, but Banff was a natural choice since he had grown up there and had most recently been manager of the Banff Springs golf course. The opportunity arose at a personal level when the former operator of the boat tours made it known to the Mackies that he was interested in selling the business.

Brenda had also been working in Banff and was not particular about whether or not Ian was self-employed, but was supportive of the business idea and of staying in Banff. In a family business, she says, 'you are a master of your own destiny.'

Over the years a number of nieces and nephews have worked seasonally for the Mackies at the lake and stayed with Ian and Brenda in Banff. Without children of their own, the Mackies had to look to other relatives if they wanted the business to stay in the family. A nephew was considered for full-time employment, but that did not work out.

Diane started to work during summers at the lake in 1987 and she in particular became much like a family member. Nevertheless, in 1998 she was surprised to be contacted in Vancouver, where she worked, and asked by Ian to become manager of Minnewanka Tours. Her university education had been in economics, and she had gained experience in almost all aspects of the business, so she felt confident but challenged. The idea of living in a small town appealed to her a great deal, and she had always enjoyed her summers spent in the mountains.

Bank financing has been used to purchase and develop the business. At first their personal guarantees were required, but later the business became successful enough to secure loans without them. Possibly a planned new tour boat will be leased, rather than purchased outright. Since there is no land ownership in the national park, the company's assets consist of boats, goodwill, and the value of a long-term lease.

The three Mackies are the only permanent workers, but the summer season requires about 20 additional employees. Some are all-year residents of Banff who work at ski resorts in the winter, and others are summer-help only. Up to eight of these staff stay in the lakeside house. A key seasonal employee is the operations manager. He is a vital part of the business and might eventually become a partner, with Diane, in its ownership.

Ian is President of Minnewanka Tours and makes the major decisions. He had to work over a period of years to secure the latest lease from Parks Canada, and was greatly relieved to get it in place.

Brenda does the company books, and while she used to run the snack bar she now only assists Diane in that task. Together with Ian they have an annual schedule of trade shows to attend for marketing purposes.

Diane, as Manager, is taking an ever-increasing role in the business with a view to becoming senior partner when Ian and Brenda retire. Although already familiar with most of the operations at the lake, she is now learning all the other aspects of the business.

They have been very lucky with staff. In addition to employing nieces and nephews, they get a lot of repeat seasonal workers. Being out of town actually helps, as it attracts a different kind of employee. They tend to be young (20s and

30s for the more responsible positions like boat operation) or local school children.

The early years of running Minnewanka Tours were difficult for Ian and Brenda, requiring a great deal of work but with inadequate financial returns. Brenda recalls that the summer workdays were very long, but did not seem tough. Both of them worked elsewhere in Banff in the off-season to generate sufficient income.

For all three Mackies work is seldom if ever left behind. Having an office at home is convenient, but also further cements the home–work union: 'It's an integral part of everything you do'. Although specific roles are played by each of the three Mackies, flexibility is also important. For example, Brenda and Diane work together to operate the snack shop.

They have informal business meetings and work together on a daily basis to get things done; sometimes they go to lunch together and discuss business. Within this family opinions get expressed freely as issues are discussed and resolved.

There is a great deal of customer contact in this business, with a high level of personal service required, but much of this is enjoyable. As well, this business does not bring customers to the owners' home, even if work responsibilities are always present.

Business dimensions

Rather than undertaking physical expansion, the company has been active in improving the quality of its equipment and service. Boats get refitted and replaced, and all equipment is kept up-to-date. Increasing numbers of tourists, in line with growing visitation to Banff National Park in general, has put pressure on the provision of service, but has also generated more revenue.

For the 4 years prior to 2000 the Mackies had been without a lease, owing mainly to delays by Parks Canada. While the parks people were not worried about renewal, this gap meant that the business could not be developed without undue risk, and banks would not lend them money for developments. Following signing of a new, long-term lease, a certain amount of work can now be done. This includes completely new

docks at the lake, replacement of several fishing boats they had sold (to get back to the complement of 21), and possibly purchasing a brand new, fourth tour boat to expand the capacity of that popular service.

In 1999 the Mackies also leased additional office space above their current location in Banff, in preparation for hiring new staff. Their main need is for a full-time marketing and sales professional. That person could replace Ian and Brenda in some ways, thereby easing their work (for example attending off-season trade shows), plus do a better marketing job then is currently possible. A part-time accountant is also being considered.

Absolute seasonality marks this business, as it cannot run in the cold months nor outside the 5-month lease period. During the off-season a lot of marketing and paper-work has to be done. Ian and Brenda have travelled a lot to trade shows and this allows the combining of work with pleasure. However, the travel can also be wearying.

Although an all-year operation would have its benefits, the option of adding a winter operation has been rejected. Opportunities for acquisitions in other locations have also been rejected over the years, as they would have generated a lot of additional travel and responsibility. Ian feels that adding a winter business would have been 'overpowering'. He preferred to stay focused and 'do things right'.

Ownership dimensions

Brenda and Ian will not retire in the immediate future, but are grooming Diane to assume more responsibility and eventually become senior partner in owning and operating the business along with the operations manager. This is a type of family inheritance, and although the legal and financial details have not been worked out, it appears to be a practical solution. Diane will get support from the senior Mackies for a number of years to come and will ultimately have an experienced operations manager and new permanent staff.

The option of selling the business was considered, but the Mackies wanted a family connection with Minnewanka Tours to continue.

Selling would generate more cash immediately, but the process of transferring ownership to the new partnership will also generate income for them, albeit spread out over time. Their ambition has never been to get rich.

Case 9.3 Åreguiderna

Background

'Founder' Ole (pronounced Ow-la) Kristianson was trained as a car mechanic and ended up working on the ski lifts while at school. He got into guiding as a sideline, hardly charging anything for his services. He has also worked in the local hospital and at the campsite in Åre (pronounced Or-a). Over the past 15 years, since 1985, Ole Kristianson has developed the leading guide service in Sweden's mountain resort of Åre. His motto is 'adventure and harmony', but now he is planning to sell out and move on to another, more personally harmonious, line of work. He is a self-described entrepreneur, now a professional, but once part of a group of three young, 'naive guys' who set up a 'fun business'. What changed? Is this a success story?

Family dimensions

Åreguiderna is a 'sole proprietor company', but there has been family involvement. Ole's father, now aged 86 and retired, has been a permanent but unpaid fixture at their camps and is much loved by the clients. He is a 'character' who seems to provide cultural authenticity to the experiences, while performing necessary services. Ole's mother has provided baking for the camps. Ole is not married, but his partner, a graduate student, likes to contribute to the business. He does not want her to sacrifice her studies for this paid, part-time work.

On family involvement, Ole has several opinions. His family has had a big involvement in the growth of the business, always discussing things and helping out. Gradually his father came to see it as a legitimate and successful business. On the negative side, Ole proclaims that it is difficult to be a boss to family members.

As owner and manager of the business, his personal life became integrated with the business; work was always being brought home with him. In this past year Ole has drawn a firm line between work and home, particularly to ensure that he spent weekends with family. If he worked all the time, which was his normal operating procedure, his staff would also feel obliged to do so.

Business dimensions

For the first two years Åreguiderna provided guide services to private clients for hiking and to bus tours for sightseeing. They could not afford to pay any staff, and Ole's father kept reminding him to 'get a real job'. A hotel came to them and asked if they could produce camps and meals for a canoe trip, and this became their first function ('arrangement'). The range of activities they guided expanded (see their website, in Swedish only: www.areguiderna.se) and in particular they added snowmobile safaris – using purchased vehicles initially, but later with 20 leased vehicles.

A few years ago Åreguiderna arranged and sold tourist packages to the area, but this service was made redundant when the major ski-lift and hotel company in the resort began its own packaging and booking business. Now Åreguiderna mostly serves groups tied to meetings and conventions, both as guides and producers of functions. They can mobilize up to 200 local people when necessary to serve a large event.

Outdoor adventure is a seasonal business, but there are opportunities all year round. Winter predominates, with guided ski and snowmobile safaris, and the summer season has actually been in decline.

His customers are mostly Swedes, who as a nation prefer to go fishing and hunting on their own, but will gladly employ a guide service for winter mountain adventures aimed at corporations and other groups. Other clients include English, Russians and some Norwegians. Individual clients come to Åre first, and then look for activities, while group business is generally tied to pre-arranged meetings and conventions.

The company does not employ full-time staff, but there are regulars who guide on a part-time basis. They are all males bar one, as physical strength has been a major criterion for driving snowmobiles. The snowmobile mechanic and office administrators work the longest season, from September to May. Numerous occasional workers are employed when needed at functions.

Åreguiderna is the dominant guide service, but there is competition. Ole says that 'fun businesses' like this attract people for the lifestyle, but they tend to burn out or fail after a few years. Why has he been successful? The number one reason has to be hard work and increasing professionalism, evolving from fun to sound business practices.

Ole says that relationship-building has been a critical success factor, particularly as in a small resort town everyone gets to know everyone else. His office is located in a hotel and he shares space with several crucial contact bodies, including the on-hill restaurant management, apartment leasing agency and conference booking. He works closely with hotels, the main reservation system and ski-lift company.

For marketing, Åreguiderna relies on the many contacts that generate group business and referrals, and on their own website. A network of people sell his product on commission. They once had a sales office in Stockholm, but it was not as effective as it should have been to justify the cost.

Ownership dimensions

The original three-way partnership was built out of friendship, not contracts. Over the years Ole became the one to spend the most time and effort on the business. It evolved into a shareholding company with a board of directors and a hired managing director, and eventually

he bought back all the shares to take complete ownership and managerial control.

Ole maintains he always had an exit plan. Currently he is negotiating with two potential buyers who would acquire very little in the way of tangible assets. They can buy the company name, three wilderness camps, some equipment, goodwill with many contacts, and Ole's advice. He would stay on as a paid consultant for a year or more.

A new company is in place and ready for his commitment. He will remain in Åre and run a one-man firm, with emphasis on harmony through team building. Perhaps his work can become international, but Ole is tired of managing employees and has slowed from a 'run to a walk'. He makes it sound like burnout, but perhaps what this entrepreneur really craves is a new challenge.

Chapter Summary

These cases studies demonstrate that an additional dimension of creativity, enterprise and enthusiasm is evident in family-owned/ -operated tour companies. The focus on providing the customer with a unique and enjoyable experience is also a common desire in these businesses and there is a high level of interaction between customers and family members. In two of the cases (9.1 and 9.3) the strength of character of the tour leader becomes a feature of the business, which is also one of the businesses' major assets and points of difference from other non-family firms in tourism. All three businesses case-studied have plans for expansion in their programmes and (in case 9.2) for the people they employ, which again differentiates them from so many other tourism businesses that are locked in to existing infrastructure and capacity.

10

Family-owned Tourist Attractions and Wineries

_____

Introduction

The three businesses in this chapter occupy an important position in the tourism industry – that of attractions. Like many tourist attractions though, they began operations not as tourist attractions, but in another industry altogether. These businesses would be what Leiper (1997) referred to as 'on the fringe' of the tourism industry. Case 10.1, Pelham Family Estate Winery was established to produce quality wine but eventually became a tourist attraction as the appeal of wine and the Niagara region of Ontario grew, especially in the populace cities of south-eastern Canada and north-eastern USA. Case 10.2, Rivendell Gardens was originally intended as a working farm and market garden providing fresh produce to local buyers, and pickling and preserving any surplus. Case 10.3, Billabong Sanctuary took many years to establish as much for conservation of Australia's unique and endangered wildlife as for tourism. These three cases illustrate how the owners have made the transformation from the fringe of tourism to become 'industrialized' tourism attractions (Leiper, 1997).

Case 10.1 Pelham Family Estate Winery

Background

Henry of Pelham Family Estate Winery is a small premium estate winery located on the Niagara Bench, Ontario, Canada. Owned and operated by the Speck family since 1988, the land now planted with grapevines was first deeded to their great-, great-, great-grandfather in 1794. With the premise that fine wine is grown and not made, they take low yields and tend the 225-acre estate vineyards with meticulous care. Their dedication to high quality in viticulture and oenology has been rewarded with over 50 international awards (www.henryofpelham. com). The winery offers a tasting bar and cellar store and in 2002 the Coach House Café adjacent to the cellar door sales room. Winery tours, picnic areas, art exhibitions and events are part of the winery experience and an annual Shakespearean performance is popular amongst visitors from Toronto. They also opened two historic walking trails around the property close to the Short Hills Park and the Bruce trail which run along the Niagara bench.

The early association of Henry Smith (who used the pseudonym 'Henry of Pelham' after the English Lord) is a unique and historical point of difference for this business. The real story of the family history is played out in the branding of the wines and on all of the marketing collateral including the web site (www.henryofpelham. com). The message is that the land and business is owned by the family, the wine is made and delivered by the family and that it is a true family business.

©D. Getz et al. 2004. _The Family Business in Tourism and Hospitality_
(D. Getz, J. Carlsen and A. Morrison)

Family dimensions

It was the founder, Mr Paul Speck Senior's decision to establish the vineyard as a family business, after initially buying back the land once owned by his forefathers. His vision was to create a small winery prior to retirement from a career that predominantly involved the running of a private school in Toronto, Ontario. Part-way into the project Mr Speck became ill, and it fell upon the eldest son, Paul to take over the running of the vineyard, while the middle son, Matthew took on the role of maintaining the original 55 acres of vines that the family had planted. Paul was going to attend Law School but then took a year off to help establish the vineyard. Eventually the youngest son, Daniel, became involved in the business as well, at a time when wine in Ontario was just beginning to make a name for itself within Canada. The decision to establish the business then was a unilateral one by Mr Speck and the circumstances dictated that the rest of the family would become involved. Out of this crisis of the loss of the founder came a closer association between the brothers, who rallied together to make the business turn the corner and break-even.

Having made the commitment to the business, the reputation and quality of the wines continued to grow, as did Paul's level of involvement in the industry. In May 1999, Paul was named chairman of the Wine Council of Ontario. Henry of Pelham is a founding member (Paul is Vice Chair) of the Vintners Quality Alliance (VQA), a government-sanctioned regulatory system that ensures the quality of Canadian wines that carry the distinctive VQA label.

There are three brothers in the business – Paul, Daniel and Mathew Speck. Paul (aged 36) is President, Mathew (aged 33) is Vice President and Viticulturist and Daniel (aged 28) is Vice President and Director of Sales. All three are university educated (Philosophy Major) and all are married. Paul has children aged 5 and 2 and Mathew has a baby boy. The business employs an estimated 30 full-time staff and ten part-time staff in its vineyard and tasting room and they are opening a small kitchen and takeaway facility in the near future. Currently the tasting room receives about 50,000 visitors per year, mostly from the 'Golden Horseshoe' area around Lake Ontario and the Greater Toronto Area, a market

area of 6 million Canadians. The wine tourism season begins in June and runs through to December of each year. Even though the winery is less than an hour's drive from the US border, they do not draw a lot of US visitors, although there has been significant new interest.

Business dimensions

Paul believes that all family businesses are entrepreneurial by nature, and take risks to achieve their goals. This is true for start-up businesses, when growth is important, but depends on the generation of business owners; more established (second and third generation) businesses might not need to take as many risks as start-up businesses. It may also be true that risk-taking becomes less necessary over the life of the business.

For example, it was necessary to borrow from merchant banks in the earliest stages of the business during development, but as the business became more established more conventional forms of business financing were put in place. This had the effect of returning more financial control to the owners, and providing a greater degree of freedom over the operation of the business. When asked about his entrepreneurial skills, Paul suggested it came from his father, who ran a private school and invested in Toronto real estate before taking on the challenge of making fine wine. Unfortunately Mr Speck passed away in 1993, but his entrepreneurial spirit lives on through his sons.

Following the difficulties and uncertainty of the early establishment years, Paul decided to place the business on a more formal footing. The roles and responsibilities of the family members were clearly defined and quarterly board meetings were used to monitor business performance. Formalized structures for employees on employment contracts and job structures were also put in place during the early 1990s.

Paul also worked hard on developing good relationships with his financiers and accountants and set up a business plan and cash flow statements that turned 'turmoil to profit' for the business. While there was no formal marketing plan, a series of specific drives to target the high-quality end of the wine market were developed, and continue to develop with each vintage and new planting of *Vinifera* planted. Currently Pelham offers a wide range of wines and styles, including white wines (Chardonnay, Riesling, Sauvignon Blanc and Gewürztraminer); sweet wines (Vidal Late Harvest, Riesling Late Harvest, Riesling Botrytis and Riesling Ice wine); red wines (Baco Noir, Gamay, Gamay-Zweigelt, Cabernet-Baco, Cabernet Merlot, Merlot and Pinot Noir); rosé (Pinot-Zweigelt) and sparkling wines (made from Chardonnay and Pinot Noir).

Growth is very customer-driven, with plantings matching what the owners anticipate that the wine market will demand, not what the industry chooses to supply. The Baco variety is a perfect example of a wine that is in demand, but for some reason is in limited supply in the Niagara region as growers give preference to other red varietals. The diverse range of wines also reflects that inchoate nature of the Canadian wine markets, with tastes and preferences continuing to develop over time.

In fact, Paul indicated that the customer focus enabled the business to overcome the lack of experience in the wine industry. An interesting feature of this business is that none of the owners have had any formal training in the positions that they hold – in management, marketing and sales or viticulture.

Ownership dimensions

Like many family businesses, especially those with young owners, there is no succession or disposition plan, nor do any of the owners have plans for retirement as they are still enjoying the business and family life in Niagara. None of the spouses are involved in the business, thereby avoiding any potential conflicts between family and business concerns. Ideally, Paul would like to see the business continue as a fully independent operational winery, which is viable, profitable and ongoing. The independence to make decisions about the future directions of the winery is most important, so selling or taking an equity partner is not an option. As long as the family enjoys the challenges, takes pride in their success and receives a reasonable return it will remain a family-owned and -operated winery.

The business has grown with the region and benefited from the decision to set the structure in place as soon as possible after Paul took over. It remains a medium-sized player in the Niagara wine region, but a miniscule player in the global wine trade, with exports limited to other Canadian provinces, the USA and Asia. The business will continue to overcome the challenges and uncertainty that have characterized its establishment and growth period, in the same way that the vines overcome the winter assault and summer heat in order to produce simply fine wines.

Case 10.2 Rivendell Gardens

Background

Established by Lu and Peter Standish in 1983 and first opened to the public in 1985, Rivendell Gardens in the Margaret River wine region of Western Australia was originally a vegetable growing operation, turning any surplus into preserves for sale locally. Now Rivendell Wines offers a range of services for tourists, including accommodation, winery, bistro, gallery, attractive gardens and a wide range of preserves made from local produce.

Rivendell produced its first wine in 1990 and now offers a range of whites (made from varietals and blends of Semillon and Sauvignon Blanc) and reds (made from Shiraz, Cabernets, Merlot and some specialized Portuguese varieties). Fruit is sourced from the farm and local vineyards with Lu and Peter's son Mark overseeing the fruit production. The local theme extends to the use of local pottery in the bistro as well as a range of paintings and ceramics by local artists. Brandywine Lodge, a two-storey, bushpole, jarrah-clad house set in the bushland overlooking the vineyard, offers a unique style of accommodation catering with ease for large family groups for special celebrations or reunions. Many craft groups, mixed-generation holiday makers and stressed executives have taken advantage of its tranquil setting.

Rivendell has evolved into a well-established and diversified family business incorporating a bistro (currently leased to a local family), wine tastings, wine sales and home-made preserves, wine-making consulting service, extensive cottage gardens, and a unique accommodation facility. Tourism is an important part of the business activities with cellar door sales (wines and preserves), accommodation revenue and the bistro lease contributing more than 80% of business turnover. The tourism market is mainly individual families, but smaller coach groups are also welcomed.

Family dimensions

Lu and Peter Standish named the business Rivendell (after the haven for weary travellers in J.R.R. Tolkien's epic *The Lord of the Rings*) and began to develop a business based on sales of local produce to tourists in the rapidly expanding South West region of WA. The vineyard was started in the late 1980s, in conjunction with an investment syndicate. It was small in size (30 hectares), with the land being provided by Lu and Peter and the development capital provided by the investors. Unfortunately, financial problems led to several of the investors choosing not to continue, so the vineyard was sold only 3 years later. Mark had been studying at agricultural college and had begun to take an interest in the vineyard. Mark leased the vineyard back from the new owners for several years and was able to develop his skills to such an extent that he could offer wine-making services to nearby small vineyards.

Their daughter-in-law, Wendy has gained hands-on knowledge, firstly as an employee and then (after marriage to Mark and the formation of the new family company) as Company Secretary since 1999 of Rivendell Wines Pty Ltd. Another son, Tony, is a shareholder in the company, but is a 'sleeping partner' as he pursues his teaching career, whilst their eldest son and university professor, Russell, lives in Sydney with his family but visits Rivendell on holidays whenever possible.

the South West, but Lu was always a 'people person' and recognized that tourism would be an opportunity to live on the property while generating extra income. After considering the establishment of various forms of accommodation (including a caravan park, chalets and/or horse riding camps), they eventually went into partnership with another family who began to build the Lodge as their private residence. Meanwhile, Peter had established a successful market garden and sold produce directly from the farm to local buyers. Any surplus was made into chutneys, sauces and jams. This was the start of the home-made preserve business that carries the Rivendell label today. As production increased, a packing shed and farm stall were built on the property and visitors and tourists were welcomed to buy the range of produce and view the gardens. In 1990 their business partners assumed the role of making all of the preserves while Peter tended the garden and Lu managed the farm produce sales. Lateral thinking led to the garden produce diversifying into 'gourmet' vegetables, which were sold through a growers' market in an affluent suburb of Perth. Eventually, in 1995, the partners moved away to a property of their own, and their home was renovated to become Brandywine Lodge.

Lu and Peter have always sought to avoid high borrowings, although their first vineyard was funded that way. Retaining equity and control of Rivendell's assets is an objective of the business. Other capital-raising options, such as sub-dividing and selling off some of the land, have occurred, but Shire restrictions prevent any further option to do this. Plans for growing the business required considerable input of capital, as the business had been undercapitalized during the first few years of operation. Instead of raising funds from the public, Lu and Peter approached other family members to invest their time and funds into the business.

Business dimensions

Lu and Peter had some common goals in establishing Rivendell and used their accumulated knowledge and interests to start up the business. Peter had originally intended to run sheep on the property that they had just purchased in

Ownership dimensions

In establishing a vineyard, a considerable amount of capital was required and in this case it was raised through equity financing. This financial arrangement was tax effective for investors, who controlled about 50% of the vineyard operation. The vineyard was not expected to realize a profit for the first 7 years of operation, and losses could be offset against the other income of investors. However, the sharing of financial control of the vineyard operation proved to be problematic and, after a few years, the vineyard was sold to appease the investors.

Rivendell has been Lu and Peter's vision and they have pursued it with a passion since the early 1980s. During that time there have been a number of partnerships, with family members and non-family partners, lease arrangements and equity funding that provided the much-needed capital. However, this also limited the control that Lu and Peter had to protect the integrity of the business and the quality of the food, wine and preserves, which is associated with the name Rivendell. Retaining control within the family has come at a high cost (both in financial and emotional terms) and problems have emerged with trying to mix business with both friends and family.

When they were building the family business, there were not a lot of family meetings or involvement in decision making. In this regard, the business was perhaps 'not very business-like'. When Mark and Wendy began their own family, it became necessary for the business to expand in order to support two families – Lu and Peter (in semi-retirement) and Mark and Wendy (plus their children). This raised the problem of capitalization and how best to fund the on-going operations and expansion. Past experiences in raising funds through equity had left the families wary of this form of borrowing. Most of the existing capital in the business was tied up in the land values, but further subdivision and land sales were not an option due to local government zoning restrictions.

This issue is further complicated by the expectation that all family members will ultimately inherit a proportion of the proceeds from the sale of the land. Wendy and Mark may consider that they are entitled to a larger share of the proceeds, due to the work and capital they have put in, compared with the other two sons Tony and Russell. Tony has had a financial involvement in the business, while Russell has had no involvement at all. Lu and Peter desire to keep the business in the family for as long as possible.

Despite being a well-established tourism business in the thriving Margaret River wine region, Rivendell also shares some of the common issues that face all family businesses in rural areas. Principal among these is the fact that much of the capital value of the business is locked up in the land, and it is this capital that provides the key to growing the business. The high value of the land is also a source of some family tension and it seems that each family member holds his or her own view as to how best to manage that asset. Their involvement raises the second issue that confronts all family businesses, that is, how to grow the business to a level where it will support a growing family while not surrendering family control. Lu and Peter are now semi-retired and have reduced their involvement in the day-to-day running of the business. The bistro has been leased out to a local family, and Lu is fulfilling a long-held dream of completing a university degree by external studies.

Finally, Mark and Wendy have indicated that they would like to be released from their commitment to the business to be in a position to spend more time with their children, as well as run a business in their own right. As all of the capital is tied up in the land, there are no cash reserves to buy out Mark and Wendy's share in the business. On top of this, Lu and Peter feel that they no longer have the energy to run the business by themselves. Thus, the decision has been made to sell the property and the business. After payment of all outstanding liabilities, Mark and Wendy should be able to walk away with a modest amount to enable them to start their own business and Tony will have his original investment returned. Lu and Peter will then invest their capital in a variety of options, so that they may hopefully retire on the interest, with the three boys inheriting equally in their estate when the time comes.

Case 10.3 Billabong Sanctuary

Background

Billabong Sanctuary (Billabong) near Townsville, Queensland, was established in 1981 and opened to the public in 1983. Like Rivendell Wines Pty Ltd, the business started as a partnership with another couple but the owners Bob and Adel Flemming assumed full ownership of the business in 1995. Their son Brett has recently joined the business and it also employs two indigenous people (descendants of traditional owners of the land where Billabong is located) and four non-aboriginal employees.

Visitors to this Australian native animal sanctuary average 130 per day or about 300,000 a year. As an outdoor tourist facility, visitor flows are weather dependent. Visitor origins are approximately 60% from overseas, 20% from Queensland and 20% from other Australian states. For example, a breakdown of visitor surveys conducted in August–September 2000 provides an indication of visitor origins (Table 10.1).

Note that the year 2000 was a low visitor number year due to global economic conditions in international markets. The domestic Australian tourism flows are somewhat seasonal with the busiest times being school holidays in the months of July, August, September and October. Visitor flows from Europe are constant all year round and the German and other European markets are very important to Billabong. Other important markets include school groups, which provide about 4000 students per year. More recently Billabong has developed packages for the conference market such as breakfasts at the billabong or evening cocktails with a crocodile, which can cater for an average of 100, but can accommodate up to 500 guests, and can include aboriginal dancing and night tours.

Other packages available include Club Billabong, a membership scheme that provides for free entry to Billabong annually, and

Table 10.1.   Billabong Sanctuary visitor origins.

Visitor origin	Proportion of all visits in August/September 2000 (%)
Other Australia	24
Other QLD	10
Townsville	8
Germany	17
Other Europe	17
UK	12
New Zealand	7
USA and Canada	5

Source: James Cook University tourism students.

packages 'all 4 fun', which provide for savings on entry to four tourist attractions in Townsville, including Billabong. Bob also offers educational programmes, such as the 'people to people' programme that brings students out from the USA each year. Bob places high value in visitor education and believes that this is the key to offering a positive ecotourism experience.

Family dimensions

Bob's personal goals were set during his teaching career, when after 15 years he reached Deputy Principal at a school in Newport, Sydney. However, Bob wanted a career change and made the decision to go independent and leave Newport. His wife, Adel was willing to 'go with the flow.' During his teaching career, Bob developed a strong commitment to the environment and conservation and incorporated these themes into his teaching.

Originally, Bob and Adel were looking at established business and considered a business in Cairns, now running as Wildworld. After the real estate deal did not go ahead, they decided to establish a business in Townsville, the regional centre of North Queensland. They took 6 months to find land (25 acres/10 ha) with good water and correct zoning, approximately 20 km south of Townsville. The business took 2 years to establish and Bob wrote environmental educational units for the Queensland Education Department on a consultancy basis to generate an income during that period. Bob continues in this educational role and offers tourism training through the Queensland Department of State Development aimed at increasing profitability of tourism businesses. Bob runs training sessions on the use of information technology and website development, and the Billabong website provides a good example of the educational theme of Billabong (www.billabongsanctuary.com.au).

After opening in 1983 the first years were tough, with low cash flow. However, they were lucky with acquiring animals for the sanctuary because they could take all of those illegally collected animals that Queensland National Parks did not want. Bob has now established an extensive sanctuary with displays of many of Australia's wild fauna, including feeding of crocodiles and a breeding programme of the endangered bird, the southern cassowary. True to the name of the business, it does provide a sanctuary and habitat for free-ranging water-birds and reptiles. Bob manages the business part-time and Adel manages the accounts and finances, also on a part-time basis (2 days/week). They employ a manager full-time, which allows them time away from the business together. Their son Brett commenced working at Billabong in November 2002 as Sales and Marketing Manager.

Business dimensions

After almost 20 years, Bob and Adel still enjoy the business and will stay in business until they are aged 70 years plus (Bob is now 55 and Adel is 53). Bob has a strong focus on recruiting and training the right staff and has appointed a Manager, Chris, who runs the business when Bob and Adel take time off. Unlike many family businesses this enables Bob and Adel to take an annual holiday – 1 month a year – and Bob cites this as the main reason for being able to stay in business for so long. In terms of recruit-ment of staff, Bob and Adel are highly selective and only appoint outstanding applicants. In their view, it is the staff at Billabong Sanctuary that make the business successful. The regional university, James Cook University (JCU), is a good source of staff and all staff at Billabong from there have a degree in zoology. Bob does not employ unqualified 'animal people' and prefers staff to have a higher level of education. In terms of retaining staff in the very competitive wildlife business where workers are mostly nomadic, Bob has introduced a number of innovations. Firstly, a 4-day week for staff has been in place for a number of years, making employment at Billabong more attractive. Sec-ondly, Bob is inclusive of all staff in all aspects of running the business and especially values their input when establishing new displays. The staff at Billabong are very 'hands-on' and seem to enjoy imparting their knowledge of Australia's wild animals to visitors through interactive sessions programmed throughout the day (see the website for feeding and other interactive programmes). Highly skilled and motivated staff

are offered a career path to management or curator level within the business.

Bob has plans to increase awareness of the region and has applied for a regional tourism grant to entice visitors to explore the region around Townsville. Within Billabong, Bob plans to establish a new rainforest display and wants to keep growing the business and introducing something new for tourists to enjoy and to keep locals interested. Bob has excellent relations with the local media, which often contact him for stories about new developments. Bob taps into the 'visiting friends and relatives' market through a Billabong Privilege card provided to locals, which provides one free local entry for every two visitors they bring to Billabong.

Bob wants to continue to target the European market, mostly high-spending back-packers and the self-drive market. Bob markets Billabong as 'Australia's best interactive wildlife park' and recognizes the value of favourable word-of-mouth promotion. The main source of information about Billabong is friends, relatives, residents of Townsville and other word-of-mouth, which was cited by 35% of the visitors in the 2000 survey. Another indication of the favourable reputation of Billabong is the propor-tion of repeat visitors, which was the second largest group in the 2000 survey.

Bob also owns land on Magnetic Island (offshore from Townsville) and plans to establish an ecotourism business with accommodation at some time in the future. He may target wealthy European backpackers who have the money to spend on up-market accommodation in a unique location.

Ownership dimensions

As previously stated, Bob and Adel intend to stay on running Billabong for another 20 years (at least) and Bob holds the view that 'if you retire you die.' They do have a son aged 22 who grew up at Billabong (a fascinating child-hood if ever there was one). He holds a degree in Hotel Management and was employed as a Purser on the *Coral Princess*, a 40-passenger cruise ship operating between Townsville and Cairns. Having shown no previous interest in joining the business, Brett is now involved in building the conventions market for the business as well as increasing the European segment and special interest-group market. However, there are no plans for him to take over the business at the moment.

A key theme of this business is education – probably as a result of Bob's background and experience in teaching, Bob believes that visitor education must be entertaining but must also involve interaction with the wildlife. Bob encourages hand-feeding of animals by visitors and does not charge for having photos taken with animals such as koalas (other Australia wildlife attractions charge for this facility). Bob has no problem balancing conservation with increasing tourism numbers and says that the site copes well with as many as 350 visitors on site at any one time.

In terms of personal goals, independence and the desire to leave teaching were the main reasons that Bob and Adel established Billabong. Bob's personal conservation and environmental interests were also important. No specific business goals were identified; however, Billabong appears to be a successful business and has won numerous local, regional and state tourism awards. Bob's goals for developing the business are shared with his partner Adel and staff, who are a valuable part of the business.

Visitor education is also an important part of the business and this occurs through the skills and efforts of the staff, who are all qualified zoologists. Billabong has a well-established reputation as a wildlife attraction and has targeted the European market (mainly Germans) on self-drive tours. Billabong produces a German version of the brochure and the latest promotional brochure features mainly European-looking people interacting with wildlife. Billabong has excellent road signage on the main highways from the north and south, and highway billboards were the second largest single source of information about Billabong in the 2000 survey (16%). Billabong also values the local market and encourages local visitation through Club Billabong membership, Billabong Privilege cards and keeping the local media informed of new developments and achievements.

Bob and Adel have no plans for disposition and in any case their son is now interested in working in the business. They plan to continue running the business for another 20 years and have put the management and staff in place to enable this to occur.

Chapter Summary

These three cases all faced different challenges in very different environments in making the transition from their primary or 'core' business to a point where they are now achieving success in more than one field of endeavour. In cases 10.1 and 10.2, success in wine and food production has underpinned the development of tourism products and services. In case 10.3, the founder's primary concern for conserving the habitat of Australian fauna and flora has been achieved and that has enabled them to deliver environmental education in an authentic and meaningful setting for tourists. In all cases, tourism was always considered as a strategic direction for the business, if only in the minds of the founders, but their ability to devise a means of strategically targeting and attracting tourists to their businesses has eventually paid dividends (after a decade or more) and now generates a substantial proportion of business turnover. The investment decisions and ownership issues confronted were difficult and the lessons learned from partnerships and equity financing are salient for any family business, particularly wineries that intend to move into the tourism industry.

Reference

Leiper, N. (1997) *Tourism Management*. TAFE Publishing, Melbourne, Australia.

11

Cross-case Analysis

_____

Introduction

Cross-case analysis is a means of grouping together common responses to interviews as well as analysing different perspectives on central issues (Patton, 1990; Carlsen and Getz, 2001). Cross-case analysis begins with writing a case for each unit studied (each family business) then grouping responses together according to questions, themes or central issues. In this way the issues that emerge in the case studies are integrated within the descriptive analytical framework that provides the basis for comparison and contrast. The themes for this cross-case analysis are those that have been used in the theoretical and case study sections of this book based on Gersick *et al.* (1997) – family, business and ownership. Previous chapters illustrate how these three themes or dimensions of family business research not only represent the most important aspects but also fit well with the structure and approach used in the 15 cases presented in Chapters 6–10. There are other approaches to conducting cross-case analysis based on the historical development of the business – the chronological approach. That is, case studies present the issues over time, describing the family business from conception through establishment and development and ultimate plans for disposition. Other strategies for analysing case studies focus on key events or decision points, business settings and environment, social/psychological processes or business strategies. While all of these have some relevance to the current cases studied, the thematic approach to cross-case analysis provided the optimum means of grouping together common issues for the family businesses studied.

Interviews leading to the preparation of case studies were conducted between 1999 and 2002. Questions covered basic business information including ownership, the roles of family members involved in the business, number of staff, business operations, when the business was established or acquired, financial turnover, and the education level and previous business experience of owners. The interviews focused on broad issues, but specifically addressed these questions:

- What were your personal motives or goals when starting up (or purchasing) this business?
- Did all family members share these goals?
- Were there other reasons for commencing in business?
- How was the decision to commence the business made?
- What was your role in the business?
- What is your personal involvement in the business?
- Have you any plans to develop the business?
- What do you want to see happen to the business?
- Will you sell the business or will it stay in the family?
- What do you prefer to do with the business in the future?

©D. Getz et al. 2004. *The Family Business in Tourism and Hospitality*
(D. Getz, J. Carlsen and A. Morrison)

Interviews were conducted with individual family members at a time and location convenient for respondents, mostly at the place of business or family home. While every effort was made to involve as many family members as possible in the case study interviews, the cross-case analysis pertains mainly to issues for founders and owners, not those of other family members working in the business.

The businesses selected for study are not necessarily representative of all family businesses in tourism, but are based on a convenience sample from the geographical region of the researchers. They were selected on the basis of personal contacts, and in some cases with a minimum of advance knowledge about the nature of ownership and family involvement. It was intended to interview only businesses with children or other family members directly involved in order that they fit the definition of a family business. The cases selected for this analysis consisted of accommodation providers, tourist attractions and tour operators. Some of these businesses incorporate more than one type of revenue source, with the simplest being cabins for rent and the most complex consisting of a campsite, cabins, motel, café, rental house, catering, and recreational activities. Direct comparison of identical types of businesses was not possible with such limited coverage. To facilitate comparisons and demonstrate examples of cases based on the issues identified, a coding system which is cross-referenced to the case studies in Chapters 6–10 is used as follows:

Case 6.1   Alborak Stables
Case 6.2   Taunton Farm Holiday Park
Case 6.3   Ol' MacDonald's
Case 7.1   The Bergstedt's
Case 7.2   Cricklewood Hotel
Case 7.3   Millestgården
Case 8.1   Crystal Creek Rainforest Retreat
Case 8.2   O'Reilly's Rainforest Guesthouse
Case 8.3   River Valley Ventures
Case 9.1   Wild Over Walpole
Case 9.2   Minnewanka Tours
Case 9.3   Åreguiderna
Case 10.1   Pelham Family Estate Winery
Case 10.2   Rivendell Gardens
Case 10.3   Billabong Sanctuary

Based on the 15 cases cross-analysed as well as other research findings in the family business literature it is possible to identify a set of issues that are salient to all family businesses in tourism and hospitality. These issues relate to the family, the business and the ownership dimensions previously discussed. Within each dimension there are a number of issues that are common to family businesses as well as issues where businesses digress. It is important to note that whilst most issues are found to be common, they cannot be considered as generic to all family businesses in tourism and hospitality. Nor are they presented in order of importance in the following sections of family, business and ownership issues.

Family Issues

Family issues that emerge in the cross-case analysis are as follows:

A degree of family consensus in decision making

The decision to establish or purchase a family business is fundamental as it affects the future of the family in almost every way possible. This decision then should rarely be taken unilaterally (as was the case in 10.1) and all family members should be involved in the decision process. Many factors are taken into consideration when establishing or developing a family business, and in most cases family members agree that lifestyle and location are the most important factors (cases 6.1, 6.2, 6.3, 7.1, 9.1, 9.3 and 10.2). Whilst consensus is desirable, it is not essential to have agreement between all family members when setting up or expanding a business, as case 6.3 demonstrates.

Shared hobbies, leisure interests and values within the family

Many tourism businesses were established in order that the owners could pursue their own leisure interests and hobbies whilst making a living for the family – an idyllic mix of business and pleasure. However, in order for that ideal to be realized, all family members must have common leisure interests. These interests were many and varied between cases, including nature and conservation (8.1, 9.1 and 10.3), snow skiing (9.3), horse riding (6.1) or gardening and viticulture (10.2). These interests and values have informed the vision of family businesses, for example in case 6.1, Sandra desired to run her own horse stables and her parents shared in that vision and realized that ambition. For rural-based family business, living in and raising children in the rural environment was important in many cases (for example, 6.3). It is also important that family leisure and business interests coincide because family holidays are rare, so the business takes the place of family leisure pursuits, especially in the first years of establishment (for example, 8.3).

Some level of support and involvement of all family members

This is an interesting family issue that illustrates that support of the family is desirable but not essential to successful family businesses. In some cases, involvement of the whole family in the business was limited due to the other commitments of some family members to activities such as farming (6.1, 6.3), education (6.1, 8.1, 10.1) or full-time employment elsewhere (7.2. 8.1 and 10.3). In other cases, the copreneurs and the extended family, including in-laws and children (8.2 and 8.3), committed to the business. Yet a third type of support was shown after the business had been established for a while, when family members chose either to become more actively involved in some aspect of the business (8.2 and 10.1) or support the family business in a financial sense whilst maintaining a separate occupation, effectively involved as a 'silent partner' (10.2) or financial adviser (6.1).

Family involvement in the business from an early stage

This issue relates more to the benefits of instilling a sense of responsibility and involvement of family members in the business, as was the case in 8.2. However, it could equally be argued that involvement of family members later in the

life of the business can be just as effective in ensuring good business practices, albeit with a 'steeper learning curve' for family members not involved from the start (10.1).

Involvement of all siblings in the business

Involvement of brothers and sisters in the family business is an issue during all stages of the business and has implications for all aspects of the business, particularly succession. In one case (8.3) the siblings all became involved in the business, fulfilling important roles. In case 7.1, three brothers have all developed cabins on adjacent parcels of land and are jointly acquiring more land to support their business and maintain their traditional lifestyle in the mountains of mid-Sweden. Siblings in business are also evident in cases 8.2 and 10.1 and all have complementary skills that support the business. In all cases, the involvement of spouses in the business is an issue that is carefully considered, particularly when children are also involved. When one sibling is involved extensively in the business, and others have little or nothing to do with the day-to-day running of it, issues arise as to the succession plans and inheritance. Are all siblings entitled to an equal share of the business? What if the business is located on a family farming property? These are pertinent issues that arise among family members when considering equity and ownership of family businesses (for example, 10.2).

A family tradition of business/entrepreneurship

A family business tradition in running a business or enterprise is more evident in the case of accommodation, such as hotels (7.1) or guest houses (8.2) and is more of an 'old world' concept. None the less, tradition can embedded in the psyche of the family and form a path that can be followed as in case 10.1. Tradition also implies some stock of knowledge, and perhaps capital that can be drawn upon in running a family business. The source of the entrepreneurial spirit in the family is usually the founder (10.1) but in one case the desire to start a business was engendered in the founder by her mother (6.3) and the desire to fulfil the mother's dream of a better life for her family was a powerful and emotional reason for Jean venturing into the tourism business.

A commitment to keeping the property under family ownership in farm-based or family home-based businesses

Similar to the previous issue, a commitment to living 'on the land' or maintaining ownership of traditional family property is desirable for farm/estate-based business, especially as farming activities can 'cross-subsidize' the establishment of tourism activities on-farm (6.1). In many farm-based family businesses, most family members felt that keeping the farm 'in the family' and recognizing that diversification into tourism was one means of achieving this was evident (6.1, 6.2, 6.3). Likewise, keeping the family property, in this case an historical guesthouse, was also important (8.3) to all family members involved in the business. In case 7.1, the family interest in tourism extends back over four generations, and the desire to cater for tourists to mid-Sweden has remained in the family even though the original shop and hotel have not.

Flexibility for family members to self-define roles and responsibilities

Family conflict can arise when roles and responsibilities overlap or workloads are not clearly defined of shared equally. In all of the case studies for this book there is no evidence that this occurred. However, there is also little evidence that roles and responsibilities were clearly defined. Instead, family members were encouraged to self-define their roles in the business based on their particular skills, interests and experience (for example, 10.1). This is perhaps one luxury afforded to family business owners, the flexibility to self-define roles and involvement may be important to prevent family disharmony. Most family members were comfortable with the shared roles in the business for example; in case 6.1 'everyone helps with everything in order to get things done'. There is

a risk that some family members will be allocated less important and challenging tasks in the business and will consequently lose interest, so to counter this everyone should be allocated a significant role, or responsibilities should be rotated around family members. One family business was adamant that if they did employ their children it would be in 'real jobs' in a paid capacity (7.3).

Good relations between siblings and within the family

Open and honest relations between family members were evident in many of the cases, both between parents and children in the business (6.1, 8.1, 8.3 and 9.1) as well as between siblings (8.2 and 10.1). That is not to say that family disharmony does not occur, but that relationships are such that any conflict can be resolved through family meetings or informally through negotiation and understanding.

Family adversity issues

Again, mutual respect and intimacy in a family setting is a useful precursor for overcoming the difficult periods that confront every business from time to time. Some families respond very well to business pressures by making decisions together as a family, thereby sharing the burden of family pressures. Other families are deeply impacted by family tragedy (6.3 and 7.1), but somehow have the strength and ability to support each other while maintaining the business.

Business Issues

Business planning and management skills

Family members that have formal training in management, including business planning and management, are a good asset for family businesses. In many cases it will be the children, not the founders of the business, who have received formal business management training, either through tertiary education programmes (8.1, 10.2) or informal training through work experience (10.3) and voluntary roles (6.3). The business networks developed by the children of founders often bring benefits to the family business and lead to more formal business structures and operations that reflect good business practice. In one case (10.3) the family business can play a mentoring role for other small businesses.

Entrepreneurial issues

The debate about the level of entrepreneurialism in family businesses is ongoing, with examples of businesses that have succeeded without the founders engaging overtly in entrepreneurial ventures, but acting in an entrepreneur guise (6.1, 6.3, 7.3, 8.1, 8.3). Other family businesses claim that everything they do is entrepreneurial (10.1) and case 9.3 is another example of an entrepreneurial individual starting a tourism business.

The case studies indicate that family businesses in tourism are mostly non-entrepreneurial and are averse to risk. After all, if the business venture fails, the family unit is also exposed to failure so the degree of risk is much greater than for non-family businesses ventures. However, at some point in the life of the family businesses, some are compelled to back their business judgement and take risks in order to succeed. It may be that the entrepreneurial family businesses must have at least one entrepreneur in the family, someone who desires a challenge and feels that they have the skills to succeed (for example, see case 6.3). The level of experience and knowledge of the family business entrepreneur can be critical to the success of the start-up family business, and also comes into play when businesses pursue their expansion plans. It is important to note that many of the family businesses case-studied do have expansion ideas (6.3, 8.1, 8.2, 8.3, 9.1 and 10.1) involving either an increase in capacity or an augmentation of their existing products and services.

Financial management

A family member with financial management skills is invaluable for a business, especially those that are externally financed. Some level of training in computerized financial management is desirable, or at the very least a level of skill in bookkeeping and accounting practices. Invariably it is the female family members that manage the finances of family businesses (9.1 and 10.3) but in other cases it is a shared responsibility. It is also important that family members gain experience in financial management by 'learning the lessons' from other business or professional employment, as case 8.3 demonstrates.

Sound decision-making processes

Most businesses seemed to be able to work under a mixture of formal and informal meetings, as they were largely comprised of family members who knew each other well, so that decisions made were comparable to what the family as a whole wanted. Case 6.1 demonstrates how the parents made the decision to develop the stables as a business, but the daughter Sandra was 'party to the detailed planning process.' Successful businesses understood that there must be a clear definition of roles and tasks; however, the family as a whole had to be happy with major/relevant decisions for them to go ahead.

An example of an *ad hoc* decision-making was case 10.2, where there were very little family meetings, which led simply to working harder (not smarter!). Finally case 10.1 shows that a key decision to commence a family business venture can be made unilaterally in the hope that other family members will follow in the footsteps of the founder/decision maker.

Computer/information technology issues

These skills were helpful in cases related to marketing the business, such as by using the Internet to generate business (7.1) or by being on a collective website through a booking company (7.3). In other cases, technology was an issue for the businesses for accounting (9.1), computerized reservation systems (8.1) and the design of a website for the business (6.1,

6.3, 7.1). One business case in particular (10.3) demonstrated the excellent information technology skills of the owner, Bob Flemming, in both their website and the fact that Bob delivers training programmes in information technology and website development for the Queensland Department of State Development.

Business networking/marketing

The importance of good networking and marketing cannot be overstated for small, family businesses. Networking with other family tourism businesses, tourism associations, convention and visitor bureaux and coach tour operators is a characteristic of most successful tourism businesses. Only one family business (6.2) was formally affiliated with a national marketing group through a franchise arrangement, which produced benefits for the business through bookings and customer loyalty. Another (8.3) was approached to franchise their business formula in New Zealand, but decided against it.

There is an over-reliance on favourable word-of-mouth and repeat business (for example, 7.1) which reflects the limited funds available for other conventional forms of marketing. Others realized the need for a more professional approach, such as hiring a full-time sales and marketing professional (9.2) and being a part of a booking company (7.3) in addition to the ubiquitous promotional brochures. All businesses case-studied, except 7.1, had promotional brochures. Other techniques include family brand extension/product diversification (8.2, 9.1); familiarization tours (8.1) and trade show promotion (9.2). Benefits from television specials focusing on the relevant areas (9.1) and tourism promotional magazines were also used (8.1). Sales commissions are also used by one business (9.3), and other techniques include clear market segmentation (6.1, 8.2) with strategies in place (8.2) as well as marketing meetings (8.2). The use of industry awards as a promotional tool has not been embraced by many family businesses in this set of case studies, but those that have entered and won national tourism awards always advertise their success (see case 8.1).

Human resource management

The ability to manage staff effectively was common to all family businesses that employed non-family staff members. In most cases, the majority of the staff members were in fact family members such as husbands, wives, sons, daughters and even a niece; managing staff effectively came down to understanding the desires and skills of family members in order to allocate roles within the business. Indeed, the accepted approach to human resource management does not apply within family businesses because it is not always possible to treat children or parents as employees (see case 8.1). Similarly any non-family members employed in the business must fit in with the family as well as fulfilling their role within the business (see case 6.1). Problems came from the fact that the owners tended to have to work long hours and mix business and personal life in order to complete necessary tasks, because they were the only people who knew the business and its operations sufficiently to do them (6.1, 8.1). Titles and job specifications were used, however there is still the issue of how many tasks each person should be allocated to effectively run the business. Another issue was managing higher levels of part-time/casual staff, both from within the family and outside (6.1, 6.3). Seasonality affects human resource management as workers are only employed at certain times of the year due to peaks and troughs in tourist demand.

Business planning and strategic management

This refers to the need to plan in the short- and long-term for the survival and success of a tourism business. Most expressed long-term goals for the business, but few had a sound plan as to how to strategically achieve those goals. In one case (8.3) the founders failed in business due to a lack of planning, financial controls and business experience.

Long-term success involves partly being able to separate themselves from the business and work 'on it' rather than 'in it' (8.1, 10.3) through employing more staff, and also by having interested/qualified family members taking over the business in the future (9.2). In case 8.2

the business was in the third generation, with family members competing against non-family applicants for positions, and only appointed if they were suitably qualified.

With regards to business planning and growth, some businesses were more concerned with trying to make their businesses profitable before considering expansion (6.1). Other businesses extended both their services as well as their business name to external activities, such as case 9.1, where Gary was involved in consulting, computer-assisted design, environmental science and guiding, and case 10.3 where Bob was involved in education and training. Other businesses extended themselves into related areas such as case 8.2, with the opening of a winery.

It was also evident that family businesses conduct very little research to support strategic planning or marketing. Business, financial, marketing and site feasibility studies were not undertaken in the family businesses case-studied, but basic cost estimates were made (6.1). Some sought useful advice from business and management planning seminars, but in one case found them of limited use (6.2). At the same time, some government departments did prove beneficial in the feasibility stage in providing models and predictions for the proposed tourist development (6.2). However, it is judgement supported by hard work and commitment that appears to be the fundamental planning approach of family businesses. Most businesses however had no real plan for continuing the business, being caught between trusting in their successors to take over, finding external ownership/management or disposing of the business for the best possible price.

Seasonality and demand issues

Seasonality is a key issue that influenced both the opening hours/dates of the business as well as the service offered. In the example of 6.3, seasonality serves both effectively to limit revenues by cutting off services at certain times of the year, as well as to act as a forced holiday for employees to have a hiatus from work. Depending on the environment and setting, most businesses operated year-round whilst others focused on other aspects of the business

such as farming or viticulture (6.1, 10.1) during the low season for tourism. Another business (6.3) considered seasonality as a double-edged sword, with the positive aspect being the free time for owners in the low season and the negative being the costs associated with start-up and shutdown for the brief high season. Indeed, the expansion plans in case 6.3 are designed specifically to create an all-year accommodation facility and employ staff on a full-time basis, in order to 'combat' seasonality (see Chapter 5).

It was also evident that many businesses did not realize the 24 hours-a-day, 7-days-a-week nature of the tourism business when commencing in business. Fortunately, family members made themselves available during the busy periods to assist with running the business on a part-time basis (6.1, 6.3, 8.1, 8.3) while others did not have this support option (10.3). The demanding nature of the tourism business is a critical issue for all family businesses; especially those that either cannot afford to employ staff (7.1) or don't have the option of employing family members on a part-time or full-time basis (8.1). In many cases, family business owners find themselves 'tied' to the business and are unable to take a break from the demands of their guests, unable to afford to employ support staff or a manager and unable to find the right people to run the business for them in their absence (8.1). Clearly, the desirable lifestyle that often motivates family business start-ups in tourism regions is not always realized due to the highly seasonal and demanding nature of the tourism business.

Good customer service

Customer service is vital to the success of all these businesses, especially considering that good customer service results in favourable word of mouth which is important for most businesses. If customer service is not satisfactory, word of mouth may be negative and the business may suffer, especially in niche markets such as in case 8.1. In most cases, good customer service is enjoyable for business owners and may even form part of the lifestyle benefits they chose when commencing in business (6.1).

Good customer services in areas such as reservations and bookings can be demanding but can also be considered as an enjoyable part of running a family business (7.3). Targeting the top end of the market by providing quality tourism experiences is a strategy employed by a number of family businesses (8.1, 8.3)

However, most businesses case-studied did not have a focus on customer service even though it was implicit in all of their business activities, and in one case improving customer service was stated as a business goal (6.3). Personal service is sometimes promoted as a unique selling point of family businesses, where the customer knows that they are dealing with the people that both own and operate the business. There can also be a market perception that family businesses are unique and offer a different product or service to non-family businesses. This belief that it is better to be unique than to try and compete with existing businesses was apparent in case 6.2, with Rob claiming 'it is better to be different than it is to be better'. When there is a high degree of social interaction with visitors, the privacy of family members is lost and it can also make it difficult to complete the daily tasks of running the business (6.1). However, one business does give priority to social interaction and customer service (6.2) ahead of the other tasks in the running the business and Rob doesn't mind if it 'takes one and a half hours to empty the rubbish bins' if he is socializing with visitors around the caravan park.

Few businesses case-studied used a customer feedback form to monitor the satisfaction and suggestions of guests (see case 8.1), despite this being an effective means of improving customer service.

Ownership Issues

Family partnerships

A number of family businesses case-studied commenced in business in conjunction with another family (10.2, 10.3) but in both cases the partnership was terminated after a few years. The issues associated with two-family businesses were not explored, but the outcomes in both cases were evident. Where two families have different views and interests in the business,

dissolution of the partnership is inevitable, especially when both families seek to place their own interests first. This termination can be acrimonious, given that both families have claim to the intellectual property, goodwill and equity in the business. In other cases, family businesses can work co-operatively to cross-promote their independent businesses (7.1 and 8.3 for example), in provision of accommodation.

Formation of a family trust

Formation of family trusts is an effective means of setting up legal ownership of a family business in most cases, depending upon the corporation and taxation regimes in the countries involved. For example in Australia, case 8.2 is owned by two family trusts, being established in 1994 especially to ensure effectively that ownership arrangements are acceptable to all family members concerned. Family trusts can assist in maintaining harmony and retaining family control of the business and preserving the assets of the business for the benefit of future generations of family members.

However, trusts also have the effect of locking away all family assets and placing them under the control of a single trustee, thereby unbalancing ownership and control of the business. This becomes an issue when siblings seek to obtain a greater level of control in the business or when one needs to liquidate some of the assets of the family as their personal share. The other effect of a trust arrangement is to obligate family members to work in the family business in order to contribute to the asset value growth.

Functional ownership structure

In more than one case, the original ownership structure proved to be unsuitable and did not allow the business founders to pursue their goals independently. This was the case in capital-intensive businesses such as tourist attractions, hotels and wineries that were originally owned or developed in joint partnership with another family (10.3) or with non-family investors (10.2). In other cases, ownership of the business changed to enable the business to survive (8.3). In all cases, any change in owner-ship structure is an issue that must be handled extremely carefully if problems such as that arising in case 7.2 are to be avoided. The reasons for diversifying or divesting ownership of all or part of the business are often sound, especially as this can enable the workload and financial obligation to be shared.

Family equity in the business

In very few businesses are family members will-ing to invest and share equity in the business with no expectation of a regular return, either in the form of profit share (if available) or realizing on the value of capital growth. Likewise, it is not always acceptable for family members to invest their time in the business without receiving regular wages or dividends, but gaining 'sweat equity' (8.3) in return for their efforts. In most cases, profits or capital growth tend to be re-invested in the business (8.1, for example).

This raises the issue of family equity being linked to land value and therefore expansion plans of business (e.g. 10.2). The extent to which family members take equity in the business can have a direct influence on the business decisions, especially the development and disposition of the business. Increasing returns on the business may be needed to support a growing number of family members (8.2) or provide an income to founding members of the family business when they retire (9.1, 10.2). Indeed, the business may represent the founder's retirement fund (7.1) or have been purchased with the proceeds of superannuation or redundancy payouts (8.1). The issuing of shares in the business to all family members can also be considered, but has the effect of diluting the control of the business (see case 8.2). In case 8.3 a number of shares have been placed in a family trust, thereby affording the family members some protection in case of business failure.

Manageable financial structures

Debt, rather than equity, was the main source of capital for establishing or acquiring family businesses in most cases, with the possible exception of farm-based and family home-based businesses. Land and property purchases were financed with bank loans which meant that interest expense was probably the highest monthly figure in the family business accounts on the expenditure side of the ledger. The cases could not divulge the extent to which business expenses were met through revenue or the drawing down of the business profits or the owner's savings, but for most family businesses it is probably a combination of the two. At least one business (7.3) had banking arrangements where credit was extended prior to the peak season.

This is a significant ownership issue for all small businesses, but especially family businesses, which must manage their debt and equity more carefully than other types of busi-nesses. In case 7.1, the limiting of borrowings (instilled by the father of the owner) enabled the family business to survive a decline in the value of their property during a period of over-supply and bankruptcy sales. Lease arrangements are an option for some family businesses but lease arrangements must only be entered into after professional and competent legal advice, if problems are to be avoided – as in case 7.2. In case 8.1 the resort was developed over time and this allowed the owners to avoid over-borrowing as well as ensuring that the theme and ambience of the site was maintained.

Access to sufficient capital

Most family businesses case-studied appeared to be under-capitalized, particularly where their expansion plans were concerned. In the exam-ple of 10.2 there was a need to raise capital out-side the family in order to expand, but raising funds through equity proved to be unsatisfac-tory for the owners. Most family businesses face the dilemma of having capital 'tied up' in land or in the value of the business, but are reluctant to sell any part of their land or business as a means of raising funds. In only one case (6.1) was a family member willing to raise funds through land sales in order for the family busi-ness to pay off loans if required. In another case (6.3), access to a government grant accelerated the development of the rural business and business development was cross-subsidized by non-business income (6.3, 10.3). Yet another response to this issue (7.3) was to consider closing down part of the business (accommodation) in order to expand another part of the business (conference and meeting venue). A well-established business has more options for raising capital and may have subsidiary businesses (such as in case 8.2 with Canungra Valley Vineyards) for full or partial sale. Family businesses access a range of sources for operating funds include income from teaching and primary production (10.2, 10.3) and private consultancy (9.1).

Separation of family and business assets

It is important that major family assets, such as the family home, be owned separately from the business in case business problems arise. In some cases family-owned farmland, but not the family home, may be offered as collateral for a business loan. Again the asset arrangements of the family businesses case-studied have not been included for reasons of privacy, but in all cases family homes have been separated from the fortunes of the business. In cases where the family resides in the business location (6.1, 6.2, 6.3, 7.1, 8.2, 8.3, 10.2) deeds and titles for the land that the home is on should be separate from the land on which the business is based, and in one case (6.1) this structure was put in place very early in the life of the business.

Disposition/succession planning issues

Untimely disposition of the family business is seldom planned, although there is usually some agreement as to how family business ownership will change in case of the death of the owners, divorce or family break-up. This is not surprising, as few families want to contemplate these matters. However, it is a reality that all family businesses must ultimately face and it is desirable that agreed succession or disposition plans are in place. The succession and ownership issues identified in previous chapters and the case studies indicate that few have disposition

plans and many confront barriers to the smooth transition of business ownership. Barriers to inheritance can be related to the financial viability of the business and the willingness of the second generation to take on the responsibilities (and liabilities) of the business owners. When the children of family business owners do not share the same level of commitment to the business, the issue of succession becomes more difficult (10.2).

Cultural issues

In some cultures it may not be considered appropriate to have children working in a family business with parents (as was the case in the Swedish businesses case-studied – 7.1, 7.3 and 9.3), whilst in other cases the continued involvement of children and even grand-children of the founders was the family tradition and accepted cultural norm (6.2, 6.3, 8.2). A limitation of the cases included for analysis was that they did not include businesses owned by people with different ethnic backgrounds, and most were of Anglo-Saxon ethnicity. Inclusion of Asian ethnic businesses might have revealed other ownership issues such as the preference for male successors in Chinese family businesses (see Chapter 5). Indeed, primogeniture may be a characteristic of many family businesses (regardless of ethnic background) and this raises gender and equity issues in terms of ownership and succession.

Gender and generational issues

Again, ownership can also be a function of gender with some owners having concerns that females may not be sufficiently skilled or interested in carrying out some of the infrastructure and maintenance aspects of the business (6.3), or it may be that male members of the business possess the technical knowledge to maintain the infrastructure but have not yet passed on that knowledge to the children or grandchildren (especially daughters). Given the predominance of females employed, it would be appropriate to have equivalent proportions in ownership and management of family businesses in tourism. In some cases (8.3 and 9.2) it is the female family member that has the best potential to take over the role of management and ownership of the family business.

Chapter Summary

This chapter has identified commonalities between case study findings of the 15 family businesses as detailed in Chapters 6–10 inclusive. Even though the cases were selected on the basis of convenience, the core activities of tourism – accommodation, attractions and tours – are all represented in the cases. Two important implications of the cross-case analysis are worth noting here, although the wider implications will be discussed in the final two chapters.

The first point is that there is a remarkable degree of commonality between the family businesses case-studied, despite the differences in their business environment, business culture, services offered, markets, location, destination and business characteristics. The fact that some 30 areas of common concern were identified in this cross-case analysis has implications for future family business research in tourism and hospitality. The issues have been presented under the headings of family, business and ownership, but there are many that cut across these three dimensions and could be studied in much more detail. Communication for example, can be investigated from the family perspective (i.e. how do the family members communicate effectively?); from the business perspective (what are the most appropriate forms of business communication for family businesses?); from the ownership perspective (which forms of communication are most commonly used to resolve family business ownership issues?). There is also an opportunity to prioritize the issues identified in this cross-case analysis, to provide a quantitative basis for identifying and progressing important areas of family business research.

The second implication of the cross-case analysis is that the common issues identified may be representative of the issues confronting the multitude of family businesses in tourism and hospitality around the world. Whilst there is no statistical test of the representativeness of the cross-case analysis findings, the range of businesses and the geographic and temporal scope of the case studies would mitigate against the myopia and bias that is inherent in single-case or single-country case studies. It would be very interesting to develop new case studies of family businesses in other countries and cultures around the world to test the extent to which these commonalities can be found in other tourism destinations.

References

Carlsen, J. and Getz, D. (2001) Cross-case analysis of family businesses in rural tourism. In: Pforr, C. and Janeczko, B. (eds) *Proceedings of the Capitalising on Research Conference*. University of Canberra, Canberra, Australia.

Gersick, K., Davis, J., Hampton, M. and Lansberg, I. (1997) *Generation to Generation: Life Cycles of Family Business*. Harvard Business School Press, Boston, Massachusetts.

Patton, M.Q. (1990) *Qualitative Evaluation and Research Methods*. Sage Publications, Fresno, California.

12

Implications for Family Businesses and Tourism Destinations

Introduction

Until very recently the family business dimensions within tourism and hospitality were only occasionally acknowledged, and not subjected to systematic analysis. Yet, as this book demonstrates, the family vision and goals are the foundation of small business management and entrepreneurship. One cannot understand the dominant small-business component of tourism and hospitality without understanding the individual and family dimensions. Consequently, the policy, planning and marketing of destinations, and economic development based on tourism or hospitality, are also dependent on better appreciation of the family perspective on business.

In the first part of this chapter we examine practical implications for family businesses in tourism and hospitality, based on our evaluation of their needs and the family-dependent dimensions of business enterprise. It is organized roughly in the same sequence in which major issues were covered in the preceding chapters, although a certain amount of cross-referencing and integration has been incorporated.

The second part covers general implications for tourism and destination management. Family businesses are often the dominant business form in destinations, especially in resorts, rural and peripheral areas, and an understanding of how they affect competitiveness is essential to destination management. As well, economic and community development policies – especially those aimed at creating employment – must take the family business into account to be effective.

Practical Implications for the Family Business in Tourism and Hospitality

This section aims to provide practical advice to those running or contemplating investment in a family business. The advice is not all-encompassing, as it is derived from this book's focus on identifying unique and salient issues facing family businesses in the tourism and hospitality industry.

We start with the issues raised in Chapter 1, including the most fundamental – are you a family business? If so, what are the general implications for ownership, business and family evolution? We then attempt to draw on all sections of the book, including the case studies, to provide a great deal of advice – some of which consists merely of asking the reader to contemplate potential implications for their own business or business plans. Answers are not always available!

Are you a family business?

Surprisingly, many owners do not think of their enterprise as a 'family business'. In some cultures it is not a differentiated form of business, while in others the term might be considered to have negative connotations such as 'it's only a mom-and-pop operation'. Sole proprietors might not consider theirs to be a family business because their partners, children or other relatives are not formally involved as owners or employees. Couples working together (i.e. 'copreneurs') might feel that only the involvement or potential inheritance by children would qualify theirs as a 'family business.'

We have taken a broad, inclusive interpretation of what constitutes a family business, including all those who consider theirs to be such, plus all sole proprietors, copreneurial businesses, and others with some degree of family involvement. Our inclusiveness is based on the desire not to focus overly on technical points of ownership and control, but rather to concentrate on family-related issues. The most important differentiating aspect of family business, as argued by Chua et al. (1999), lies in the vision of its dominant family members. The vision must be to use the business for the betterment of the family – potentially across more than one generation.

In terms of practical implications, owners should ask themselves to what degree family members are involved, if family takes priority in any aspect of the business, and if they hold a family vision of using the business for betterment of their family. If family is important, then there are many implications contained in this book. As well, owners must ask themselves what are their primary motives and goals for being in business. We look at implications of that key question later.

Interdependencies in the evolution of family, business and ownership

The evolutionary perspective contained in the model developed by Gersick et al. (1997) has many important implications for the family business. Ownership, business and family evolve together, in many interdependent ways. It is the essence of a family business that shifts in one component will impact on others. For example, getting children involved in the business as they get older will potentially lead to control and ownership issues including inheritance, while business operations are also impacted by the need to find each family member challenging

and responsible work. Case studies and cross-case analysis provide examples where the involvement and support of all family members is not always possible nor desirable, due to the challenges this entails. Figure 1.2 presents a summary of challenges through the life cycle.

On the other hand, this book makes it clear that many tourism and hospitality businesses – probably a large majority – never progress beyond the foundation stage. Owners continue to control the business, keeping it small, and children either do not get involved or the potential for them to take control or inherit the venture is not realistic. Even in these family businesses, owners should understand the basic principle that all families and their businesses evolve to some extent, and that the ultimate disposition of the business is a critical issue. Strategic thinking, if not formal planning, is clearly necessary. However, the research and case studies provide little evidence of business planning, let alone strategic planning, by family businesses in tourism and hospitality.

The business environment and industry-specific modifiers

The business environment for tourism and hospitality is an important consideration for owners, and in some ways it is unique. The case studies elucidate business opportunities that allow people to pursue their leisure interests or live in attractive surroundings such as resorts, small towns and out-of-the-way places. Many ventures in this industry fulfil basic needs to socialize, meet interesting people, be self-employed and even to earn extra money (beyond the primary economic activity) to support a farm or a family.

It is also a service industry in which people skills are often paramount, host–guest contacts are frequent and often in the home environment, and long hours are the norm – especially in the peak seasons. There is fulfilment in pleasing other people, and this is a powerful motivator, yet burn-out is a real risk. Owners and families in these service businesses must develop effective strategies for preserving some degree of privacy and quiet time, for balancing family and business life.

The business environment is also risky and challenging. Numerous tourism and hospitality businesses are highly substitutable and do not possess competitive advantages. Others are too small to make much revenue, or are subject to extreme seasonality of demand, thereby generating cash-flow problems. Locating in a rural or remote area is appealing to many owners, but predictable costs and problems accompany such decisions. Family businesses in remote areas face higher costs, greater seasonality of demand, less opportunity for networking and marketing collaboration, and greater difficulty in securing suitable employees. On the other hand, there might be government grants and technical assistance available, as was identified in some of the case studies.

Owners must also be aware of the implications of the 'destination life cycle'. When operating in a tourism environment, as opposed to catering exclusively to local-area residents, it can be expected that opportunities and challenges will vary over time as the destination matures. The fate of the individual business might depend to a greater or lesser degree on the success of the destination in achieving sustainable competitiveness and occasionally re-positioning itself. Conversely, the competitiveness and profitability of numerous small and family businesses can certainly affect the destination's success chances.

The business environment also includes culture and level of economic development. Some cultures are very supportive of entrepreneurship and especially family businesses, while in others these actions are not well-established or valued. It will certainly be more challenging to develop a successful family business in lesser-developed economies that lack physical infrastructure or marketing support. In the special case of business initiatives by indigenous people, a number of additional challenges might occur, such as communal ownership of resources or the need to share all decision-making at the community level.

Easy in – easy out!

Too many owners in the tourism and hospitality industry create or purchase their business without proper thought about their skills and resources and the nature of the work that lies ahead. Many are disillusioned and give up or fail. Turnover rates in many areas are high, with one family or sole proprietor taking over from others. Potential investors should realize that if it is easy to get into this line of enterprise, it might equally be easy to fail.

A strong interest in the type of work might be sufficient to assure business success, such as where lifestyle and leisure interests are at the heart of the business. As with many of the cases in this book, having generic management skills and experience will prove to be adequate, assuming the owner can adapt to different settings and environmental challenges. On the other hand, having worked in the industry does not necessarily prepare one for ownership.

The bottom line is that owners and potential investors should seek training and professional advice, while destinations and government agencies should take these services to the family businesses that need them.

Are you an entrepreneur?

Chapter two examined in detail the nature and application of entrepreneurship to family businesses in tourism and hospitality. Whether or not one believes in the personality-trait approach to defining entrepreneurship, everyone in business should examine their motives, goals, attitudes and practices with the purpose of identifying their fundamental driving forces. Many owners will be quite comfortable with their autonomy and lifestyle-oriented businesses, but a minority will not.

Understanding the entrepreneurial process should help every owner and manager do a better job. Being able to objectively assess risk is a necessity in the business world, but so to is knowing ones' own acceptable degree of risk-taking. Innovation is inherent in entrepreneurship, but it can be manifested in many ways. In some of our case studies, this means a completely new venture or way of doing business, while to others it is an element in providing better customer service or more creative packaging or programming

Mobilizing resources is an essential element in the entrepreneurial process. How well do family-business owners secure, invest and achieve acceptable returns from available resources – including a return on their own effort? Many small family businesses are too small ever to become profitable or support a family – does that matter? Taking on debt exposes one to increased risk, but is essential for growth – is it an unacceptable risk in the context of the family's security, or protection of its legacy? What is necessary to create and sustain a business capable of being inherited by the next generation? Some businesses are built up to a point where they can be sold for the best price, while others (especially farm-based businesses) would rarely be sold. This book contains examples of both highly entrepreneurial and highly risk-averse family businesses.

Business and strategic planning

Formal planning is associated with business success, although it is sometimes unclear if talent leads to planning efforts or planning leads to improved performance. Advice has been given in Chapter 4 about preparing a business plan, with a number of key planning issues being identified. These include control of the business, careers for family members, capital and reinvestment, conflict resolution, and dealing with a family culture (Carlock and Ward, 2001). Those authors also recommended a parallel system of planning for the business and the family, including a 'family enterprise continuity plan' which specifies the vision and strategies to achieve it.

Strategies and options

Generic business strategies can be pursued by the family business. For example, the 'defender' strategy involves sticking to what the firm knows best, the 'innovator/prospector' strategy embodies taking risks and is therefore most suited to the growth-oriented entrepreneur, and the 'analyser' strategy seeks competitive advantage through adoption of proven strategies (Miles and Snow, 1978). Carlock and Ward (2001) discussed three generic strategies

that have applicability to family businesses, especially at the point of succession. A 'renewal' strategy focuses the owner's attention on getting more out of current capabilities and markets, such as through value-adding investments. 'Reformulation' implies improvement of the business strategy, such as by developing new markets. 'Regeneration' applies when a new owner or inheritor has to make fundamental changes or investments to ensure viability of the business.

More importantly, family-business owners should look to the specific competitive advantages that a family business entails, such as sacrifice, use of family resources, family networks, unified management and strategy, integrity, loyalty and dedication, tradition, special knowledge, continuity and a long-term orientation to achieving results (Donnelly, 1964). Inherent weaknesses must also be avoided. These can include conflicts between business and family interests, lack of discipline over resources, failure to adapt – or quickly respond to – opportunities, and nepotism.

Niche marketing

Small businesses almost inevitably pursue niche markets, not mass markets, and the trick is to find those customers willing to pay higher prices for the services and atmosphere that only a family business can provide. The case studies and research found limited use of target marketing, which implies that there is a potential for family businesses to pursue this form of marketing strategy in the future.

Networking and collaboration

Being small and often isolated, family businesses in tourism and hospitality can benefit greatly from business-to-business networking and the kind of family or social networking that provides support. Informal and formal marketing alliances or other collaborations among businesses can be essential for marketing effectiveness and innovation, as the case studies have demonstrated.

Other options

When the goal is to remain small and under control, but profitable, it can be called the 'sustainability option'. Nevertheless, specific strategies and investments may be required – it does not imply doing nothing. Regardless of growth orientation, virtually every family business can benefit from a planned 'value-adding' strategy. This might include investment in technology or internet advertising, quality and efficiency improvements, and new services that generate money. Filling unused occupancy by tapping new markets is value adding, as is the practice of 'yield management' to maximize revenues.

'Family Branding' is an option only available to family businesses. It features the family behind the services offered and makes it part of the product. The family name can become a trade-mark (for example, O'Reilly's Guesthouse), and family members can develop reputations and even legends. Family branding stresses 'relationship marketing' with specific segments, and features the intangible 'brand attributes' of quality, value, tradition and personality. Ethnicity might also be a factor.

'Diversification' into other types of business or other areas is sometimes tempting, but usually rejected by autonomy-seekers and those who value small businesses, because of the costs and strains it can impose. Experts agree that going outside one's area of expertise and experience is highly risky, yet adding new markets (e.g. residents plus tourists) or developing products for export, was a viable strategy for a number of family-business owners in Bornholm (see Chapter 5).

Responses to seasonality

Evidence from Bornholm, Denmark, demonstrated several strategic responses by family businesses to extreme seasonality of demand. A majority of owners accepted the limitations imposed by seasonality and coped with it by closing for part of the year. For small, part-time businesses this might not be a problem, and for some owners it could be a welcome respite. Families have to adjust to these changes, both

in terms of cash-flow and work-load. 'Combating' strategies were practised by owners who sought to reduce demand fluctuations by expanding their season and/or broadening their market base. Some developed export markets, while others catered to residents in the off-peak seasons.

In extreme cases, 'capitulation' might be forced on owners, such as selling the business, shrinking or terminating it. Most of the Bornholm respondents wanted a longer tourism season, realizing that would greatly enhance their profitability.

Financial management

A major issue facing many families is that of taking money out of the business for personal uses versus having a plan that requires savings and re-investment. Those not seeking growth might think that there is no need for accrual of working capital, but they will probably find it necessary, sooner or later, for maintenance, improvements and value-adding investments.

Case studies and cross-case analysis show that many family businesses are undercapitalized. This becomes an issue when they expand (or even disband) the business, and access to capital is needed to fund further expansion or 'buy-out' the shares of exiting family members.

Ownership, organization and governance

Simple forms of direct ownership are most common, but the growth- and profit-oriented entrepreneur generally seeks company status in order to protect family assets and help generate external capital. If the business develops into a multi-generational firm, ownership probably has to evolve as well, with consideration given to a family trust or sibling/family partnerships. It might be wise to separate ownership of the tourism/hospitality business from other family assets including the land (as some of our case studies demonstrate), although lenders often require these assets as collateral.

Because most family businesses in this industry are small and operated by autonomy-seekers, their organizational structure remains very simple and top–down. Often the owners do everything! Growth, and the hiring of professional staff, may lead to more sophisticated and formal management systems. Retaining family ownership and control might become an issue where professional managers have day-to-day oversight of the business. The establishment of a Board of Directors, including external experts, is a recommended development for the larger and growth-oriented family firm.

Parallel to the Board, a formal Family Council can be established to oversee the ownership and long-term strategy. Also, a Family Agreement can be drafted to govern ownership, such as a family-member's rights to acquire and/or dispose of shares. The Family Trust, as exhibited in the O'Reilly's case, is a specific form of ownership designed to sustain family ownership and control through the generations, but it might eventually give rise to problems when descendents cannot realize a cash value for their inheritance.

The meaning and causes of failure

Failure in a family business can have disastrous consequences for the family, which helps explain the tendency of owners to be risk-averse. Given that the rate of outright failure among small businesses in general is high, and tourism/hospitality enterprises would appear to fare no better than average, it is wise for owners to consider reasons for failure and strategies for success. Even though our research showed that many respondents were not profit- and growth-oriented, in the entrepreneurial sense, almost all of them explicitly desired to make and keep the business profitable. The next-most common goal among family-business owners in general is to increase the firm's value. Success and failure can best be evaluated against the owners' goals and needs. For some, mere survival will be a sufficient indicator of success, while for others leaving a sustainable family legacy will signify success. Getting children involved and passing on the business to them is a very specific and evidently rare definition of success, although some of our case studies indicate that this is possible.

Common causes of failure for small and family businesses include a lack of business expertise, high costs (especially in isolated areas), under-capitalization and small size (which limit growth and profit potential), a harsh business environment (particularly extreme seasonality of demand and unlimited competition) and the absence of marketing alliances or other forms of cooperation and support. There is little evidence to determine if avoidance of debt is a success or failure factor.

Although innovation and growth might be desired, researchers and industry experts all agree that owners should stick to what they know best. Diversification beyond one's immediate area of expertise and experience could prove fatal for the business.

Preconditions and barriers to growth

Although growth is shunned by the majority, it is vigorously pursued by others. Every family-business owner should carefully consider the pros and cons of growth and alternative long-term strategies for their business. In particular, growth (and related innovations) might be necessary to sustain a competitive position or to achieve an acceptable family income.

Resources are the main determinant of growth potential. Revenue has to be saved in the business (i.e. working capital), borrowed, or attracted from investors. Family sacrifices might be necessary, trading the desired immediate gains for longer-term income potential. The resource-based theory of the firm suggests that families might possess unique bundles of tangible resources (including family investments and land) that can be the basis of growth. As well, the knowledge-based theory of the firm suggests that families might possess intangible resources, especially specialized knowledge of markets or products/services, which give them advantages.

Specific barriers to growth for family firms in tourism and hospitality were discussed. They include the kind of family vision that results in a lack of motivation; a family *impasse* over goals or strategies; a lack of market intelligence; and inability to be competitive within the market area, laws or regulations. All these have to be assessed when formulating strategy.

Achieving growth and maximizing profits

Owners have the option of following a strategy of sustaining the business, in the interest of preserving autonomy and maximizing lifestyle benefits, or risking more and striving for growth and higher profit. Anyone seeking this latter path should have sound knowledge of business management and strategy in general, and of their tourism/hospitality business environment in detail.

Our research points to a number of factors associated with successful growth and increased profitability among family business owners in this industry, namely:

- They respond strongly in the affirmative to the statement 'I want to keep the business growing'.
- They are opportunists, and this includes consciously seeking to purchase businesses with higher profits and growth potential.
- They are more likely to invest in hotels and restaurants, or attractions, as opposed to small accommodation units (e.g. pensions or B&B) or arts and crafts operations.
- They are more likely to be copreneurs than sole proprietors without family involvement in the business (as these latter owners tend to be females either running a secondary or micro business).
- They are more likely to own a limited company, as this legal arrangement protects their family and allows easier acquisition of capital from lenders and investors.
- They are more likely to involve children (although this might be a chicken-and-egg situation – i.e. is growth necessary for involvement of children or intended to permit their involvement?).
- They are more likely to be male (although the exact causes of this difference are not known; there might be profound cultural differences at work).
- They adopt deliberate strategies that include market and product diversification, such as catering to both residents and tourists (owing to seasonality of demand) and developing export markets.
- They recognize the need for employees, debt, and innovation.

- They love the challenge of growing the business.
- They are also motivated by lifestyle benefits.

Involving the next generation and succession

Owners of family businesses who have children must decide at some point whether children are to be involved in the business, and if so is inheritance a prospect? A related issue is that of the family 'legacy' – perhaps a farm or other real estate – that is intended to be kept permanently in the family.

Apparently inheritance happens in only a small minority of family businesses in tourism and hospitality, and there are a number of reasons. The absence of potential heirs is the most fundamental barrier, and is often created or exacerbated by parents making a decision to establish or purchase the tourism/hospitality business as a second career or even with retirement in mind; by then, the children have usually gone elsewhere. Permanent out-migration by youth for purposes of advanced education and employment is typical of remote and economically disadvantaged regions. As well, children exposed to the business from an early age might be turned off by the long hours, lack of privacy, nature of the work, or its low levels of income. They might become interested in establishing their own business, rather than taking over, as occurred in several of our case studies.

Another barrier is the common practice of not separating the business from other assets, usually farmland. This inseparability reduces or eliminates the chances for continuance of the tourism/hospitality business. Gender can also be a problem, as many females are not given serious consideration as inheritors, or even to becoming involved seriously in a family business. Where the business is run by females it is often secondary to a farm or other economic activity, and will not survive the founder.

When parents want their children to be involved or to inherit, they have to plan it carefully – yet research continuously reveals a very low rate of succession planning in family businesses of all types. We provided expert opinion on how best to get children involved and to prepare for succession. According to Lansberg (1988) there should be a shared vision within the family, and this appears to be the fundamental pre-condition. Numerous tourism and hospitality businesses simply do not have what it takes to inspire the next generation, and many owners in fact would prefer their offspring to seek other professional careers.

Getting children involved early is important, then developing a responsible career path for them. Knowing when to 'pass the baton', and bringing oneself to that critical point in life, is a crucial concern for business founders. Structures have to be put in place, such as a family council or continuity plan, and estate planning practiced to ensure a smooth transition that benefits both generations.

Balancing Family and Business through the Life Cycle

Although not all owners want their family to be involved or place family interests ahead of the business, balancing family with business through the life cycle is likely to be of importance to all owners, at least some of the time. Indeed, the balancing challenge will vary through stages in the life cycle of the business and the family as they evolve together.

Generic challenges identified by Carlock and Ward (2001) apply to most family-business owners. There is the matter of control and decision-making, and the related issue of family 'culture'. Is it a collaborative family or patriarchal? Developing meaningful and equal careers for couples and for children is a challenge, and means for identifying and resolving conflicts have to be found. Finally, the matter of capital and re-investment is a potential challenge, especially when families want to take money out of the business for immediate use.

Our cross-case analysis revealed the importance of achieving family consensus in decision-making, especially when couples work together. Finding work of equal value is a challenge. Getting children or other potential successors involved in meaningful ways is a key to successful transition. A strong interest in particular leisure opportunities motivates some families to establish their tourism or hospitality business, or at least shapes their locational choice, and having common family leisure pursuits could be a major balancing tool.

Roles in family businesses might be determined by gender or age, yet it is highly desirable to allow every participant to try new roles and find the ones they are comfortable with. The assumption that certain tasks are 'women's work' runs deep, especially in the hospitality services, but this can be a source of tension as well as a limiting factor when it comes to ensuring business success.

Resolving conflicts and facing adversity

Mechanisms should be put in place to identify and resolve sources of potential conflict. They might include informal meetings and more formal Family Councils or Codes of Conduct. Although unpredictable, adversity of some kind can be expected – for example, in two cases studied in this book, the eldest son and designated heir were tragically killed in accidents. Having the ability to adapt will prove to be a valuable family asset. Facing adversity involves testing the strength of family bonds during the difficult periods in the life cycle of the business.

Existing family relationships also have bearing on the ability of a family to prevent disharmony – and indeed this rates highly as a business goal for many family businesses we have studied. Cross-case analysis identified ways that businesses avoid conflict by including all family members in decision-making, attempting to achieve consensus, having siblings involved in the business and having family members involved from an early stage in business development.

Support mechanisms

The level of family support for a business venture is a key success factor. Sole proprietors draw on other family members, often informally, while couples at least sometimes need the help of children or other family members. This principle might extend to larger family and friend networks, or ethnic communities, and certainly applies to joint marketing and other forms of collaboration among small and family businesses. Private financing is one hallmark of the family business.

Public-sector support is often directed at small and medium businesses, but seldom takes into account the specific needs and preferences of family business. The assumption that all owners want to grow and maximize profits is false, and probably hinders effective support for this sector.

Family business traditions

Enterprise does run in some families, although there is no certainty that inheriting an entrepreneurial orientation will lead children to become involved or take over a family business – they might very well want to create their own! Family continuity has its advantages, not least of which is the knowledge gained over many years or several generations, but parents might have to help their children use this knowledge to go out on their own ventures. Where tradition is a force for involving one or more children in the business (often the eldest son is pressured) it can have negative consequences, such as rebellion by the child or a mismatch between talents, interests and ownership responsibilities.

The legacy

The desire to create or perpetuate a family legacy can be a powerful motivator, especially when farmland or other real estate is involved, such as 'the family home'. Tourism might provide one means to help preserve property in the family, or enable continuation of otherwise unsustainable farm operations. Certainly the case studies demonstrate that retaining ownership of family farms or homes is a powerful motivator for starting a tourism business. Legacy can also be something intangible, such as maintaining a family tradition of service to visitors which may have commenced in previous generations.

Gender

Gender has been a major issue in the tourism and hospitality literature, although the emphasis has not been on gender within a family context, but on the unique challenges facing female entrepreneurs. Many family businesses are started and operated by women, often without moral or financial support, and encompassing the need to balance housework, mothering and business pressures. In many family businesses, however, couples start and manage the business as equals. Another important issue is that of getting daughters involved in a family business and preparing them for inheritance, as in many cultures they are ignored.

Most studies have focused on rural and specifically farm-related ventures, so the evidence on gender issues is somewhat limited. However, McGibbon's (2000) detailed study of women and guest houses in the resort town of St Anton, Austria, provides detailed insights in a different environment. From this and other research, it becomes clear that cultural differences directly affect the family and business roles of women and their entrepreneurial activities.

One major implication of the available research is that there are clear incentives, rewards, costs and challenges related to women in business. Not the least of these is the issue of so-called 'women's work' which is a cultural bias towards the kinds of work expected of and acceptable for women to perform. In developed economies, with plenty of alternatives for women, it is not such an issue. In those economies, such as the ones studied in this book, copreneurial activities are of equal or greater importance. Our research showed that when it comes to goals, male and female respondents showed no significant differences.

Strategies for managing family and business

Because home and business often overlap in the tourism and hospitality industry, especially in the provision of accommodation, ways must be found to ensure a degree of privacy and to maximize family-time, without the intrusions of guests. Physical or psychological barriers can be erected, including signs, fences, and locks on doors. Most owners we spoke to expressed a desire to find (and be able to afford) trustworthy staff to help relieve the burden, yet human resource management can also become a major headache as a company grows. Time management has to be effectively practised, and this goes with a positive attitude both towards the work and the need for relief from it.

Family business and the environment

Our survey in Western Australia sought to determine if family business owners were concerned about the environment and implemented practices specifically for conservation or enhancement. There was some evidence that this was the case, but more research will be needed on that point. There is no doubt, however, that family businesses in tourism and hospitality are often tied to the land (e.g. on farms) or directly linked to natural and heritage resources. Accordingly owners should be concerned about sustainability of the resource base, and in rural and remote areas in particular they are often in a position to have influence on policy and accepted business practices. Intergenerational equity in terms of access to the natural environment could also be expected to come in to play in nature-based family businesses.

Implications for Tourism and Destination Management

Very little recognition has been given in the tourism and hospitality literature to the importance of the family or the individual entrepreneur in shaping community and economic development or destination competitiveness. Attention has been paid to the entrepreneurs and to issues applicable to small and medium-sized enterprises, but as this book has demonstrated it is often the family vision that lies behind the visible actions or inactivity.

We did not set out specifically to study implications for tourism, destinations, economic or community development, but some did

emerge. To articulate them requires a certain amount of repetition, but in a different light from the implications drawn for specific family businesses and owners. The predominance of family businesses in many tourism destinations is also justification for examining the implications for tourism and destination management.

Destination competitiveness and marketing

Tourism scholars have traditionally paid much more attention to the destination than to individual business units, while hospitality scholars have focused on management issues within the firm rather than its ownership and governance by individuals and families.

In a paper delivered at a conference with the theme 'Reinventing the Destination', Getz and Petersen (2002) argued that the individual business was not merely a factor in destination competitiveness – as some models have suggested – but that the purpose of destination management and marketing organizations was to make businesses competitive. Without profitable and sustainable family businesses, and without growth-oriented entrepreneurs, destinations cannot develop or sustain a competitive advantage.

The fact that most small, family businesses are not growth-oriented, and many are competitively weak, presents a serious challenge to economic development agencies and to destination marketing organizations. Other authors have cautioned that lifestyle-oriented owners might not want to make a commitment to various business support schemes or even to seek out information (e.g. Shaw and Williams, 1997). Brownlee (1994) argued that the owners of small businesses must be engaged to assess their goals and the help they need relative to their goals and resources.

Hall and Jenkins (1997) identified 18 types of instruments used by governments to promote the development of rural tourism. These included regulations, monetary investment, capital expenditures, training, advice, research and establishment of business incubators. Determining which actions or combinations work best for family businesses should be a priority.

Destination marketing

Is it logical to promote family businesses separately, or as particular assets within the context of destination marketing? There might be a case made for this strategy if the family-business sector is sufficiently well developed and provides high-quality or unique services. However, Destination Marketing Organizations (DMOs) tend to pay little attention to the small and family businesses in their domain because they lack funds for co-marketing efforts, or because they are simply perceived to be irrelevant to the bigger job of establishing a positive destination image and competitive attractions. Some attitudes in DMOs have to be changed, because in many instances their marketing is useless if the small- and family-business sector cannot match the promises being made.

Fostering and contributing to marketing consortia by small and family businesses should be a standard operating procedure for DMOs. Particular attention should be given to networking for purposes of learning, stimulating innovations and achieving economies of scale in purchasing or advertising. A separate small- and family-business marketing campaign might very well be justified.

Economic development

The primary connection to economic development is through the creation of jobs, and most family businesses in tourism and hospitality remain small and struggle to be able to afford to hire full-time staff. Can this be influenced? A two-pronged strategy will be required, with one focused on identifying and cultivating the growth-oriented entrepreneur and the other working with more conservative, autonomy- and lifestyle-oriented owners.

Data from Canmore and Bornholm clearly identified the existence of growth-oriented entrepreneurs and went some distance in characterizing them, their businesses and their goals and strategies. This knowledge should be used to help identify, attract and cultivate those entrepreneurs with the greatest potential to create employment and wealth.

Typical approaches to small-business nurturing might have to be altered. For example, why assist in the establishment of businesses that have little or no prospect of growth because the owners do not want it? Assistance for entrepreneurs to both establish and purchase businesses with a view to profit maximization and growth makes a lot more sense.

As for the lifestyle-oriented owners who abound in this industry, is there any reasonable hope that some of them can be induced to grow their businesses? It is logical to assume that latent entrepreneurship exists in the industry – that many are actually 'constrained entrepreneurs' as identified by Shaw and Williams (1997). If so, then identification of the very specific constraints holding them back, and ways to counter them, is a necessity. A number of those constraints have been highlighted in this book.

The first major constraint is a fear of incurring debt and the risks that implies for a family. Can ways be found to reduce the risk or perceived risk? One of our case studies illustrated how borrowing to develop the business was justified financially because the value of underlying assets (the farm land) exceeded the liability – is this a model that can be refined and applied through policy? Can loans be linked with training and advice to increase the likelihood of success? Taking the learning materials and expert advice directly to family-business owners is probably a necessity, as few of them will be able to leave their operations.

A second major constraint is the fact that many, if not most of the owners in this industry are not particularly well qualified through experience and training. Not only do they require educational assistance, but they need models and a vision of what they can become. Benchmarking against successful family businesses that have grown will probably help to stimulate latent entrepreneurship, as will provision of detailed growth models (i.e. the financial, strategic and operational steps needed).

Within the context of economic development another priority should be to examine how family businesses create and invest wealth through tourism and hospitality services, how their developments and legacies tangibly affect regions and nations, and what can be done to maximize wealth creation. Tax laws, particularly related to inheritance, should be evaluated in view of the desirability of perpetuating and growing family legacies, as opposed to diminishing or preventing them.

Community development

Family businesses can be important anywhere, but are often the cornerstone of community development in small towns, rural and remote areas. The specific roles they can play relate to the provision of leadership (e.g. for economic and environmental policy), stability across the generations (which can perpetuate valuable local knowledge and traditions), self-confidence in the community's ability to survive and prosper (through the example of successful businesses), and support for other locally-owned businesses. As well, the mere fact that families are sustainable in some areas helps to ensure the survival of schools and other social infrastructure. If an area cannot attract and hold families, its population will most probably decline, beginning or reinforcing a downward spiral.

Chapter Summary

This first of two concluding chapters has summarized important implications from the literature and research documented in this book specific to the individual family business. Secondly, it has drawn implications for the broader policy domains of tourism and destination competitiveness, economic and community development. In doing so it has raised a number of issues to do with the structure, ownership, location, education, management, orientation and continuation of family businesses.

Achieving a balance between family and business commitments throughout the life cycle of the business remains a major challenge which has implications not only for the family business, but also for the tourism destinations, destination management organizations and the community in which these businesses operate.

References

Brownlee, D. (1994) Market opportunity analysis: a DIY approach for small tourism enterprises. *Tourism Management* 15(1), 37–45.

Carlock, R. and Ward, J. (2001) *Strategic Planning for the Family Business*. Palgrave, Basingstoke, UK.

Chua, J., Chrisman, J. and Sharma, P. (1999) Defining the family business by behaviour. *Entrepreneurship Theory and Practice* 24(4), 19–39.

Donnelley, R. (1964) The family business. *Harvard Business Review* 42(2), 93–105.

Gersick, K., Davis, J., Hampton, M. and Lansberg, I. (1997) *Generation to Generation: Life Cycles of Family Business*. Harvard Business School Press, Boston, Massachusetts.

Getz, D. and Petersen, T. (2002) Growth-oriented Entrepreneurs and Destination Competitiveness. Paper presented at the Re-Inventing the Destination Conference, Dubrovnik, Croatia.

Lansberg, I. (1988) The succession conspiracy. *Family Business Review* 1(2), 119–144.

McGibbon, J. (2000) Family business: commercial hospitality in the domestic realm. In: Robinson, M., Long, P., Evans, N., Sharpley, R. and Swarbrooke, J. (eds) *Reflections on International Tourism: Expressions of Culture Identity and Meaning in Tourism*. Business Education Publications, Sunderland, UK.

Miles, R. and Snow, C. (1978) *Organizational Strategy, Structure, and Process*. McGraw-Hill, New York.

Shaw, G. and Williams, A. (eds) (1997) *The Rise and Fall of British Coastal Resorts: Cultural and Economic Perspectives*. Pinter, London.

13

Implications for Research and Theory

Introduction

The first part of this final chapter returns to the beginning of the book in search of research gaps and to formulate a research agenda. Gaps are identified by assessing the extent and nature of tourism and hospitality-specific literature (as presented throughout this book), compared to the three-axes model of family business, and to the identified themes and topics found in generic family-business literature.

The second part addresses theory development. It has been argued that the nature of the tourism and hospitality industry, especially the settings or business environments in which family businesses operate, modifies family businesses in a number of ways. A model was presented in Chapter 1, and we return to that framework to formulate a number of major propositions that can be used in building theory.

Developing a Research Agenda

The three-axis model of Gersick *et al.* (1997) provides the starting point. First, ownership is examined. What do we know about unique forms of family business ownership within tourism and hospitality, and how these forms might change as the business evolves? Ownership also covers control and governance. The second axis to be summarized is business evolution, and the third is family.

Ownership

Control is a generic family business theme that has been neglected in the tourism and hospitality literature. Related questions include the problem of how to ensure that children receive benefits from the family business while control remains within the family. There has been no attention paid to unique forms of ownership, nor their evolution, in these sectors, even though it is apparent that many such businesses are tied to family property or lack tangible assets.

Because a majority are run by couples, there is a need to examine how they arrange ownership; at least one study (McGibbon, 2000) noted that women can be disenfranchised in some cultures. Succession within a family and between generations has barely been considered in the tourism and hospitality literature, yet it is the dominant generic family business theme. The study by Getz and Carlsen (2000) concluded that a majority had no succession plan. Specific barriers to inheritance should be examined in different settings.

Longitudinal research is the best way to deal with many issues pertaining to the family business life cycle. Case studies of success and failure stories will be useful, but comparisons over time will probably be more valuable theoretically. For example, researchers could examine family business start-ups and evolution within a specific area over many years.

©D. Getz *et al.* 2004. *The Family Business in Tourism and Hospitality*
(D. Getz, J. Carlsen and A. Morrison)

Business

Motives and goals have been studied to some degree, enough at least to conclude that in tourism and hospitality enterprises, lifestyle and locational preferences are extremely important. Failure has been studied, but not specifically linked to the core family vision. Does family business in these sectors perform worse than corporations? The involvement of professionals as managers, staff or directors in family businesses has not been addressed.

Analysis of staff–family interaction is a potential research topic. The lack of entrepreneurship has been identified, but not tested systematically. The notion of 'constrained entrepreneurship' should be explored more fully, including determination of what mechanisms would best facilitate greater entrepreneurial activity among family businesses. Also, almost all the literature pertains to micro and small businesses, even though some family businesses grow to a large size.

There is a great need for systematic and comparative research of several topics: of settings (e.g. rural versus urban and resort environments); family versus non-family businesses; sole-proprietor versus copreneurs and larger family businesses; developed versus remote rural areas with dispersed infrastructure; small versus large businesses, and so on. To evaluate what is unique about tourism and hospitality businesses will require comparisons within these sectors, and with other types of service businesses.

Family

Gender has received the most attention, particularly female entrepreneurs in home-based tourism and hospitality businesses. Curiously, the couple as copreneurs has been neglected, even though this ownership form is probably most typical in family businesses. As well, children have been overlooked – their introduction to the business, involvement over time with its management and ownership, and whether or not they share the core family vision.

It is known that family-first, or lifestyle entrepreneurship, probably dominates these sectors, but no researchers have examined the minutiae of decision making in family businesses. How exactly do family vision or lifestyle preferences interfere with business? Why can't they be successfully combined? How do family businesses that grow differ from static enterprises in terms of changing family attitudes, roles and challenges?

Generic family business themes and topics

We re-visit Fig. 1.3 for a summary of generic family business themes and topics, as derived from Sharma et al. (1996). Not all of these major themes and specific topics have been considered or adequately developed in the tourism and hospitality literature.

Definitions

There is no need to invent new definitions on an industry-by-industry basis. However, it is important to realize that in tourism and hospitality the vast majority of 'family businesses' are not classic, multi-generation firms; most never go beyond the foundation stage in terms of ownership, business or family evolution. Thus, the most important point is for researchers to recognize that it is the 'family vision' that defines and distinguishes these ventures from others.

Appropriate research questions:

- What is the extent (a definitional and measurement problem) and significance (requiring evaluation from multiple perspectives) of 'family business' in various tourism and hospitality environments?
- What are the unique components of the 'family vision' in tourism and hospitality (e.g. related to leisure interests, locational preferences, service orientation, autonomy-seeking)?

In terms of types of family business, the most common in tourism and hospitality are the copreneurial venture in which husband and wife (and sometimes other partners) work the business together and often equally. Those involving children are special cases, and those leading to inheritance are rare.

Appropriate research questions:

- Are there unique forms of family business in tourism and hospitality? (i.e. Are copreneurial structures different because of the nature of the business environment or the motives and goals of owners?)

Uniqueness of family business

Generically, we have already defined the fundamental uniqueness of the family business in terms of the family vision and how it shapes the evolution of business, ownership and family inter-dependencies over time. This should hold true regardless of the industry, although no-one has challenged that hypothesis. One topic of particular interest, hitherto unexplored, is family branding in tourism and hospitality businesses.
Appropriate research questions:

- Are there unique aspects of tourism and hospitality that influence the inherent strengths or weaknesses of family business?
- Are there unique opportunities and aspects of family branding in tourism and hospitality (e.g. because of the nature of the services and the business environments)?

Life cycle

Most family businesses in tourism and hospitality appear to remain frozen in the first stage where founders dominate, the business is not grown, and succession is not even a possibility. More and comparative cases of multi-generational families are needed to make a meaningful contribution to understanding evolutionary forces and to determine if they are in any way unique to the industry or setting.
Appropriate research questions:

- How do family businesses in tourism and hospitality evolve over time in terms of inter-dependencies among business, ownership and family?
- Is there anything unique about the evolution of family businesses in tourism and hospitality other than the observation that most do not go beyond the foundation stage?

Succession and inheritance

This theme has dominated the generic family business literature, but has seldom been raised in the tourism and hospitality literature. The research from Bornholm reported in this book is ground-breaking in this context.
Appropriate research questions:

- Does the observed rarity of inheritance in family businesses in tourism and hospitality vary by setting or particular features of the business environment (e.g. is it different in developing economies or highly developed resorts and cities)?
- How can the severe barriers to inheritance be mitigated (e.g. by tax policies, assistance to grow the family business, improvements to the work environment, education and training opportunities, etc.)?

Governance

Because the whole subject of family business in tourism and hospitality has either been subsumed under the broader topic of 'small and medium-sized business', or ignored because of a pre-occupation with large, public companies, the topics of ownership, control and governance in family businesses have largely been ignored. The unique opportunities and implications of family trusts deserve further exploration, especially in light of the O'Reilly's case documented in this book.
Appropriate research questions:

- Do family businesses in tourism and hospitality invent or adopt unique forms of ownership, control or governance?
- What are the implications and relative degrees of effectiveness of various means (such as family trusts) of preserving family control across generations? (This question should also be linked to the one related to family branding.)

Strategic management

The theme of 'family vision' is problematic when most owners in this industry do not plan for succession or inheritance, or it is simply not practical for them. The family vision in these businesses has more to do with personal and copreneurial lifestyles, autonomy-seeking, and realizing a decent economic return on effort. A special case exists when a 'family legacy' of real property is at stake.

Business and strategic planning is weak across the industry, and the full range of business strategies available to the family-business owner is often not evaluated.

Appropriate research questions:

- What are the variations on 'family vision' found in tourism and hospitality businesses?
- Why do some families give importance to the concept of a 'family legacy'? How does that influence the decisions of parents and children?
- How can autonomy and lifestyle-oriented owners be assisted to adopt business and strategic planning?

The founders

We have explored founding motives and goals in depth, finding that lifestyle and autonomy are predominant considerations, while profit- and growth-oriented entrepreneurs are in the minority in this industry. Because succession is generally not an issue, leadership is more a question of how sole proprietors shape their business and how copreneurs work together towards common goals. 'Passing the baton' is a rare issue, although there is no evidence for saying that founders in this industry are more or less reluctant than those in other types of family business to let go of control.

More research on motives and goals in different settings, and how they might change over time, will be important. Also, goal incongruence and divergence among family members should be examined in multi-generational businesses. The details of how decisions are made have not been examined, nor have the subtleties of family dynamics in tourism and hospitality businesses. There are, *a priori*, reasons for suspecting that the service orientation and other aspects of the tourism/hospitality business environment will shape decision-making (e.g. related to gender roles), the evolution of goals (e.g. getting burned-out), and the practical questions of viable succession.

Entrepreneurship must become a major theme in tourism and hospitality studies. It has been shown in many studies to be lacking, or at least limited, yet it is highly desired by tourism destination managers and economic or community policy-makers. By examining in detail the motives and goals of family-business owners we have been able to demonstrate why so few businesses in this industry pursue growth and why so few are innovative or even competitive. This raises the matter of how policy and planning might attract or generate higher levels of entrepreneurship, even among autonomy- and lifestyle-seekers. Can a formula be developed, for example, to encourage small, family-business owners to adopt growth-oriented goals, re-invest in their businesses and become more competitive?

Appropriate research questions:

- Do founders' motives and goals vary according to setting or other environmental factors?
- How are business- and family-related decisions actually made and enforced in various types of family? Does the type of business make a difference?
- How might entrepreneurship be increased among the lifestyle- and autonomy-seekers that dominate tourism and hospitality?

Family influence and dynamics

Family culture has not been systematically researched, especially with regard to values, the importance of a family legacy, or entrepreneurship. Gender has been examined in some detail, but mainly in the context of female entrepreneurs establishing tourism or hospitality ventures – and primarily in farm or rural settings. The other topics under this theme (copreneurship, sibling rivalry, intergenerational relationships, nepotism) appear to be completely new for tourism and hospitality researchers.

Appropriate research questions:

- Are there unique aspects of family culture within and leading to family businesses in tourism and hospitality?
- How does gender relate to family-business formation and management in different settings (e.g. comparing rural with resort and urban)?

Culture and ethnicity

Culture as a determinant of the business environment has yet to be examined in the context of the family business in tourism and hospitality. It seems reasonable that the family business in tourism and hospitality vary across cultures, both in terms of opportunities and business types. Ethnicity is known to be a factor in family business generically, such as its close association with ethnic-immigrant communities and networking among business owners of the same cultural background.

Appropriate research questions:

- Are some cultures more supportive of family-business formation in tourism and hospitality?
- How does ethnicity (or other cultural factors) shape networking among family-business owners?

Professionalism

Working with employees is a common issue for owners in tourism and hospitality businesses, whereas transition to a professionally-managed firm is a rather rare occurrence. Although a number of goals and challenges related to family–staff relationships have been identified in this book, the research evidence is slim.

Appropriate research questions:

- What are the benefits and costs or risks for family-business owners who want or need to hire and manage employees? (e.g. Does the home-based accommodation sector restrict the choices and increase scope for owner–employee tension?)
- What sizes and types of business in this industry lend themselves to professional management?
- How does professional management affect the potential for involving children and ultimate inheritance of the business?

The family in society

We explored the environmental attitudes and practices of family-business owners, but that was a fairly superficial introduction to this broader theme. From a community-development perspective, family businesses should be valued and nurtured. The ways in which they network and do business are important for local politics and community viability.

Appropriate research questions:

- Are family businesses in tourism and hospitality inherently oriented toward achieving environmental responsibility and community viability?
- How can community and environmental sustainability be increased within the family-business sector?

There are an endless number of potential research questions that could benefit this field. Those mentioned above should be viewed as examples, based on obvious gaps in the literature. In the ensuing section, propositions are used in theory-building, and while they are put forward with some degree of confidence, it is also recognized that they should be expressed as hypotheses and tested.

Theory-building

Although a case has been made for taking an industry-specific approach to family business studies, which would have the affect of broadening family-business studies, the main theoretical concern in this book is to encourage systematic application of a family-business perspective within tourism and hospitality. To accomplish this aim, a conceptual framework has been developed to advance theory and shape research on family-business issues within the tourism and hospitality fields.

This framework (Fig. 1.4) places the family at the core, suggesting that some or most business decisions are rooted in a family vision that makes the family firm unique. Understanding the family vision and how it shapes a business is the essential starting point of family-business studies. Mainstream entrepreneurship and small-business studies do apply to a point, but there is a great need to start with the premise that owner-operators will behave differently.

Family-business studies embody an evolutionary perspective in which ownership, family and the business change over time, interdependently. Family ownership has been neglected in hospitality and tourism, and considered mostly as a minor variant within small-business and entrepreneurship themes. Inter-generational ownership issues and succession are also neglected issues.

A number of industry-specific modifiers have been identified, and certainly more can be expected to emerge from research. It is important to explore these connections as they shape the appeal of tourism and hospitality business ventures as well as many of the family-related rewards and challenges. A new theme to emerge, not covered in generic family business studies, is that of families and development. It has been highlighted in tourism and hospitality because the family business is often of critical importance in peripheral and rural areas – to the community, economy and environment. This theme also introduces the importance of setting modifiers, as family business is greatly impacted by location, culture and level of economic development.

Use of this framework will provide a more theoretically integrative base for exploring family business issues in tourism and hospitality. By way of focusing attention on the key research gaps and theoretical issues, a set of major propositions can be advanced for consideration. They should be viewed as starting points for researchers interested in developing theory in this field.

The propositions stated in this section are quite different from the research questions suggested above. Those were derived from an analysis of gaps, whereas the propositions below are derived from the authors' existing understanding of this field. Addressing the research questions mentioned above will advance theory in this field, as will testing these propositions.

Family vision

At the core of family business studies is the fact that many owners put family interests ahead of purely business interests; they behave differently from profit- and growth-oriented entrepreneurs and corporations. Many owners have a vision for what the business can do to help the owners and their families realize personal goals, typically related to autonomy (being one's own boss and hands-on work), living in the right environment (especially in resorts, islands, small towns and rural areas), and enjoying a desired lifestyle (often specific to leisure interests). As a result of the family vision, many family-business owners are content to remain small and tend to avoid debt and risks.

The family vision, surprisingly, usually does not include the involvement of children, or passing the business on to the next generation. Involvement of children, and inheritance within the family, are very infrequent occurrences within the tourism and hospitality industry for a variety of reasons, not the least of which are the facts that many such businesses cannot be separated from the family home or farm, or are not viable entities that can support children. As well, many children do not share the family vision and get away from the home as soon as possible. The nature of the work itself probably discourages many from even considering tourism or hospitality businesses.

There are many issues to explore related to the family vision and its impact on tourism and hospitality businesses, communities and destinations. We will examine a number of propositions, below, that are derived from the literature and the authors' collective research efforts. The nature of propositions is that they are put forward as being true, based on available evidence, but should nevertheless be tested in a variety of settings, using a range of methodologies. As the propositions become hypotheses for testing, they directly assist in theory-building.

Propositions

P 1. The core family vision in most family businesses in tourism and hospitality is focused on the lifestyle, autonomy and locational preferences of the founders; it is therefore a barrier to business growth, profit maximization and new venture creation.

There appears to be some degree of universality in people seeking autonomy through business, but it is possible that the lifestyle vision is much more feasible in developed economies. Conversely, in lesser-developed economies it might be expected that many family businesses are established because of a lack of choice. Many family businesses are known to be established by immigrants in new countries as well as by returning migrants who have made money elsewhere. In these circumstances, do the owners and families behave differently? How does business performance, including growth, vary according to the family vision or other founding motives?

A key research question has to be: under what circumstances, or with what assistance, will family businesses grow? It is likely that most cannot grow because of structural limitations (i.e. personal financing and hands-on management), even if the owners desire it. Will training opportunities achieve more growth than financial incentives? To what extent can partnerships and new technology assist the family-business owner in becoming more efficient and therefore more profitable?

> P 2. The unique opportunities for tourism and hospitality businesses in rural and peripheral areas will result in a preponderance of lifestyle-oriented, family-business owners.

No systematic comparison has been made of motives and goals in different business settings, but the research evidence strongly suggests that in rural, island and resort settings there are definitely unique opportunities within tourism and hospitality that do attract and sustain lifestyle-oriented families. But what of large resorts and cities? Are they more likely to attract the profit- and growth-oriented entrepreneur? Can family businesses compete with the big corporations and chains in these settings?

> P 3. Following on from P1 and P2, most family-business owners in tourism and hospitality will display low levels of entrepreneurship, specifically in terms of risk-taking, innovation, growth and new ventures.

Research has demonstrated the existence of profit- and growth-oriented entrepreneurs as a small minority of tourism and hospitality family businesses. They tend to be attracted to businesses with greater potential for profit and growth, and to involve more children. But what comes first – family involvement or profit? They also tend to purchase rather than set up new businesses, so agencies seeking economic growth and new jobs might be wiser to fund these entrepreneurs rather than putting money into the creation of new, small businesses.

It is possible that innovation and growth might vary by setting, culture, and level of economic development. A comparison of a newer, mountain resort (Canmore, Alberta) with an older, more traditional seaside resort (Bornholm, Denmark) revealed that the family-business owners in Canmore were in general more profit- and growth-oriented. Did the

environment – especially lower seasonality of demand – make the difference? Or was this a cultural difference reflecting underlying values and attitudes in Denmark and Canada?

> P 4. Goals of male and female owners in copreneurial businesses (i.e. those operated by couples) are likely to be identical.

> P 5. Female entrepreneurs, specifically those involved in home-based businesses, display a different set of motives and challenges from those exhibited by the copreneurial family business. In female-led family businesses there is greater scope for dissention on goals and business roles.

A great deal of research and discussion in the literature has focused on female entrepreneurs, and on the disadvantages or barriers they typically face, but in businesses owned and operated by couples, the limited evidence suggests that male and female goals are largely identical. This observation deserves more detailed examination, including a comparison between females acting alone and those working with partners in running a business. Family business researchers should, in fact, be more interested in family dynamics, such as the interplay between family members by gender, age, and degree of interdependence. One focus for this line of research should be the examination of how families identify and resolve issues pertaining to their business.

> P 6. Sole proprietors, although more likely to adhere to mainstream entrepreneurial business goals and practices, nevertheless involve family in business operations and decisions.

Sole proprietors might not consider their business as a family business, yet they will find it difficult to separate completely their business and family lives. Many do involve spouses or other family members, formally or informally, although not in ownership. In couples, where one partner runs a business and the other has separate employment (which is particularly the case with many female-operated, small accommodation and retail operations), there is ample scope for either informal assistance or for conflict.

> P 7. Larger firms are more appealing for purchase by growth- and profit-oriented

entrepreneurs; in turn, these will offer more scope for employing and challenging family members.

As mentioned earlier, does family involvement come before or after business growth? It has been claimed that business founders do not create family firms, and the 'family business' part comes later. Certainly larger firms offer more scope for employing and challenging family members, but is that in itself a motive for growing the business?

Propositions relating to ownership, family and business evolution

P 8. Most family businesses in tourism and hospitality will not be passed on within the family.

P 9. A primary barrier to inheritance of family businesses in this industry will be a lack of shared vision between the generations.

This can be stated with a high degree of certainty, based on available research within the industry and family business data in general, but does it hold true everywhere? The family vision does not seem to endure across generations. It might be that living in resorts, islands, small towns and rural areas is desirable only later in life, and by the time inheritance becomes possible the children have left.

P 10. Children in family businesses in this industry are likely to consciously reject taking over the family business because of perceptions of hard work and low profitability.

The very nature of tourism and hospitality work discourages many people from entering or continuing, either in employment or ownership. Data are needed from children growing up in these businesses, or perhaps college students reflecting on their childhood experiences, to see what effect it has on their attitudes and careers. A logical sample would be of tourism and hospitality students, with a specific hypothesis being: tourism and hospitality students from a family business background are more likely to reject involvement in the family firm and potential ownership of a similar business.

P 11. Family businesses in tourism and hospitality are most likely sold and taken over by other family businesses.

Research should be directed at examining the life cycle of individual businesses within different settings to see if purchase by different families is a repeat phenomenon. And if the vision does occur to children later in life, will they emulate their parents but in a different place or business?

P 12. Farm-based family businesses are more likely to involve a conscious attempt by the owners to create or pass on a legacy of land to the next generation.

Many people desire to create a legacy of land, money or a business for their inheritors. The notion of 'legacy' deserves more attention from researchers. To what extent is it rooted in various cultures? Or has it more to do with strong ties to the land? Certainly in the tourism and hospitality research cited in this book, the desire for creating a legacy appears to be linked to farming in particular. A related issue is that of separating the tourism business from the farming operation.

P 13. In remote and lesser-developed settings, returning migrants and in-migrants are likely to be the predominant form of business ownership in tourism and hospitality.

Research in the Spey Valley of Scotland (Getz, 1986) revealed that in-migrants were the dominant entrepreneurial group in tourism and hospitality, although many B&B establishments were founded by natives of the area. Other academics have noted that returning migrants have the money and expertise to establish businesses. A number of issues are raised by these phenomena, including cultural (is indigenous culture threatened?), social (the politics of newcomers versus natives) and economic (control over the industry).

P 14. Family business in tourism and hospitality will display lower profitability and higher failure rates than other forms of business.

This is a more contentious proposition, not backed by systematic testing but only by direct observation of the industry. It is based on the fact that the majority of tourism and hospitality businesses studied to date, by multiple researchers, have been small and not growth-oriented, and the industry generally experiences a high turn-over in ownership. Research should therefore concentrate on comparing family businesses between industry sectors.

Propositions relating to industry-specific modifiers

P 15. The nature of tourism and hospitality services, often involving a high degree of host–guest interaction, is both a motivator for many family businesses and a source of family branding (in which the family is the attraction).

This proposition reflects the positive side of running a tourism/hospitality business. Many family-business owners seek both autonomy and hands-on work in this industry, obviously enjoying meeting and pleasing people. It can grow tiring and intrusive, but certain personality types relish the contacts. The desire for social contacts has been noted to be a motivator, especially for females in remote and rural areas.

Family branding has not been given much attention in the tourism and hospitality literature. The O'Reilly case study demonstrates its poten-tial power for ensuring a sustainable, profitable family business, but what are the exact benefits and costs? If the success of a business is tied to a family name, what happens when ownership changes or a scandal occurs?

P 16. Cyclical demand, especially seasonality, has a major negative impact on family business viability and inter-generational succession.

Tourism in most destinations experiences some degree of seasonality of demand, and in many rural, remote and resort settings the fluctuations are extreme. This causes major problems for family businesses, and requires specific coping strategies that directly effect family life. The Bornholm research clearly demonstrated how most family businesses had to shut down for part of the year, but also pointed out strategies that can be successful in combating or even overcoming seasonality. The exact link between seasonality and inheritance has not been tested, but this proposition follows logically from available data on the low levels of

inheritance and the marginal nature of many of the businesses.

P 17. Families adopt both personal and business strategies that are unavailable to corporations to diminish or cope with seasonality.

P 18. Some family-business owners prefer seasonal breaks from work, but these businesses will remain small in terms of employment and profit potential.

These two propositions also get at the core of family-business studies. For some, seasonality is not a crucial issue because their business is secondary to another activity, such as farming, or even counter-cyclical to other activities like fishing or forestry. For these family-business owners, seasonality is a fact of life and not a threat. To others, the low-demand period (or 'off-season') comes as a relief, enabling rest, vacations, and time for necessary work around the house and business. These families simply cope with seasonal demand and will generally remain small and lack high profitability. Others, however, combat it vigorously. To economic development agencies and destination market-ers, the 'combaters' are to be valued and encour-aged. What sets them apart is both a theoretical and a practical question that cannot yet be fully answered.

P 19. Families engage in value-adding to their business in order to generate sufficient income to hire staff, not for profit maximization.

The majority of 'development' within fam-ily businesses in tourism and hospitality appears to be of the 'value-adding' kind, and not devel-opment for the sake of growth or attainment of maximum profits. Owners realize the need for greater profits, and can achieve this goal through improved marketing, technology, cost controls, and possibly expansion. The case studies cited in this book suggest that expansion is carefully thought out and usually linked to the desire to obtain relief from the burdens of being owner-operators.

P 20. A high concentration of small, family businesses contributes to resort decline.

This proposition is bound to be contro-versial. It follows in part from the observations of Shaw and Williams (1997) concerning the decline of British coastal resorts, and in part from the other research cited in this book that points to the general absence of growth motivations and entrepreneurship in family businesses. Researchers might find that it is not the concentration of small, family businesses that leads to decline, or as argued by Getz and Petersen (2002), prevents destination repositioning, but the low number of profit- and growth-oriented entrepreneurs in a given economy. If that is the case, special attention must be given to attracting and encouraging this type of family business.

> P 21. There are more opportunities for family-business creation by residents in the early stages of destination development, but more opportunities for in-migrant family-business creation and for family-business growth in the later stages.

The destination life cycle (from Butler, 1980) has been applied to many facets of tourism and hospitality studies, but little attention has been given to the possible links between stages of the life cycle and family-business opportunities. This proposition, therefore, is more tenuous than many of the others.

> P 22. Family-business owners in tourism and hospitality are willing to accept the many challenges and limitations imposed on them because of the compensating benefits relating to lifestyle.

This contention follows from previous discussion, and it should be possible to put it to a simple test in any given business environment. What it does not say, however, is that many owners do not accept the trade-off between work conditions and lifestyle, or cannot sustain it over time, and they leave the sector. To get a complete picture will require surveys of owners and past-owners of failed, lapsed and sold family businesses.

Propositions relating to setting modifiers

> P 23. Family businesses in remote and rural settings have a substantial, positive impact on community and economic development as well as on cultural and environmental sustainability.

Some families are motivated to develop a tourism or hospitality business in order to stay on their land or in their family home, while others consciously choose to re-locate to a preferred setting. Either way, the family in business in remote areas, small towns, islands and other peripheral settings, is potentially an important asset to that fragile economy and community. Even when the individual family business fails or is sold, other families are likely to take it over. No-one has documented this process or evaluated all its implications. Case studies would be a logical starting point.

> P 24. Networks of family businesses are essential for development in rural, remote and lesser-developed settings.

Where there is a long tradition of family business, it is likely that they have closer links than with external or non-family businesses. Partly this will rest on extended family ties, and partly on preference. Such networks can provide financial and moral support, increase the marketing reach of small businesses, and even act to keep out competitors. But where does it work this way in tourism and hospitality? How exactly do the networks work?

> P 25. Opportunities for profitable family business are maximized in highly developed economies, cities and popular resorts.

Presumably the more tourism and leisure demand there is, the more opportunities exist for family business. But are they crowded out by large corporations and chains? Is there a position in the life cycle of the destination that maximizes or minimizes opportunities for families?

> P 26. In lesser-developed economies, tourism and hospitality sectors offer new opportunities for family-business creation, but these will be constrained by culture, capital and economic dualism.

Many developing countries and regions rely on tourism to attract foreign investment and currency, to help build infrastructure and modernize the economy. Aside from the potential negative implications of this process, such as economic dualism, it does create opportunities for indigenous and returning (i.e. re-patriated) investors. The trouble is that in some cultures there are severe barriers: cultural (e.g. gender bias, attitudes towards business owners); legal (taxation, inheritance or monetary controls), or economic (lack of capital or difficulty in borrowing).

> P 27. Family business in traditional and indigenous cultures will be uniquely shaped by issues pertaining to communal ownership of resources and control of culture.

Dimensions of family business in indigenous cultures have yet to be examined. Even though communal ownership applies, there are still opportunities for individuals and families (sometimes extended to the tribal level) to operate a tourism and hospitality business. It could be accommodation on communal land, or guiding services using personally owned equipment such as boats or snowmobiles, but the ownership of culture is another issue. How do personal or family business ambitions get reconciled with community decision-making? Does the community block innovations in the name of cultural protection?

> P 28. Female entrepreneurship is in many areas restricted by culture, yet in itself offers an opportunity to break tradition and realize women's goals for greater independence.

Quite a lot of attention has been given to the female entrepreneur in tourism and hospitality, particularly because so many micro and small businesses are established and operated by women. Research is needed on incentives and barriers specific to women, trade-offs between family and business, conflict resolution, and cultural implications.

Chapter Summary

There is a huge scope for theory-building in the family-business sector in general, and for industry-specific developments in particular. We have argued from the book's very beginning that an industry-specific approach will benefit the generic field of family business studies, and that it is important within the context of understanding tourism and hospitality.

This concluding chapter started with our assessment of gaps between what should be known or studied, and what is known about family business within tourism and hospitality. Gaps were identified specifically by reference to

the Gersick *et al.* (1997) life cycle model incorporating the three axes of business, family and ownership, as well as through reference to the generic, family-business themes and topics identified by Sharma *et al.* (1996).

What are the most important research gaps? As this is a new line of inquiry for tourism and hospitality scholars, there are certainly many gaps, and more will be identified as research advances. Without repeating all the questions raised above, it has to be emphasized that the most important research projects are those that either help identify the unique or common aspects of family business in this industry (compared with other industries, preferably over time), and those that help formulate generic, family-business theory (such as the nature of constrained or latent entrepreneurship within families).

In the second part of this chapter a series of inter-related propositions were advanced as a step in theory-building. Propositions follow directly from the authors' collective knowledge and research evidence and represent what we believe to be the truth. They can and should be tested in many settings and across industries, but they can be used as emergent theories.

If this book has one over-riding benefit to the field of tourism and hospitality studies, to the industry and its countless family-business owners, we hope it is in elevating the profile of family-business issues. If successful in realizing that goal, it should result in more and better research, more effective policies, better-managed businesses, more competitive destinations, and more students inspired to study the family business in tourism and hospitality.

References

Butler, R. (1980) The concept of the tourist area cycle of evolution; implications for management of resources. *Canadian Geographer* 24, 5–12.

Gersick, K., Davis, J., Hampton, M. and Lansberg, I. (1997) *Generation to Generation: Life Cycles of Family Business.* Harvard Business School Press, Boston, Massachusetts.

Getz, D. (1986) Tourism and population change: long term impacts of tourism in the Badenoch–Strathspey District of the Scottish Highlands. *The Scottish Geographical Magazine* 102(2), 113–126.

Getz, D. and Carlsen, J. (2000) Characteristics and goals of family and owner-operated businesses in the rural tourism and hospitality sectors. *Tourism Management* 21(6), 547–560.

Getz, D. and Petersen, T. (2002) Growth-oriented Entrepreneurs and Destination Competitiveness. Paper presented at the Re-inventing the Destination Conference, Dubrovnik, Croatia.

McGibbon, J. (2000) Family business: commercial hospitality in the domestic realm. In: Robinson, M., Long, P., Evans, N., Sharpley, R. and Swarbrooke, J. (eds) *Reflections on International Tourism: Expressions of Culture Identity and Meaning in Tourism*. Business Education Publications, Sunderland, UK.

Sharma, P., Chrisman, J. and Chua, J. (1996) *A Review and Annotated Bibliography of Family Business Studies*. Kluwer, Boston, Massachusetts.

Shaw, G. and Williams, A. (eds) (1997) *The Rise and Fall of British Coastal Resorts: Cultural and Economic Perspectives*. Pinter, London.

Bibliography

Alcorn, P. (1982) *Success and Survival in the Family-Owned Business*. McGraw Hill, New York.

Allcock, J. (1989) Seasonality. In: Witt, S. and Moutinho, L. (eds) *Tourism Marketing and Management Handbook*. Prentice Hall, London, pp. 387–392.

Ambrose, D. (1983) Transfer of the family-owned business. *Journal of Small Business Management* 21(1), 49–56.

Andersson, T., Carlsen, J. and Getz, D. (2002) Family business goals in the tourism and hospitality sector: case studies and cross-cases analysis from Australia, Canada, and Sweden. *Family Business Review* 15(2), 89–106.

Antoncic, B. and Hisrich, R. (2001) Intrapreneurship: construct refinement and cross-cultural validation. *Journal of Business Venturing* 16(5), 495–528.

Apostolopoulos, Y., Sonmez, S. and Timothy, D. (eds) *Women as Producers and Consumers of Tourism in Developing Regions*. Praeger, Westport, Connecticut.

Armstrong, K. (1978) Rural Scottish women: politics without power. *Ethnos* 43(1/2), 51–72.

Aronoff, C., Astrachan, J. and Ward, J. (1996) *Family Business Sourcebook 2*. Business Owner Resources, Marietta, Georgia.

Astrachan, J. (1989) Family firm and community culture. *Family Business Review* 1(2), 165–189.

Astrachan, J. (1993) Preparing the next generation for wealth: a conversation with Howard H. Stevenson. *Family Business Review* 6(1), 75–83.

Ateljevic. I. and Doorne, S. (2000) Staying within the fence: lifestyle entrepreneurship in tourism. *Journal of Sustainable Tourism* 8(5), 378–392.

Australian Bureau of Statistics (1998) *Australian Social Trends*. Cat. 4102.0, pp. 10–14.

Baines, S. and Wheelock, J. (1998) Working for each other: gender, the household and micro-business survival and growth. *International Small Business Journal* 17, 11–16.

Barney, J. (1991) Firm resources and sustained competitive advantage. *Journal of Management* 17(1), 99–120.

BarOn, R. (1975) Seasonality in tourism: a guide to the analysis of seasonality and trends for policy making. *Economist Intelligence Unit*, Technical Series No. 2, London.

Barry, B. (1975) The development of organisation structure in the family firm. *Journal of General Management* 3(1), 42–60.

Baum, T. (1998) Tourism marketing and the small island environment: cases from the periphery. In: Laws, E., Faulkner, B. and Moscardo, G. (eds) *Embracing and Managing Change in Tourism: International Case Studies*. Routledge, London, pp. 116–137.

Baum, T. (1999) Human resource management in tourism's small business sector: policy dimensions. In: Lee-Ross, D. (ed.) *HRM in Tourism and Hospitality: International Perspectives on Small to Medium-sized Enterprises*. Cassell, London, pp. 3–16.

Baum, T. and Hagan, L. (1997) Responses to seasonality in tourism: the experience of peripheral destinations. Conference paper, International Tourism Research Conference on Peripheral Area Tourism. Research Centre of Bornholm, Denmark, pp. 8–12.

Baum, T. and Lundtorp, S. (eds) (2001) *Seasonality in Tourism*. Pergamon, Amsterdam.

Beckhard, R. and Dyer, W. (1993) Managing change in the family firm – issues and strategies. *Sloan Management Review* 24(3), 59–65.

Benson, B., Crego, E. and Drucker, R. (1996) Family councils. In: *The Family Business Management Handbook*. From the editors of Family Business Magazine. Family Business Publishing Co, Philadelphia, Pennsylvania, pp. 45–46.

Birley, S. (1986) Succession in the family firm: the inheritor's view. *Journal of Small Business Management* 24(3), 36–43.

Birley, S. (1997) *The Family and the Business*. Grant Thornton, London.

Birley, S. (2001) Owner-manager attitudes to family and business issues: a 16-country study. *Entrepreneurship Theory and Practice* 26(2), 63–76.

Birley, S. (2002) Attitudes of owner-managers' children towards family and business issues. *Entrepreneurship Theory and Practice* 26(3), 5–19.

Birley, S. and Cromie, S. (1988) Social networks and entrepreneurship in Northern Ireland. Enterprise in Action Conference, Belfast, UK.

Birley, S., Ng, D. and Godfrey, A. (1999) The family and the business. *Long Range Planning* 32(6), 598–608.

Bjuggren, P. and Sund, L. (2001) Strategic decision-making in intergenerational successions of small- and medium-sized family-owned businesses. *Family Business Review* 14 (1), 11–23.

Blackburn, R.M. (1999) Is housework unpaid work? *International Journal of Sociology and Social Policy* 19(7/8), 1–20.

Blotnick, S. (1984) The case of reluctant heirs. *Forbes* July, 134, 180.

Boer, A. (1998) An assessment of small business failure. In: Thomas, R. (ed.) *The Management of Small Tourism and Hospitality Firms*. Cassell, London, pp. 39–57.

Boger, C. and Buchanan, R. (1991) *A Study of Bed and Breakfast Facilities in Indiana*. Indianan University, The Indiana Extension Service, Indianapolis, Indiana.

Bouquet, M. and Winter, M. (1987) (eds) *Who From Their Labours Rest? Conflict and Practice in Rural Tourism*. Avebury Press, Aldershot, UK.

Bransgrove, C. and King, B. (1996) Strategic marketing practice amongst small tourism and hospitality businesses. In: Thomas, R. (ed.) *Spring Symposium Proceedings of International Association of Hotel Management Schools*, Leeds Metropolitan University, Leeds, UK, pp. 29–38.

Breathnach, P., Henry, M., Drea, S. and O'Flaherty, M. (1994) Gender in Irish tourism employment. In: Kinnaird, V. and Hall, D. (eds) *Tourism: a Gender Analysis*. John Wiley & Sons, Chichester, UK, pp. 52–73.

Britton, S. (1981) Tourism, dependency and development: a mode of analysis. Occasional Paper No. 23, Development Studies, Australian National University.

Brockhaus, R. (1980) Risk-taking propensity of entrepreneurs. *Academy of Management Journal* 23(3), 509–520.

Brockhaus, R. (1994a) Family business: a blessing or a curse? Keynote Address, Proceedings of the Small Enterprise Association of Australia and New Zealand Conference.

Brockhaus, R. (1994b) Entrepreneurship and family business: comparisons, critique, and lessons. *Entrepreneurship Theory and Practice* 19(1), 25–38.

Brown, B. (1987) Recent tourism research in South East Dorset. In: Shaw, G. and Williams, A. (eds) *Tourism and Development: Overviews and Case Studies of the UK and the South West Region*. Working Paper 4, Department of Geography, University of Exeter, UK.

Brown, F. and Hall, D. (eds) (2000) *Tourism in Peripheral Areas: Case Studies*. Channel View Publications, Clevedon, UK.

Brownlie, D. (1994) Market opportunity analysis: a DIY approach for small tourism enterprises. *Tourism Management* 15(1), 37–45.

Buhalis, D. and Cooper, C. (1998) Competition or cooperation? Small and medium-sized tourism enterprises at the destination. In: Laws, E., Faulkner, B. and Moscardo, G. (eds) *Embracing and Managing Change in Tourism*. Routledge, London, pp. 324–346.

Butler, R. (1980) The concept of the tourist area cycle of evolution; implications for management of resources. *Canadian Geographer* 24, 5–12.

Butler, R. (1994) Seasonality in tourism: issues and problems. In: Seaton, A. *et al.* (eds) *Tourism: the State and the Art*. John Wiley & Sons, Chichester, UK, pp. 332–339.

Caballe, A. (1999) Farm tourism in Spain: a gender perspective. *Geojournal* 48(3), 245–252.

Cameron, A. and Massey, C. (1999) *Small and Medium-sized Enterprises: a New Zealand Perspective*. Addison Wesley Longman, New Zealand Ltd, Auckland.

Carland, J., Hoy, W., Boulton, F. and Carland J.C. (1984) Differentiating entrepreneurs from small business owners: a conceptualisation. *Academy of Management Review* 9(2), 354–359.

Carlock, R. and Ward, J. (2001) *Strategic Planning for the Family Business*. Palgrave, Basingstoke, UK.

Carlsen, J. and Getz, D. (2001) Cross-case analysis of family businesses in rural tourism. In: Pforr, C. and Janaczko, B. (eds) *Proceedings of the Capitalising on Research Conference*. University of Canberra, Canberra, Australia.

Carlsen, J., Getz, D. and Ali-Knight, J. (2001) Environmental attitudes and practices of family businesses in the rural tourism and hospitality sectors. *Journal of Sustainable Tourism* 9(4), 281–297.

Carrier, C. (1996) Intrapreneurship in small business: an exploratory study. *Entrepreneurship Theory and Practice* 21(1), 5–51.

Carson, D., Cromie, S., McGowan, P. and Hill, J. (1995) *Marketing and Entrepreneurship in SMEs: an Innovative Approach*. Prentice Hall, London.

Carter, S. (2001) Multiple business ownership in the farm sector: differentiating monoactive, diversified and portfolio enterprises. *International Journal of Entrepreneurial Behaviour and Research* 7(2), 43–59.

Carter, S., Anderson, S. and Shaw, E. (2001) *Women's Business Ownership: a Review of the Academic, Popular and Internet Literature*. Small Business Service, Department of Trade and Industry, London.

Carter, S., Tagg, S., Ennis, S. and Webb, J. (2002) *Lifting the Barriers to Growth in UK Small Businesses*. Federation of Small Business, London.

Chua, J., Chrisman, J. and Sharma, P. (1999) Defining the family business by behavior. *Entrepreneurship Theory and Practice* 23(4), 19–37.

Chua, J., Chrisman, J. and Sharma, P. (2002) Family and non-family priorities in family firms: preliminary evidence. In: Chrisman, J., Holbrook, J. and Chua, J. (eds) *Innovation and Entrepreneurship in Western Canada: From Family Businesses to Multinationals*. University of Calgary Press, Calgary, Canada, pp. 299–320.

Clarke, J. (1995) Sustainable tourism: marketing of farm tourist accommodation. PhD thesis, School of Hotel and Catering Management, Oxford Brookes University, UK.

Collins, J. (2002) Chinese entrepreneurs: the Chinese diaspora in Australia. *International Journal of Entrepreneurial Behaviour and Research* 8(1/2), 113–133.

Cooper, C. (1997) Parameters and indicators of the decline of the British seaside resort. In: Shaw, G. and Williams, A. (eds) *The Rise and Fall of British Coastal Resorts: Cultural and Economic Perspectives*. Mansell, London, pp. 79–101.

Cooper, C., Fletcher, J., Gilbert, D. and Wanhill, S. (1993) *Tourism: Principles and Practice*. Pitman, London.

Coopers and Lybrand Consulting (1996) Special report on off- and shoulder season marketing, for the Canadian Tourism Commission. Ottawa.

Commonwealth of Australia (1997) *A Portrait of Australian Business*. Department of Industry, Science and Tourism, Canberra, Australia.

Cory, J. (1990) Preparing your success: family ownership. *Hardware Age*, July, p. 74.

Craig, J. and Lindsay, N. (2002) Incorporating the family dynamic into the entrepreneurship process. *Journal of Small Business and Enterprise Development* 9(3), 416–430.

Cromie, S. and O'Sullivan, S. (1999) Women as managers in family firms. *Women in Management Review* 14(3), 76–88.

Cromie, S., Adams, J., Dunn, B. and Reid, R. (1999) Family firms in Scotland and Northern Ireland: an empirical investigation. *Journal of Small Business and Enterprise Development* 6(3), 253–266.

Cromie, S., Dunn, B., Sproull, A. and Chalmers, D. (2001) Small firms with a family focus in the Scottish Highlands and Islands. *Irish Journal of Management* 22(2), 45–66.

Cukier, J., Norris, J. and Wall, G. (1996) The involvement of women in the tourism industry of Bali, Indonesia. *The Journal of Development Studies* 33(2), 248–270.

Dahles, H. (1998) Tourism, government policy and petty entrepreneurs. *South East Asia Research* 6, 73–98.

Dahles, H. and Bras, K. (1999) Entrepreneurs in romance tourism in Indonesia. *Annals of Tourism Research* 26(2), 267–293.

Dailey, C. and Dollinger, M. (1992) An empirical examination of ownership structure in family and professionally managed firms. *Family Business Review* 5(2), 117–136.

Dana, L. (2001) The education and training of entrepreneurs in Asia. *Education and Training* 43(8/9), 405–416.

Danes, S. (1998) *Farm Family Business*. University of Minnesota Extension Service.

Davis, J. (1996a) Values and mission statements. In: *The Family Business Management Handbook* (1996). From the editors of Family Business Magazine. Family Business Publishing Co, Philadelphia, Pennsylvania, pp. 20–23.

Davis, J. (1996b) Boards of Directors. In: *The Family Business Management Handbook*. From the editors of Family Business Magazine. Family Business Publishing Co, Philadelphia, Pennsylvania, pp. 90–93.

Davis, J. and Tagiuri, R. (1989) The influence of life-stage on father–son work relationships in family companies. *Family Business Review* 2(1), 47–74.

Davis, P. and Harveston, P. (1998) The influence of family on the family business succession process: A multi-generational perspective. *Entrepreneurship Theory and Practice* 22(3), 31–53.

Davis, S. (1968) Entrepreneurial succession. *Administrative Science Quarterly* 13, 402–416.

Dawson, C. and Brown, T. (1988) B&Bs: a matter of choice. *Cornell Hotel and Restaurant Administration Quarterly* 29 (1), 17-21.

Day, J. (2000) Commentary: the value and importance of the small firm to the world economy. *European Journal of Marketing* 34(9/10), 1033–1037.

Dean, S. (1992) Characteristics of African American family-owned businesses in Los Angeles. *Family Business Review* 5(4), 373–395.

Deloitte and Touche (1999) $1.3 trillion at stake as Canada's family businesses face leadership crisis. www.deloitte.ca

Deloitte Touche Tomatsu (1994) *Small Business Survey 1994: New Zealand Tourism Industry.* Deloitte Touche Tomatsu Tourism and Leisure Consulting Group, Christchurch, New Zealand.

Department of Trade and Industry (2001) *Small and Medium-sized Enterprise Statistics for the UK, 2000.* DTI, Sheffield, UK.

Dernoi, L. (1991a) About rural and farm tourism. *Tourism Recreation Research* 16(1), 3–6.

Dernoi, L. (1991b) Canadian country vacations: the farm and rural tourism in Canada. *Tourism Recreation Research* 16(1), 15–20.

Dewhurst, P. and Horobin, H. (1998) Small business owners. In: Thomas, R. (ed.) *The Management of Small Tourism and Hospitality Firms.* Cassell, London, pp. 19–38.

Din, H. (1992) The 'involvement stage' in the evolution of a tourist destination. *Tourism Recreation Research* 17(1), 10–20.

Dodd, S. (1997) Social network memberships and activity rates: some comparative data. *International Small Business Journal* 15(4), 80–87.

Dondo, A. and Ngumo, M. (1998) Africa: Kenya. In: Morrison, A. (ed.), *Entrepreneurship: an International Perspective.* Butterworth Heinemann, Oxford, UK, pp. 15–26

Donnelley, R. (1964) The family business. *Harvard Business Review* 42(2), 93–105.

Drucker, P. (1985) *Innovation and Entrepreneurship: Practice and Principles.* Heinemann, London.

Drucker, P. (1986) *Innovation and Entrepreneurship: Practice and Principles.* Pan Books, London.

Dumas, C. (1992) Integrating the daughter into family business management. *Entrepreneurship: Theory and Practice* June, 41–55.

Dunkelberg, W. (1995) Presidential address: small business and the US. *Business Economics* 30, 13–18.

Dunlop, M. (1993) Parents' beliefs can cause trouble in family firms. *The Toronto Star* Nov. 20, pp. K2.

Dunn, B. (1995) Success themes in Scottish family enterprises: philosophies and practices through the generations. *Family Business Review* 8(1), 17–28.

Dyer, W. (1988) Culture and continuity in family firms. *Family Business Review* 1(1), 37–50.

Dyer, W. and Handler, W. (1994) Entrepreneurship and family business: exploring the connections. *Entrepreneurship Theory and Practice* 19(1), 71–83.

Evans, N. and Ilbery, W. (1989) A conceptual framework for investigating farm-based accommodation and tourism in Britain. *Journal of Rural Studies* 5(3), 257–266.

Evans, N. and Ilbery, W. (1992) Advertising and farm-based accommodation: a British case study. *Tourism Management* 13(4), 415–422.

Fairbairn-Dunlop, P. (1994) Gender, culture and tourism development in Western Samoa. In: Kinnaird, V. and Hall, D. (eds) *Tourism: a Gender Analysis.* John Wiley & Sons, Chichester, UK, pp. 121–141.

File, K., Prince, R. and Rankin, M. (1994) Organisational buying behaviour of the family firm. *Family Business Review* 7(3), 263–272.

Flognfeldt, T. (2001) Long-term positive adjustments to seasonality: consequences of summer tourism in the Jotunheimen area, Norway. In: Baum, T. and Lundtorp, S. (eds) *Seasonality in Tourism.* Pergamon, Amsterdam, pp. 109–117.

Frater, J. (1982) *Farming Tourism in England and Overseas.* Research Memorandum 93, Centre for Urban and Regional Studies, Birmingham, UK.

Frideres, J. (1988) *Native Peoples in Canada: Contemporary Conflicts,* 3rd edn. Prentice-Hall Canada Inc., Scarborough, Canada.

Friel, M. (1998) Marketing. In: Thomas, R. (ed.) *The Management of Small Tourism and Hospitality Firms.* Cassell, London, pp. 117–137.

Friel, M. (1999) Marketing practice in small tourism and hospitality firms. *International Journal of Tourism Research* 1, 97–109.

Garcia-Ramon, D., Canoves, G. and Valdovinos, N. (1995) Farm tourism, gender and the environment in Spain. *Annals of Tourism Research* 22(2), 267–282.

Gartner, W. (1988) 'Who is the entrepreneur?' is the wrong question. *American Journal of Small Business* 12, 11–32.

Gartner, W. (1990) What are we talking about when we talk about entrepreneurship? *Journal of Business Venturing* 5(1), 15–28.

Geeraerts, G. (1984) the effect of ownership on the organization structure in small firms. *Administrative Science Quarterly* 29, 232–237.

Gersick, K., Davis, J., Hampton, M. and Lansberg, I. (1997) *Generation to Generation: Life Cycles of Family Business.* Harvard Business School Press, Boston, Massachusetts.

Getz, D. (1986) Tourism and population change: Long term impacts of tourism in the Badenoch–Strathspey District of the Scottish Highlands. *The Scottish Geographical Magazine* 102(2), 113–126.

Getz, D. and Carlsen, J. (2000) Characteristics and goals of family- and owner-operated businesses in the rural tourism and hospitality sectors. *Tourism Management* 21, 547–560.

Getz, D. and Jamieson, W. (1997) Rural tourism in Canada: issues, opportunities and entrepreneurship in aboriginal tourism in Alberta. In: Page, S. and Getz, D. (eds) *The Business of Rural Tourism: International Perspectives.* International Thomson Business Press, London, pp. 93–107.

Getz, D. and Petersen, T. (2002) Growth-oriented entrepreneurs and destination competitiveness. Paper presented at the Re-inventing The Destination conference, Dubrovnik, Croatia.

Gilder, G. (1971) *Spirit of Enterprise.* Simon and Schuster, New York.

Gladstone, J. and Morris, A. (2000) Farm accommodation and agricultural heritage in Orkney. In: Brown, F. and Hall, D. (eds) *Tourism in Peripheral Areas: Case Studies.* Channel View, Clevedon, UK, pp. 91–100.

Glezer, L. (1988) Business and commerce. In: Jupp, J. (ed.) *The Australian People: an Encyclopedia of the Nation, its People and Origins,* Angus and Robertson, Sydney, Australia, pp. 860–864.

Goffee, R. (1996) Understanding family businesses: issues for further research. *International Journal of Entrepreneurial Behaviour and Research* 2(1), 36–48.

Goffee, R. and Scase, R. (1985) *Women in Charge: the Experiences of Female Entrepreneurs.* George Allen and Unwin, London.

Goffee, R. and Scase, R. (1995) *Corporate Realities: The Dynamics of Large and Small Organisations.* Routledge, London.

Goldberg, S. and Wooldridge, B. (1993) Self-confidence and managerial autonomy: Successor characteristics critical to succession in family firms. *Family Business Journal* July, 60–65.

Gorton, M. (2000) Overcoming the structure–agency divide in small business research. *International Journal of Entrepreneurial Behaviour and Research* 6(5), 276–292.

Greenbank, P. (2000) Micro-business start-ups: challenging normative decision-making? *Market Intelligence and Planning* 18(4), 206–212.

Greenbank, P. (2001) Objective setting in the micro-business. *International Journal of Entrepreneurial Behaviour and Research* 7(3), 108–127.

Gruidl, N., Cooper, R. and Silva, D. (1990) *Structure, Conduct, and Performance of the Bed and Breakfast Industry in Wisconsin.* Recreation Resource Center, University of Wisconsin-Extension, Madison, Wisconsin.

Gyimothy, S. (2000) The quality of visitor experience: a case study in peripheral areas of Europe. Research Centre of Bornholm, Denmark, Report 17/2000.

Habbershon, T. and Williams, M. (1999) A Resource Based Framework for Assessing the Strategic Advantages of Family Firms, Working Paper Series No. 101, The Wharton School, University of Pennsylvania, Pennsylvania.

Haber, S. and Lerner, M. (2002) Small tourism ventures in peripheral areas: the impact of environmental factors on performance, In: Krakover, S. and Gradus, Y. (eds) *Tourism in Frontier Areas.* Lexington Books, Lanham, Maryland, pp. 141–163.

Hair, J., Anderson, R., Tatham, R. and Black, W. (1998) *Multivariate Data Analysis* 5th edn. Prentice Hall, Upper Saddle River, New Jersey.

Hall, C. and Jenkins, M. (1997) The policy dimensions of rural tourism and recreation. In: Butler, R., Hall, C. and Jenkins, J. (eds) *Tourism and Recreation in Rural Areas.* John Wiley & Sons, New York.

Handler, W. (1992) The succession experience of the next generation. *Family Business Review* 5(3), 283–307.

Handler, W. (1994) Succession in family businesses: a review of the research. *Family Business Review* 7(2), 133–157.

Handler, W. and Kram, K. (1988) Succession in family firms: the problem of resistance. *Family Business Review* 1(4), 361–381.

Hankinson, A. (1989) Small hotels in Britain: investment and survival. *The Cornell HRA Quarterly* 30(3), 80–82.

Harper, M. (1984) *Small Businesses in the Third World: Guidelines for Practical Assistance.* John Wiley & Sons, Chichester, UK.

Harrison, D. (1992) The social consequences. In: Harrison, D. (ed.) *Tourism and the Less Developed Countries.* Belhaven Press, London, pp. 19–34.

Harrison, R. and Leitch, C. (1996). Whatever you hit call the target. An alternative approach to small business policy. In: Danson, M. (ed.) *Small Firm Formation and Regional Economic Development.* Routledge, London.

Hegarty, C. and Ruddy, J. (2002) The role of family in entrepreneurial development in Irish rural tourism. Paper presented at the conference: Re-inventing the Destination. Dubrovnik, Croatia.

Herremans, I. and Welsh, C. (1999) Developing and implementing a company's ecotourism mission statement. *Journal of Sustainable Tourism* 7(1), 48–76.

Hisrich, R. and Drnovsek, M. (2002) Entrepreneurship and small business research: a European perspective. *Journal of Small Business and Enterprise Development* 9(2), 172–222.

Hisrich, R. and Grachev, M. (1995) The Russian entrepreneur: characteristics and prescriptions for success. *Journal of Managerial Psychology* 10(2), 3–9.

Hjalager, A. (1996) Agricultural diversification development into tourism. Evidence of a European Community development programme. *Tourism Management* 17(2), 103–112.

Ho, Y. and Tanewski, G. (2002) An examination of leadership in fast-growth family businesses: a conceptual framework. IFSAM Conference, Gold Coast, Australia.

Hofer, C. and Bygrave, W. (1992) Researching entrepreneurship. *Entrepreneurship Theory and Practice* 16, 91–100.

Hofstede, G. (1991) *Culture and Organisations.* McGraw-Hill, London.

Hoy, F. and Verser, T. (1994) Emerging business, emerging field: entrepreneurship and the family firm. *Entrepreneurship Theory and Practice* 19(1), 9–23.

Hurley, A. (1999) Incorporating feminist theories into sociological theories of entrepreneurship. *Women in Management Review* 14(2), 54–62.

Iannarelli, C. (1992) The socialization of leaders: a study of gender in family business. Unpublished doctoral dissertation, University of Pittsburgh, Pennsylvania.

Jeffrey, D. and Barden, R. (2001). An analysis of the nature, causes and marketing implications of seasonality in the occupancy performance of English hotels. In: Baum, T. and Lundtorp, S. (eds) *Seasonality in Tourism.* Pergamon, Amsterdam, pp. 119–140.

Jennings, G. and Stehlik, D. (1999) The innovators are women: the development of farm tourism in central Queensland, Australia. In: Hsu, C. (ed.) *New Frontiers in Tourism Research.* Proceedings, International Society of Travel and Tourism Educators Annual Conference, Vancouver, Canada, pp. 84–98.

Jones, K. (2000) Psychodynamics, gender, and reactionary entrepreneurship in metropolitan Sao Paulo, Brazil. *Women in Management Review* 15(4), 207–217.

Katz, J. (1994) Modelling entrepreneurial career progressions: concepts and considerations. *Entrepreneurship Theory and Practice* 19(2), 23–29.

Katz, J. (1995) Which track are you on? *Inc.*, 17, 27–28.

Kennedy, E. and Deegan, J. (2001) Seasonality in Irish tourism, 1973–1995. In: Baum, T. and Lundtorp, S. (eds) *Seasonality in Tourism.* Pergamon, Amsterdam, pp. 51–74.

Kets de Vries, M. (1993) The dynamics of family controlled firms: the good news and the bad news. *Organisational Dynamics* 21(3), 59–71.

Kets de Vries, M. (1996) *Family Business: Human Dilemmas in the Family Firm.* Thomson International Business Press, London.

King, B., Bransgrove, C. and Whitelaw, P. (1998) Profiling the strategic marketing activities of small tourism businesses. *Journal of Travel and Tourism Marketing* 7(4), 45–59.

King, R. (1995) Tourism, labour and international migration. In: Montanari, A. and Williams, A. (eds) *European Tourism: Regions, Spaces and Restructuring.* John Wiley & Sons, Chichester, UK, pp. 177–190.

Kinnaird, V. and Hall, D. (eds) (1994) *Tourism: a Gender Analysis.* John Wiley & Sons, Chichester, UK.

Kirzner, I. (1979) *Perception, Opportunity and Profit Studies in the Theory of Entrepreneurship.* London University Chicago Press, Chicago, Illinois.

Klenell, P. and Steen, M. (1999) I am in charge – small business problems and insolvency in Jamtland. Cited in: Public Support for Tourism SMEs in Peripheral Areas: The Arjeplog Project, Northern Sweden.

Komppula, R. (2000) Definitions of growth and success – case studies in Finnish rural tourism industry. Paper presented at the 12th Nordic Conference on Small Business Research, Kuopia, Finland. University of Kuopia Department of Business Management.

Kousis, M. (1989) Tourism and the family in a rural Cretan community. *Annals of Tourism Research* 16(3), 318–332.

Kovassy, M. and Hutton, C. (2001) Why do restaurants succeed in the Dandenong Ranges tourism region? Unpublished seminar paper, RMIT University, Melbourne, Australia.

Krakover, S. and Gradus, Y. (eds) (2002) *Tourism in Frontier Areas.* Lexington Books, Lanham, Maryland.

Kuratko, D. and Hodgetts, R. (1998) *Entrepreneurship: a contemporary Approach.* Dryden Press, New York.

Lane, S. (1989) An organizational development/ team-building approach to consultation with family businesses. *Family Business Review* 2(1), 5–16.

Lank, A. (1995) *Key Challenges Facing Family Enterprises.* IMD Publication, Lausanne, Switzerland.

Lank, A., Owens, R., Martinez, J., Reidel, H., de Visscher, F. and Bruel, M. (1994) The State of Family Business in Various Countries Around the World. *The Family Business Newsletter* May, 3–7.

Lansberg, I. (1988) The succession conspiracy. *Family Business Review* 1(2), 119–144.

Lansberg, I. (1996) Twelve tasks in succession. *The Family Business Management Handbook*. From the editors of Family Business Magazine. Family Business Publishing Co, Philadelphia, Pennsylvania, pp. 108–111.

Lansberg, I. (1999) *Succeeding Generations: Realizing the Dream of Families in Business*. Harvard Business School Press, Boston, Massachusetts.

Leat, P., Williams, F. and Brannigan, J. (2000) Rural competitiveness through quality and imagery across lagging regions of the European Union. In Proceedings of the Conference on European Rural Policy at the Crossroads. The Arkleton Centre, University of Aberdeen, UK.

Leiper, N. (1997) *Tourism Management*. TAFE Publishing, Melbourne, Australia.

Leontidou, L. (1994) Gender dimensions of tourism in Greece: employment, subcultures and restructuring. In: Kinnaird, V. and Hall, D. (eds) *Tourism: a Gender Analysis*. John Wiley & Sons, Chichester, UK, pp. 74–105.

Littlejohn, D., Foley, M. and Lemmon, J. (1996) The potential of accommodation consortia in the Highlands and Islands of Scotland. Proceedings of the IAHMS Spring Symposium, Leeds Metropolitan University, UK, pp. 55–66.

Litz, R. and Kleysen, R. (2002) Old men will dream dreams, your young men will see visions: a conceptualization of innovation in family firms. In: Chrisman, J., Holbrook, J. and Chua, J. (eds) *Innovation and Entrepreneurship in Western Canada: From Family Businesses to Multinationals*. University of Calgary Press, Calgary, Canada, pp. 269–298.

Lockyer, C. and Morrison, A. (1999) *Scottish Tourism Market: Structure, Characteristics and Performance*. Scottish Tourism Research Unit/Fraser of Allander Institute, University of Strathclyde, Glasgow, UK.

Long, P. and Edgell, D. (1997) Rural tourism in the US: the peak to peak scenic byway and KOA. In: Page, S. and Getz, D. (eds) *The Business of Rural Tourism: International Perspectives*. International Thomson Business Press, London, pp. 62–76.

Long, V. and Kindon, S. (1997) Gender and tourism development in Balinese villages. In: Sinclair, T. (ed.) *Gender, Work and Tourism*. Routledge, London, pp. 91–119.

Lundgren, J. (1994) Tourist impact/island entrepreneurship in the Caribbean. Conference paper cited in Shaw and Williams (1994), p. 126.

Lundtorp, S. (2001) Measuring tourism seasonality. In: Baum, T. and Lundtorp, S. (eds) *Seasonality in Tourism*. Pergamon, Amsterdam, pp. 23–48.

Lundtorp, S., Rassing, C. and Wanhill, S. (1999) The off-season is 'no season': the case of the Danish island of Bornholm. *Tourism Economics* 5(1), 49–68.

Lynch, P. (1996) Microenterprises and micro-firms in the hospitality industry: the case of bed and breakfast enterprises. In: Thomas, R. (ed.) *Spring Symposium Proceedings of International Association of Hotel Management Schools*. Leeds Metropolitan University, UK, pp. 231–236.

Lynch, P. (1999) Host attitudes towards guests in the homestay sector. *Tourism and Hospitality Research* 1(2), 119–144.

Lynch, P. and MacWhannell, D. (2000) Home and commercialized hospitality. In: Lashley, C. and Morrison, A. (eds) *In Search of Hospitality: Theoretical Perspectives and Debates*. Butterworth Heinemann, Oxford, UK, pp. 100–117.

Margerison, J. (1998) Business planning. In: Thomas, R. (ed.) *The Management of Small Tourism and Hospitality Firms*. Cassell, London, pp. 101–117.

Massachusetts Mutual Life Assurance (1993) *Major Findings of the Family Business Survey*. Springfield, Massachusetts.

McCann, J., Leon-Guerrero, A. and Haley, J. (2001) Strategic goals and practices of innovative family businesses. *Journal of Small Business Management* 39(1), 50–59.

McEniff, J. (1992) Seasonality of tourism demand in the European Community. Economist Intelligence Unit. *Travel and Tourism Analyst* No. 3, pp. 67–88.

McGibbon, J. (2000) Family business: Commercial hospitality in the domestic realm. In: Robinson, M. *et al.* (eds) *Reflections on International Tourism: Expressions of Culture Identity and Meaning in Tourism*. Business Education Publications, Sunderland, UK, pp. 167–181.

McKay, R. (2001) Women entrepreneurs: moving beyond family and flexibility. *International Journal of Entrepreneurial Behaviour and Research* 7(4), 148–165.

McKercher, B. (1998) *The Business of Nature-Based Tourism*. Hospitality Press, Melbourne, Australia.

McKercher, B. and Robbins, B. (1998) Business development issues affecting nature-based tourism operators in Australia. *Journal of Sustainable Tourism* 6 (2), 173–188.

Medlik, S. (1994) *The Business of Hotels*. Butterworth-Heinemann, Oxford, UK.

Mendonsa, E. (1983) Tourism and income strategies in Nazare, Portugal. *Annals of Tourism Research* 10(2), 213–238.

Middleton, V. (2001) The importance of micro-businesses in European Tourism. In: Roberts, L. and Hall, D. (eds) *Rural Tourism and Recreation: Principles to Practice*. CAB International, Wallingford, UK, pp. 197–201.

Middleton, V. and Clarke, J. (eds) (2001) *Marketing in Travel and Tourism*. Butterworth-Heinemann, Oxford, UK.

Miles, R. and Snow, C. (1978) *Organizational Strategy, Structure, and Process*. McGraw-Hill, New York.

Mintzberg, H. and Waters, J. (1990) Tracking strategy in an entrepreneurial firm. *Family Business Review* 3(3), 285–315.

Morrison, A. (1994) Small tourism business: product distribution system. Proceedings of CHME Spring Symposium, Edinburgh, Napier University, UK.

Morrison, A. (1996) Small firm cooperative marketing in a peripheral tourism region. *International Journal of Contemporary Hospitality Management* 10(5), 191–197.

Morrison, A. (1998a) Small firm statistics: a hotel sector focus. *The Service Industries Journal* 18(1), 132–142.

Morrison, A. (ed.) (1998b) *Entrepreneurship: an International Perspective*. Butterworth-Heinemann, Oxford, UK.

Morrison, A. (2000a) Entrepreneurship: what triggers it? *International Journal of Entrepreneurial Behaviour and Research* 6(2), 59–71.

Morrison, A. (2000b) Initiating Entrepreneurship in Enterprise and Small Business. Carter, S. and Jones-Evans, D. (eds). Pearson Education, London, pp. 97–114.

Morrison, A. (2001) Entrepreneurs transcend time: a biographical analysis. *Management Decision* 39(9), 784–790.

Morrison, A. (2002) Small hospitality business: enduring or endangered? *Journal of Hospitality and Tourism Management* 9(1), 1–11.

Morrison, A. and Teixeira, R. (2002) Small Hospitality Firms: Business Performance Obstacles. Paper presented at the International Small Hospitality and Tourism Firm Conference, Leeds Metropolitan University, Leeds, UK, September.

Morrison, A., Rimmington, M. and Williams, C. (1999) *Entrepreneurship in the Hospitality, Tourism and Leisure Industries*. Butterworth-Heinemann, Oxford, UK.

Morrison, A., Baum, T., Andrew, R. and Andrew, R. (2001) The lifestyle economics of small tourism businesses. *Journal of Travel and Tourism Research* 1, 16–25.

Murphy, P. (1985) *Tourism: a Community Approach*. Methuen, New York.

Naffziger, D., Hornsby, J. and Kuratko, D. (1994) A proposed research model of entrepreneurial motivation. *Entrepreneurship: Theory and Practice* 18(3), 29–43.

Neubauer, F. and Lank, A. (1998) *Family Business: its Governance for Sustainability*. Routledge, New York.

Nickerson, N., Black, R. and McCool, S. (2001) Agri-tourism: motivations behind farm/ranch business diversification. *Journal of Travel Research* 40, 19–26.

Nilsson, P., Petersen, T. and Wanhill, S. (2003) Public support for tourism SMEs in peripheral areas: The Arjeplog project, northern Sweden. *The Service Industries Journal*.

Nonaka, I. (1994) A dynamic theory of organizational knowledge creation. *Organization Science* 5(1), 14–37.

Notzke, C. (1999) Indigenous tourism development in the Arctic. *Annals of Tourism Research* 26(1), 55–76.

Omar, A. and Davidson, M. (2001) Women in management: a comparative cross-cultural overview. *Cross Cultural Management* 8(3/4), 35–67.

Opperman, M. (1996) Holidays on the farm: a case study of German hosts and guests. *Journal of Travel Research* 34(1), 63–67.

Opperman, M. (1997). Rural tourism in Germany – farm and rural tourism operators. In: Page, S. and Getz, D. (eds) *The Business of Rural Tourism: International Perspectives*. International Thomson Business Press, London, pp. 108–119.

Orhan, M. and Scott, D. (2001) Why women enter into entrepreneurship: an explanatory model. *Women in Management Review* 16(5), 232–247.

Ozar, B. and Yamak, S. (1997) Financing of small hospitality establishments. Paper presented at the Eurochrie Conference on Hospitality Business Development, Sheffield, UK.

Page, S. and Getz, D. (1997) *The Business of Rural Tourism: International Perspectives*. International Thomson Business Press, London.

Page, S., Forer, P. and Lawton, G. (1999). Small business development and tourism: Terra incognita? *Tourism Management* 20(4), 435–459.

Patrick, A. (1985) Family business: the offspring's perception of work satisfaction and their working relationship with their father. Unpublished doctoral dissertation, The Fielding Institute, Santa Barbara, California.

Patton, M.Q. (1990) *Qualitative Evaluation and Research Methods*. Sage Publications, Fresno, California.

Pearce, I. (1980) Reforms for entrepreneurs to serve public policy. In: Seldon, A. (ed.) *The Prime Mover of Progress: the Entrepreneur in Capitalism and Socialism*. The Institute of Economic Affairs, London.

Pearce, P. (1990) Farm tourism in New Zealand: a social situation analysis. *Annals of Tourism Research* 17(3), 117–125.

Peiser, R. and Wooten, L. (1983) Life cycle changes in small family businesses. *Business Horizons* 26(3), 58–65.

Peters, M. and Weirmair, K. (2001) Theoretical constructs and empirical evidence of entrepreneurial growth modes in the hospitality industry. Paper presented at the conference Entrepreneurship on Tourism and the Contexts of Experience Economy, University of Lapland, Finland.

Pfeffer, J. and Salancik, G. (1978) *The External Control Of Organizations: a Resource Dependence Perspective*. Harper and Row, New York,

Pizam, A. and Upchurch, R. (2002) The training needs of small rural tourism operators in frontier regions. In: Krakover, S. and Gradus, Y. (eds) *Tourism in Frontier Areas*. Lexington Books, Lanham, Maryland, pp. 117–140.

Poon, A. (1993) *Tourism, Technology and Competitive Strategies*. CAB International, Wallingford, UK.

Porter, M. (1980) *Competitive Strategy*. The Free Press, New York.

Porter, M. (1985) *Competitive Advantage*. The Free Press, New York.

Poza, E. (1988) Managerial practices that support interpreneurship and continued growth. *Family Business Review* 1(4), 339–359.

Queensland Tourist and Travel Corporation (1993) *Tourism – Taking the First Steps: Getting Started Series*. Brisbane, Australia.

Quinn, U., Larmour, R. and McQuillan, N. (1992) The small firm in the hospitality industry. *International Journal of Hospitality Management* 1, 11–14.

Ram, M. (1994) Unravelling social networks in ethnic minority firms. *International Small Business Journal* 12(3), 42–53.

Ram, M. and Halliday, R. (1993) Relative merits: family culture and kinship in small firms. *Sociology* 27, 629–648.

Ram, M., Abbas, T., Sanghera, B. and Hillin, G. (2000) Currying favour with the locals: Balti owners and business enclaves. *International Journal of Entrepreneurial Behaviour and Research* 6(1), 41–55.

Ram, M., Sanghera, B., Abbas, T. and Barlow, G. (2000) Training and ethnic minority firms: the case of the independent restaurant sector. *Education and Training* 42(4/5), 334–341.

Risker, D. (1998) Toward an innovation typology of entrepreneurs. *Journal of Small Business and Entrepreneurship* 15(2), 27–41.

Roberts, L. and Hall, D. (2001) *Rural Tourism and Recreation: Principles to Practice*. CAB International, Wallingford, UK.

Rodenburg, E. (1980) The effects of scale on economic development in Bali. *Annals of Tourism Research* 7(1), 177–196.

Romano, C., Smyrnios, K. and Dana, L. (2000) *Succession Matters: the Australian Family Business Survey 2000*. Family Business Research Unit, Monash University, Melbourne, Australia.

Rosenblatt, P., de Mik, C., Anderson, R. and Johnson, P. (1985) *The Family in Business: Understanding and Dealing With the Challenges Entrepreneurial Families Face*. Jossey-Bass, San Francisco, California.

Rue, L. and Ibrahim, N., (1996) The status of planning in smaller family owned businesses. *Family Business Review* 9(1), 29–43.

Russell, B. (1996) Innovation in small Irish tourism businesses. In: Thomas, R. and Shacklock, R. (eds) *Spring Symposium Proceedings of International Association of Hotel Management Schools*. Leeds Metropolitan University, Leeds, UK, pp. 116–120.

Ryan, C. (1998) Dolphins, canoes and marae: ecotourism products in New Zealand. In: Laws, E., Faulkner, B. and Moscardo, G. (eds) *Embracing and Managing Change in Tourism*. Routledge, London, pp. 285–306.

Saker, J. (1992) Cited in: Ram, M. (1994) Unravelling social networks in ethnic minority firms. *International Small Business Journal* 12(3), 42–53.

Santarelli, E. and Pesciarelli, E. (1990) The emergence of a vision: the development of Schumpeter's theory of entrepreneurship. *History of Political Economy* 22(4), 677–696.

Scase, R. and Goffee, R. (1989) *The Real World of the Small Business Owner*. Routledge, London.

Schein, E. (1994) Commentary: what is an entrepreneur? *Entrepreneurship Theory and Practice* 19, 87–88.

Schumpeter, J. (1934) *The Theory of Economic Development*. Translated by R. Opie. Harvard University Press, Cambridge, Massachusetts.

Scott, J. (1996) Chances and choices: women and tourism in Northern Cyprus. In: Sinclair, T. (ed.) *Gender, Work and Tourism*. Routledge, London, pp. 60–90.

Sexton, D. and and Kent, C. (1981) Female executives versus female entrepreneurs. In: Vesper, K. (ed.) *Frontiers of Entrepreneurship Research: the Proceedings of the 1981 Babson Conference on Entrepreneurship*. Babson College, Wellesley, Massachusetts, pp. 40–45.

Shanker, M. and and Astrachan, J. (1996) Myths and realities: Family businesses' contribution to the US economy – a framework for assessing family business statistics. *Family Business Review* 9, 107–119.

Shapero, A. and Sokol, L. (1982) The social dimensions of entrepreneurship. In: Kent, C., Sexton, D. and Vesper, K. (eds) *Encyclopedia of Entrepreneurship*. Prentice-Hall, Englewood Cliffs, New Jersey, pp. 72–88.

Sharma, P., Chrisman, J. and Chua, J. (1996) *A Review and Annotated Bibliography of Family Business Studies*. Kluwer, Boston, Massachusetts.

Shaw, E., Shaw, J. and Wilson, M. (2002) *Unsung Entrepreneurs: Entrepreneurship for Social Gain*. University of Durham Business School, Durham, UK.

Shaw, G. and Williams, A. (1987) Firm formation and operating characteristics in the Cornish tourist industry – the case of Looe. *Tourism Management* 8(4), 344–348.

Shaw, G. and Williams, A. (1990) Tourism, economic development, and the role of entrepreneurial activity. In: Cooper, C. (ed.) *Progress in Tourism, Recreation and Hospitality Management*, Vol. 2. Belhaven Press, London, pp. 67–81.

Shaw, G. and Williams, A. (1994) *Critical Issues in Tourism: a Geographical Perspective*. Blackwell, Oxford, UK.

Shaw, G. and Williams, A. (eds) (1997) *The Rise and Fall of British Coastal Resorts: Cultural and Economic Perspectives*. Pinter, London.

Shaw, G. and Williams, A. (1998) Entrepreneurship, small business, culture and tourism development. In: Ioannides, D. and Debbage, K. (eds) *The Economic Geography of the Tourist Industry: a Supply-Side Analysis*. Routledge, London, pp. 235–255.

Shaw, G. and Williams, A. (eds) (2001) *Critical Issues in Tourism: a Geographical Perspective*, 2nd edition. Blackwell, Oxford, UK.

Sherwood, A.-M., Parrott, N., Jenkins, T., Gillmor, D., Gaffey, S. and Cawley, M. (2000) Craft Producers on the Celtic Fringe: Marginal Lifestyles in Marginal Regions? Paper presented at 15th International Society for the Study of Marginal Regions Seminar, Newfoundland, Canada.

Sinclair, T. (ed.) (1997) *Gender, Work and Tourism*. Routledge, London.

Singer, J. and Donahu, C. (1992) Strategic management planning for the successful family business. *Journal of Business and Entrepreneurship* 4(3), 39–51.

Smallbone, D., Evans, M., Ekanem, I. and Butters, S. (2001) *Researching Social Enterprise, Small*

Business Service. Department of Trade and Industry, London.

Smith, C. (2000) Managing work and family in small 'copreneurial' business: an Australian study. *Women in Management Review* 15(5/6), 283–289.

Smith, R. (1967) *The Entrepreneur and the Firm*. Bureau of Business and Economic Research, MSU, East Lansing, Michigan.

Smith, V. (1998) Privatization in the Third World: small-scale tourism enterprises. In: Theobald, W. (ed.) *Global Tourism*, 2nd edn. Butterworth-Heinemann, Oxford, UK, pp. 205–215.

Smyrnios, K. and Romano, C. (1999) The 1999 Australian Family Business Lifestyle Audit. AXA Australia Family Business Research Unit, Monash University, Melbourne, Australia.

Smyrnios, K., Romano, C. and Tanewski, G. (1997a) *The Australian Family and Private Business Survey*. Monash University, Melbourne, Australia.

Smyrnios, K., Romano, C. and Tanewski, G. (1997b) *Distinguishing Factors of High- and Low-Growth Family Firms*. Working Paper Series, AXA Australia Family Business Reseearch Unit, Monash University, Melbourne, Australia.

Stavrou, E. (1999) Succession in family businesses: exploring the effects of demographic factors on offspring intentions to join and take over the business. *Journal of Small Business Management* 37(3), 43–61.

Stavrou, E. and Swiercz, P. (1998) Securing the future of the family enterprise: a model of offspring intentions to join the business. *Entrepreneurship Theory and Practice* 23(2), 19–39.

Stavrou, E. and Winslow, E. (1996) Succession in entrepreneurial family business in the US, Europe and Asia: a cross-cultural comparison on offspring intentions to join and take over the business. International Council for Small Businesses. *Proceedings of World Conference 1996*, Vol. 1. ICSB, Stockholm, pp. 253–273.

Storey, D. (1994) *Understanding the Small Business Sector*. Routledge, London.

Stoy Hayward Consulting (1999) *Staying the course: Survival Characteristics of the Family Owned Business*. Stoy Hayward Consulting, London.

Stringer, P. (1981) Hosts and guests: the bed and breakfast phenomenon. *Annals of Tourism Research* 8(3), 357–376.

Sundgaard, E., Rosenburg, L. and Johns, N. (1998). A typology of hotels as individual players: the case of Bornholm, Denmark. *International Journal of Contemporary Hospitality Management* 10(5), 180–183.

Szivas, E. (2001) Entrance into tourism entrepreneurship: a UK case study. *Tourism and Hospitality Research* 3(2), 163–172.

Tagiuri, R. and Davis, J. (1992) On the goals of successful family companies. *Family Business Review* 5(1), 263–281.

Tayeb, M. (1988) *Organisations and National Culture.* Sage, London.

Taylor, S., Simpson, J. and Howie, H. (1998) Financing small businesses. In: Thomas, R. (ed.) *The Management of Small Tourism and Hospitality Firms.* Cassell, London, pp. 58–77.

The Family Business Management Handbook (1996) From the editors of Family Business Magazine. Family Business Publishing Co., Philadelphia, Pennsylvania.

Thomas, R. (ed.) (1998a) *The Management of Small Tourism and Hospitality Firms.* Cassell, London.

Thomas, R. (1998b) An introduction to the study of small tourism and hospitality firms. In: Thomas, R. (ed.) *The Management of Small Tourism and Hospitality Firms.* Cassell, London, pp. 1–17.

Thomas, R. (1998c) Small firms and the state. In: Thomas, R. (ed.) *The Management of Small Tourism and Hospitality Firms.* Cassell, London, pp. 78–98.

Thomas, R., Friel, M., Jameson, S. and Parsons, D. (1997) *The National Survey of Small Tourism and Hospitality Firms, Annual Report 1996–97.* Centre for the Study of Small Tourism and Hospitality Firms, Leeds Metropolitan University, Leeds, UK.

Thomas, R., Friel, M. and Jameson, S. (1999) Small business management. In: Brotherton, B. (ed.) *The Handbook of Contemporary Hospitality Management Research.* John Wiley & Sons, Chichester, UK, pp. 497–512.

Thomas, R., Lashley, C., Rowson, B., Xie, G., Jameson, S., Eaglen, A., Lincoln, G. and Parsons, D. (2001) *The National Survey of Small Tourism and Hospitality Firms: 2001.* Centre for the Study of Small Tourism and Hospitality Firms, Leeds Metropolitan University, Leeds, UK.

Thomassen, A. (1992) European family-owned businesses: emerging issues for the 1990s. In: *The Family Firm Institute, Family Business at the Crossroads.* Proceedings of the 1992 Conference, Boston, Massachusetts, pp. 188–191.

Thompson, J., Alvy, G. and Lees, A. (2000) Social entrepreneurship: a new look at the people and the potential. *Management Decision* 38(5), 328–338.

Timmons, J. (1994) *New Venture Creation: Entrepreneurship for the 21st Century.* Irwin, Boston, Massachusetts.

Tinsley, R. and Lynch, P. (2001) Small tourism business networks and destination development. *International Journal of Hospitality Management* 20(4), 367–378.

Tourism Victoria (n.d.) *Starting Up in Tourism.* Melbourne, Australia.

Tsang, E. (2002) Learning from overseas venturing experience: the case of Chinese family businesses. *Journal of Business Venturing* 17(1), 21–40.

Twining-Ward, L. and Baum, T. (1998) Dilemmas facing mature island destinations: cases from the Baltic. *Progress in Tourism and Hospitality Research* 4, 131–140.

Twining-Ward, L. and Twining-Ward, T. (1996) Tourist destination development: the case of Bornholm and Gotland. Research Centre of Bornholm, Denmark. Report 7/1996.

Ucbasaran, D., Westhead, P. and Wright, M. (2001) The focus of entrepreneurial research: contextual and process issues. *Entrepreneurship Theory and Practice* Summer, 57–80.

Upton, N., Teal, E. and Felan, J. (2001) Strategic and business planning practices of fast growth family firms. *Journal of Small Business Management* 39(1), 60–72.

Vander Horst, H. (1996) *The Low Sky: Understanding the Dutch.* Scriptum, The Hague, The Netherlands.

Velasco, M. (1999) Andalusian women and their participation in rural tourist trade. *Geojournal* 48(3), 253–258.

Vesper, K. (1980) *New Venture Strategies.* Prentice Hall, Englewood Cliffs, New Jersey.

Walker, S., Valaoras, G., Gurung, D. and Godde, P. (2001) Women and mountain tourism: redefining the boundaries of policy and practice. In: Apostolopoulos, Y., Sonmez, S. and Timothy, D. (eds) *Women as Producers and Consumers of Tourism in Developing Regions* Praeger, Westport, Connecticut, pp. 211–234.

Walton, J. (1978) *The Blackpool Landlady – a Social History.* Manchester University Press, Manchester, UK.

Wanhill, S. (1980) Tackling seasonality: a technical note. *Tourism Management* 1(4), 243–245.

Wanhill, S. (1997) Peripheral area tourism: a European perspective. *Progress in Tourism and Hospitality Research* 3(1), 47–70.

Wanhill, S. (2000) Small and medium tourism enterprises. *Annals of Tourism Research* 27(1), 132–147.

Ward, J. (1987) *Keeping the Family Business Healthy: How to Plan For Continuing Growth, Profitability, and Family Leadership.* Josey-Bass, San Francisco, California.

Ward, J. (1988) The special role of strategic planning for family businesses. *Family Business Review* 2(1), 105–117.

Ward, J. (1990) The succession process: 15 guidelines. *Small Business Forum* 8(3), 57–62.

Ward, J. and Aronoff, C. (1990) To sell or not to sell. *Nation's Business* 78(1), 63–64.

Webster, M. (1998) Strategies for growth. In: Thomas, R. (ed.) *The Management of Small Tourism and Hospitality Firms.* Cassell, London, pp. 207–218.

Westhead, P. (1997) Ambitions, 'external' environment and strategic factor differences between family and non-family companies. *Entrepreneurship and Regional Development* 9(2), 127–157.

Westhead, P. and Cowling, M. (1998) Family firm research: the need for a methodological rethink. *Entrepreneurship Theory and Practice* Autumn, 31–56.

Westhead, P. and Wright, M. (eds) (2000) *Advances in Entrepreneurship* Vol. 3. Elgar Reference Collection, Cheltenham, UK.

Whatmore, S. (1991) *Farming Women: Gender, Work and Family Enterprise.* Macmillan, Basingstoke, UK.

Williams, A., Shaw, G. and Greenwood, J. (1989) From tourist to tourism entrepreneur, from consumption to production: Evidence from Cornwall, England. *Environment and Planning* A21, 1639–1653.

World Tourism Organisation (1997) *Rural Tourism: a Solution For Employment, Local Development and Environment.* WTO, Madrid.

Wortman, M. (1994) Theoretical foundations for family-owned business: a conceptual and research-based paradigm. *Family Business Review* 7(1), 3–27.

Wortman, M. (1995) Critical issues in family business: an international perspective of practice and research. In: Proceedings of the 40th International Council for Small Business Conference, Sydney. NCP Printing, University of Newcastle, Newcastle, Australia.

Yacoumis, J. (1980) Tackling seasonality: the case of Sri Lanka. *Tourism Management* 1(2), 84–98.

Yu, T.F.-L. (2001) The Chinese family business as a strategic system: an evolutionary perspective. *International Journal of Entrepreneurial Behaviour and Research* 7(1), 22–40.

Index